AMAZING ANIMAL KINGDOM

LIFE IN THE WILD

AMAZING ANIMAL KINGDOM

LIFE IN THE WILD

HOW WILD ANIMALS SURVIVE IN THEIR DIFFERENT HABITATS, FROM DESERTS AND JUNGLES TO OCEANS AND THE SKIES

CONSULTING EDITOR **MICHAEL CHINERY**

HERMES HOUSE

Contents

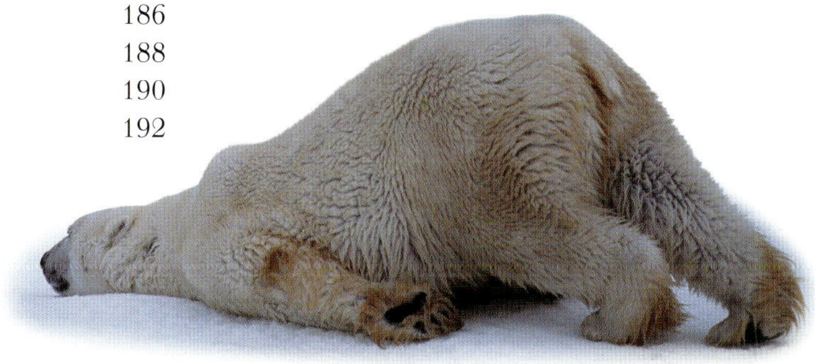

Introduction

We are unique in the universe in inhabiting the only planet that is known to have life on it: and what an extraordinary diversity of life forms there are. Scientists believe there could be between 14 million and 100 million species of animals and plants existing today. They cannot even be sure exactly how many, because most of these life forms are either too small to find or are dwelling in unexplored places, such as the tropical rainforest or the deep sea.

Lions must hunt down and kill their own food. They do this in groups, enabling them to bring down prey far bigger than themselves.

Wolves are very agile animals and this helps them to escape from predators; they can leap upwards, sideways and even backwards.

Of all the potential 100 million species on our planet only 1.3 million have been studied scientifically, including about 750,000 insects and 50,000 vertebrates (animals with backbones), so there is still a great deal for us to learn. Around 10,000 new species are described annually, so it is an extraordinary thought that at this rate it will take well over 1,000 years to complete a catalogue of the living creatures of the Earth that we currently know little or nothing about.

The creatures we do know about range from the huge blue whale, weighing up to 150 tonnes, down to microscopic creatures so small that several could sit comfortably on the head of a pin. As well as huge variations in size, animals display an equally wide range of behaviour patterns, but what links them all is they have the same basic need for somewhere to live that will provide them with food and some degree of protection or shelter. Because individual animals cannot live forever, they all also need to be able to produce more of their own kind – otherwise the species would die out.

Zebras eat mainly grass and, like all equids, they graze for many hours a day.

The production of new generations is called reproduction and it usually involves the meeting and mating of a male and a female of the same species. Some form of communication is necessary to bring the males and females together. Animals also communicate with each other to warn of danger or to tell each other about good food sources. Communication is especially well developed among insects, such as ants and many bees and wasps, which live in colonies and work together for the good of the whole community.

This book is designed to reveal all the secrets of the wildlife world, using 1,200 wonderful pictures to investigate and illustrate every element of animal behaviour and characteristics. The book begins by looking how each animal type works; where animals live and what kinds of home they make; the fantastic skills and attributes they develop and evolve to adapt themselves to their environment and prosper in it; and the techniques and methods they use simply to survive the changing seasons, landscape and climatic conditions.

There is an fascinating look into the methods different animals seek out and hunt for food, some in groups and some singly; the ways animals mate and give birth in order to protect the future of their species; and how animals communicate, in families, in groups, within their own species and also with other species, to attract, warn or threaten. The book ends with a focus on animals in danger of extinction, an investigation of some conservation successes and some failures, and a review of what is being done and what should be done to protect these irreplaceable species for future generations.

There are 17,500 known species of butterfly in the world. Of these about 300 are endangered.

HOW ANIMALS WORK
Why They Are Their Size and Shape, Why They Eat What They Do

What we know about the inner workings of different animals is laid out in the the following chapter and illustrated with revealing cut-away diagrams. We find out how every creature is adapted to the habitat in which it lives, whether this is on land or in the sea. Each animal's ability to survive depends not only on its size or shape, but also by what goes on inside its body, and this chapter peels away the layers to demonstrate the complex inside mechanisms of all kinds of animals. We discover how almost every animal on the planet depends on plants for food and energy, whether it eats vegetation directly (a herbivore or plant-eater, such as horses, elephants and many insects) or hunts and kills other animals (a carnivore or meat-eater, such as lions, crocodiles and tigers). All have the means to gather or catch their chosen food and then process it and turn it into valuable energy.

Apes are our closest animal relatives. Gorillas are the largest of the great apes.

Hippopotamuses spend all day resting in the water or asleep in the sun. They go ashore at night to feed.

ANIMAL HABITATS
Where Animals Live and How They Adapt

Animals have explored and colonized just about every place on earth, from the deepest and coldest oceans to the hottest deserts and the highest mountain tops. Only the permanent ice fields around the Poles lack resident animals, although emperor penguins spend several months guarding their chicks on the bare Antarctic ice. Most species are associated with particular habitats, such as forests or deserts, and each species is generally well adapted to the conditions in which it lives. Camels, for example, have many adaptations enabling them to survive in hot, dry deserts: broad feet help them to walk on loose sand; long eyelashes keep the sand out of their eyes, and the ability to go without water for long periods. Many smaller desert animals avoid the heat by sleeping in burrows during the day and coming out to feed only during the cool of the night. Mammals living in cold environments usually have thick fur or a layer of insulating blubber under the skin. Camouflage is another valuable adaptation, enabling animals to blend in with their surroundings and hide from their enemies.

AMAZING ANIMALS
Adapting to the Environment – Extraordinary Feats, Skills and Attributes

Polar bears have thick fur so they can live in the Arctic where the temperature can drop as low as -50°C.

Animals go to extraordinary lengths to survive in an often hostile world, and many have developed or refined fantastic new skills and techniques to get an advantage over their rivals or over their environment. Like some human military equivalents, some animals indulge in chemical warfare, both for attack and defence, with an astonishing range of bites, jabs, poisons and venoms. Then there are 'stealth' animals that use camouflage to make themselves invisible, while 'advertisers' have gaudy patterns to startle, confuse, mislead and frighten. Some animals, like chimps, have developed the facility to use tools; others have evolved the ability to sleep for six months of the year and wake only when the climate it suitable for their lifestyle. In this chapter we find out that animals really are 'amazing', and none more so than those that travel enormous distances across the world, relying on the sun, stars and the Earth's magnetic field to find their way across featureless oceans and deserts. Migratory animals escape extremes in the weather, while others hibernate, and some just keep going in all seasons, even in the harshest of places, such as hot deserts, the oceans' abyss and the icy Arctic wilderness, making changes to their skin, fur, diet or routine in order to keep functioning successfully.

ANIMAL SURVIVAL
Mother Nature, Evolution and the Survival of the Fittest

Animals need to be able to find their way about, locate food and detect the predators that are out to hunt them down. They must be able to move from one place to another to be in the best spot to maximize their chances of eating, to escape from predators, and also to track down a mate so that they can reproduce. This chapter explores the senses of sight, smell, hearing, and touch, and discovers other senses that humans do not have and do not even understand. It reveals how animals have taken up every means to travel on land, under the sea and in the air, and it tells how Mother Nature adopted the same solution to the same challenge in different groups of animals that evolved many millions of years apart.

Snakes move in the shape of a wave. Their bendy backbones enable them to climb trees, move along the ground, and swim through water.

THE HUNT FOR FOOD
Diet, Appetite and the Skills of the Ruthless Killers

Few animals can go for more than a few days without eating. Food provides energy and the building materials needed for growth. Most animals are herbivores – plant eaters. As well as the herds of grazing mammals, they include vast numbers of leaf-chewing and sap-sucking insects. Meat eaters or carnivores include lions, crocodiles and spiders, and then there are the omnivores – animals that eat both plant and animal matter. They include many household pests, such as rats, mice and cockroaches. Some insects have decidedly odd diets: dung, carpets, and solid wood are all eaten by various species. This chapter is all about how animals find food to eat. It includes some of the animal kingdom's most ruthless killers – big cats, sharks, alligators, bears, birds of prey and wolves – and also some of the most cunning and clever trappers and ambushers, such as spiders, snakes and poisonous bugs.

The owl is built to fly silently and to locate prey that it cannot see but can hear, so it can hunt in the dark.

NEW LIFE
Procreation, Birth, Rearing the Family and Ensuring the Future

Corals and some sea anemones can produce branches that break off and grow into a new individual, but this kind of reproduction is unusual in the animal kingdom. Most animals lay eggs or give birth to babies. This usually happens after a male and female pair up and mate, although aphids and some other insects can give birth without mating. Most insects and fishes take no interest in their offspring at all, working on the principle of delivering babies or eggs in their hundreds or even thousands and beating adverse environmental conditions or aggressors by sheer weight of numbers. At the other end of the scale mammals are born in much smaller families, so that individual infants can be fed milk from their mothers' bodies and given tender and loving care for many months. In fact, young chimps and baby elephants are intensively reared by their mothers for several years after they are born.

The lioness will remain close to her cubs until they are large enough to protect themselves.

HOW ANIMALS COMMUNICATE
Talking, Signs and Signals for Attracting Mates or Threatening Enemies

A dolphin's clicking sounds allow it to navigate through the water, find food, and communicate with other dolphins.

The dawn chorus of spring and early summer is a well-known example of animal communication. The male birds sing to attract females and also to let other males know that a territory is occupied. Gibbons and several kinds of monkeys also make a lot of noise to warn their neighbours to keep away. Most kinds of animals emit some sort of signal to attract mates and many animals give out scents that excite the opposite sex. Parents and offspring also communicate with each other. Baby birds, for example, squawk when hungry, and the parents use various calls to warn their babies of danger. Some animals or insects live in elaborate colonies which have developed incredibly sophisticated systems for relaying instructions, sharing information and alerting the community.

ANIMALS IN DANGER
The Threat of Extinction and the Need for Conservation in Man's Changing World

What lies ahead? This book shows us an incredible global collection of animals and explores the remarkable ways in which all these creatures live and work. Animals that are well adapted to their habitat and good at finding food and evading their enemies are most likely to survive and produce more of their own kind. They will pass their good qualities to their offspring and the species as a whole will continue to flourish. However, wherever they are and whatever they do to survive, nothing prepared animals for the activities of people. In the short space of time that modern man has evolved – about two million years – animals have been disappearing more rapidly than ever before, and that decline is accelerating. Of the 1.3 million known species, between five per cent and twenty per cent are threatened with extinction. Half of them live in the tropical rainforests, and 50–100 species are disappearing every single day. The blame for their downfall lies squarely on the shoulders of humankind. This important chapter shows that unless there is a change in our attitude to the natural world, many species face a bleak future.

Giant pandas are a very rare, endangered species. Forest clearing, the expansion of farmland, and poachers, threaten the pandas' food source and habitat.

How Animals Work

Inside every animal is an extraordinary story waiting to be told. This section provides an insight into how all kinds of animals feed, hunt and survive – examining the different physical characteristics that allow them to live in wild and dangerous conditions.

How Animals Work

Polar bears can swim in the icy sea because they are protected by insulating fur and layers of thick fat.

Over a million different kinds or species of animals inhabit the Earth. They live on land and in the water and exhibit an amazing range of shapes and sizes, but they all have a number of things in common. They all move, feed, breathe, reproduce, grow and get rid of waste. These features are characteristic of all living things, but the animals' bodies are constructed to carry them out in many different ways. You will discover how various animals live, and how their bodies are made to do the jobs necessary to keep them fit and healthy.

Muscles for Movement

Animals can run, hop, crawl, fly or swim, and these movements are all brought about by muscles. Each end of a muscle is firmly fixed to a part of the body and, when the muscle contracts, it makes something move. Among the vertebrates (animals with backbones) – most of the muscles are attached to bones. Contraction of the muscles at the top of a wolf's leg, for example, pulls on the bones lower down in the leg and lifts the leg up. Other muscles swing it forward and put it down again – the faster this happens, the faster the wolf runs. All vertebrates are built on a similar plan, but the shape, arrangement and density of their bones vary. The skeleton of a bird's wing, for example, has the same basic structure as that of an ape's arm, but birds' bones, unlike mammals, are usually hollow. This makes them lighter, so flying is easier.

The muscles in the neck, shoulders and hindquarters of wolves are very well developed. They give the wolf strength, stamina and speed.

Invertebrate animals do not have bony skeletons, they have tough and sometimes very hard shells or cases (exoskeletons). Insects and spiders have lots of joints, rather like suits of armour. The joints are moved when they are pulled by muscles fixed to the insides of the armour.

Feeding

Food provides animals with energy and the materials needed for growth. Digestive juices break it down into simple substances that are absorbed into the body. Most animals specialize in either liquid or solid food.

Bugs and butterflies feed on liquids, such as plant sap and nectar, which they suck up through slender tubes. The drinking tubes of bugs have sharp tips that pierce the plants to reach the sap. Spiders feed on insects and other small animals, but they cannot eat solid matter, so they liquefy their prey with digestive juices before they swallow it. Beetles and many other insects have biting jaws and eat solid food, but their jaws are outside their mouths and they chew their food before pushing it into their mouths.

Insects are protected by a hard outer layer called an exoskeleton which is waterproof and also prevents the insect from drying out in hot weather.

Most vertebrates have strong teeth, the shape and arrangement of which depend on the kind of food that is eaten. Cats and other carnivorous animals (meat-eaters) have sharp-edged teeth that slice through the meat. Baleen whales have no teeth: they filter small creatures from the water with the horny plates that hang from the roof of the mouth like curtains. Birds also lack teeth. Their horny beaks do the same job as teeth and, being lighter, they make it easier for the birds to fly.

Breathing

Oxygen is necessary for life, and animals get oxygen from the air or water around them. Vertebrates that live on the land breathe with lungs. Air is drawn into these thin-walled pouches and the oxygen passes through the lung walls and into the blood vessels to be carried around the body. Fish breathe with gills. These are clusters of tiny thin-walled fingers in the throat section. Water is taken in through the mouth and pumped over the gills, where the oxygen dissolved in it passes into the blood. The water then passes out through the gill slits. These slits are easily seen in sharks, but in most fish they are covered with a flap called an operculum. Insects' bodies have a number of tiny holes on each side. These holes are called spiracles and are easily seen in large caterpillars. They lead into a network of minute tubes, called tracheae, that carry air to all parts of the insect's body.

The cheetah is the world's fastest land animal and is fine-tuned for speed. It has wide nostrils to breathe in as much oxygen as possible and has specially adapted paws for running fast.

Nature's Success Story

People like to think that humans dominate Earth, but insects could in many ways be seen as far more successful. There are over one million species (kinds) of insects, and because they breed very quickly they can adapt to all kinds of conditions and can live just about anywhere.

Scientists divide insects into groups called orders. The insects in each order share certain features. Beetles and bugs are two of the largest insect orders. The main difference between them is that beetles have biting jaws and bugs have sucking mouthparts. So far, 350,000 different kinds of beetles and 80,000 different kinds of bugs have been found, but there are probably many more species.

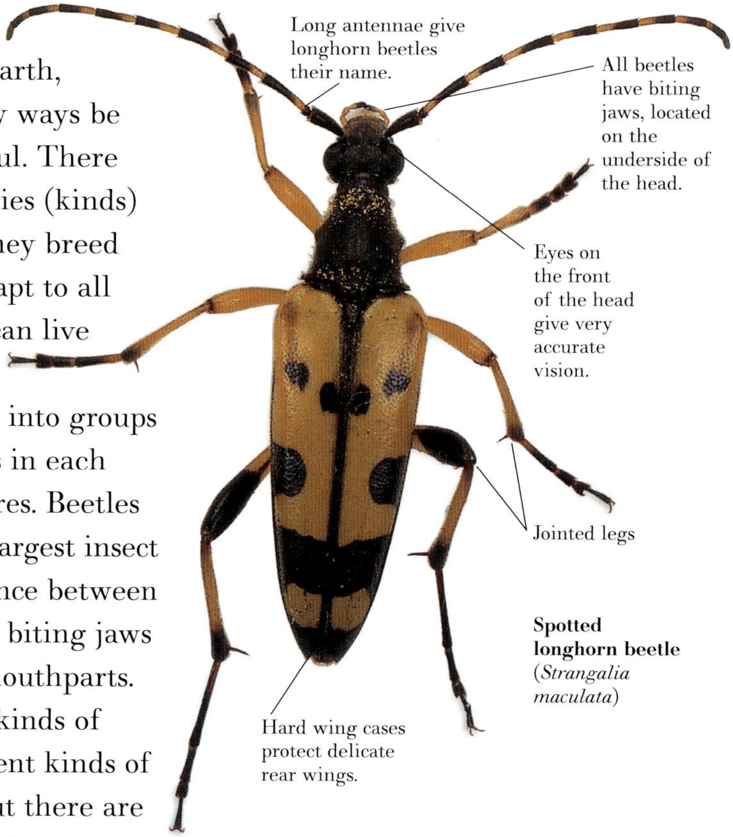

Spotted longhorn beetle (*Strangalia maculata*)

▲ THE BEETLE ORDER
Beetles belong to the order Coleoptera, which means 'sheath wings'. Most beetles have two pairs of wings. The tough front wings fold over the delicate rear wings to form a hard, protective case, like body armour. Longhorn beetles owe their name to their long antennae (feelers), which look like long horns.

◄ LIVING IN WATER
Not all beetles and bugs live on land. Some, like this great diving beetle, live in fresh water ponds. The diving beetle hunts underwater, diving down to catch a variety of small creatures.

◀ FEEDING TOGETHER

A group of aphids feeds on a plant stem, sucking up liquid sap. Most beetles and bugs live alone, but a few species, such as aphids, gather together in large numbers. Some insects, such as ants and bees, form communities. Living in a group gives them protection from predators.

What's in a Name?

This image comes from the animated feature film A Bug's Life. *The hero of the cartoon is not actually a bug at all, but an ant. True bugs are a particular group of insects with sucking mouthparts that can slurp up liquid food.*

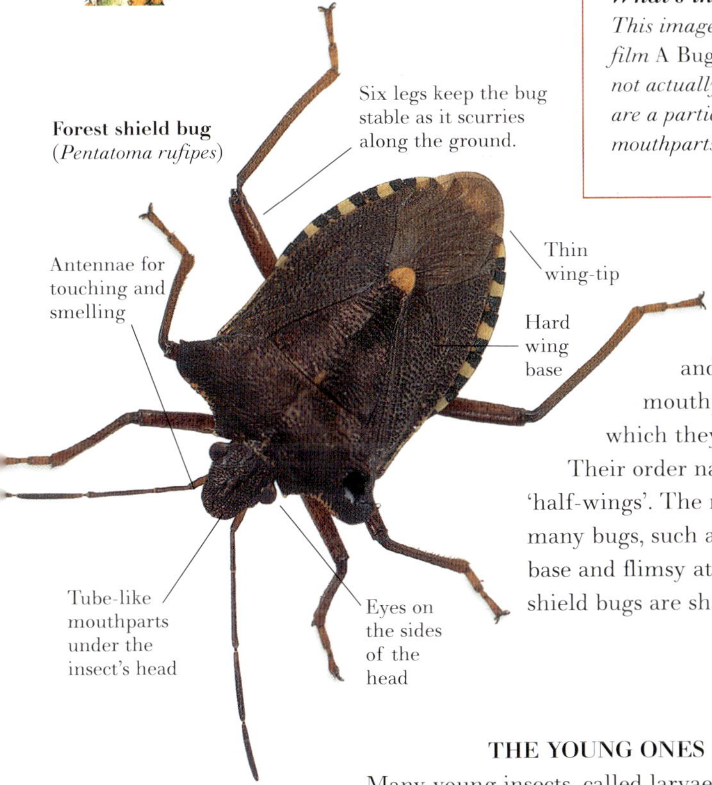

◀ THE BUG ORDER

Bugs come in many shapes and sizes. All have long, jointed mouthparts that form a tube through which they suck up liquid food, like a syringe. Their order name is Hemiptera, which means 'half-wings'. The name refers to the front wings of many bugs, such as shield bugs, which are hard at the base and flimsy at the tip. With their wings folded, shield bugs are shaped like a warrior's shield.

THE YOUNG ONES ▶

Many young insects, called larvae, look very different from the adults. This beetle larva, or grub, feeds on plant roots in the soil. Soon it will change into a winged adult. Young bugs, called nymphs, look like miniature adults when they hatch from their eggs although they have no wings.

Did you know? Insects are unique in having six legs – three on each side.

Bodies in Sections

Human bodies are supported on the inside by a bony skeleton. Insects do not have bones to support them but have a tough outer layer called an exoskeleton. This layer protects the insect's body from damage. The exoskeleton is also waterproof and helps to prevent the insect from drying out in hot weather. Holes in the exoskeleton, called spiracles, allow the insect to breathe.

The word 'insect' comes from the Latin word *insectum* meaning 'in sections'. All insect bodies are made up of three main parts. They have a head, a thorax (middle section) and an abdomen (rear section). Most adult insects have one or two pairs of wings. Many of them use long antennae to sense their surroundings.

▲ THREE SECTIONS
This beetle's main sense organs, the antennae and eyes, are on its head. Its wings and legs are attached to the thorax. The abdomen contains the most of the digestive and reproductive organs.

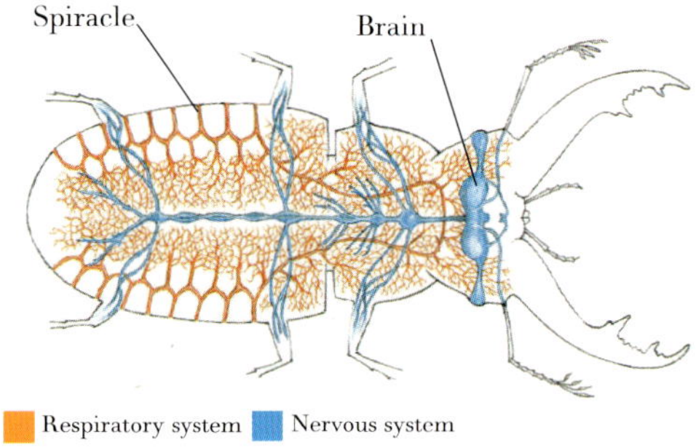

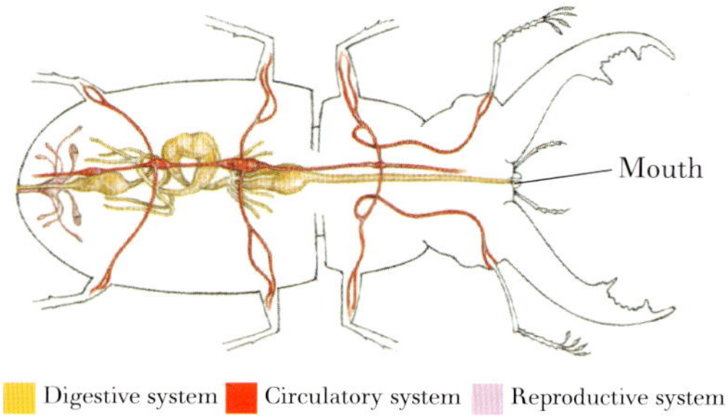

▲ BREATHING AND NERVOUS SYSTEMS
The respiratory (breathing) system has spiracles (holes) that lead to a network of tubes. The tubes allow air to reach all parts of the insect's body. The nervous system receives messages from the sense organs, and sends signals to the insect's muscles to make it move.

▲ OTHER BODY SYSTEMS
The digestive system breaks down food and absorbs it. The circulatory system includes a long, thin heart that pumps blood through the body. The abdomen contains the reproductive parts. Males have two testes that produce sperm. Females have two ovaries that produce eggs.

◀ IN COLD BLOOD

All insects, including beetles and bugs, are cold-blooded animals. This means that the temperature of their body is similar to their surroundings. Insects control their body temperature by moving about. To warm up, many insects bask in the sun, as this leaf beetle is doing. If they need to cool their bodies, they move into the shade.

SURVIVING THE COLD ▶

This tiger-beetle egg is buried in the soil. In some parts of the world, winters are too cold for adult insects to survive. The adult insects die, but their eggs, or young, survive buried in the soil. When spring arrives, the young insects emerge and become adults ready to breed before winter comes again.

Beetle Car

During the 1940s, the tough, rounded beetle shape inspired the German car manufacturer Volkswagen to produce one of the world's most popular family cars, the VW Beetle. The car's tough outer shell, just like that of a beetle, helped it to achieve a good safety record. The design proved so successful that the Beetle car was recently improved and relaunched.

Rhinoceros beetle
(*Megasoma elephas*)

▲ MOVING FORTRESS

The rhinoceros beetle is very well armoured. Its tough exoskeleton covers and protects its whole body. The cuticle (outer skin) on the head and thorax of this male forms three long points that look like a rhinoceros's horns. These points are used in battles with other males over mates.

Winged Beauties

Butterflies and moths are the most beautiful of all insects. On sunny days, butterflies flit from flower to flower. Their slow, fluttering flight often reveals the full glory of their large, vividly coloured wings. Moths tend to be less brightly coloured than butterflies and generally fly at night.

Together, butterflies and moths make up one of the largest orders (groups) of insects, called Lepidoptera. This order includes more than 165,000 different species (kinds), living in all parts of the world except Antarctica. Most moths and butterflies feed on sugary flower nectar by dipping a long proboscis (tongue) into the heart of the flower. The proboscis is rolled up under the body when it is not being used.

Geometrid moth
(*Hypochrosis bifurcata*)

▲ **MOTHS**
Most moths fly only at dusk or at night. They rest on tree trunks and in leaf litter by day, where their drab colours make them difficult to see. Moths tend to have plump bodies covered in thick hair, and their feathery antennae are used for sniffing out mates.

▼ **RESTING BUTTERFLY**
You can usually tell a butterfly from a moth by the way it folds its wings when it is resting. A moth spreads its wings back like a tent, with only the upper sides visible. However, a butterfly settles with its wings folded upright with the upper sides together, so that only the undersides show.

Green-veined white butterfly
(*Pieris napi*)

Psyche and Aphrodite
The Ancient Greeks believed that, after death, their souls fluttered away from their bodies in the form of butterflies. The Greek symbol for the soul was a butterfly-winged girl called Psyche. According to legend, Aphrodite (goddess of love) was jealous of Psyche's beauty. She ordered her son Eros to make Psyche fall in love with him. Instead, Eros fell in love with her himself.

▲ FEATURES OF A BUTTERFLY

Butterflies tend to have brilliantly coloured wings and fly only during the day. They have slim bodies without much hair, and their antennae are shaped like clubs, with a lump at the end. However, the distinction between butterflies and moths is not very clear, and in some languages they are not distinguished at all.

▼ CATERPILLARS

A many-legged caterpillar hatches from a butterfly's egg. When young, both moths and butterflies are caterpillars. Only when they are big enough do the caterpillars go through the changes that turn them into winged adults.

Privet hawk moth caterpillar
(*Sphinx ligustri*)

Did you know? Tiger moths make high-pitched clicks at night to confuse hunting bats.

Crawling Creatures

Spiders are some of the most feared and least understood creatures in the animal world. These hairy hunters are famous for spinning silk and giving a poisonous bite. There are around 35,000 known species (kinds) of spider, with probably a similar number waiting to be discovered. Only about 30 species, however, are dangerous to people. Spiders are very useful to humans, because they eat flies and other insect pests that invade our homes and gardens. Spiders live nearly everywhere, from forests, deserts and grasslands to caves. Some even live underwater. Some spin webs to catch their prey, while others leap out from a hiding place or stalk their meals like a cat. There are even spiders that fire streams of sticky silk to tangle up their prey and others that lasso flying moths.

◄ **WHAT IS A SPIDER?** Spiders are often confused with insects, but they belong to a completely different group. A spider has eight legs, while an insect has six. Its body has two parts, while an insect's has three. Many insects have wings and antennae, but spiders do not.

WEB WEAVERS ►

About half of all spiders spin webs. They know how to do this by instinct from birth, without being taught. Many spiders build a new web each night. They build webs to catch flying prey. Some of the web's silk is sticky to trap animals. The spider walks around on non-stick strands.

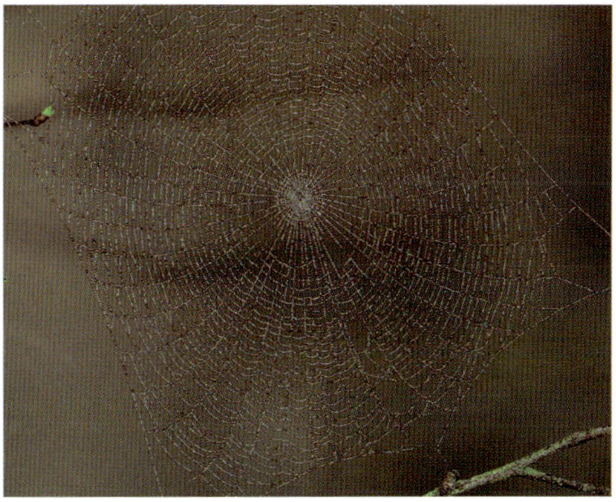

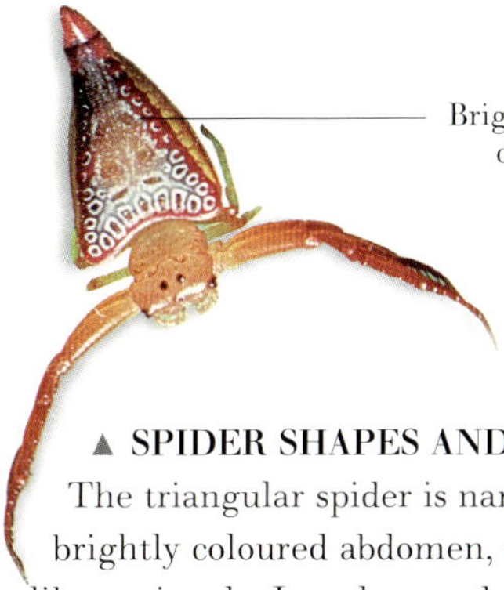

Bright colours help to conceal this spider among flowers.

▲ SPIDER SHAPES AND COLOURS

The triangular spider is named after its brightly coloured abdomen, which is shaped like a triangle. Its colour and shape help it to hide in wait for prey on leaves and flowers. Other spiders use bright colours to warn their enemies that they are poisonous or taste nasty.

Arachne's Tale

A Greek legend tells of Arachne, a girl who was very skilled at weaving. The goddess Athene challenged her to a contest, which Arachne won. The goddess became so cross Arachne killed herself. Athene was sorry and turned the girl into a spider so she could spin forever. The scientific name for spiders is arachnids, named after Arachne.

◄ MALES AND FEMALES

Female spiders are usually bigger than the males and not so colourful, though this female *Nephila* spider is boldly marked. The male at the top of the picture is only one-fifth of her size.

Did you know? All spiders are carnivores (meat-eaters) and many are cannibals.

How Spiders Work

From the outside, a spider's body is very different from ours. It has a tough outer skeleton, called an exoskeleton, and legs that have many joints. It has several eyes and a mouth, but no ears, nose or tongue. Instead, it relies on a variety of hairs and bristles to touch, taste and hear things, and it smells through microscopic pores on its feet. Inside, a spider has many features common to other animals, such as blood, nerves, a brain and a digestive system. It also has special glands for spinning silk and for making and storing poison.

▲ **SHEDDING SKIN**
A spider's exoskeleton protects its body like a suit of armour. A waxy layer helps to make it waterproof. The exoskeleton cannot stretch as the spider grows so must be shed from time to time after a new, looser skin has grown underneath. The old skin of a huntsman spider is shown here.

Male spiders use taste hairs to pick up scent trails left by females.

◀ **HAIRY SIGNALS**
The sensitive hairs covering a spider send signals to the brain alerting it to food and enemies. Tasting hairs are spread all over the spider's body. On the palps and legs, special hairs, called trichobothria, set in cup-like sockets pick up movements in the air.

▲ **PICKING UP VIBRATIONS**
A green orb-weaver devours a fly trapped in the sticky web. Spiders use special slits on their bodies to detect when an insect is trapped in their webs. These slits, called lyriform organs, pick up vibrations caused by a struggling insect. Nerve endings in the slits send signals to the spider's brain.

SPIDER POISON ►
A spider is a delicate creature compared to some of the prey it catches. By using poison, a spider can kill or paralyse its victim before the latter has a chance to do any harm. The spider pumps poison through its fangs. Spiders cannot chew solid food, and their poison turns the prey's body into a fleshy goo. The spider sucks up this liquid.

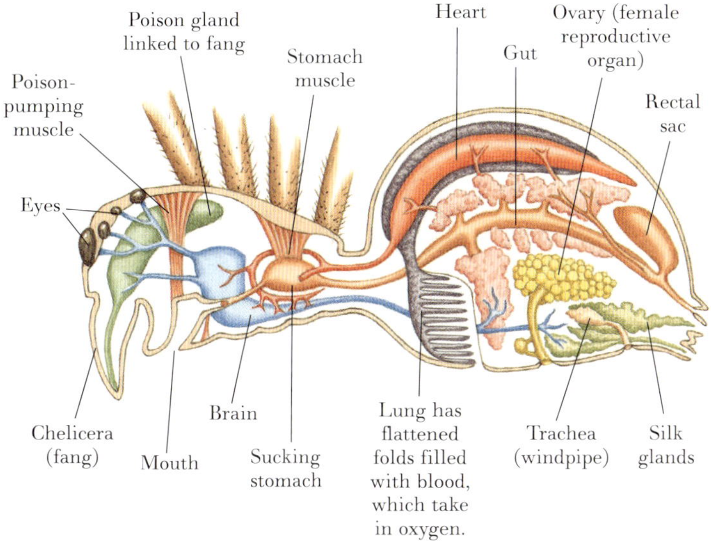

◄ INSIDE A SPIDER
The front part of a spider, the cephalothorax, contains the brain, poison glands and stomach. The abdomen contains the heart, lungs, breathing tubes, gut, waste disposal system, silk glands and reproductive organs. A spider's stomach works like a pump, stretching wide to pull in food that has been turned into a soupy pulp. The heart pumps blue blood around the body.

Raiko and the Earth Spider
People have regarded spiders as dangerous, magical animals for thousands of years. This Japanese print from the 1830s shows the legendary warrior Yorimitsu (also known as Raiko) and his followers slaying the fearsome Earth Spider.

Snake Life

Snakes are reptiles, closely related to lizards and more distantly to crocodiles and turtles. Altogether, there are about 2,700 different kinds of snake, but only 300 or so are able to kill people. In Europe or North America, you are more likely to be struck by lightning than to be bitten by a poisonous snake. All snakes have long bodies covered with waterproof scales. They are meat-eaters and swallow their prey whole. Snakes have always had a special place in myths and legends, being used as symbols of both good and evil.

◄ **A SNAKE'S TAIL**
The tail of a snake is the part behind a small opening called the cloaca, where the body wastes pass out. The snake narrows slightly where the tail begins.

Grass snake
(*Natrix natrix*)

◄ **SNAKE HEADS**
Most snakes have a definite head and neck. But in some snakes, one end of the body looks very much like the other end!

Rattlesnake
(*Crotalus*)

◀ **FORKED TONGUE**

Snakes and some lizards have forked tongues. A snake flicks its tongue out to taste and smell the air. This gives the snake a picture of what is around it. A snake does this every few seconds if it is hunting or if there is any danger nearby.

Colombian rainbow boa
(*Epicrates cenchria maurus*)

▲ **SCALY ARMOUR**

A covering of tough, dry scales grows out of a snake's skin. The scales usually hide the skin. After a big meal, the skin stretches so that it becomes visible between the scales. A snake's scales protect its body while allowing it to stretch, coil and bend. The scales may be either rough or smooth.

Red-tailed boa
(*Boa constrictor*)

Did you know? Snakes never feel slimy to the touch.

Medusa

An ancient Greek myth tells of Medusa, a monster with snakes for hair. Anyone who looked at her was turned to stone. Perseus managed to avoid this fate by using his polished shield to look only at the monster's reflection. He cut off Medusa's head and carried it home, dripping with blood. As each drop touched the earth, it turned into a snake.

Did you know? A boa squeezes its prey to death in its coils.

Egg-eating snake (*Dasypeltis fasciata*)

◀ **STRETCHY STOMACH**
Luckily, the throat and gut of the egg-eating snake are so elastic that its thin body can stretch enough to swallow a whole egg, shell and all. Strong muscles in the throat force food down into the stomach.

Inside a Snake

A snake has a stretched-out inside to match its long, thin outside. The backbone extends along the whole body with hundreds of ribs joined to it. There is not much room for organs such as the heart, lungs, kidneys and liver, so they are thin shapes to fit inside the snake's body. Many snakes have only one lung. The stomach and gut are stretchy so that they can hold large meals. When a snake swallows big prey, it pushes the opening of the windpipe forward from the back of its mouth in order to keep breathing. Snakes are cold-blooded, which means that their body temperature is the same as their surroundings.

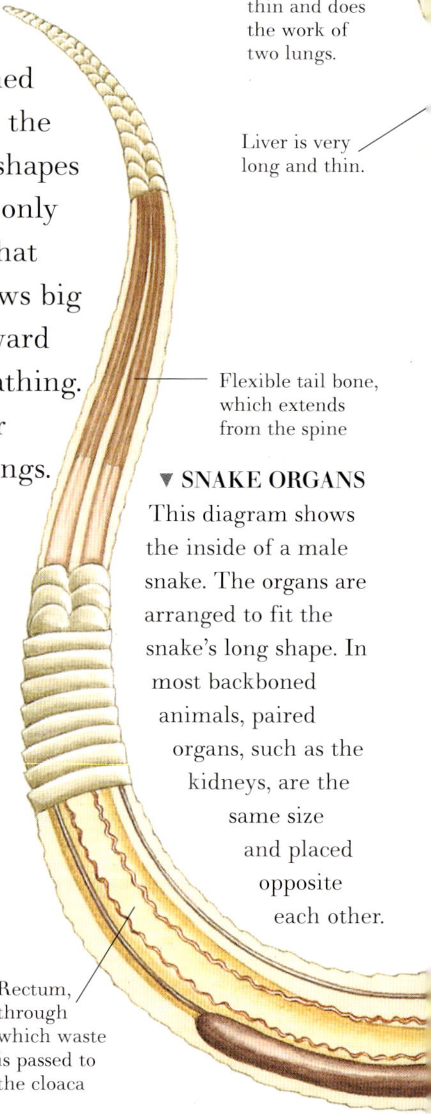

▼ **SNAKE ORGANS**
This diagram shows the inside of a male snake. The organs are arranged to fit the snake's long shape. In most backboned animals, paired organs, such as the kidneys, are the same size and placed opposite each other.

▲ **RATTLER**
Rattlesnakes have dried scales on their tail. When cornered, the snake shakes its tail to produce a warning rattle.

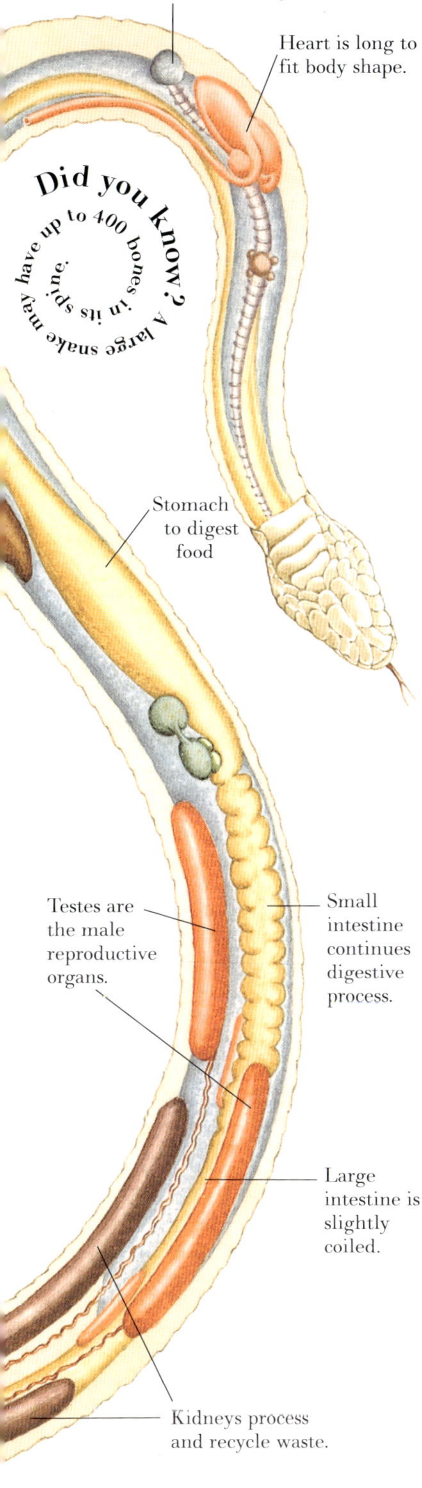

Did you know? A large snake may have up to 400 bones in its spine.

▲ SNAKE BONES
This X-ray of a grass snake shows the delicate bones that make up its skeleton. There are no arm, leg, shoulder or hip bones. The snake's ribs do not extend into the tail.

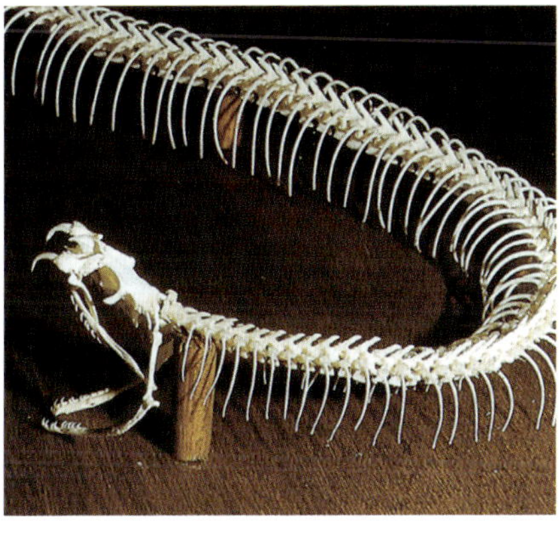

◄ SKELETON
A snake's skeleton is made up of a skull and a spine with ribs arching out from it. The jawbones can be separated so large meals can pass through.

Fierce Creatures

Crocodilians are scaly, armour-clad reptiles that include crocodiles, alligators, caimans and gharials. They are survivors from a prehistoric age – their relatives first lived on the Earth with the dinosaurs nearly 200 million years ago. Today, they are the dinosaurs' closest living relatives, apart from birds.

Crocodilians are fierce predators. They lurk motionless in rivers, lakes and swamps, waiting to snap up prey with their enormous jaws and sharp teeth. Their prey ranges from insects, frogs and fish to birds and large mammals, such as deer and zebras. Crocodilians usually live in warm, tropical places in or near fresh water, but some live in the sea. They hunt and feed mainly in the water, but crawl on to dry land to sunbathe, build nests and lay their eggs. Crocodilians rarely attack humans, even saltwater crocodiles, the largest species.

▲ **SCALY TAILS**
Like many crocodilians, an American alligator uses its long, strong tail to swim through the water. The tail moves from side to side to push the alligator along. The tail is the same length as the rest of the body.

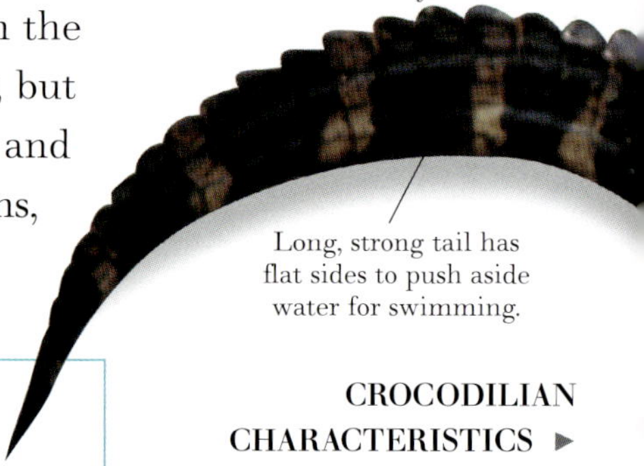

CROCODILIAN CHARACTERISTICS ►
With its thick, scaly skin, huge jaws and powerful tail, this American alligator looks like a living dinosaur. Its eyes and nostrils are on top of its head so that it can see and breathe when the rest of its body is underwater. On land, crocodilians slither along on their bellies, but they can lift themselves up on their four short legs to walk.

The Chinese Dragon

People in China have worshipped the dragon, a mythical creature, for centuries. The original stories surrounding the dragon may have been based on the real-life Chinese alligator. According to ancient texts, the dragon was a supernatural creature that could take on many different forms. It could change instantly from thick to thin or long to short, and could soar into the heavens or plunge to the depths of the sea.

▲ TALKING HEADS

Huge, powerful jaws lined with sharp teeth make Nile crocodiles killing machines. They are some of the world's largest and most dangerous reptiles. The teeth are used to attack and grip prey, but are useless for chewing. Prey has to be swallowed whole or in chunks.

SHUTEYE ►

Although this spectacled caiman has its eyes shut, it is probably not asleep, just resting. Two butterflies are basking in safety on the caiman's head. Animals will not dare to come near because the caiman is still sensitive to what is going on around it, even though its eyes are shut.

SOAKING UP THE SUN ►

Nile crocodiles sun themselves on a sandbank. This is called basking and it warms the body. Crocodilians are cold-blooded, which means that their body temperature is affected by their surroundings. They have no fur or feathers to keep them warm, nor can they shiver to warm up. They sunbathe to warm themselves and slip into the water to cool down.

The scales on the back are usually much more bony than those on the belly.

Scaly skin covers the whole body for protection and camouflage.

Eyes and nostrils are on top of the head.

The digits (toes) of each foot are slightly webbed.

American alligator (*Alligator mississippiensis*)

Long snout with sharp teeth to catch prey

Did you know? Most crocodilians live for about 50 years but some live up to 100.

Crocodilian Bodies

The crocodilian body has changed very little over the last 200 million years. It is superbly adapted to life in the water. Crocodilians can breathe with just their nostrils above the surface. Underwater, ears and nostrils close and a transparent third eyelid sweeps across the eye for protection. Crocodilians are the only reptiles with ear flaps. Inside the long, lizard-like body, a bony skeleton supports and protects the lungs, heart, stomach and other soft organs. The stomach is in two parts, one part for grinding food, the other for absorbing (taking in) nutrients. Unlike other reptiles, which have a three-chambered heart, a crocodilian's heart has four chambers, like a mammal's. This stronger heart can pump more oxygen-rich blood to the brain during a dive. The thinking part of its brain is more developed than in other reptiles, and crocodilians learn their hunting skills rather than just acting on instinct.

▲ **THROAT FLAP**
A crocodilian has no lips so it is unable to seal its mouth underwater. Instead, two special flaps at the back of the throat stop water flowing from its mouth into its lungs. This enables the crocodile to open its mouth underwater to catch and eat prey without drowning.

Did you know? A saltwater crocodile can stay underwater for more than an hour.

◄ **OPEN WIDE**
Crocodilians have mighty jaws. However, the muscles that close the mouth are much stronger than the ones that open it. This American alligator is relaxing with its mouth agape. Gaping helps to cool the animal down.

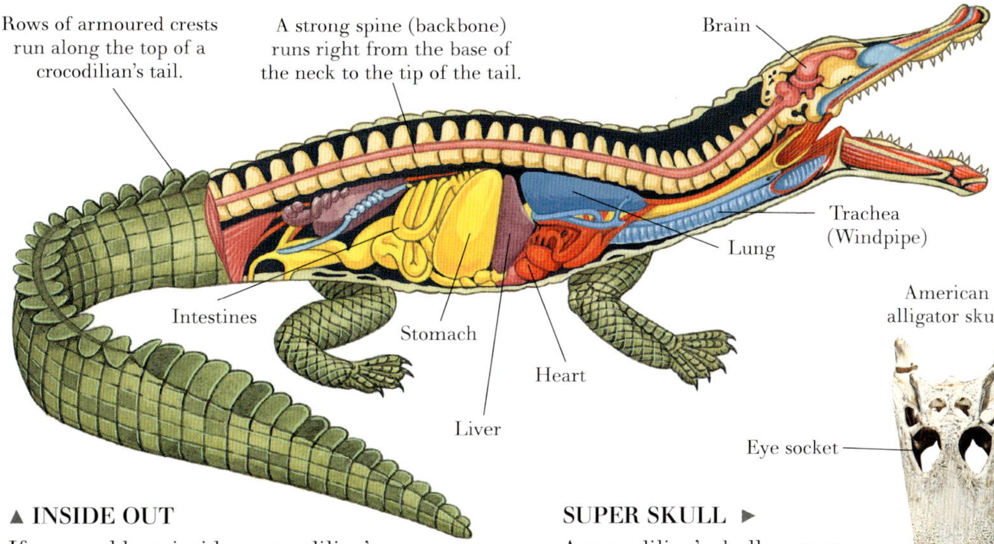

▲ INSIDE OUT

If you could see inside a crocodilian's body, you would see a mixture of reptile, bird and mammal features. The crocodilian's brain and shoulder blades are like a bird's. Its heart, diaphragm and efficient breathing system are similar to those of mammals. The stomach and digestive system are those of a reptile, as they deal with food in unchewed chunks.

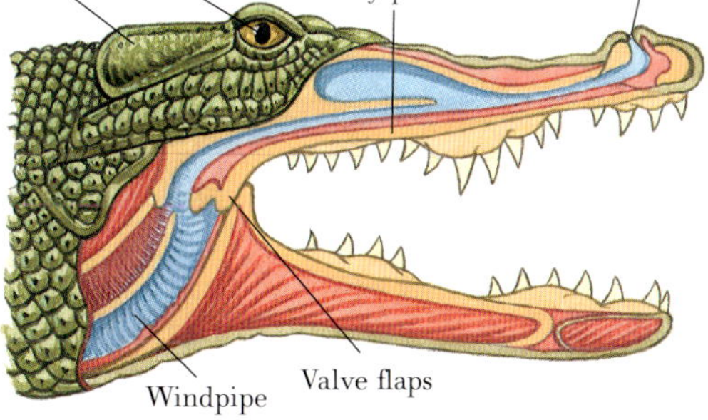

▲ WELL DESIGNED

A view inside the head of a crocodilian shows the ear, eye and nostril openings set high up in the skull. The bones in the roof of the mouth are joined together to create a bony palate that separates the nostrils from the mouth. Flaps of skin form a valve, sealing off the windpipe underwater.

SUPER SKULL ►

A crocodilian's skull protects the animal's large reptile brain. The skull is wider and more rounded in alligators (*top*), and long and triangular in crocodiles (*bottom*). Behind the eye sockets are two large holes where strong jaw muscles emerge and attach to the outer surface of the skull.

► STOMACH STONES

Crocodilians swallow objects, such as pebbles, to help mash up their food. These gastroliths (stomach stones) churn around inside part of the stomach, helping to break up food so it can be digested. Not all gastroliths are stones. Bottles, coins and a whistle have been found inside crocodilians.

Winged Hunters

There are nearly 9,000 different species (kinds) of birds in the world. Most of them eat plant shoots, seeds, nuts and fruit, or small creatures such as insects and worms. However, around 400 species, called birds of prey, hunt larger creatures or scavenge carrion (the flesh of dead animals). Birds of prey are called raptors, from the Latin *rapere* meaning 'to seize', because they grip and kill their prey with sharp talons (claws) and hooked beaks. Raptors have very sharp eyes and good hearing, so they can locate their prey on the wing. Most raptors, including eagles, falcons and hawks hunt by day. Vultures are active in the day, too, searching for carrion. Owls are raptors that hunt by night.

▼ HANGING AROUND
The outstretched wings of the kestrel face into the wind as the bird hovers like a kite above a patch of ground in search of a meal. The bird also spreads the feathers of its broad tail to keep it steady in the wind.

▼ IN A LEAGUE OF THEIR OWN
Five young tawny owls cluster together on a branch. Owls are not closely related to the other birds of prey. However, like other raptors they have talons, hooked beaks and excellent eyesight. Most hunt silently during the hours of darkness. Their rounded faces act like satellite dishes that collect the slightest sounds and direct them to the birds' ears.

Tawny owls
(*Strix aluco*)

◂ HAWKEYE

The sparrowhawk has large eyes that face forward. The bill is hooked, for tearing flesh. These are typical features of hunters.

Eurasian sparrowhawk
(*Accipiter nisus*)

▴ BUILT FOR SPEED

The peregrine falcon is one of the swiftest birds in the world, able to dive at up to 224 km/h. Its swept-back wings help it cut through the air at speed. Their shape has been copied by aircraft designers for the wings of fighter planes.

▾ THE EAGLE HAS LANDED

In the snow-covered highlands of Scotland, a golden eagle stands over a rabbit it has just killed. Eagles kill with their talons which are so long, sharp and deeply curved that one swipe is usually enough to kill the rabbit.

Golden eagle
(*Aquila chrysaetos*)

God of the Sky

Horus was one of the most important gods in ancient Egypt. He was the god of the sky and the heavens. His sacred bird was the falcon, and Horus is often represented with a human body and a falcon's head. The Egyptian hieroglyph (picture symbol) for 'god' in ancient Egyptian is a falcon.

How Birds of Prey Work

Birds of prey are expert fliers. Like other birds, they have powerful chest and wing muscles to move their wings. Virtually the whole body is covered with feathers to make it smooth so that it can slip easily through the air. The bones are very light, and some have a honeycomb structure, which makes them even lighter but still very strong. Birds of prey differ from other birds in a number of ways, particularly in their powerful bills (beaks) and clawed feet, which are well adapted for their life as hunters. Also, like many other birds, they regurgitate (cough up) pellets. These contain the parts of their prey they cannot digest.

▲ NAKED NECK
A Ruppell's vulture feeds on a zebra carcass in the Masai Mara region of eastern Africa. Like many vultures, it has a naked neck, which it can thrust deep inside the carcass. As a result, it can feed without getting its feathers too covered in blood.

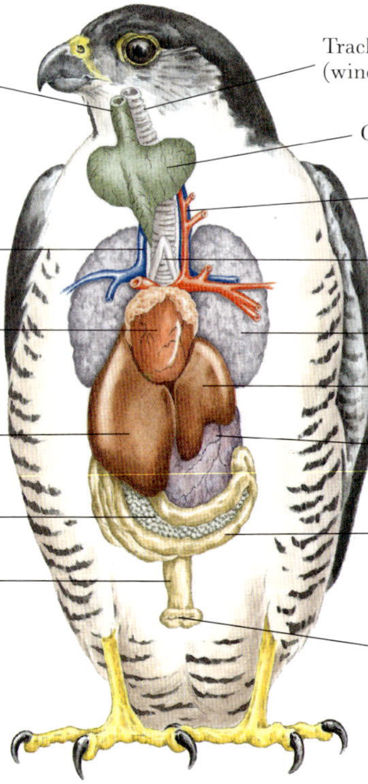

◄ BODY PARTS
Underneath their feathery covering, birds of prey have a complex system of internal organs. Unlike humans, most birds have a crop to store food in before digestion. They also have a gizzard to grind up hard particles of food, such as bone, and to start the process of making a pellet. Birds also have a syrinx (the bird equivalent of the human voice box).

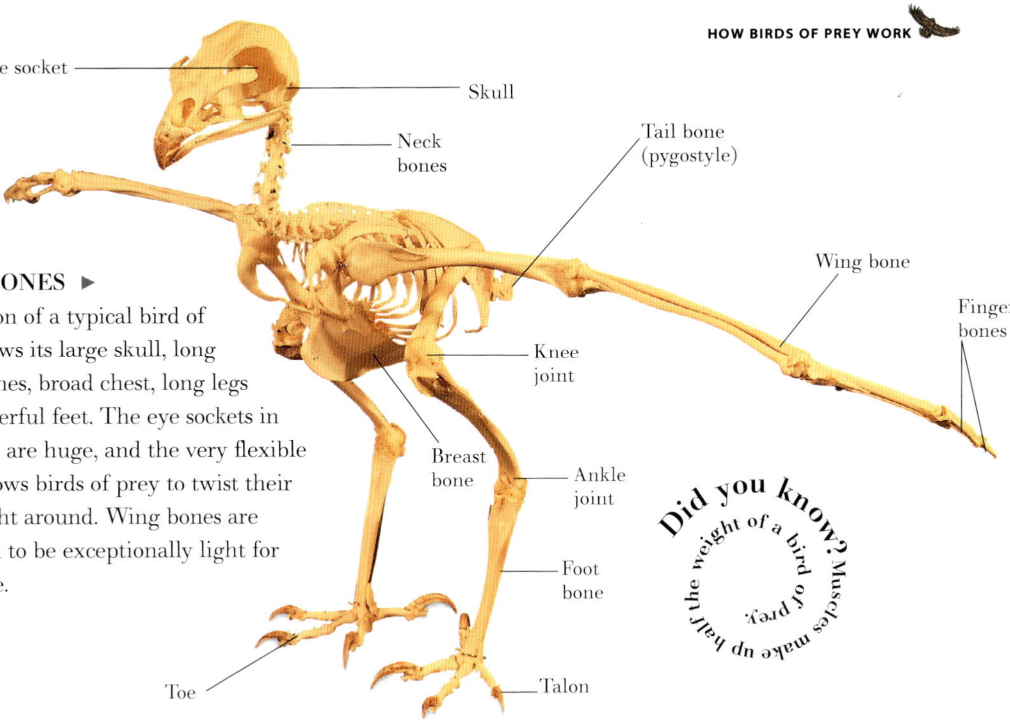

BARE BONES ▸

A skeleton of a typical bird of prey shows its large skull, long wing bones, broad chest, long legs and powerful feet. The eye sockets in the skull are huge, and the very flexible neck allows birds of prey to twist their head right around. Wing bones are designed to be exceptionally light for their size.

Did you know? Muscles make up half the weight of a bird of prey.

▾ BACK TO FRONT

This peregrine falcon appears to have eyes in the back of its head. Its body is facing away, but its eyes are looking straight into the camera. All birds of prey can twist their heads right around like this, because they have many more neck bones than mammals. They can see in any direction without moving their body, but they cannot move their eyeballs in their sockets.

Peregrine falcon
(*Falco peregrinus*)

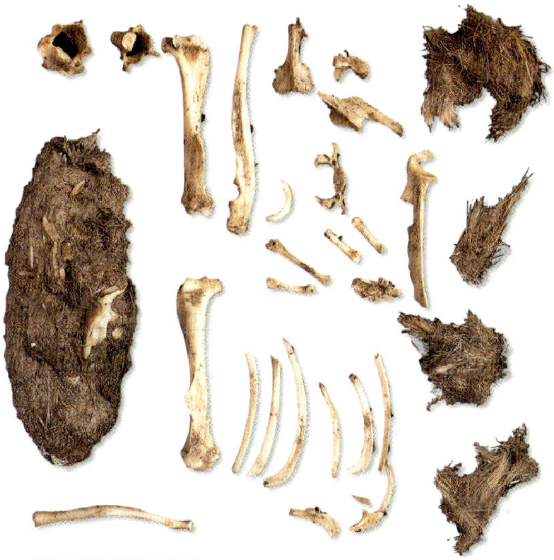

▴ INDIGESTION

On the left of the picture above is the regurgitated (coughed-up) pellet of a barn owl, and on the right are the indigestible parts it contained. The pellet is about 5cm long. From the scraps of fur and fragments of bone in it, we can tell that the owl has just eaten a small mammal.

Built for Speed

Equids are designed to be able to flee from predators. Their skeletons are lightweight, strong and geared for maximum speed with minimum energy. A horse's upper leg bones, for example, are fused into a single, strong bone, while in humans their equivalents are two separate bones. The joints are less flexible than those of a human. Instead, they are strong in an up-and-down direction to support and protect powerful tendons and muscles. A horse's skeleton is designed to absorb the weight and impact of its body as it moves over the ground.

▲ **RESTING ON AUTOMATIC**
When horses are standing at rest, the patella (kneecap) slots into a groove in the femur (leg bone). This locks their back legs into an energy-saving position, just like our knees. Another mechanism keeps the horse's head from dropping to the ground. A ligament in the neck acts like a piece of elastic, returning the head to an upright resting position when the horse is not grazing.

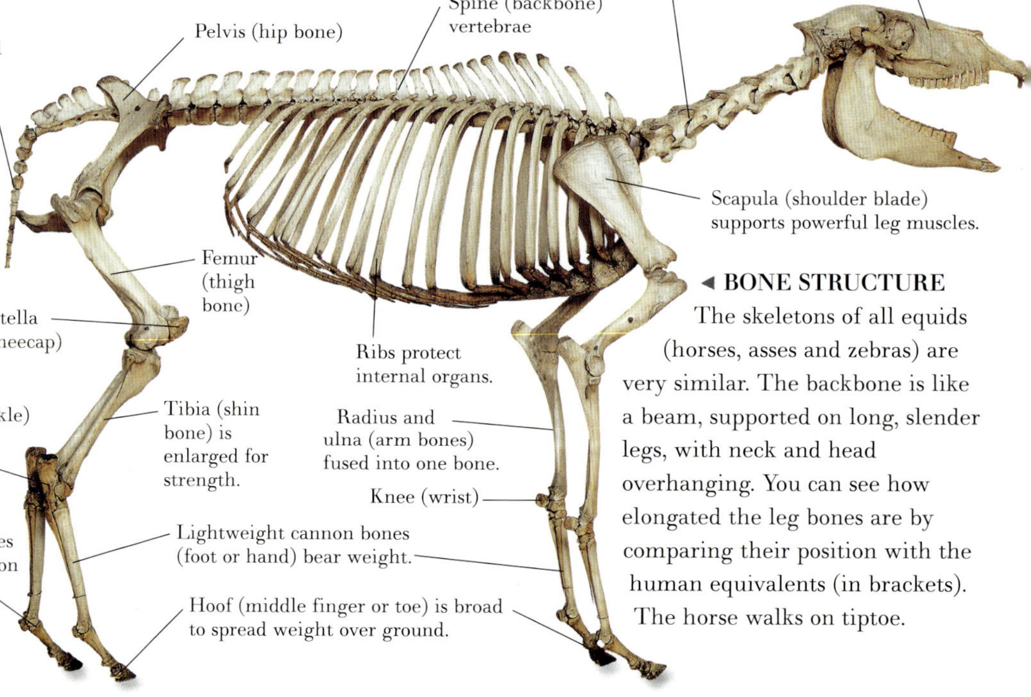

◀ **BONE STRUCTURE**
The skeletons of all equids (horses, asses and zebras) are very similar. The backbone is like a beam, supported on long, slender legs, with neck and head overhanging. You can see how elongated the leg bones are by comparing their position with the human equivalents (in brackets). The horse walks on tiptoe.

◄ SPACE FOR CHEWING

The long and narrow skull provides space for the big molar teeth, and enables the eye sockets to fit in behind them. This means that when the horse chews, there is no pressure on the eye. The large eye sockets give enough space for the horse to have all-round vision.

▼ FIGHTING TEETH

The small tushes (or tusker) teeth, just behind the big incisors, are used in fights between stallions (males). Mares (females) have very small tushes teeth or none at all.

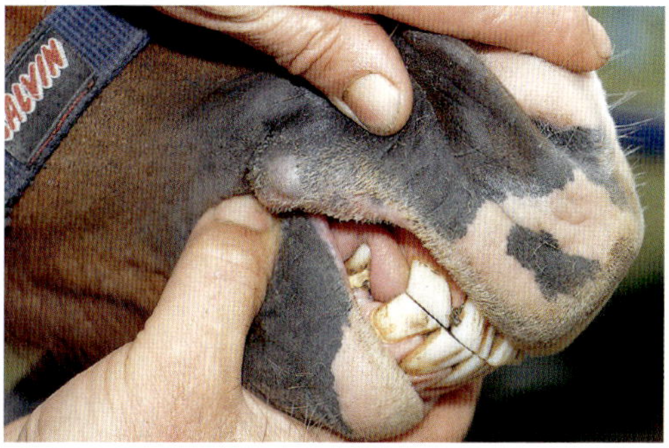

Pegasus

Greek mythology tells of a winged horse called Pegasus. He sprang fully grown from the dead body of the evil Medusa after she was beheaded. Pegasus was ridden by the hero Bellerophon. Together they defeated the fire-breathing monster, the Chimera. Bellerophon tried to ride Pegasus to heaven but the gods were angry and he was thrown off and killed. Pegasus became a constellation in the night sky.

TEETH FOR THE JOB ►

Mares have 36–40 teeth and stallions 44 teeth. A horse's teeth are specially adapted for its diet. Chisel-shaped incisors at the front snip through grass. Molars in the side of the mouth grind down the grass before it is swallowed. The degree of wear on teeth is sometimes used to calculate a horse's age. This can be misleading, as some foods wear down the teeth more than others do.

Powerful Bodies

The horse is one of the fastest long-distance runners in the animal world. Its digestive system processes large quantities of food in order to extract sufficient energy. The digestive system is in two parts. The food is partly digested in the stomach, then moves quickly through to the hindgut (cecum and colon). Here, bacteria break down the tough cell walls of the plants. The nutrients are released, and cells lining the gut are ready to absorb them.

Equids also have a big heart and large lungs. This allows them to run quickly and over a long distance. Horse tendons connecting muscles to bones are very elastic, especially those in the lower leg. Together with the ligaments, which bind bones together at joints, they can stretch and give to save energy and cushion impact of the hooves on the ground when the horse is on the move.

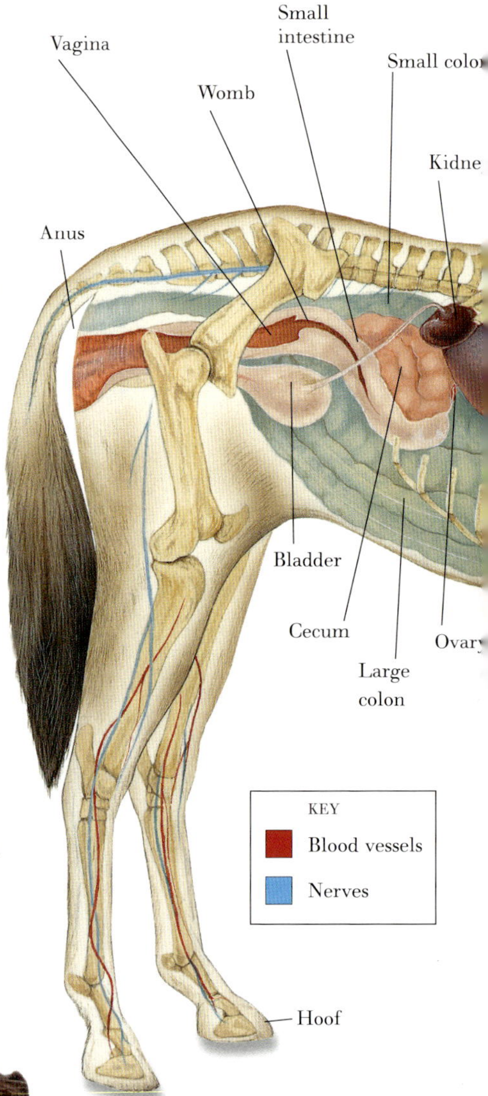

◂ FLEXIBLE LIPS
The horse's mobile, sensitive lips are described as prehensile (able to grasp). They are used to select and pick food. When a horse wants to use its power of smell to full effect, it curls its lips back.

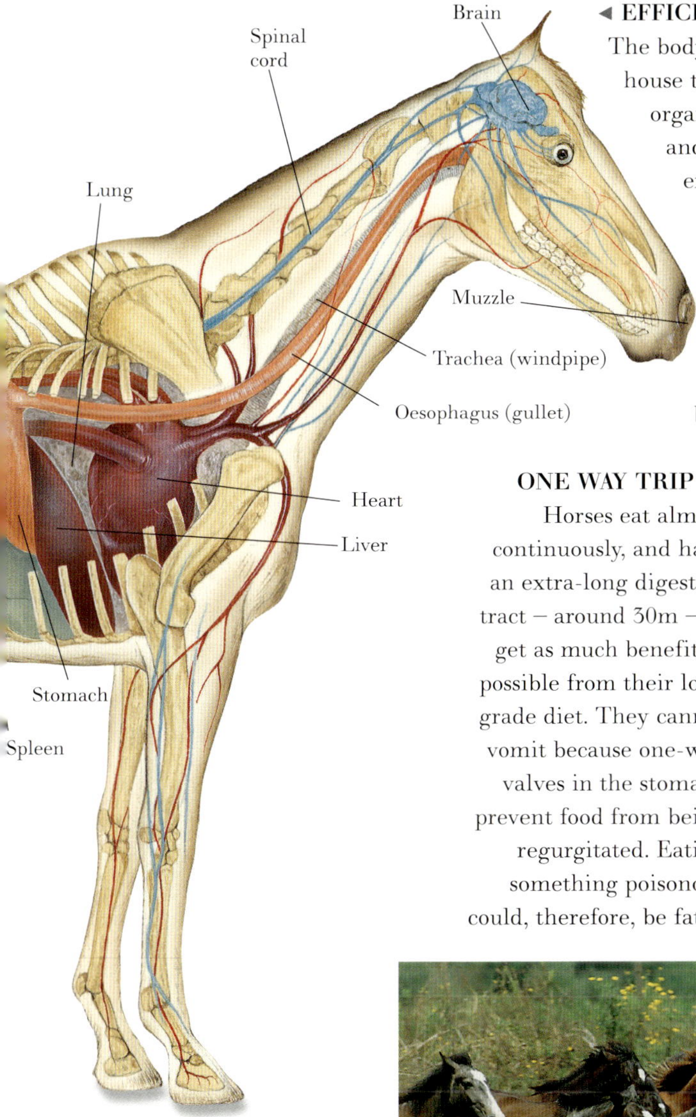

◀ EFFICIENT BODYWORKS

The body of the horse is big enough to house the powerful muscles and large organs that the animal needs for speed and endurance. The large heart, for example, pumps at 30–40 beats per minute when resting – about half the rate of a human's. This can rise to a top rate of 240 – nearly twice the rate of a human's – when working hard. This means that blood circulates around the body very efficiently.

ONE WAY TRIP ▶

Horses eat almost continuously, and have an extra-long digestive tract – around 30m – to get as much benefit as possible from their low-grade diet. They cannot vomit because one-way valves in the stomach prevent food from being regurgitated. Eating something poisonous could, therefore, be fatal.

LONG LEGS ▶

Horses' feet have a single toe, tipped with a fingernail-like hoof. Horses stand on this single toe. Their heel bone never touches the ground, making their legs very long – ideal for running and jumping.

Gentle Giants

Elephants are the largest and heaviest creatures on land. An African male (bull) elephant weighs as much as 80 people, six cars, 12 large horses or 1,500 cats. Elephants are extremely strong and can pick up whole trees with their trunks. They are also highly intelligent, gentle animals. Females live together in family groups and look after one another. Elephants are mammals – they can control their body temperature and they feed milk to their babies. After humans, elephants are the longest lived of all mammals. Some live to be about 70 years old. Two species (kinds) of elephant exist today – the African elephant and the Asian elephant. Both have a trunk, thick skin and large ears, although African elephants have larger ears than Indian ones. Not all elephants have tusks, however. Generally, only African elephants and male Asian elephants have tusks.

▲ **WORKING ELEPHANTS**
In India, domesticated (tamed) elephants are used by farmers to carry heavy loads. In some Asian countries they also move heavy logs by pulling them.

Tail, has a brush of thick hair at the end.

African elephant (*Loxodonta africana*)

Indra and the Elephant
One of the most celebrated Hindu gods, Indra, rides a mighty white elephant called Airavata. In Hinduism (the main religion of India), elephants are sacred animals. One of Indra's emblems is the ankus, a special pointed stick used to control elephants. Indra is shown holding an ankus in this painting.

▼ UNUSUAL FEATURES

The mighty elephant is a record-breaking beast. Not only is it the largest land animal, it is also the second tallest (only the giraffe is taller). It has larger ears, teeth and tusks than any other animal. The elephant is also one of the few animals to have a nose in the form of a long trunk.

FAMILY LIFE ▲

Adult male and female elephants do not live together in family groups. Instead, adult sisters and daughters live in groups led by an older female. Adult males (bulls) live on their own or in all-male groups.

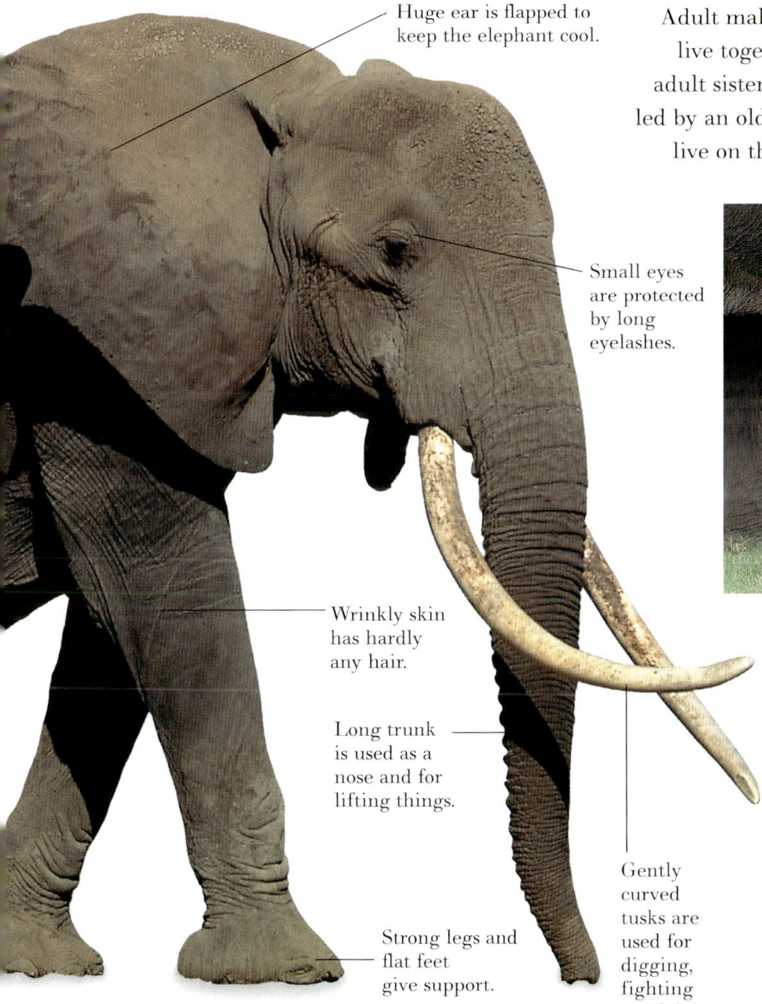

BABY ELEPHANTS ▲

An elephant baby feels safe between its mother's front legs. It spends most of the first year of its life there. Mother elephants look after their young for longer than any other animal parent except humans. Daughters never leave the family group unless the group becomes too big.

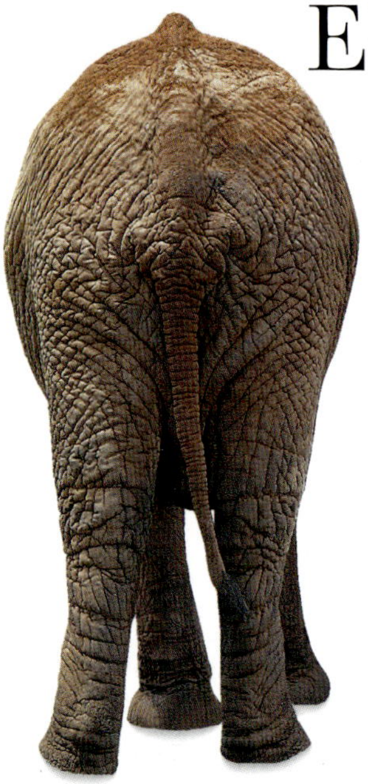

Elephant Bodies

An elephant's skin is thick, grey and wrinkly, and surprisingly sensitive. Some insects, including flies and mosquitoes, can bite through it. Often, elephants roll around in the mud to keep flies from biting them (as well as cooling themselves down). Underneath the skin, the elephant has typical mammal body parts, only very large. The heart, for example, is about five times bigger than a human heart and weighs up to 21kg – the weight of a small child. Also, an elephant's huge intestines can weigh nearly a tonne, including the contents. The powerful lungs are operated by strong muscles. These let the elephant breathe underwater while using its trunk as a snorkel.

▲ **THICK SKIN**
An elephant's skin is 2.5cm thick on the back and in some areas of the head. But in other places, such as around the mouth, the skin is paper thin.

▲ **PINK SKIN**
An elephant gets its colour from dots of grey pigment (colouring) in the skin. As it ages, this grey pigment may gradually fade so that the skin looks pink.

Did you know? Some very rare Asian elephants have white skin.

◄ **ELEPHANT HAIR**
The hairiest part of an elephant is the end of its tail. The tail hairs are many times thicker than human hair and grow into thick tufts. Apart from the end of the tail, the chin and around the eyes and ears, the adult elephant has very little hair.

▲ **FLY SWATTER**
Although they can swish their tufted tails to get rid of flies, elephants also use leafy branches to swat annoying insect pests. They pick a branch up with their trunks and brush it across their backs to wipe the pests away.

Flying Elephants
According to an Indian folk tale, elephants could once fly. This ability was taken away by a hermit with magical powers when a flock of elephants woke him from a deep trance. The elephants landed in a tree above him, making a lot of noise and causing a branch to fall on his head. The hermit was so furious that he cast a magical spell.

▼ **INSIDE AN ELEPHANT**
If you could look inside the body of an elephant, you would see its huge skeleton supporting the organs. The cross-section shown here is of a female African elephant.

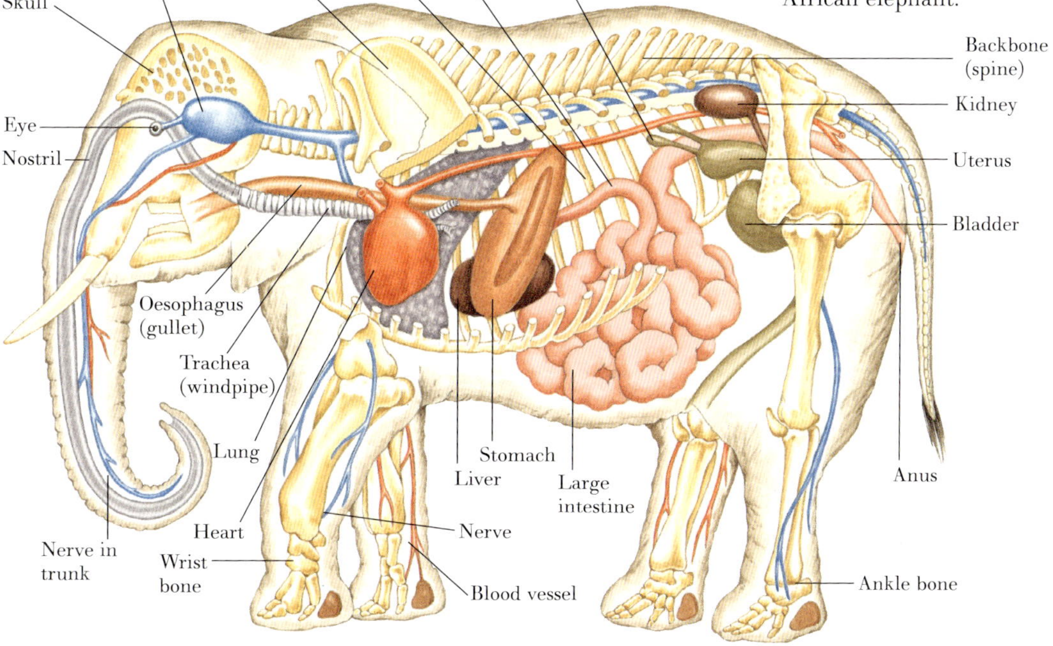

Big Bones

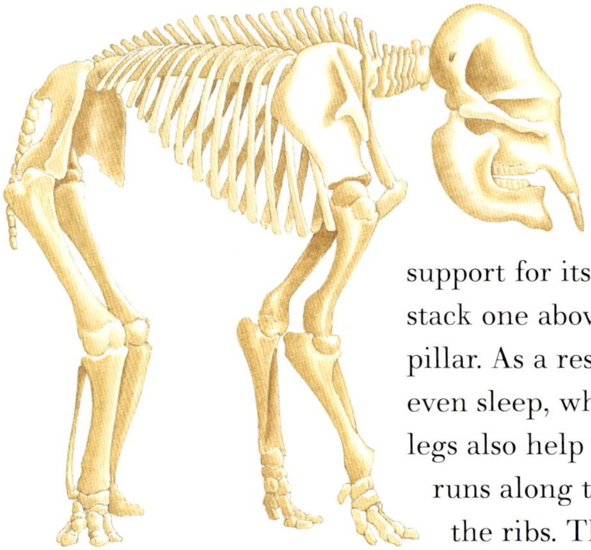

An elephant's legs are placed directly underneath its body, like a table's legs. This arrangement provides a firm support for its great weight. The leg bones stack one above the other to form a strong pillar. As a result, an elephant can rest, and even sleep, while standing up. The pillar-like legs also help to hold up the backbone, which runs along the top of the animal and supports the ribs. The backs of Asian elephants arch upwards, while African elephants' backs have a dip in them. These different shapes are produced by bones that stick up from the backbone. The elephant's skeleton is not just built for strength, however. It is also flexible enough to let the elephant kneel and squat.

▲ **BONY BACK**
Crests of bone stick up from the backbone of the Asian elephant's skeleton. The muscles that hold up the head are joined to these spines and to the back of the skull.

Elephant's skull

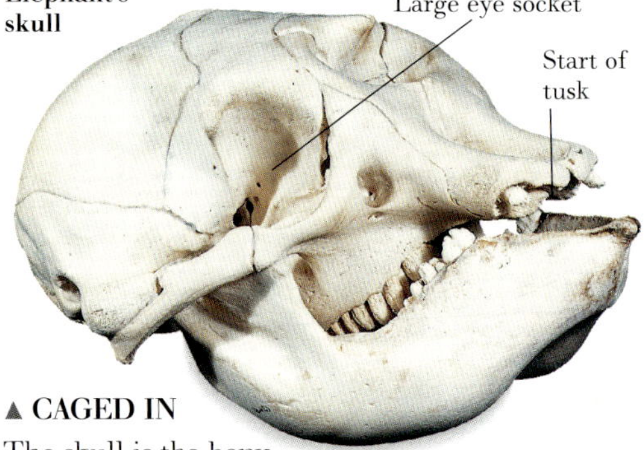

▲ **CAGED IN**
The skull is the bony box that protects the brain and holds the huge teeth and tusks. The skull above is that of a young male elephant with undeveloped tusks. On an adult male, the upper jaw juts out farther than the lower jaw because it contains the roots for the heavy tusks.

Skull cut in half

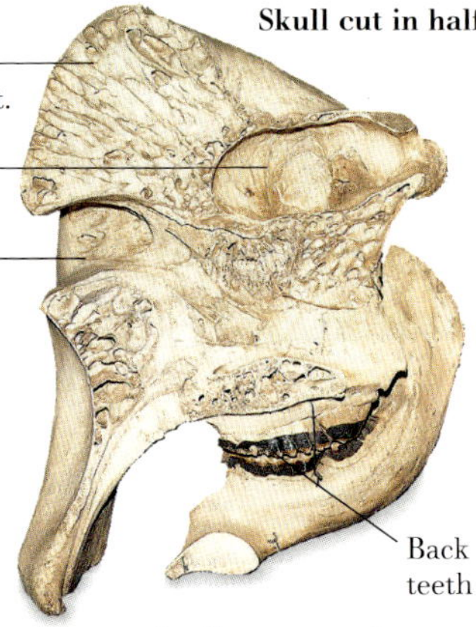

▲ **AIR HOLES**
An elephant has a large skull compared to the size of its body. However, a honeycomb of air holes inside the skull makes it lighter than it looks from the outside.

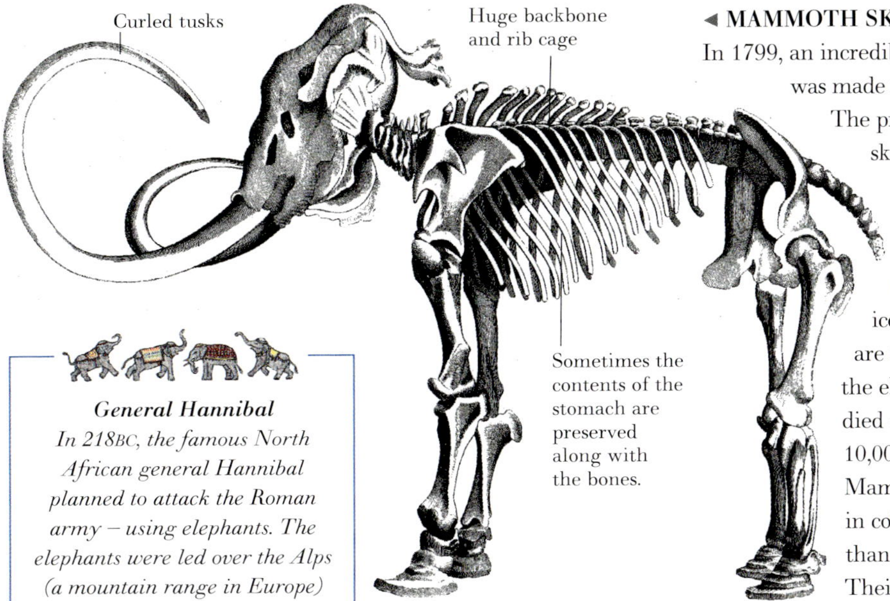

◄ MAMMOTH SKELETON

In 1799, an incredible discovery was made in Siberia. The preserved skeleton of a woolly mammoth was found buried in the ice. Mammoths are relatives of the elephant that died out about 10,000 years ago. Mammoths lived in colder places than elephants. Their long body hair kept them warm.

General Hannibal

In 218BC, the famous North African general Hannibal planned to attack the Roman army – using elephants. The elephants were led over the Alps (a mountain range in Europe) and taken across rivers by raft. Sadly, most of them died and Hannibal had to admit defeat.

AFRICAN SKELETON ►

The African elephant's forehead is smooth and rounded, whereas an Asian elephant's skull and head have two domes on top. The large hole in the skull is the trunk opening, and the tusks fit into the skull through the upper jaw.

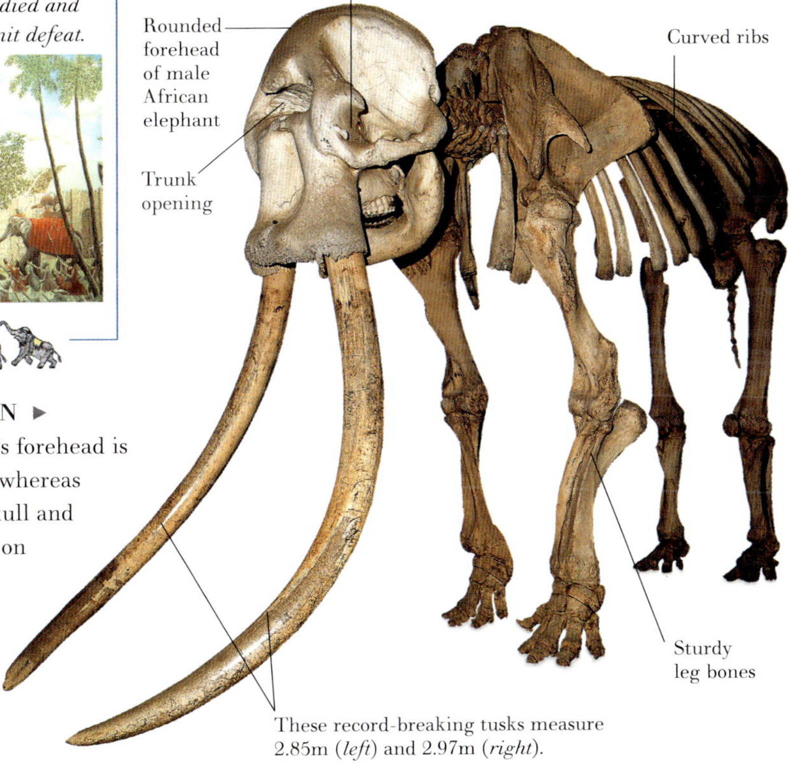

The Bear Facts

Bears may look cuddly and appealing, but in reality they are enormously powerful animals. Bears are mammals with bodies covered in thick fur. They are heavily built with a short tail and large claws. All bears are basically carnivores (meat-eaters), but most enjoy a very mixed diet with just the occasional snack of meat. The exception is the polar bear, which feasts on the blubber (fat) of seals. There are eight species (kinds) of bear: the brown or grizzly bear, American black bear, Asiatic black bear, polar bear, sun bear, sloth bear, spectacled bear and giant panda. They live in both cold and tropical regions of the world. The sun bears of South-east Asia are the smallest at 1.5m long, while Alaska's brown bears are the largest at 2.7m long.

Winnie-the-Pooh

The lovable teddy bear Winnie-the-Pooh was created by A.A. Milne. Like real bears he loves honey. Teddy bears became popular as toys in the early 1900s. The President of the USA, Teddy Roosevelt refused to shoot a bear cub on a hunting trip. Toy bears went on sale soon after known as "Teddy's bears".

◄ **BEAR FACE**
The brown bear shares the huge dog-like head and face of all bears. Bears have prominent noses, but relatively small eyes and ears. This is because they mostly rely on their sense of smell to help them find food.

▲ **BIG FLAT FEET**
A polar bear's feet are broad, flat and furry. The five long, curved claws cannot be retracted (pulled back). One swipe could kill a seal instantly.

◄ POINTS OF A BEAR

The brown bear is called the grizzly bear in North America. Fully-grown brown bears weigh nearly half a tonne. They fear no other animals apart from humans. They can chase prey at high speed, but they rarely bother as they feed mainly on plants.

▲ GIANT PANDA

China's giant panda, with its distinctive black and white face, is a very unusual bear. Unlike most other bears, which will eat anything, pandas feed almost exclusively on the bamboo plant.

◄ ARCTIC NOMAD

Most bears lead a solitary life. The polar bear wanders alone across the Arctic sea ice. Usually it will not tolerate other bears. The exceptions are bears that congregate at rubbish dumps, or mothers accompanied by their cubs, as shown here.

Bear Bodies

Bears are the bully-boys of the animal kingdom, using their size, strength and deep roar to scare off other animals. Most species (kinds) can stand up on their back legs for a short time to make themselves look even more fierce. At other times, a bear will put its powerful forelimbs to good use in digging, climbing, fishing and fighting. Bears do not like each other's company and will often attack other bears that cross their path. During fights, bears can do considerable damage with their teeth and claws and survive by sheer brute force. Male bears are generally much larger than females of the same species.

▲ **CLAWS DOWN**
The sun bear has particularly large, curved claws for climbing trees. It spends most of the day sleeping or sunbathing in the branches. At night it strips off bark with its claws, looking for insects and honey in bees' nests.

◄ **PUTTING ON WEIGHT**
This grizzly bear is at peak size. Most bears change size as the seasons pass. They are large and well-fed in autumn, ready for their winter hibernation. When they emerge in spring, they are scrawny with sagging coats.

Beowulf
An Anglo-Saxon poem tells of the hero Beowulf (bear-wolf). He had the strength of a bear and went through many heroic adventures. Beowulf is famous for slaying a monster called Grendel. Here, Beowulf as an old man lies dying from the wounds inflicted by a fire-breathing dragon.

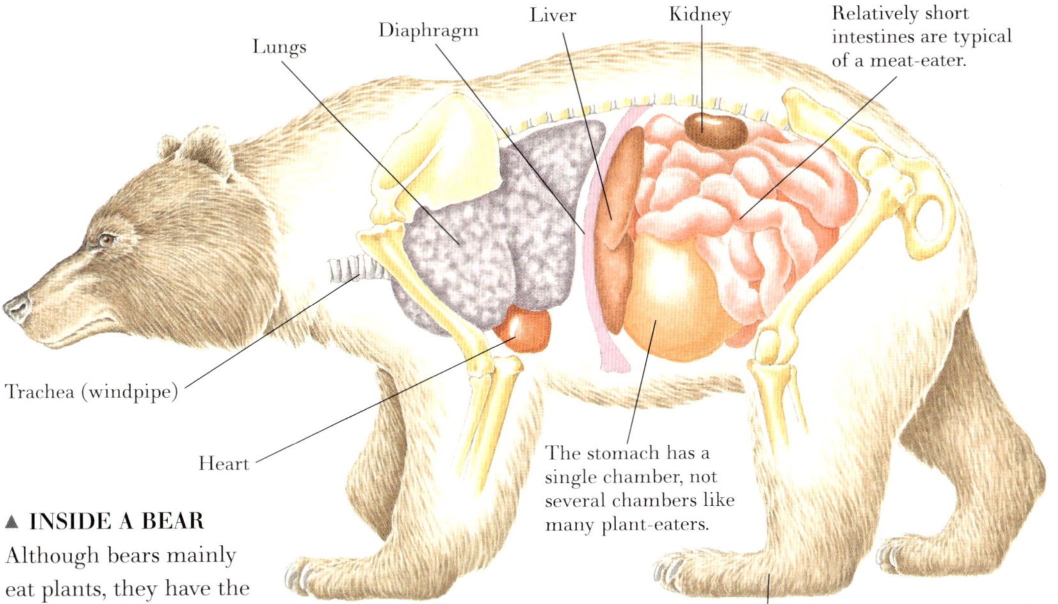

▲ **INSIDE A BEAR**

Although bears mainly eat plants, they have the relatively short intestines more characteristic of a meat-eater, rather than a long gut like a cow. This makes it hard for them to digest their food. Curiously, the bamboo-eating giant panda has the shortest gut of all. Because of this it can digest no more than 20 per cent of what it eats, compared to 60 per cent in a cow.

▲ **SHORT BURSTS**

Bears are not particularly agile and swift, but they can run fast over short distances. The brown bear can charge at 50km/h (lions reach about 65km/h) and does sometimes chase its food. A bear at full charge is a frightening sight.

▲ **SWEET TOOTH**

The sun bear's long slender tongue is ideal for licking honey from bees' nests and for scooping up termites and other insects. Like all bears, it has mobile lips, a flexible snout and strong jaws.

Stealthy Hunters

Cats are native to every continent except Australia and Antarctica. They are mammals with fine fur that is often beautifully marked. All cats are meat-eaters, being skilled hunters and killers with strong agile bodies, acute senses and sharp teeth and claws. Cats are stealthy and intelligent animals, and most kinds live alone and are very secretive. Although cats vary in size from the domestic (house) cats kept by people as pets to the huge Siberian tiger, both wild and domestic cats share many features and behave in very similar ways. In all, there are 38 different species (kinds) of cat.

▲ LONG TAIL
A cat's long tail helps it to balance as it runs. Cats also use their tails to signal their feelings to other cats.

▲ PRIDE KING
Unlike other cats, most lions live in groups called prides. Each pride is ruled by a single large adult male. The other adult members are all lionesses (females). The lionesses hunt as a team, usually at dusk. Most lions live in the grasslands of Africa, where they feed on large antelopes, such as wildebeests and gazelles.

▲ BIG BITE
As this tiger yawns, it reveals its sharp teeth and strong jaws which can give a lethal bite. Cats use these long canine teeth for killing prey.

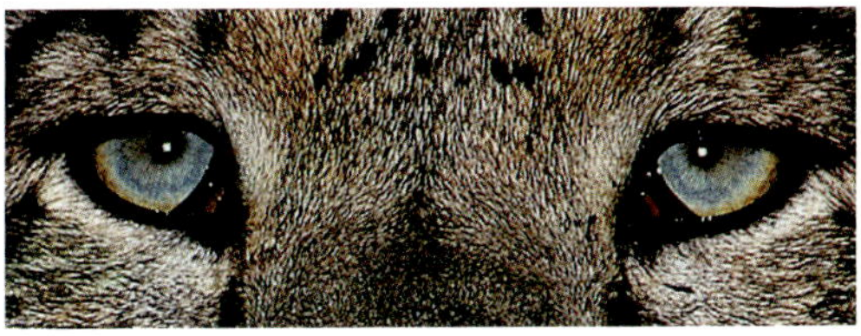

▲ NIGHT SIGHT

The pupils (dark centres) of cats' eyes close to a slit or small circle during the day to keep out the glare. At night they open up to let in as much light as possible. This enables a cat to see clearly at night as well as during the day.

The Lion and the Saint

St Jerome was a Christian scholar who lived from about AD331 to 420. According to legend, he found an injured lion in the desert with a thorn in its paw. Instead of attacking him, the lion befriended the saint when he removed the thorn. St Jerome is often shown with a lion sitting at his feet.

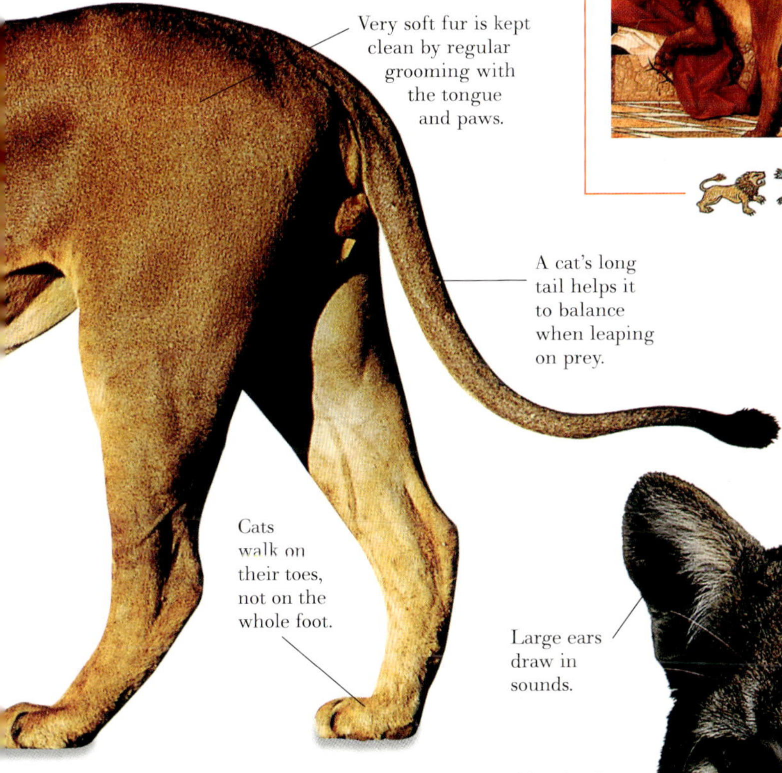

Did you know? Some Arctic cultures believe that cats represent the spirits of the dead.

CAT'S EARS ▶

A cat's ears are set high on its head. This gives a keen hunter the best possible chance of picking up sounds. Cats can also swivel their ears to pick up sounds from almost any direction.

Inside a Cat

The skeleton of a cat gives it its shape and has about 230 bones (a human has 206). A cat's short and round skull is joined to the backbone (spine), which supports the body. Vertebrae (bones of the spine) protect the spinal cord, which is the main nerve cable in the body. The ribs are joined to the spine, forming a cage that protects a cat's heart and lungs. Cats' teeth are designed for killing and chewing. Wild cats have to be very careful not to damage their teeth, because with broken teeth they would quickly die from starvation.

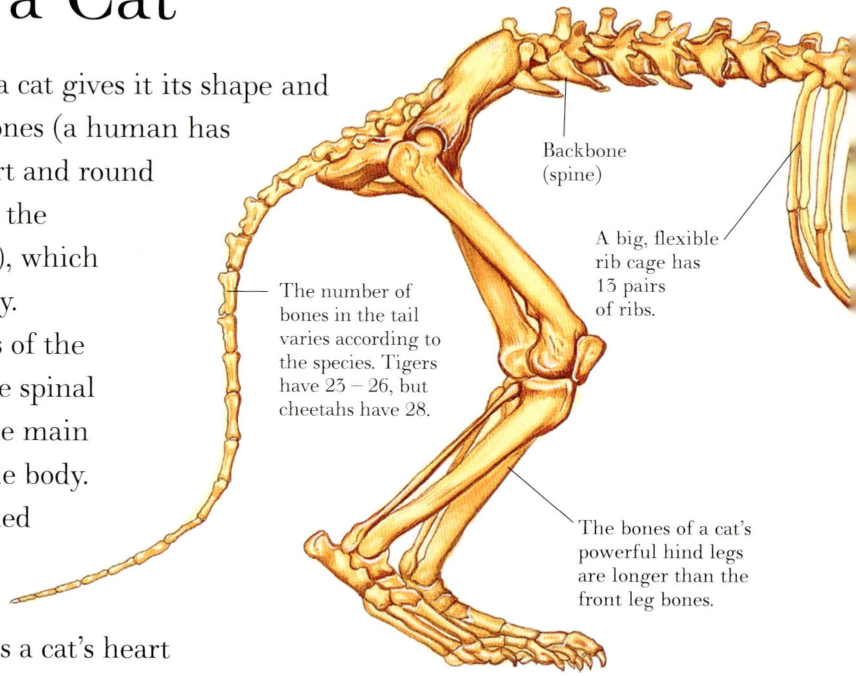

▲ **THE FRAME**
The powerfully built skeleton of a tiger is similar to all cats' skeletons. Cats have short necks with seven compressed vertebrae. These help to streamline and balance the cat so that it can run at great speeds. All cats have slightly different shoulder bones. A cheetah has long shoulder bones to which sprinting muscles are attached. A leopard, however, has short shoulder bones and thicker, tree-climbing muscles.

◀ **CANINES AND CARNASSIALS**
A tiger reveals its fearsome teeth. Its long, curved canines are adapted to fit between the neck bones of its prey to break the spinal cord. Like all carnivores, cats have strong back teeth, called carnassials. These teeth work like scissors, slicing through meat.

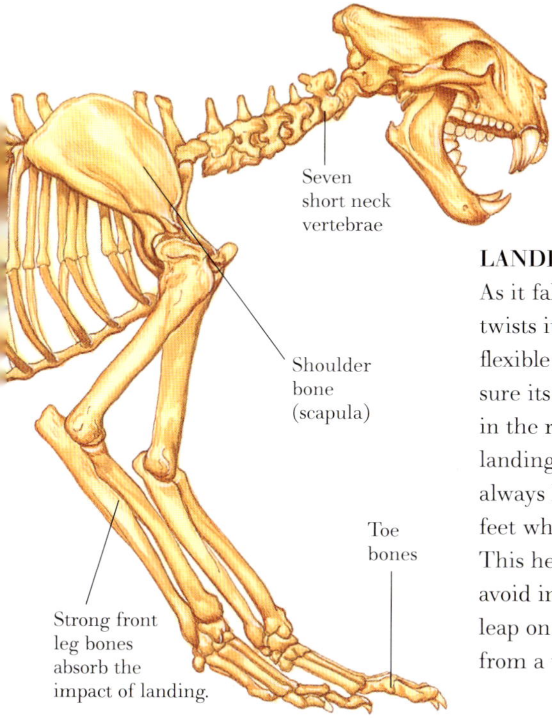

LANDING FEET ▶
As it falls, this cat twists its supple, flexible spine to make sure its feet will be in the right place for landing. Cats almost always land on their feet when they fall. This helps them to avoid injury as they leap on prey or jump from a tree.

▼ CHEWING ON A BONE
Ravenous lions feast on the carcass of their latest kill. Cats' jaws are hinged so that their jaw bones can move only up and down. Because of this, cats eat on one side of their mouths at a time and they often tilt their heads when they eat.

▼ CAT SKULL
Like all cats' skulls, this tiger's skull has a high crown at the back giving lots of space for the attachment of its strong neck muscles. The eye sockets hold large eyes that allow it to see well to the sides as well as to the front. Its short jaws can open wide to deliver a powerful bite.

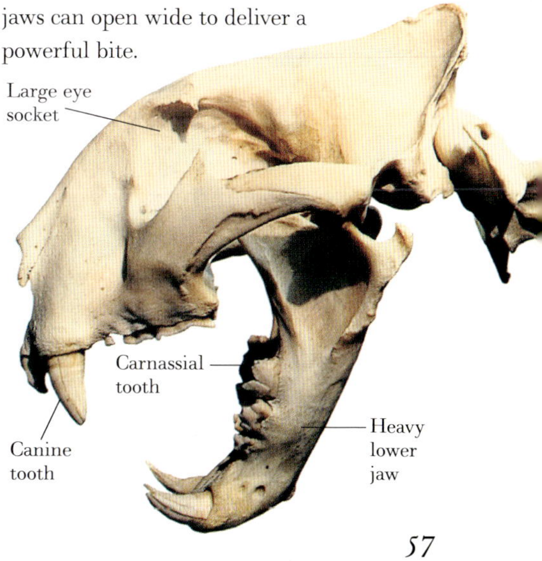

Killing Machines

Both inside and out, cats are designed to be killers. Thick back and shoulder muscles make them powerful jumpers and climbers. Long, dagger-like teeth and sharp, curved claws that grow from all of their digits (toes) are their weapons. One of the digits on a cat's front foot is called the dew claw. This is held off the ground to keep it sharp and ready to hold prey. Cats are warm-blooded, which means that their bodies stay at the same temperature no matter how hot or cold the weather is. The fur on their skin keeps them warm when conditions are cold. When it is hot, cats cool down by sweating through their noses and paw pads.

Hercules and the Nemean Lion
The mythical Greek hero Hercules was the son of the god Zeus and tremendously strong. As a young man he committed a terrible crime. Part of his punishment was to kill the Nemean lion. The lion had impenetrable skin and could not be killed with arrows or spears. Hercules chased the lion into a cave and strangled it with his hands. He wore its skin as a shield and its head as a helmet.

▼ KNOCKOUT CLAWS
Cheetahs have well-developed dew claws that stick out from their front legs. They use these claws to knock down prey before grabbing its throat or muzzle to finish it off. Other cats use their dew claws to grip while climbing or to hold on to prey. Cats have five claws, including the dew claw, on their front paws. On their back paws, they have only four claws.

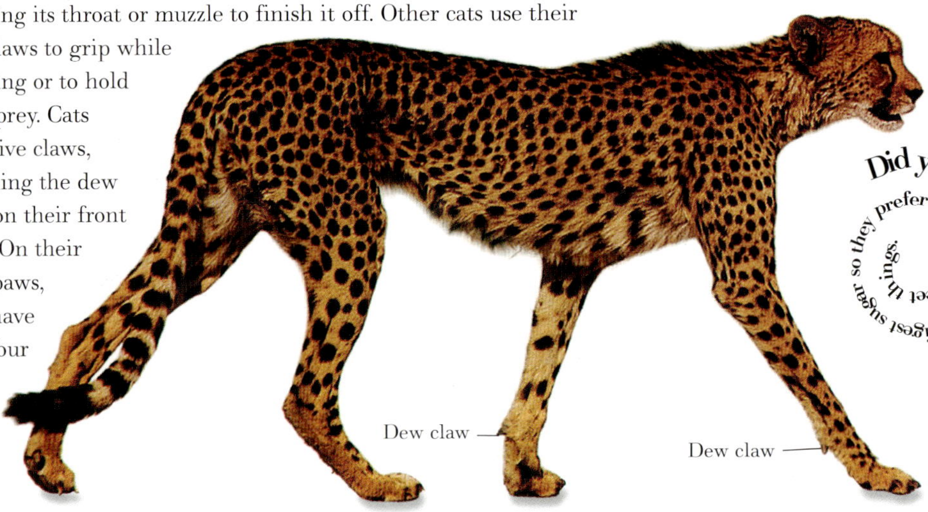

Did you kno
cannot digest sugar so they prefer not to eat sweet things.

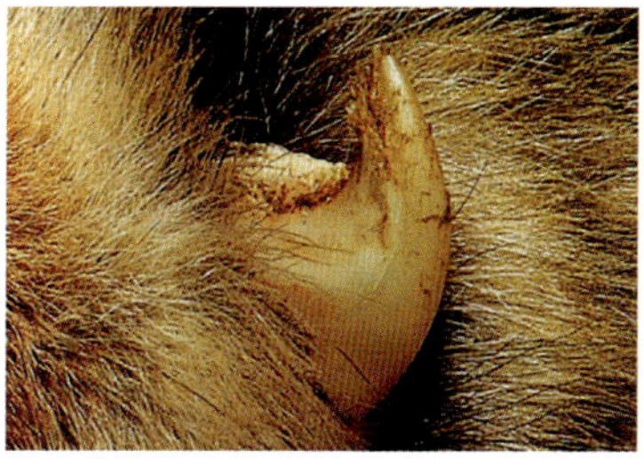

▲ TIGER CLAW

This is the extended claw of a tiger. Cats' claws are made of keratin, just like human fingernails. They need to be kept sharp all the time.

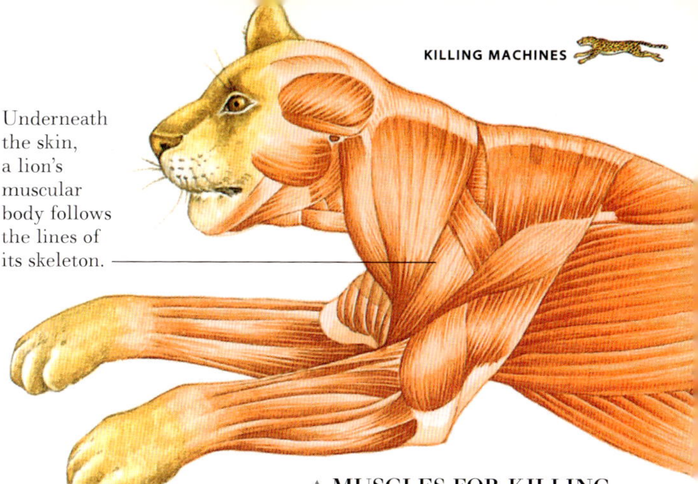

▲ MUSCLES FOR KILLING

Cats have very strong shoulder and neck muscles which give it power to attack prey. The muscles also absorb some of the impact when the cat pounces.

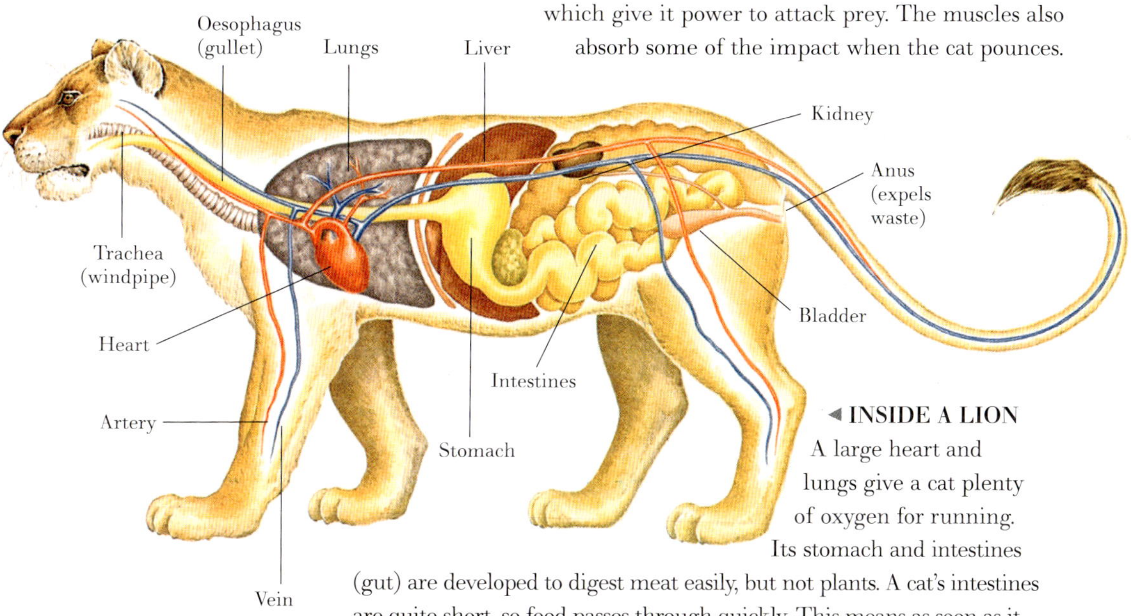

◄ INSIDE A LION

A large heart and lungs give a cat plenty of oxygen for running. Its stomach and intestines (gut) are developed to digest meat easily, but not plants. A cat's intestines are quite short, so food passes through quickly. This means as soon as it needs more food, a cat is light enough to run and pounce. However, once a lion has had a big meal, it does not need to eat again for several days.

CLAW PROTECTION ►

Cats retract (pull back) their claws into fleshy sheaths to protect them. This prevents them from getting blunt or damaged. Only cheetahs do not have sheaths.

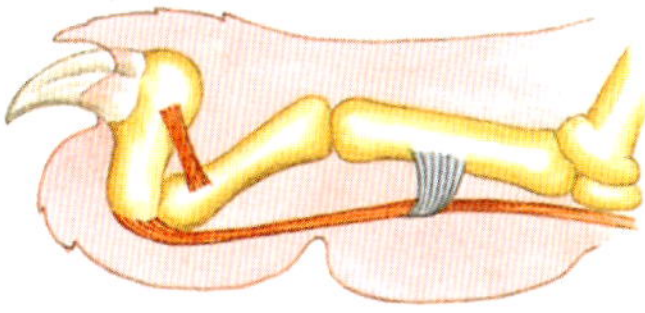

Sheathed claw is protected by a fleshy covering.

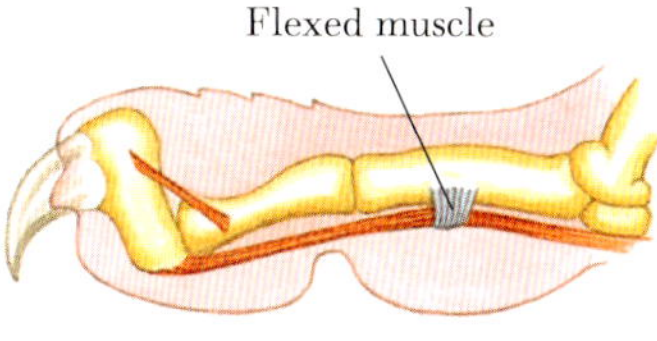

The claw is unsheathed when a muscle tightens.

Running Wild

Wolves are wild members of the dog family (canids). They have gleaming yellow eyes and lean, muscular bodies. The 37 different species (kinds) of canids include jackals, coyotes, foxes and wild and domestic dogs, as well as wolves. Canids are native to every continent except Australia and Antarctica. All of them share a keen sense of smell and hearing, and are carnivores (meat-eaters). Wolves and wild dogs hunt live prey, which they kill with their sharp teeth. However, many canids also eat vegetable matter and even insects. They are among the most intelligent of all animals. Many, including the wolves, are highly social animals that live together in groups called packs.

▲ **PRODUCING YOUNG**
A female wolf suckles (feeds) her cubs. All canids are mammals and feed their young on milk. Females produce a litter of cubs, or pups, once a year. Most are born in an underground den.

BODY FEATURES ►
The wolf is the largest wild dog. It has a strong, well-muscled body covered with dense, shaggy fur, a long, bushy tail and strong legs made for running. Its muzzle (nose and jaws) is long and well developed and its ears are large. Male and female wolves look very similar, although females are generally the smaller of the two.

◀ KEEN SENSES

The jackal, like all dogs, has very keen senses. Its nose can detect faint scents and its large ears pick up the slightest sound. Smell and hearing are mainly used for hunting. Many canids also have good vision.

The Big, Bad Wolf

Fairy tales often depict wolves as wicked, dangerous animals. In the tale of the Three Little Pigs, the big, bad wolf terrorizes three small pigs. Eventually he is outwitted by the smartest pig, who builds a brick house that the wolf cannot blow down, and all the pigs are safe.

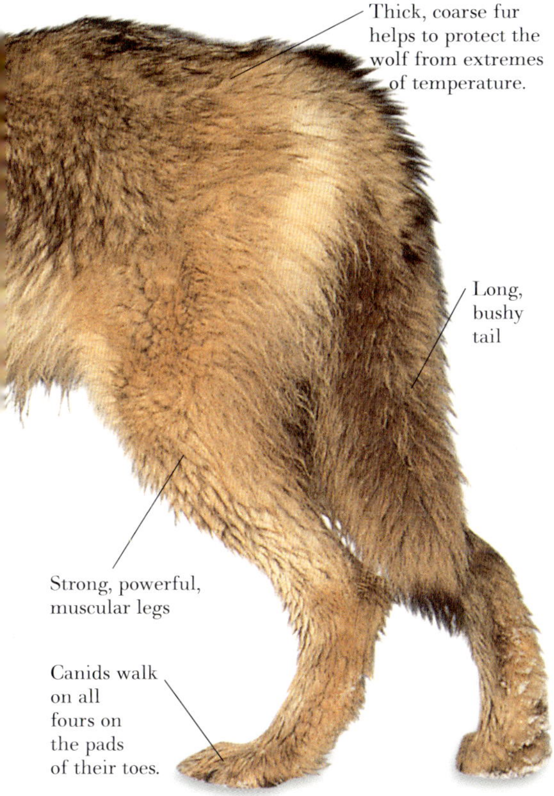

▲ LIVING IN PACKS

Wolves and many other wild dogs live in groups called packs of about eight to 20. Each pack has a hierarchy (social order) and is led by the strongest male and female.

EXPERT HUNTERS ▶

A wolf bares its teeth in a snarl to defend its kill. Wolves and other canids feed mainly on meat, but eat plants, too, particularly when they are hungry.

Body of a Wild Dog

Muscular, fast-running wolves and wild dogs are built for chasing prey in open country. Thick muscles and long, strong legs enable them to run fast over great distances. The long muzzle helps the wolf to seize prey on the run. The wolf has a large stomach that can digest meat quickly and hold a big meal after a successful hunt. Wolves, however, can also go without food for more than a week if prey is scarce. Teeth are a wolf's main weapon, used for biting enemies, catching prey and tearing food. Small incisors (front teeth) strip flesh off bones. Long fangs (canines) grab and hold prey. Toward the back, jagged carnassial teeth close together like shears to slice meat into small pieces, while large molars can crush bones.

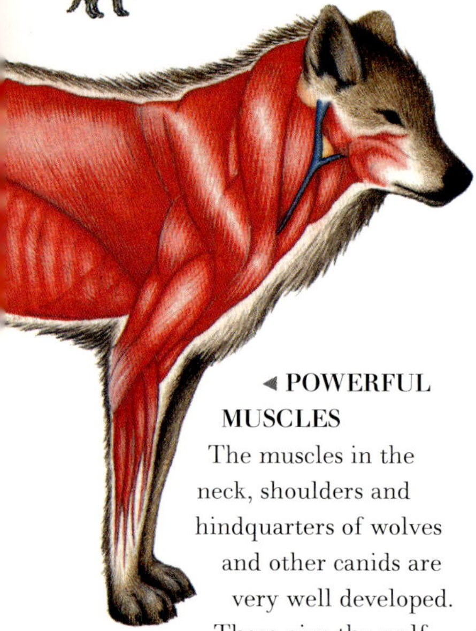

◀ **POWERFUL MUSCLES** The muscles in the neck, shoulders and hindquarters of wolves and other canids are very well developed. These give the wolf strength and long-distance stamina as well as speed. When hunting, a wolf pack chases its prey, such as a large deer, until the victim is totally exhausted. Then the pack bites the animal to death.

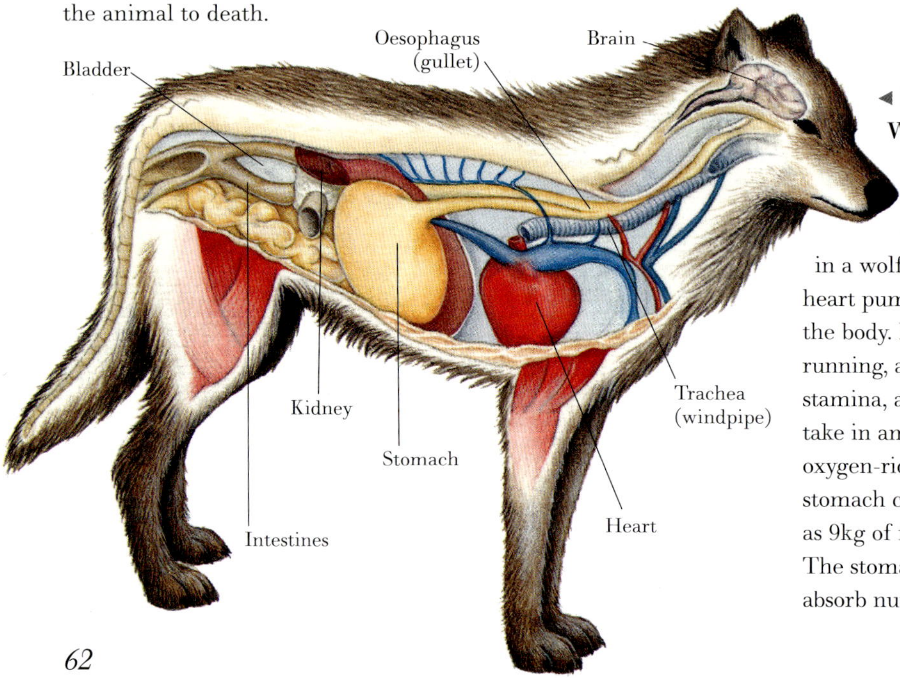

◀ **INSIDE A WOLF** This diagram shows some of the main organs in a wolf's body. A strong heart pumps blood around the body. For long-distance running, a wolf needs lots of stamina, and its large lungs take in ample supplies of oxygen-rich air. A wolf's stomach can hold as much as 9kg of food at a time. The stomach and intestines absorb nutrients in the food.

▼ WOLF'S SKULL

A wolf's head has a broad crown and a tapering muzzle. The bones of the skull are strong and heavy. They form a tough case that protects the animal's brain, eyes, ears and nose. The jaws have powerful muscles that can exert great pressure as the wolf sinks its teeth into its prey.

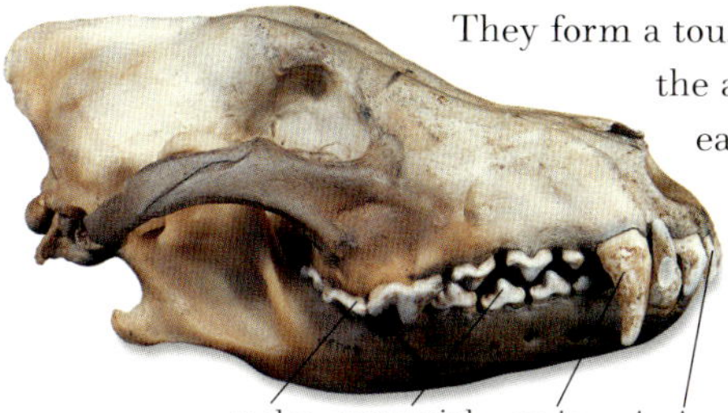

▼ BAT-EARED FOX SKULL

The bat-eared fox has a delicate, tapering muzzle. Its jaws are weaker than a wolf's and suited to deal with smaller prey, such as insects. This fox has 46–50 teeth, which is more than any other canid. Extra molars at the back of the animal's mouth enable it to crunch insects, such as beetles, which have a tough outer casing on their bodies.

▲ TIME FOR BED

A wolf shows its full set of meat-eating teeth as it yawns. Wolves and most other canids have 42 teeth. In wolves, the four large, dagger-like canines at the front of the mouth can grow up to 5cm long.

COOLING DOWN ►

Like all mammals, the wolf is warm-blooded. This means that its body temperature remains constant whatever the weather, so it is always ready to spring into action. Wolves do not have sweat glands all over their bodies as humans do, so in hot weather they cannot sweat to cool down. When the wolf gets too hot, it opens its mouth and pants with its tongue lolling out. Moisture evaporates from the nose, mouth and tongue to cool the animal down.

Monkey Power

The primates are a group of mammals that include monkeys, apes and also humans. Many of them have large brains and are among the most intelligent of animals, but their bodies are still largely the same as those of most other mammals. Small primate bodies are built for flexibility and agility, with hinged joints supported by long, elastic muscles to allow maximum range of movement. Body shapes vary according to whether the animals climb and leap through trees or move along the ground. Head shape and size depend on whether brainpower or the sense of smell or sight is top priority.

▲ **DENTAL PRACTICE**
Monkeys and prosimians (monkey relatives) have four types of teeth – incisors for cutting, canines for stabbing and ripping, and molars and premolars for grinding tough leaves and fruit into a paste.

▼ **INTERNAL VIEW**
A monkey's bones and strong muscles protect the vital organs inside its body. Its facial muscles allow it to make expressions. Monkey legs are generally shorter in relation to their bodies than lemur legs. This gives them more precise climbing and reaching skills, especially in the treetops.

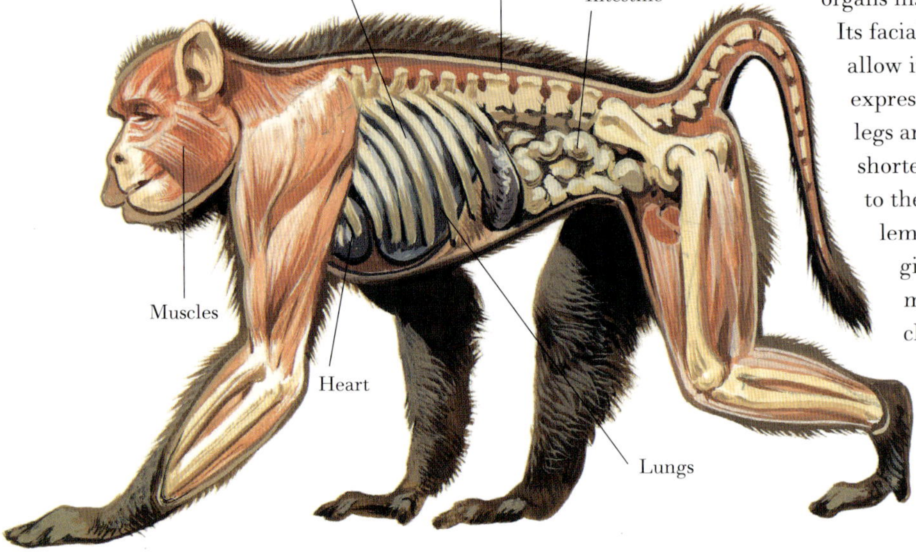

▼ BIG EYES

The tarsier has the biggest eyes of any animal in relation to its body size. There is not much room left in its skull for a brain and each of the eyes is heavier than the brain. Prosimians have simpler lives than monkeys and do not need big brains. Instead, they have an array of sharp senses – more sensitive than a monkey's – that help them to survive. As well as its huge eyes, this tarsier has large ears that pick up the slightest sounds in the quiet of the night.

▲ A STRONG STOMACH

A baboon's digestive system can cope with raw meat as well as plant food. These big monkeys catch and eat rodents, hares and even small antelopes as well as lots of insects. Most monkeys and prosimians eat mainly plants and have relatively large stomachs and long guts because leaves and other plant foods are hard to digest.

INSIDE LOOK AT A LEMUR ►

Lemurs belong to a group of monkey relatives called prosimians. These are less advanced than the monkeys. This skeleton of a ruffed lemur has a long, narrow head, which has less space for the brain, and its legs are very long compared to the length of its body. Their long legs help lemurs to leap great distances from tree to tree and enable them to cling in a relaxed fashion to vertical tree trunks.

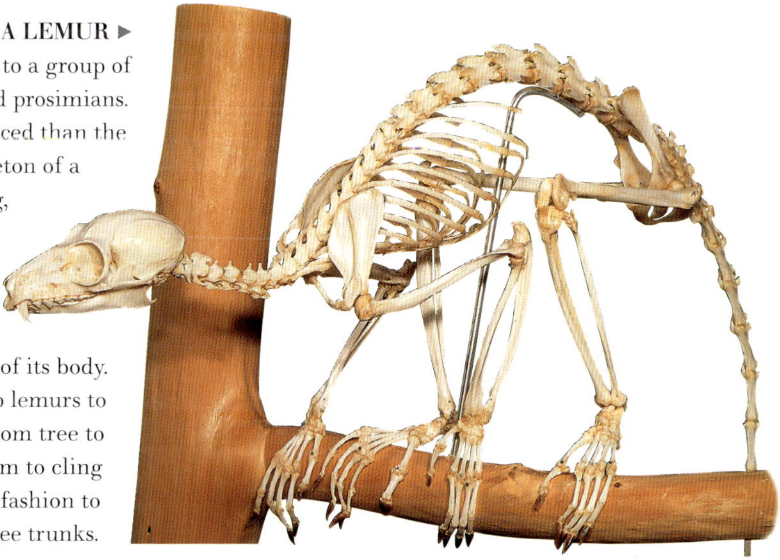

What is a Great Ape?

The four great apes – the chimpanzee, bonobo, gorilla and orang-utan – look similar to us because they are our closest animal relatives. Humans are sometimes called the fifth great ape. Great apes are also closely related to the lesser apes, called gibbons. Nearly 99 per cent of our genes are the same as those of a chimpanzee. In fact, chimpanzees are more closely related to humans than they are to gorillas. Like us, the other great apes are intelligent, use tools, solve problems and communicate. They can also learn simple language, although their vocal cords cannot produce enough sounds to speak words.

▼ APE FEATURES
Gorillas are the largest of the great apes. Typical ape features include long arms (longer than their legs), flexible wrist joints, gripping thumbs and fingers, and no tail. Apes are clever, with big brains.

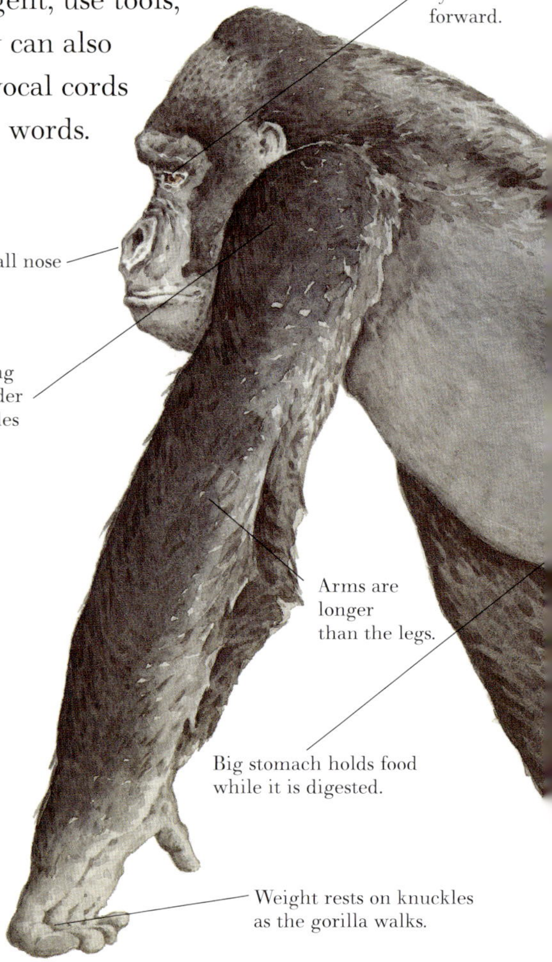

▲ RED APE
Red, shaggy orang-utans are the largest tree-living animals in the world. Their name means old-man-of-the-forest. Orang-utans live on the islands of Borneo and Sumatra in South-east Asia.

▲ **STUDYING APES**
Much of what we know today about wild apes is based on the work of scientists such as Dr Dian Fossey, who spent many years carefully observing gorillas in the wild.

GROUPS ▶
Family groups of between five and 40 gorillas live together in the misty rainforests and mountains of central Africa. Each group is led by an adult male. He decides where the group will feed, sleep and travel.

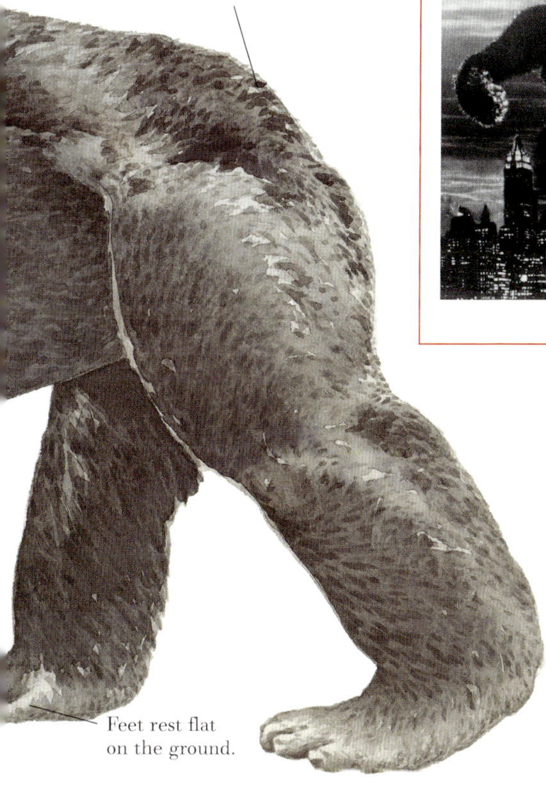

King Kong
At the beginning of the 1930s, the film King Kong *showed a giant gorilla as a dangerous monster. In the movie, a team of hunters capture Kong and take him to America. We now know that gorillas are peaceful animals, very different from the movie monster.*

▼ **APE FACES**
Have you ever watched a chimpanzee in a zoo and found that it has turned to watch you? Great apes are often as interested in watching us as we are in watching them.

Inside a Great Ape

Characteristic features of great apes are their long, strong arms and flexible shoulders, which they use to clamber through the trees. They do not have tails to help them balance and grip the branches. Instead of hooves or paws, apes have hands and feet that can grasp branches and hold food very well. On the ground, an ape's strong arms and fingers take its weight as it walks on all fours. Humans are different from the other apes as they have short arms and long legs. Human arms are about 30 per cent shorter than human legs. Our bodies and bones are also designed for walking upright rather than for swinging through the trees. All the apes have a large head, with a big skull inside, to protect an intelligent brain.

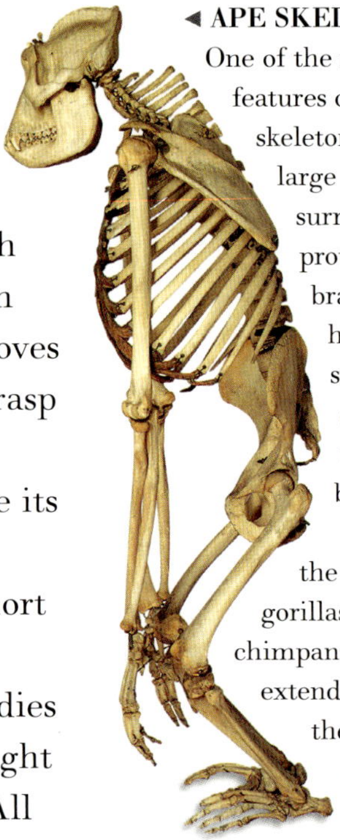

◄ **APE SKELETON**
One of the notable features of an ape skeleton is the large skull that surrounds and protects the big brain. Apes also have long, strong finger and toe bones for gripping branches. The arm bones of the orang-utans, gorillas and chimpanzees are also extended, making their arms longer than their legs.

Did you know? Female orang-utans can weigh up to 40kg but males can weigh over 90kg.

▼ **THE BIG FIVE**
All great apes have similar bodies, although a human's body is less hairy and muscular than the bodies of the other apes. The main differences between ape bodies lie in the shape of the skull and also the length of the arms and legs. Orang-utans have extra-long arms to hang from branches, while humans have long legs for walking upright.

Orang-utan Gorilla Bonobo Chimpanzee Human

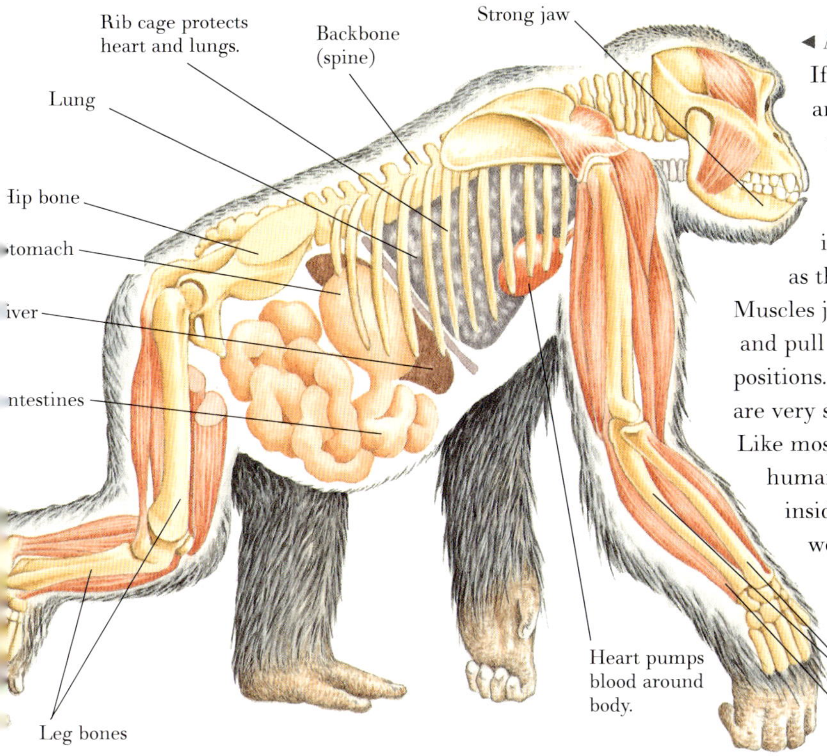

◄ APE ORGANS

If you could look inside an ape, you would see its skeleton supporting and protecting the internal organs, such as the heart and lungs. Muscles join on to the bones and pull them into different positions. The insides of an ape are very similar to our own. Like most mammals, ape and human babies develop inside their mother's womb, or uterus, taking in food and oxygen from her blood.

▲ NO TAIL

Apes, such as chimpanzees, do not have tails, but most monkeys do. Apes clamber and hang by their powerful arms. Monkeys walk along branches on all fours, using the tail for balance.

EXTRA HAND ►

Unlike the apes, monkeys that live in the dense rainforests of Central and South America have special gripping tails, called prehensile tails. The tails also have sensitive tips that work like an extra one-fingered hand, allowing the apes to cling to the branches when gathering fruit.

Wonderful Whales

Whales are mammals and more closely related to furry land animals than to other fish. Over many millions of years, whales have developed features that suit them to a life spent mostly underwater. They have long, rounded bodies and smooth, almost hairless skin. There are two types of whale: toothed whales, such as dolphins, feed on fish, while baleen whales strain smaller creatures from seawater.

▼ BIG MOUTH

This grey whale is a baleen whale. Its baleen – curtains of fine plates – can be seen hanging from its upper jaw. The whale filters food from gulps of seawater by straining it through gaps between the plates of the baleen. Baleen whales have large mouths to take in a lot of water.

Jonah and the Whale

This picture from the 17th century tells one of the best known of all Bible stories. The prophet Jonah was thrown overboard by sailors during a terrible storm. To rescue him, God sent a whale, which swallowed him whole. Jonah spent three days in the whale's belly before it coughed him up on to dry land. The picture shows that many people at this time had little idea of what a whale looked like. The artist has given it shark-like teeth and a curly tail.

▼ LEAPING DOLPHINS

A pair of bottlenose dolphins leap effortlessly several metres out of the water. Powerful muscles near the tail provide them with the energy for fast swimming and leaping. They leap for various reasons – to signal to each other, to look for fish or perhaps just for fun.

▲ HANGERS ON

This humpback whale's throat is covered with barnacles, which take hold because the whale moves quite slowly. They cannot easily cling to swifter-moving whales, such as dolphins. A dolphin sheds rough skin as it moves through the water. This also makes it harder for a barnacle to take hold.

LOUSY WHALES ►

The grey whale's skin is covered with light-coloured patches. These patches are clusters of ten-legged lice, called cyamids, which are 2–3cm long. They feed on the whale's skin.

◄ BODY LINES

A pod, or group, of melon-headed whales swim in the Pacific Ocean. This species is one of the smaller whales, at less than 3m long. It shows the features of a typical whale – a well-rounded body with a short neck and a single fin on the back. It has a pair of paddle-like front flippers and a tail with horizontal flukes.

Did you know? Whales have whiskers on their faces.

Shark Attack

Sharks are perfect underwater killing machines. All sharks are fish, related to rays and dogfish. Unlike most other fish, sharks do not have bones. Instead their bodies are supported by springy cartilage. Although most sharks are cold-blooded – their bodies are always the same temperature as the seawater – some sharks, such as the great white and mako, can keep their bodies warmer than the water around them. Warm bodies are more efficient, allowing the sharks to swim faster. Sharks have a huge, oil-filled liver that helps to keep them afloat. However, most ocean sharks must swim all the time. If they were to stop, not only would they sink, but they would also be unable to breathe. Some sharks can take a rest on the seabed by pumping water over their gills to breathe.

▲ **GILL BREATHERS**
Like almost all fish, this sixgill shark breathes by taking oxygen-rich water into its mouth. The oxygen passes through the gills into the blood, and the water leaves through the gill slits.

▲ **OCEAN RACER**
The shortfin mako shark is the fastest shark in the sea. Using special, warm muscles, it can travel at speeds of 35–50km/h. The sharks use their speed to catch fast-swimming swordfish.

◀ **SUSPENDED ANIMATION**
The sandtiger shark can hold air in its stomach. The air acts like a life jacket, helping the shark to hover in the water. Sandtiger sharks stay afloat without moving, lurking among rocks and caves as they wait for shoals of fish.

KEEP MOVING ▶
Like many hunting sharks, the grey reef shark cannot breathe unless it moves forward. The forward motion pushes water over its gills. If it stops moving, the shark will drown. Sharks have to swim even when they are asleep.

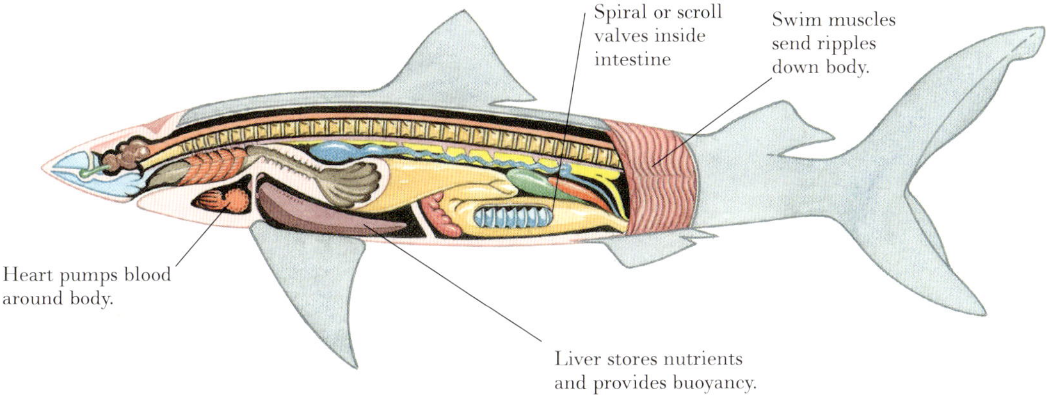

▲ INSIDE A SHARK
A shark has thick muscles, a spiral or scroll valve in the intestine, which increases the area for absorbing digested food. It also has blood vessels that carry oxygen from the gills around the body.

Did you know? Mako sharks have been seen to leap 6m clear of the water.

◀ ABLE TO REST
The tawny nurse shark pumps water over its gills by lifting the floor of its mouth. This allows it to rest on the seabed, yet still breathe. Whitetip reef sharks, lemon sharks, catsharks and nursehounds also do this.

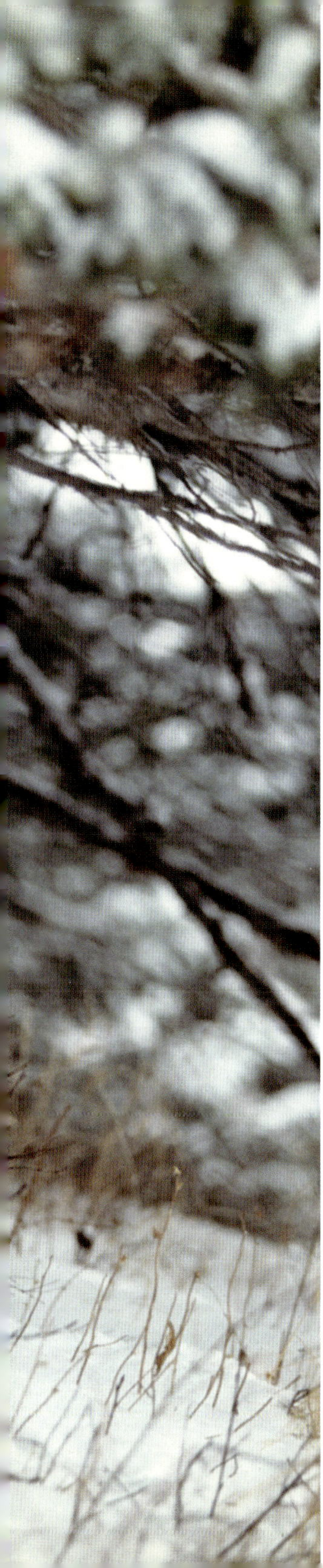

Animal Habitats

Animals live in a wide range of climates and habitats, from grasslands and vast tracts of forest, to rivers and deep oceans. This section explores the problems that animals face living in the wild and what they do to overcome these problems.

A Place to Live

Wolves can live in a range of habitats, from forests to open areas. Most wolves live in cool, temperate parts of the world, but some live in the deserts of south-west Asia.

Ever since life began, different species have competed with each other for food and living space. This competition has led to each kind of animal becoming more or less specialized for a particular way of life in certain surroundings, known as its habitat, which may be a woodland, a savanna grassland, a small pond or a vast ocean. Wherever it lives, the animal must be well suited to its habitat, otherwise it will not survive. Most animals keep to one kind of habitat, but some species can survive in different surroundings, so long as they can find food.

Weather conditions

The climate – the temperature and amount of rainfall in an area – is the major factor that determines whether animals can exist in a particular place. Life cannot exist where the temperature is permanently below -10°C or above 45°C, but there are species that survive at all temperatures between these limits. Bears and other mammals living in very cold places generally have thick fur to keep them warm, while whales living in cold seas have a thick layer of body fat, called blubber, beneath the skin. Some insects living in cold regions have a kind of antifreeze in their blood to prevent them from freezing solid. Animals living in deserts have usually adapted their behaviour to cope with the difficult conditions. Many hide away in burrows in the heat of the day and come out only at night when the air is cooler. Beetles that roam about by day often have long legs to keep their bodies off the burning hot sand.

The grey whale migrates 10,000km between its summer feeding grounds and winter breeding grounds. Many other animals also migrate in order to find the perfect habitat.

All living things need water to survive, and this is a particular problem for animals that live in deserts. Most have internal adaptations to help them use water more efficiently. Some desert animals never need to drink because they get enough water from their food and use it very carefully.

Snakes are found in many different sorts of habitat, from deserts to rainforests. Most snakes can only live in warm climates, however, as they need the sun's heat to maintain their body temperature.

Enough to eat

Climate is not the only thing that determines where an animal can live. Within a region of suitable climate, animals can survive only where they can find the right habitat, with the right kinds of plants or other animals to eat.

Animals search for their food in several ways. Some animals or family groups of animals, such as elephants, roam freely through a habitat without having any fixed home. Most animals, however, keep within a certain area. A pride (group) of lions, for example, has a definite territory that it defends against other lions. A territory may be large or small, but it will be big enough to provide food for all the animals living in the group, and it will have somewhere safe for the animals to raise their young.

Summer and winter – the changing seasons

The cool and temperate regions of the world experience very different conditions in summer and winter. Many mammals cope with the change by growing thicker coats for winter, but some move to warmer places. Several kinds of whale make these long-distance journeys, which are called migrations. They move to tropical waters for the winter and have their babies, and then go back to the cooler waters in spring. But cold weather is not the only problem facing animals in winter. Food may be in short supply, especially in areas that get a lot of snow. Some animals, including the raccoon dog, overcome this problem by hibernating (sleeping through the winter). They gorge themselves in the summer, building up a layer of fat to help them survive the winter.

In temperate regions, many plants lose their leaves for the winter. Insects that feed on them often go into hibernation. This shield bug matches the bright green leaves in the summer and it remains well camouflaged in autumn by turning reddish-brown. During the winter, it hibernates in the fallen leaves.

Success story

Animals have been incredibly successful at adapting to different habitats and environments. Today, there is hardly any place on Earth – from the highest mountain peaks to the deepest oceans – that does not support some kind of animal life.

Beetle and Bug Environments

Our planet has a huge number of different habitats, and beetles and bugs are found in most of them. Like other insects, beetles and bugs usually live in hot, tropical regions or in mild, temperate areas. Some, though, can survive on snow-capped mountains or frozen icefields, in caves and even in hot springs. Other beetles and bugs are found in places with heavy rainfall, and a few tough species survive in deserts.

Beetles and bugs that live in very cold or very hot places often adapt their life cycle to cope with the extreme temperatures. Many survive the coldest or driest periods as eggs in the soil. In deserts, beetles and bugs tend to be active at night, when the air is cooler. The toughest species have adapted to survive for long periods without food or even water.

▲ **A WARM HOME**
Bedbugs are parasites that live and feed on warm-blooded animals. Some species suck human blood while others infest the homes of birds and furry mammals, or live among their feathers or fur. Kept warm by their host animal, some bedbugs can even survive in cold places such as the Arctic.

Did you know? Water boatmen can fly many kilometres to find a new home.

◄ **LIFE IN THE WATER**
Water boatmen are predatory bugs that have adapted to life in the water. They prey on all kinds of small water creatures, including tadpoles and tiny fish. They are also called backswimmers because they swim upside-down, using their long back legs rather like oars. The bugs come to the surface from time to time to renew their air supplies.

LIVING IN THE DARK ▶

This stilt-legged bug has adapted to pitch-black caves in the Caribbean. Its antennae and legs are long and thin, to help it to feel its way. The legs and antennae are also covered with hairs that can detect the slightest air currents, alerting the bug to the presence of other animals.

◀ DESERT SURVIVOR

The fog-basking beetle lives in the Namib Desert, in southern Africa. This beetle has an ingenious way of drinking. When fog and mist swirl over the dunes, it does a handstand and points its abdomen in the air. Moisture gathers on its body, then trickles down special grooves on its back into its waiting mouth.

NO CAMOUFLAGE REQUIRED ▶

This *Aphaenops* beetle lives in caves high in the Pyrenees mountains, between France and Spain. Its body is not well camouflaged but, in the dark of the caves, disguise is not important. Scientists believe some cave-dwelling species developed from beetles that first lived in the caves during the last Ice Age, about a million years ago.

dune beetle
(Onymacris bicolor)

◀ DUNE DWELLER

The dune beetle lives in the deserts of southern Africa. It is one of the few white beetles. White reflects the rays of the sun and helps to keep the insect cool. The pale colour also blends in well with the sand where it lives, which helps it to hide from predators. The beetle's wing cases are hard and close-fitting, and so help to conserve precious body moisture in this dry region. Long legs raise the beetle's body above the burning hot desert sand.

Insects Living

SURFACE SPINNERS
Whirligig beetles are oval, flattened beetles that live on the surface of ponds and streams. Their eyes are divided into two halves, so that they can see above and below the water at the same time. The beetles are named after a spinning toy called a whirligig, because they swim in circles.

Some beetles and bugs live in and on fresh water – not only ponds and rivers but also icy lakes, muddy pools and stagnant marshes. Different types of water-dwellers live at different depths. Some live on or just below the water surface. Other species swim in the mid-depths, or lurk in the mud or sand at the bottom. Beetles and bugs that live underwater carry a supply of air down with them so that they can breathe.

In some other insects, only the larvae (young) live in the water, where there is plenty of food. The adults live on land.

SKATING ON WATER
Pond skaters live on the water surface. They move about like ice skaters on their long slender legs. The bugs' feet make dimples on the surface of the water, but do not break it. When the bugs sense a drowning insect nearby, they skate over in gangs to feed on it.

SPINY STRAW
A water scorpion has a long, hollow spine on its abdomen. The spine has no sting, but it is used to suck air from the surface. Sensors on the spine tell the bug when it is too deep to breathe.

In and On Water

THE AQUATIC SCORPION

Water scorpions are fierce predators. This bug has seized a stickleback fish in its pincer-like front legs. It then uses its mouthparts to pierce the fish's skin and suck out its juices. Compared to some aquatic insects, water scorpions are not strong swimmers. They usually move about by crawling slowly over submerged plants.

DIVING DEEP

Saucer bugs are expert divers. In order to breathe, the bug takes in air through spiracles (holes) in its body. Tiny bubbles of air are also trapped between the bug's body hairs, giving it its silvery colour. Saucer bugs use their front legs to grab their prey. They cannot fly, but move from pond to pond by crawling through the grass.

UNDERWATER ROWING

You can often see lesser water boatmen just below the water surface, but they can also dive further down. They use their back legs to row underwater, and breathe air trapped under their wings. The females lay their eggs on water plants or glue them to stones on the stream bed. The eggs hatch two months later.

Butterfly Habitats

Almost every country in the world has its own particular range of butterflies and moths. They are surprisingly adaptable insects, and inhabit a huge variety of different environments, from the fringes of deserts to icy Arctic areas.

Butterflies and moths that live in cold climates tend to be darker than those living in warmer regions. This is because they need to be warm in order to fly, and dark colours soak up sunlight more easily. In mountainous areas, the local species usually fly close to the ground. Flying any higher than this would create a risk of being blown away by strong gusts of wind. Some female moths living in mountainous areas do not have wings at all, and move around by crawling along the ground.

orange-tip butterfly *(Anthocharis cardamines)*

◄ HEDGEROWS AND WAYSIDES
Orange-tip butterflies, named for the bright orange tips of the male's front wings, live in a wide range of grassy places, including hedgerows, woodland margins, damp meadows and roadsides. When at rest, with their front wings hidden behind the hind wings, their mottled green undersides blend in with the vegetation and make them very difficult to see.

apollo butterfly *(Parnassius apollo)*

◄ HIGH LIFE
The apollo butterfly has adapted to life in the mountains of Europe and Asia. The apollo's body is covered with fur-like scales that protect it from the extreme cold. Most apollo eggs that are laid in autumn do not hatch until the following spring because of the low temperatures. Those caterpillars that do hatch hibernate at once.

◄ WETLAND WANDERER
The marsh fritillary butterfly flourishes among the flowers of open grassland in temperate regions (areas with warm summers and cold winters). It is happy in both damp and dry areas, but it needs plenty of warm sunshine in the spring to enable its caterpillars to develop properly.

BUTTERFLY HABITATS ▸
Some butterflies, such as the large white, occur in many habitats, including town gardens. Others are more choosy about their homes. The grayling and Spanish festoon like coastal areas, while the speckled wood and white admiral prefer woodland glades. Arctic species include the moorland clouded yellow. The apollo and Cynthia's fritillary are alpine butterflies living high in mountains. Painted ladies inhabit many areas in summer, but spend the winter around the deserts of North Africa.

▾ GARDEN VISITORS
These peacock butterflies are feeding on a flower. Gardens provide food for all kinds of butterflies. Many flowers grown in gardens are related to wild hedgerow and field flowers.

The Warrior Symbol
A statue of a proud warrior stands at the ancient Toltec capital city of Tula in Mexico. An image of a butterfly appears on the warrior's breastplate. The Toltec people saw that butterflies live short but brilliant lives. Consequently, the butterfly became a symbol for Toltec soldiers who lived a brave, but often short, life and did not fear death.

Migrant Butterflies

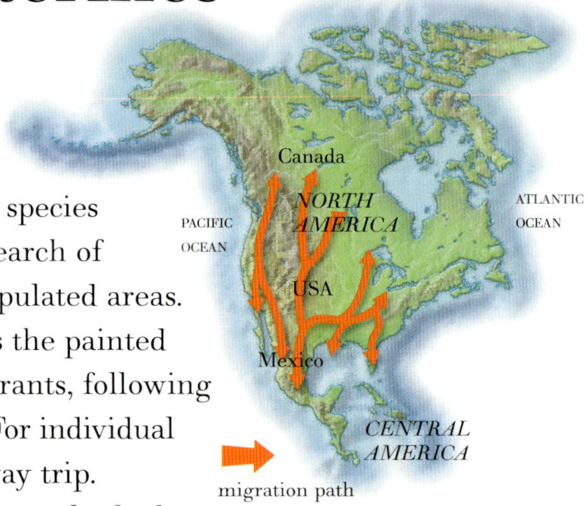

Most butterflies and moths live and die within a very small area, never moving far from their birthplace. However, a few species travel astonishing distances in search of food, or to escape cold or overpopulated areas.

Some butterfly species, such as the painted lady and monarch, are true migrants, following the same routes year after year. For individual butterflies, however, it's a one-way trip. Clouded yellow caterpillars, for example, feed in the Mediterranean region in spring. As adults, many fly northwards to feed and mate. There, they lay eggs and new generations can be seen throughout the summer. But the clouded yellow cannot survive the cold and, apart from the few that manage to get back to southern Europe, the butterflies die in the autumn.

▲ **THE ROYAL ROUTE**
Monarch butterflies migrate mainly between North and Central America. Occasionally, instead of flying south, strong winds can sweep the butterflies 5,500km north-east, to Europe.

▲ **TREE REST**
Every autumn huge numbers of monarch butterflies leave Canada and the northern USA and fly 3,000km south to spend the winter in Mexico. They make the journey as quickly as possible, resting on trees on the way.

▲ **MONARCHS ON THE MOVE**
In spring, monarchs begin their journey north. They lay their eggs on the way and then die. Once their young become butterflies, the cycle begins again. The new butterflies either continue north or return south, depending on the season.

brown-veined white butterfly
(Belenois aurota)

◀ AN AFRICAN MIGRANT

This butterfly has large wings capable of carrying it over long distances. Millions of brown-veined white butterflies form swarms in many parts of southern Africa. A swarm can cause chaos to people attempting to drive through it. Although this butterfly flies throughout the year, the swarms are seen most often in December and January.

Did you know? A large swarm of migrating butterflies can bring farm machines to a standstill by resting on them.

FAST AS A HAWK ▶

Every spring thousands of oleander hawk moths set off from their native lands in tropical Africa and head north, over the Mediterranean sea. A few of them reach the far north of Europe in late summer. Hawk moths are among the furthest flying of all moths. They are able to travel rapidly over long distances.

oleander hawk moth
(Daphnis nerii)

▲ SURVIVING THE COLD

The adult peacock butterfly hibernates during the winter. The peacock is protected by chemicals called glycols that stop its body fluids from freezing. Many other moths and butterflies survive the winter by hibernating instead of migrating.

▼ CHASING THE SUN

The painted lady butterfly lives almost all over the world. In summer it is found across Europe, as far north as Iceland. However, it cannot survive the winter frosts in temperate areas. Adults emerging in late summer head south, and a few reach North Africa before the autumn chill starts.

painted lady butterfly
(Vanessa cardui)

Spider Homes

There are few places on Earth that spiders do not live. They are found in forests, grasslands, marshes and deserts, on high mountain tops and hidden in caves. Even remote islands are inhabited by spiders, perhaps blown there on the wind or carried on floating logs. Many spiders live in our houses and some travel the world on cargo ships. Others make their home in sewage works, where there are plenty of flies for them to feed on. Spiders are not very common in watery places, however, as they cannot breathe underwater. There are no spiders in Antarctica, although some do live near the Arctic. To survive the winter in cool places, spiders may stay as eggs or hide under grass, rocks or bark. Some spiders even have a type of antifreeze to stop their bodies from freezing.

▲ **HEDGEROW WEBS**
One of the most common spiders on bushes and hedges in Europe and Asia is the hammock web spider. One hedge may contain thousands of webs with their haphazard threads.

Did you know? Some spiders live in the webs of other species of spider and steal their food.

◄ **SPIDER IN THE SINK**
The spiders that people sometimes find in the sink or the bath are usually male house spiders that have fallen in while searching for a mate. They cannot climb back up the smooth sides because they do not have gripping tufts of hair on their feet like hunting spiders.

▲ **LURKING IN THE DARK**
The cave orb-weaver almost always builds its web in very dark places, often suspended from the roof. It is found in caves, mines, hollow trees, railway tunnels, drains, wells and the corners of outbuildings in Europe, Asia and North America.

▲ **LIVING IN A BURROW**
The white lady spider lives in deserts. It hides away from the intense heat in a burrow beneath the sand. The main problem for desert spiders is lack of water. In times of drought the white lady spider may go into suspended animation, an extreme form of hibernation.

◄ **HOSTILE HOME**
This beach wolf spider is well camouflaged on the sand. It lives in a very hostile place. Waves pound on the beach and shift the sand. There is little fresh water and the sun quickly dries everything out. Food is scarce, although insects do gather on seaweed, rocks and plants growing along the edge of the shore.

RAINFOREST SPIDER ►
The greatest variety of spiders is found in tropical rainforests. Here, the climate is warm all year round and plenty of food is always available. This forest huntsman spider is well camouflaged against a tree trunk covered in lichen. To hide, it presses its body close against the tree. It lives in Malaysia where it is found in gardens as well as in the rainforest.

Snake Habitats

Every continent except Antarctica contains snakes, although they are most common in deserts and rainforests. Snakes cannot survive in very cold places because they use heat in the air around them to make their bodies work. Most snakes live in places where the temperature is high enough for them to stay active day and night. In cooler climates, snakes may spend the cold winter months asleep in hibernation.

▲ **OUT IN THE OPEN**
The European grass snake lives mainly on damp grassland. It sometimes climbs on to hedgerows to bask in the sunshine.

◄ **MOUNTAIN SURVIVAL**
The Pacific rattlesnake is sometimes found on the lower slopes of mountains in the western USA. In general, though, mountains are problem places for snakes because of their cold climates.

Pacific rattlesnake
(Crotalus viridis)

▲ **WINTER SLEEP**
Thousands of garter snakes emerge after their winter hibernation.

▲ **FOREST LIFE**

This eyelash viper lives in the Central American rainforest. The climate here is warm all year round, so snakes can stay active all the time. Snakes have adapted to every niche provided by the rainforest – there are snakes in trees, on the forest floor, in soil and in rivers.

▼ **PLENTIFUL TROPICS**

Hot, tropical rainforests contain the greatest variety of snakes, including this Brazilian rainbow boa. There is plenty to eat in a rainforest, from insects, birds and bats to frogs.

Brazilian rainbow boa
(Epicrates cenchria)

BARK TUNNEL ►

Yellow-headed worm snakes live under tree bark. Other worm snakes live underground where the soil is warm.

◄ **AT HOME IN THE DESERT**

This African puff adder lives in the deserts of southern Africa. Many snakes live in deserts because they can survive with little food and water.

Desert Snakes

Many snakes live in deserts, although the habitat is hot, dry and inhospitable. This is partly because snakes can survive for a long time without food. Mammals need energy from food to produce body heat, but reptiles take their heat from their surroundings. Snakes are also able to thrive in deserts because their waterproof skins stop them losing too much water. During the hottest part of the day, and the bitterly cold nights, snakes shelter under rocks or in the ground – often in rodent burrows.

▼ **SCALE SOUND** If threatened, this viper makes a loud rasping sound by rubbing together jagged scales along the sides of its body. This warns predators to keep away.

desert horned viper
(Cerastes cerastes)

► **GO AWAY!** A rattlesnake warns enemies that it is dangerous by shaking the rattle in its tail. Desert snakes do not hiss because they would lose precious moisture through water vapour.

SANDSHUFFLER ►
The desert horned viper is a master ambusher. It spreads its ribs to flatten its body and shuffles its way under the sand until it almost disappears and only its eyes and horns show. It strikes out at its prey from this position.

◄ DESERT MOVES
Many desert snakes, such as this Peringuey's viper, travel in a movement called sidewinding. As the snake moves, only a small part of its body touches the hot sand at any time. Sidewinding also helps to stop the snake sinking down into the loose sand.

◄ HIDDEN BOA
The colours of this sand boa make it hard for predators and prey to spot it among the rocks and sand. The snake's smooth, round body shape helps it to burrow down into the sand.

The Hopi Indians

This Native North American was a Hopi snake chief. The Hopi people used snakes in their rain dances to carry prayers to the rain gods to make rain fall on their desert lands.

Tropical

Tropical rainforests grow near the Equator, in areas with plenty of sun and rain. They are dense jungles, teeming with life. The emerald tree boa lives in the rainforests of South America. Its green body is well camouflaged among the leaves. Like other tree snakes, it moves easily among the trees, at home high above the jungle floor.

UPSIDE-DOWN ATTACK

To catch a small mammal or bird, an emerald tree boa drapes its coils over a horizontal branch and hangs its head down. As soon as a victim comes within reach, it strikes. Once the snake has a firm hold with its teeth, it coils around its prey. The boa squeezes slowly until the animal stops breathing and dies. The snake swallows its victim head-first so that it slides down easily.

PATCHY OUTLINE

The creamy-coloured bands along the back of an emerald tree boa help to break up its outline and camouflage it in the dappled light.

SLIM SLITHERER

Tree boas are longer and slimmer than boas that live on the ground. Their streamlined shape and lightweight head help them to slither through the branches easily.

Tree Boas

emerald tree boa
(Corallus canina)

COLOUR CHANGE

Young emerald tree boas are orange, pink or yellow when they are born. They gradually change to green in their first year by producing new colour pigments in their skin. No one is sure why the young are a different colour from the adults. They may live in different places and need their red colouring for effective camouflage.

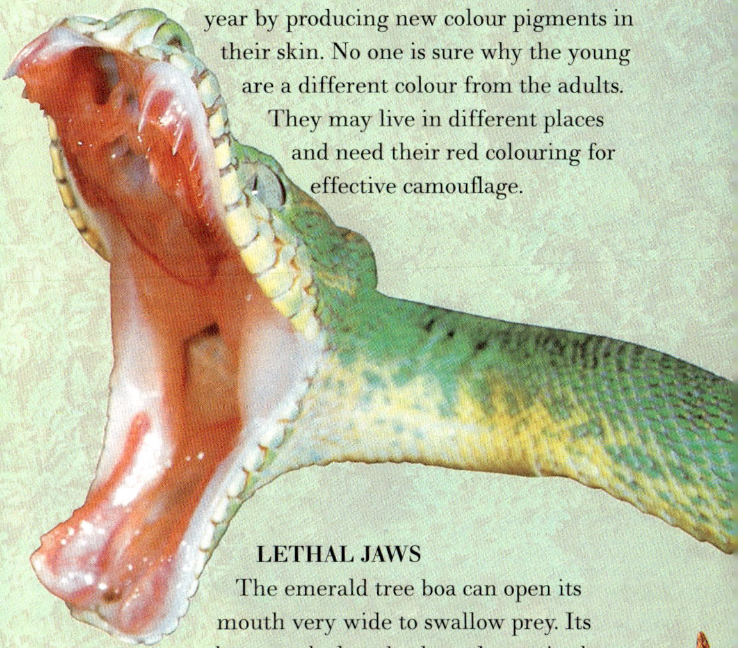

HOT LIPS

Heat-sensitive areas on the tree boa's lips help it to detect the warm-blooded animals on which it feeds.

LETHAL JAWS

The emerald tree boa can open its mouth very wide to swallow prey. Its sharp teeth slope backwards to grip the victim firmly and stop it escaping.

Crocodiles of Rivers and Lakes

Most crocodiles, alligators and other crocodilians prefer fresh water to salty water. They live in rivers, lakes and swamps, in warm climates. Crocodilians tend to live at the edge of the water because the shallows provide many plants to hide among and plenty of animals to eat.

Water is helpful in other ways, too. Like other reptiles, crocodilians draw their heat from their surroundings. Water helps to keep their body heat steady because the temperature of water does not vary as much as the temperature on dry land.

Crocodilians also save energy by moving about in rivers, because the water supports their heavy bodies. However, crocodilians can walk many kilometres on dry land. Young crocodilians may even gallop if they need to move quickly.

Aboriginal Creation Myth

Crocodiles are often shown in bark paintings and rock art made by the Aboriginals of Australia. Their creation myth, called the dream time, tells how ancestral animals created the land and people. According to a Gunwinggu story from Arnhem Land, the Liverpool River was made by a crocodile ancestor. The mighty crocodile made his way from the mountains to the sea, chewing the land as he went. This made deep furrows, which filled with water to become the river.

▲ **ALL-AMERICAN GATOR**
American alligators can be found on the south-eastern coast of the USA, around Florida. The population of alligators cannot spread further north than Virginia or further west than Texas because the winters are too cold.

▲ **RIVER DWELLERS**
The gharial is a type of crocodilian that likes fast-flowing rivers, such as the Indus in Pakistan and the Ganges in India. It prefers rivers with high banks, clear water and deep pools where there are plenty of fish.

◀ CROWDED POOL

Caimans are a type of crocodilian from South America. During the dry season, they gather in the few remaining pools along drying-up river beds. Although the pools become very crowded, the caimans seem to get along well. In some areas, caimans are forced to live in river pools for four or five months of the year. After the floods of the wet season, they can spread out again.

SUN-LOVING NILE CROCODILES ▶

These Nile crocodiles bask on the river banks to warm themselves after a night in the water. If they get too hot, they simply open their mouths and the evaporation from their huge mouths soon cools them down. If they still feel too hot, they simply slide into the water. Despite their name, these crocodiles live around many African lakes and rivers, not just the Nile.

◀ SHALLOW SWAMPS

This swamp is a billabong – a branch of a river that comes to a dead end. Billabongs provide crocodiles with water and land as well as food to eat. This one, in the Northern Territory of Australia, is home to Johnston's crocodiles. They lurk in shallow water, waiting to snap at fish, reptiles, birds and small mammals.

Saltwater Crocodiles

Most crocodilians live in fresh water, but some individuals venture into the salty water of estuaries (river mouths), and a few wander out into the sea. The species most likely to be seen at sea is the saltwater or estuarine crocodile. This is the world's biggest crocodile, and it grows up to six metres in length. It is found over a vast area, from India to northern Australia. Saltwater crocodiles are usually found in coastal rivers and swamps, but some have been seen swimming hundreds of kilometres from land. Some populations live entirely in the sea, and come ashore only to lay their eggs.

Living in salt water causes a problem for crocodiles. As they eat their food they swallow sea water, but they cannot cope with too much salt in their body. Crocodiles therefore have salt glands on their tongue that get rid of the extra salt.

▲ **GETTING RID OF SALT**
Saltwater crocodiles have up to 40 salt glands on the tongue. These special salivary glands allow the crocodile to get rid of excess salt. Freshwater crocodiles also have these glands, perhaps because their ancestors lived in the sea. Alligators and caimans do not have salt glands.

SCALY DRIFTER ►
Although it can swim vast distances far out to sea, a saltwater crocodile is generally a lazy creature. Slow, side-to-side sweeps of a long, muscular tail propel it through the water, using as little energy as possible. Saltwater crocodiles do not like swimming vigorously, so they avoid strong waves wherever possible. They prefer to drift with the tide in relatively calm water.

NEW WORLD CROC ►
The American crocodile is the most widespread crocodile in the Americas, ranging from southern Florida, USA, to the Pacific coast of Peru. It is usually about three metres long, although some grow up to six metres. The American crocodile often lives in brackish (slightly salty) water. It can be found in swamps, estuaries and lagoons as well as in rivers.

◄ TRAVELLING CAIMANS
A group of baby spectacled caimans hides among the plants. This wide-ranging species lives mainly in muddy rivers but can tolerate salt marshes. Many caimans live on islands in the Caribbean, which their ancestors probably reached by swimming through the sea or by clinging to drifting logs.

◄ LOST ARMOUR
A saltwater crocodile has less protective armour on the neck and back compared to other crocodilians. This makes it easier for the crocodile to bend its body when swimming. Thick, heavy scales would weigh it down too much at sea.

▲ ADVENTURE AT SEA
Nile crocodiles typically live in rivers, but they also inhabit salty estuaries. A strong current may sometimes sweep a crocodile out to sea. Some crocodiles survive these unplanned journeys and reach inhabitable islands.

Open Habitats for Birds of Prey

Many birds of prey make their home on grassland, moorland and other stretches of open land. Each species has adapted to a particular kind of habitat, and to hunting the prey that is found there. This prevents too much competition for the food resources available. Imperial and golden eagles hunt in mountainous country. The gyrfalcon and snowy owl are the most successful predators on the bleak expanses of the Arctic tundra. Farmland provides a hunting ground for kestrels and harriers, while the vast savanna lands of eastern and southern Africa are the home of many vultures. Here, there are rich pickings on the carcasses of zebras and antelopes killed by large predators. Many vultures also hunt small prey themselves.

▲ **GROUND NESTER**

A young Montagu's harrier spreads its wings in the nest. Like other harriers, it nests in vegetation on the ground. This harrier lives on open moors and farmland throughout Europe, northern Africa and Asia.

Did you know? The lammergeier eats bones – it smashes them by dropping them from a great height.

◀ **TUNDRA HUNTER**

A gyrfalcon devours its prey. This bird lives in the cold, wide-open spaces of the Arctic tundra, in Alaska, northern Canada and northern Europe. The picture shows a young bird with dark, juvenile plumage. The adult is much paler – grey above and white underneath. Some birds are almost pure white and blend in perfectly with their snowy habitat.

▼ **KILLING FIELDS**

A common buzzard feeds on a dead rabbit that it has found. Buzzards live in open and lightly wooded country throughout the world. They can be found in both lowland and upland areas where their food – mainly small mammals – is plentiful.

▲ **VULTURES AT THE CAPE**

The Cape vultures of southern Africa inhabit the clifftops and hilly regions around the Cape of Good Hope. They have broad wings that enable them to soar effortlessly on the warm air currents rising from the hot land below. Often, several birds soar high in the air together, watching out for a meal to share.

◀ **PLAINS WALKER**

The secretary bird of Africa's savanna grassland is the only bird of prey that walks in search of prey. Its long legs enable it to search in all but the tallest grass, and the bird usually kills its prey by stamping on it.

▼ **SUNNING ON THE SAVANNA**

A young bateleur eagle suns itself on a tree in the savanna of Africa. When fully grown, it will fly over the grasslands all day, keeping a watchful eye for prey such as small mammals and reptiles.

bateleur eagle
(Terathopius ecaudatus)

Birds of Prey in Woods and Near Water

honey buzzard *(Pernis apivorus)*

The world's forests make good hunting grounds for many different kinds of birds of prey. The goshawk and sparrowhawk, and the common and honey buzzards, all make their homes in woodlands. Many owls prefer to live in woods, too. The most formidable forest predators, however, are the enormous South American harpy eagle and the Philippine eagle. They live in rainforests and prey on monkeys high in the treetops.

Lakes, rivers and estuaries are the territory of the sea and fishing eagles and the osprey. They have rough scales on their feet to help them grip slippery fish. In Asia and Africa, the fishing owls make their homes in woodlands close to the coast or by inland waterways.

▲ **FOREST FEEDER**
The honey buzzard is quite a small bird, found in the forests of Europe. Its bill is small and delicate compared to other raptors, well suited to its diet of the larvae of bees and wasps.

◀ **IN THE MARSHES**
Three marsh harrier chicks peep out of their reed nest in a swampy region of Poland. This species is the largest harrier, measuring up to 55cm from head to tail. Marsh harriers glide over reed beds and open farmland to hunt. They are fearsome predators that eat birds, small mammals and reptiles.

◄ DOWN IN THE JUNGLE
The harpy eagle lives in the dense forests and jungles of Central and South America. It is an awesome predator, picking animals as big as sloths and monkeys from the trees, as well as birds such as parrots. Harpy eagles grow up to 1m from head to tail. They have huge talons that can grip heavy prey.

▲ DAYLIGHT OWL
Hawk owls live mainly in the forests of the far north, where there is permanent daylight in the summer. They usually sit on a perch and dart out to catch prey.

▲ FLEET FLIER
The sparrowhawk is found in the woodlands of Europe and Asia. It flies swiftly and close to the ground, using the dense vegetation as cover. However, it sometimes hunts like a peregrine, circling high and then diving steeply at its prey.

▼ EAGLE AT SEA
The white-bellied sea eagle lives high on the clifftops of an island in Indonesia, South-east Asia. Like other sea eagles, it takes fish from both coastal and inland waters and also feeds on carrion. This eagle will even eat poisonous sea snakes.

Horses of the World

There are no truly wild horses any more, but feral herds are found all over the world. Feral horses are the descendants of tame horses that escaped from people. They run wild without any human interference. Semi-wild horses also run free, although these horses are owned by people and are sometimes rounded up to be tamed. Horses can live in many different habitats because their main food, grass, grows in most open areas.

The relatives of horses – asses and zebras – are less widespread. Zebras are found only in Africa, south of the Sahara Desert. Wild asses live in scattered areas of eastern Africa and Asia. Many species of wild ass and zebra are now threatened with extinction.

◄ **OUTBACK**
Australia has the largest number of feral horses in the world. They are known as brumbies, and can be found in a wide range of habitats throughout Australia. They run wild over dry plains, wetlands, grasslands and in the mountains.

▼ **SOUTH AMERICA**
These feral horses live on the Falkland Islands, near Argentina. Their home is one of moorland, sand-dunes and rocks.

ASSES
1 Mongolia – dzeggetai
2 Turkmenia – kulan
3 Iran – onager
4 Tibet – kiang
5 India – khur
6 Somalia – Asiatic wild ass
7 Australia – feral donkey
8 North America – feral donkey

ZEBRAS
1 Southern and eastern Africa – plains
2 South Africa – mountain
3 Kenya – Grevy's

SEMI-WILD HORSES
1 Norway – Norwegian Fjord
2 Britain – Dartmoor, Exmoor, Lundy, New Forest, Shetland
3 Germany – Dülmen
4 France – Camargue

FERAL HORSES
1 Western North America – mustang
2 Sable Island, Canada – Sable Island
3 Assateague Island, USA – Assateague, Chincoteague
4 Argentina – Criollo
5 Poland – tarpan
6 Mongolia – Przewalski
7 Namibia – Namib Desert
8 Australia – brumby
9 New Zealand – Kaimanawa

▼ **RELATIVES OF HORSES**
These wild asses are khurs from India. Wild asss – like zebras – live in both temperate and dry, tropical regions. Both species roam in small herds over open landscapes such as the savannas of Africa and the dry, rocky scrubland of Asia.

Tough Horses

WATCH THEM PLAY
Scenes such as these horses at play can be enjoyed by tourists. A hide has been set up so that people can watch the Namib Desert horses. Conservationists are divided about the horses. Some want them protected, while others want to remove them so that they do not damage the fragile desert environment.

DRINKING IN THE DESERT
Water is scarce in the desert and the horses must trek many kilometres to drink. These horses have started to adapt to their desert life and they are smaller than the horses from which they descended. They also urinate less, and can go without water for up to five days.

There is just one population of feral horses that has learned to survive in the desert. These horses have lived in the Namib Desert, in south-western Africa, for over 80 years. Their ancestors were brought to Namibia by European settlers, but escaped from their owners or were released into the wild.

Horses are not natural desert dwellers, and so they have not evolved the many special features that enable other animals to thrive in hot, dry climates. The Namib horses came close to extinction in the 1970s. Just in time, people created a water supply, especially for the horses. This was enough to tip the balance towards survival. Today there are about 150 horses living in the Namib Desert – one of only two or three feral groups in Africa.

of the Desert

UPS AND DOWNS OF DESERT LIFE

Namib Desert horses have survived against all odds. They live alongside specialist desert animals such as the gemsbok, ostrich and springbok.

THE NEW GENERATION

The horses breed when the rains come and food is relatively plentiful. There are few Namib horses, and they can only breed with each other because the horses live so far away from other herds. Scientists are interested in studying the effects of such inbreeding.

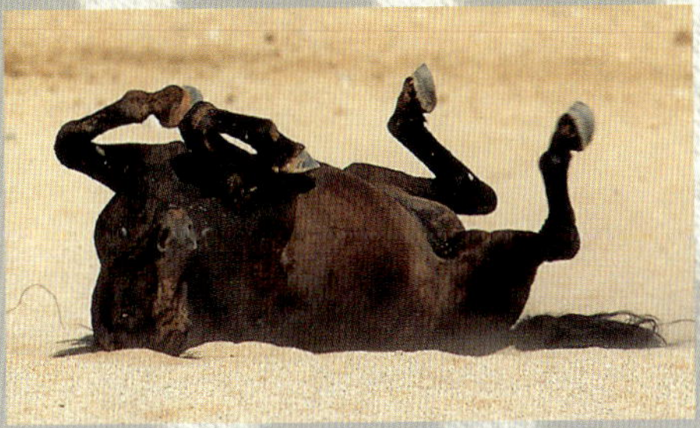

SAND BATHING

Horses keep their coats in good condition by rolling in sand. Namib horses are relatively free of parasites because of their isolation in a hot, dry desert. This unique environment is useful to scientists trying to understand how animals cope with extreme climate change.

ESSENTIAL RAIN

The Namib horses are thin for most of their lives, but they grow fatter and the population swells in years of good rains. The sudden growth of desert plants provides them with an instant food bonanza.

Elephant Habitats

The two species of elephant, African and Asian elephants, are divided into smaller groups called subspecies. The subspecies each look a little different from one another and are named after their habitats. Africa has three subspecies – the bush elephant of the open grasslands, the forest elephant of western and central Africa, and the desert elephant of Namibia. The main subspecies throughout South-east Asia is the Indian elephant. Asia is also home to two other subspecies, the Sumatran and Sri Lankan elephants.

▲ **IN A SUMATRAN SWAMP**
Sumatran elephants wade into swamps to find juicy grasses to feast on. They are the smallest of the Asian subspecies. These elephants are also the lightest in colour, and have fewer pink patches than the other Asian subspecies.

ASIAN GIANT ►
The rare Sri Lankan elephant is the biggest and darkest of the three Asian subspecies.

Did you know? The desert elephant is the tallest elephant in the world, at over four metres high.

forest elephant
(Loxodonta africana cyclotis)

◄ **ADAPTED FOR THE FORESTS**
The forest elephant is the smallest African subspecies, and its size enables it to move easily through the trees. Elephants lose heat through their ears, so it is no surprise that this species, living in the cooler forests, has smaller ears than other elephants.

◄ SURVIVAL IN THE DESERT
The hot, dry deserts of Namibia in south-western Africa are home to the rare desert elephant. This subspecies is very closely related to the African bush elephant, but it has longer legs. Desert elephants have to walk long distances to find food and water. Scientists think that this is why they have longer legs than any other subspecies.

ELEPHANT WORLD ►
African elephants live in a broad band across central and southern Africa. They became extinct in North Africa around AD300. Today, Asian elephants live in hilly or mountainous areas of India, Sri Lanka, South-east Asia, Malaysia, Indonesia and southern China. In the past, they roamed right across Asia.

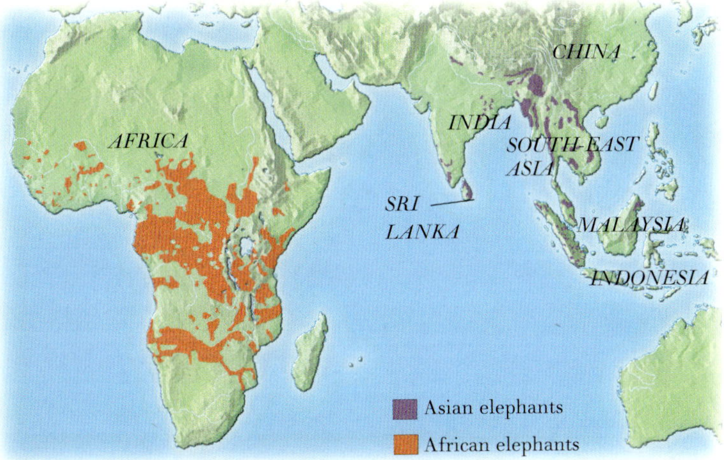

▲ IN THE SAVANNA
African bush elephants live in savanna (areas of grassland with scattered trees). However, some live in forests, marshes and even on mountains.

◄ SOLIDLY BUILT
The African bush elephant is bulkier and heavier than any other elephant. Like all elephants, its large size is a useful weapon against lions, tigers and other predators.

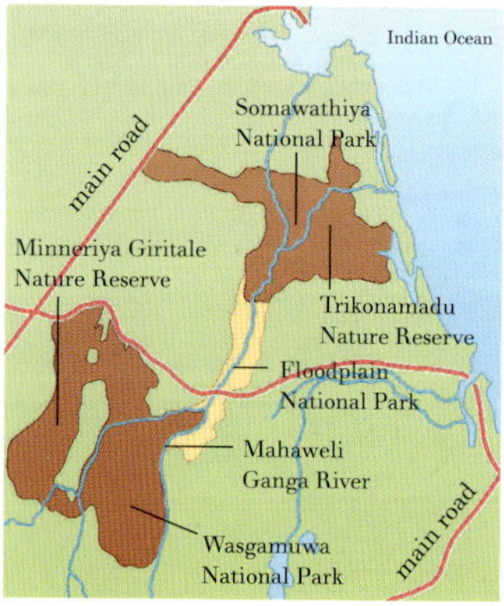

Roaming Elephants

Like horses, elephants are constantly on the move, searching for food. They travel about 25km a day, ranging over a wide area.

Twice a year, elephants make long migrations to a new area to search for food and water. They gather in large groups for these journeys. The elephants follow the same paths year after year as each generation of elephants learns the route. Today, elephants have been squeezed into smaller areas as human beings take up more and more land. As a result, their migrations are much shorter than they used to be, although they may still walk for hundreds of kilometres.

▲ **ANIMAL CORRIDORS**
Much of Sri Lanka is used for agriculture, so elephants tend to live in protected nature reserves. They move between the regions along special corridors of land, in the same way that people travel between cities along motorways.

ELEPHANT RAIDERS ▶
This maize field on the island of Sumatra lies on a traditional migration route. Elephants can do a lot of damage to crops, and farmers try to scare them away.

◀ **ELEPHANT WELLS**
During times of drought, elephants may dig holes in dry stream beds. They use their trunks, tusks and feet to reach water hidden under the ground. Elephants need to drink 70–90 litres of water each day. They have been known to travel distances of up to 30km to reach a tiny patch of rainfall. Elephant wells can be life-savers for other wildlife that come to drink the water after the elephants have gone.

LONG JOURNEYS ▸
African elephants on the savanna may wander over an area of more than 3,000 sq km. The extent of their migrations depends on the weather and other conditions. Asian elephants living in forests migrate over smaller areas of 100–300 sq km.

◂ WATCHING FROM ABOVE
Migrating elephants can be followed by aeroplane in open country. Little or no rain falls during the dry season and the elephants tend to group together in places where water is available. The thirsty animals usually mill around a river valley or a swamp. In rainy seasons, elephants spread out over a wider area.

◂ PUSHING THROUGH
Elephants will try anything to find a way through farmers' fences. They can use their tusks to break electric fence wires and even drop large rocks or logs on top of fences.

KEEPING TRACK ▸
Scientists in Africa fit a radio-collar to an elephant. This device tracks the animal's movements without disturbing its natural behaviour.

Where Bears Live

Most types of habitat are home to a species of bear. Bears live in temperate and tropical forests, on mountain slopes, scrub desert and tropical grasslands, and on the Arctic tundra. Each species, however, has its own preferred environment. The polar bear, for example, inhabits the lands and sea ice bordering the Arctic Ocean. It favours shoreline areas where the ice breaks up as this is where its main food source, seals, gather. Most other bears are less fussy about what they eat, and have the uncanny ability to turn up wherever food is abundant. However, many of the wilderness areas where bears live are under threat. Every year, more land is cultivated for farmland and forests all over the world are cut down.

▲ **IN THE BAMBOO FORESTS**
The giant panda is restricted to areas of abundant bamboo forest. It was once much more widespread across eastern Asia, but now survives in just three provinces of western China – Gansu, Shanxi and Sichuan.

▼ **MOUNTAIN BEAR**
The spectacled bear of South America feeds on fruit and juicy leaves. It is found in humid forests as well as on open grassland and rocky areas high in the Andes Mountains.

spectacled bear
(Tremarctos ornatus)

▲ **THE ADAPTABLE BROWN**
The brown bear is the most widespread of all bears. It is found in Europe and the Middle East, and across northern Asia to Japan. North American brown bears live in Alaska and the Canadian Rockies.

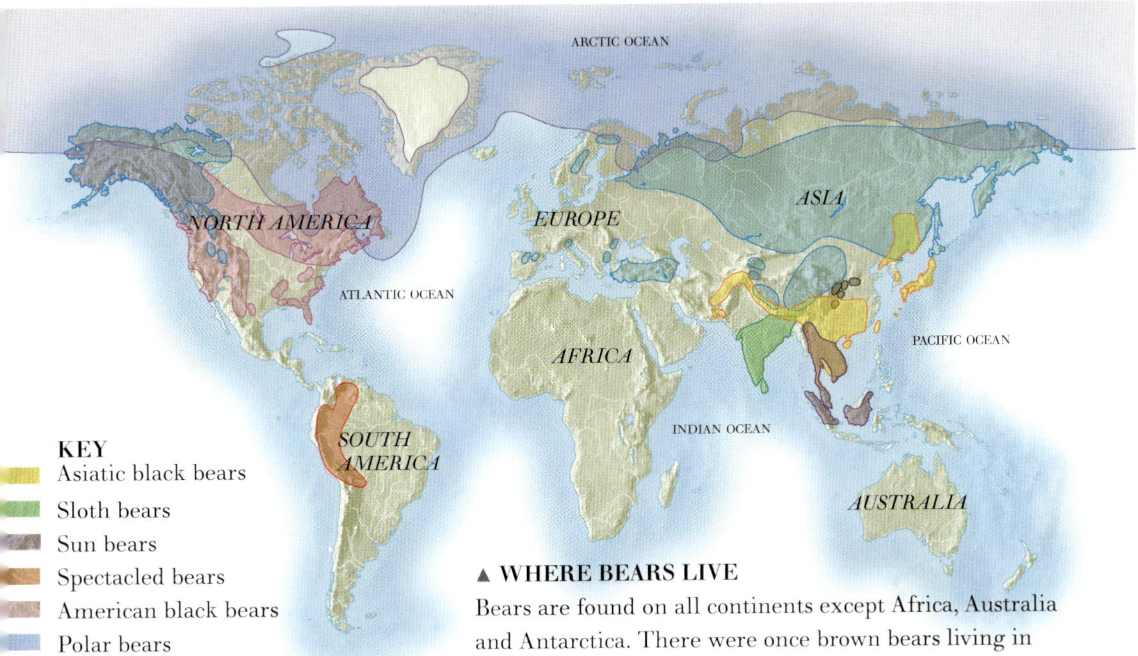

▲ WHERE BEARS LIVE
Bears are found on all continents except Africa, Australia and Antarctica. There were once brown bears living in the mountains of North Africa, but they became extinct in the 1800s.

▲ MOUNTAIN BLACK
The Asiatic black bear lives in mountainous regions. Although related to the American black bear, Asiatic bears are smaller, perhaps because the conditions they live in are harsher.

▲ LIFE IN THE FOREST
The sloth bear lives in dense, dry forests in India and Sri Lanka. It feeds mostly at night, on leaves and fruits on the forest floor. During the day, the bear rests in a tree where it is surprisingly well camouflaged. Sloth bears are agile climbers, gripping the trees with their long claws.

Pandas in

Giant pandas live in the bamboo forests of western China. For most of the year, the panda's distinctive black and white coats stand out clearly among the greenery. But in winter, the bears become difficult to see in the snow. Some scientists believe that pandas developed their coat as a camouflage at some point in their history. They have had no reason to perfect it because there are few large predators in the areas where pandas live.

Although giant pandas are very rare – there are probably only a few hundred left in the wild – they are fairly safe as long as people do not destroy their forest homes. Habitat destruction is the largest threat to pandas.

FINDING FOOD
Bamboo forms over 99 per cent of pandas' diets, although they do supplement their diet with meat when they can get it. Pandas catch rats and beetles in the bamboo, and have been known to scavenge at leopard kills. But easy prey is scarce and pandas make clumsy hunters. The abundant bamboo makes for easier picking.

THIRSTY WORK
Most of the water a panda needs comes from bamboo. If a bear is thirsty, it scoops out a hollow by a stream and drinks as much as it can. The giant panda is most active in the early morning and late afternoon. It spends 16 or more hours a day feeding.

the Bamboo Forest

ESSENTIAL FOOD

Bamboo is plentiful and easy for the bears to harvest, but digesting it is hard work. This is because the panda's digestive system is more characteristic of a carnivore. Pandas eat huge quantities of bamboo every day in order to keep going. It takes a long time for animals to evolve the perfect body to suit a new habitat.

FEEDING ALL YEAR

Even in the coldest months, bamboo is green and nutritious so the panda has a continuous supply of food. Unlike some other bears, whose food is scarce at certain times, the panda remains active throughout the winter. A thick fur coat protects it from the snow and the cold.

GOOD GRIP

A panda's front paws are specially adapted to manipulate bamboo. The wrist bones have become elongated to create a "thumb". A panda usually feeds sitting upright on its haunches. This leaves its forelegs free to handle the bamboo stalks.

Polar Bears

The polar bear is perfectly adapted to life in the Arctic, where winter temperatures can drop to -50°C. Beneath its skin lies a thick layer of fat. The bear's entire body, including the soles of the feet, is covered in insulating fur made up of thick hairs with a woolly underfur. Each hair is not actually white, but translucent and hollow. This acts like a tiny greenhouse, allowing light and heat from the sun to pass through, trapping the warm air. Sometimes, for example in zoos, the hairs are invaded by tiny algae and the polar bear's coat has a green tinge. In the wild, the fur often appears yellow, the result of oil stains from its seal prey. Beneath the fur the skin is black, which absorbs heat. This excellent insulation keeps the polar bear's body at a constant 37°C.

Respect for the Ice Bear

The polar bear is the most powerful spirit in Arctic cultures. The Inuit believe that a polar bear has a soul. It will only allow itself to be killed if the hunter treats it properly after death. It is forbidden to hunt another bear too soon. Time must be left for the bear's soul to return to its family. Some Inuit offer a dead male bear a miniature bow and arrow, and a female bear a needle holder.

◂ **SEA-GOING BEAR**

Polar bears are excellent swimmers. They must swim frequently for their icy world is unpredictable. In winter, the Arctic Ocean freezes over. But with the arrival of storms and warmer weather the ice breaks up. Then the bear must swim between ice floes in search of seals. The thick layer of fat below the skin and dense, insulating fur allow a polar bear to swim in the coldest seas without suffering. In such cold water, a human being would be dead in a few minutes.

▲ COOLING DOWN IN THE ARCTIC
Polar bears are so well insulated they are in danger of overheating on warm days. To keep cool, they lie flat out on the ice. At other times they lie on their backs with their feet in the air.

▲ BEAR SLUMBERS
A polar bear, like a human, sleeps for seven or eight hours at a time. This helps the polar bear to conserve energy and heat. Polar bears are not at risk of attack when they are sleeping, so they do not have to hide like other animals. Most often, polar bears find a sheltered area to protect them from the cold winds that blow across the Arctic.

▲ PROTECTED FROM THE COLD
The insulating fur and fat of a polar bear are so efficient that little heat is lost. In fact, if a scientist were to look at a polar bear with an infra-red camera (which detects heat given off by the body), only the bear's nose and eyes would be visible.

CHANGING ENVIRONMENT ►
Polar bears are most active at the start of the day. During summer, when the ice melts and retreats, bears may be prevented from hunting seals. Then they rest, living off their fat reserves and eating berries.

Cats of the Savanna

Large areas of Africa are covered with grasslands called savannas. Rain falls at certain times of the year, but there is not enough water for forests to grow. The tall grasses provide food for huge herds of antelope, zebra and other grazing animals. These in turn are eaten by many predators, which use various methods to catch the fast-moving prey. The big cats are among the most successful predators on the savannas. Lions, leopards and cheetahs all make their home on the African savanna, together with several smaller cats such as the serval. Similar grasslands in South America are home to the powerful jaguar.

▲ **CAMOUFLAGE CAT**
A lion strolls through the African savanna, its sandy colouring perfectly matching its habitat. When a lion hunts, it uses the cover of grass to hide from its quarry. It must creep up fairly close without being spotted.

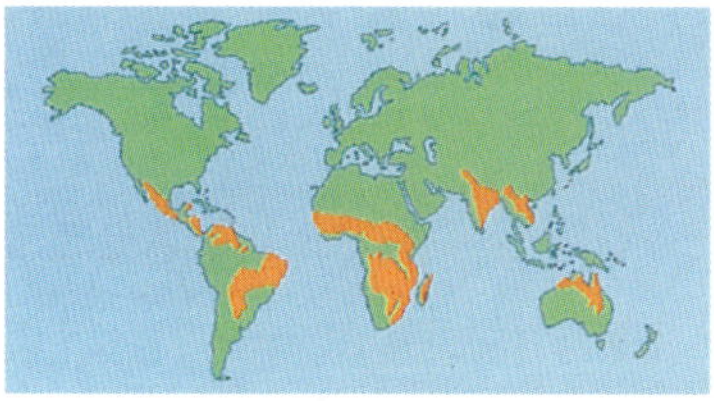

This map shows where the world's tropical grasslands are located. The largest region of savanna is in Africa.

Did you know? Cats sleep for longer than most other animals. Lions sleep for 20 hours a day.

◀ **ON THE LOOKOUT**
Cheetahs are perfectly adapted for life on the plains. Here, a cheetah stands on the top of a small mound on the Kenyan savanna. It is searching for prey with its excellent eyesight. Once it spots a vulnerable animal, it races over the open, flat terrain to catch its victim. Cheetahs are the fastest of all land mammals. They can reach speeds of 115km per hour.

◄ VIEW FROM A BRANCH

Leopards like to live in areas of grassland where there are trees. Here they can sleep hidden during the heat of the day. They avoid the insects that live in the grass below and can enjoy the afternoon breeze. Leopards also prefer to eat in a tree, out of the reach of scavengers.

The Zodiac Sign of Leo

People born between 24 July and 23 August are born under the astrological sign of Leo (the lion). They are said to be brave, strong and proud, just like lions.

▲ AT THE WATERHOLE

During the dry season in the African savanna, many grazing animals gather near waterholes to drink. Giraffes, Thomson's gazelles and zebras are shown here. Lions congregate around the waterholes, not only to drink, but also to catch prey unawares. Their favourite prey animals are antelope, zebra and warthog, but they also eat young giraffes and buffalo.

SPEEDY SERVAL ►

Servals are small cats that live on all over the African savanna. They like to live near water where there are bushes to hide in. The servals' long legs enable them to leap over tall grass when they hunt small rodents. They also climb well and hunt birds. With their long legs, servals can run quickly over short distances and so can easily escape from predators.

Forest Cats

Dense, wet rainforests are home to many insects which are eaten by birds, snakes, frogs and small mammals. In turn, these animals provide a feast for big cats. Tigers, jaguars, leopards and clouded leopards all live in rainforests, as do smaller cats including ocelots and margays. Their striped or spotted coats provide good camouflage. Forest cats hunt on the ground and in trees. They usually rest in the day and hunt at night, tracking down their prey using their superb hearing and eyesight.

▲ **UP IN THE CLOUDS**
The clouded leopard is a shy and rarely seen Asian big cat. It lives in forests from Nepal to Borneo, spending most of its time in the trees. Clouded leopards are about one metre long with an equally long tail, and weigh about 30kg. They are smaller than true leopards and they can move around easily in the trees. Clouded leopards are perfectly built for climbing, with a long, bushy tail for balance and flexible ankle joints.

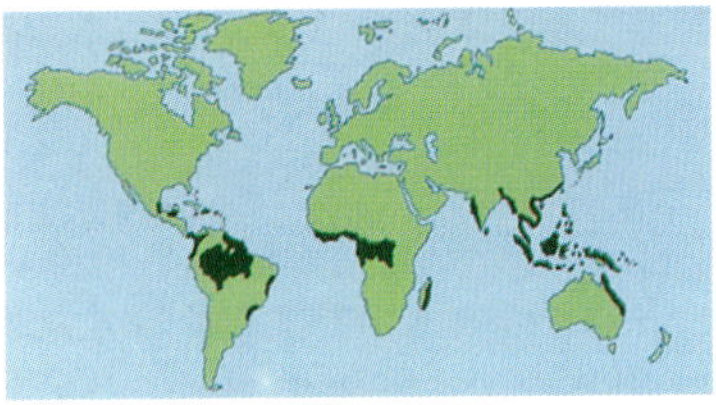

This map shows where the world's tropical rainforests are located. They lie in a band on either side of the Equator.

▼ **OUT OF REACH**
Leopards live in Africa and southern Asia in all kinds of habitat, from rainforest to dry grassland. They are great climbers and often drag their prey high into trees where they can be safe from thieving hyenas.

Did you know? The jaguar was the symbol of the sun for the Maya of Central America.

▲ **TAKING ADVANTAGE OF THE WATER**
A tiger walks stealthily into a jungle pool on the island of Sumatra. Tigers are good swimmers, and a forest pool is a good place to hunt as well as to cool off from the tropical heat. Tigers often hide the carcasses of their prey in water or in the dense undergrowth.

▲ **LOSS OF HABITAT**
Jaguars can be found all over South and Central America but they prefer thick forests. They are threatened by over-hunting and the destruction of their forest habitat.

◄ **LOST IN THE DARK**
Forest leopards and jaguars are darker than their grassland cousins. Some are even black. The dark colour helps them to virtually disappear in the shadows of their forest habitat.

▲ **TOP CAT**
Margays live in the tropical forests of Central and South America. They are the best of all cat climbers, with broad, soft feet and exceptionally flexible ankles and hind legs. They feed largely on birds and so need to be good at moving around in the tops of trees.

▲ **A TURTLE TREAT**
A jaguar catches a river turtle in a pool. Jaguars are such good swimmers that they hunt some of their prey in water. They love to eat fish and turtles. Their jaws are powerful enough to crack open a turtle's shell like a nut. They have also been known to kill caimans, a type of crocodile.

Mountain Cats

To live in the mountains, cats need to be hardy and excellent rock climbers. They also have to cope with high altitudes where the air is thin and there is less oxygen to breathe. Mountain climates are harsh, and the weather can change very quickly. To survive, mountain cats need to use their wits and to know where to find shelter. They mate so that their cubs are born in the spring. This is to ensure that they will be almost grown by the time winter closes in. Big cats that live in the mountains include leopards and the rare snow leopard. Small cats include the puma, mountain cat, bobcat and lynx.

▲ **SOUTH AMERICAN CAT**
The Andean mountain cat is a secretive, shy creature and seldom seen. It is about 50cm long and has soft, fine fur. It lives in the high Andes mountains of Chile, Argentina, Peru and Bolivia. This cat is found at altitudes of up to 5,000m above sea level.

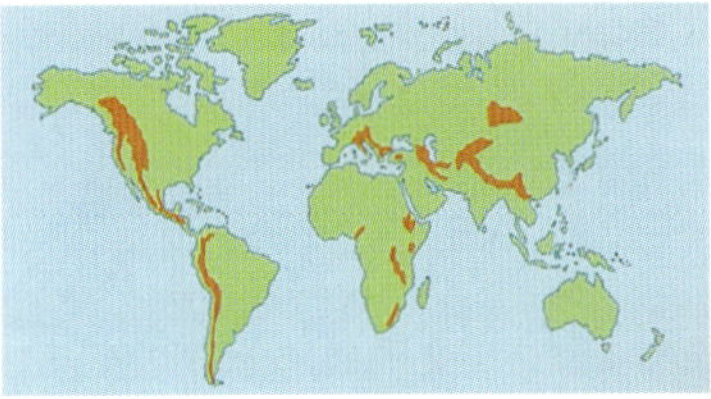

This map shows the world's major mountain ranges. The puma, lynx and mountain cat live in the Americas. Lynx also live in Europe and Asia, while the snow leopard lives in Asia.

◄ **SURVEYING THE SLOPES**
A puma, sometimes known as a mountain lion, keeps watch over its vast territory. Male pumas can grow to 2m long, and weigh 100kg. They are good at jumping and can easily leap 5m on to a high rock or into a tree. Pumas are found over a wide area, from Canada to the very tip of South America in Chile. They live along the foothills of mountains, in forests on mountain slopes and all the way up to 4,500m above sea level. Depending on where they live, pumas will eat porcupines, deer, beavers, hares and armadillos.

IN THE COLD ▸
Lynx live in mountainous regions of Asia, Europe and North America. They have unusually short tails and tufted ears. Lynx are well designed to live in very cold places. In winter they grow an especially long coat, which is light coloured so that they are well camouflaged in the snow.

◂ MOUNTAIN CHASE
A snowshoe hare darts this way and that to shake off a puma. To catch the hare, the puma makes full use of its flexible back and its long balancing tail. Pumas hunt by day as well as by night.

KING OF THE MOUNTAINS ▸
The snow leopard is one of the rarest big cats, found only in the Himalaya and Altai mountains of central Asia. It can live at altitudes of 6,000m, the highest of any wild cat. Snow leopards feed on wild goats, hares and marmots. Their bodies measure just over 1m long, with tails that are almost as long. They wrap their bushy tails around themselves to keep warm when they are sleeping. Snow leopards are agile jumpers and are said to be able to leap a gap of 15m. Their long tails help them to balance as they jump.

Did you know? Snow leopards are well adapted to the cold – even their feet are covered with fur.

Forest-living Wolves and Wild Dogs

▲ **JACKAL ON ALERT**
A side-striped jackal keeps a wary lookout for danger. In Africa, the three different kinds of jackal are found in different types of terrain. Side-striped jackals keep mostly to woods and swampy areas. Golden and black-backed jackals live in more open countryside.

Trees cover much of the world. Canada, Russia and northern Europe have many dense evergreen forests. Warmer, temperate regions contain broad-leaved woodlands. Nearer the Equator, tropical rainforests grow. In all of these areas, wolves or other species of wild dogs can be found.

Forests provide a plentiful supply of prey and dense undergrowth in which to hide and stalk. Wolves tend to live in northern regions, where large game such as deer abound. Temperate forests in Asia provide a home for the raccoon dog. Bush dogs are one of the few wild dogs to live in the rainforest. It is harder for wild dogs to survive in tropical rainforests, because most of the small prey animals live out of reach in the treetops.

◄ **HIDDEN HUNTERS**
In dark pine forests and dappled broad-leaved woodlands, the grey or blackish coats of wolves blend in with the shadows. This helps them to sneak up on moose, deer and other forest prey. In Arctic regions, wolves can have almost white coats, an effective camouflage in the snow.

◀ SOUND SLEEPERS

Raccoon dogs live in thickly wooded river valleys in eastern Asia. They are the only species of dog that hibernates in winter. In autumn, raccoon dogs gorge themselves on fruit and meat to put on a thick layer of fat. Then they retreat to their burrows and sleep right through the harsh winter.

JUNGLE PACK ▶

This wild dog is called a dhole. Packs of dholes hunt deer in the dense forests in South-east Asia. They call to one another to surround their prey as it moves through the jungle. The pack will guard its kills against bears, tigers and scavengers.

◀ RODENTS BEWARE

Bush dogs make their home in the dense rainforests and marshlands of South America. They live close to rivers and streams, where they find plenty of animals to eat. Their main prey are aquatic rodents such as pacas and agoutis. Bush dogs will even plunge into the water to hunt capybaras – the world's largest rodents, at 1.3m long.

A SCARCE BREED ▶

A wolf surveys the snowy landscape in the Abruzzo region of central Italy. Wolves are common in remote forests in Canada and Russia, but in western Europe they are scarce. They survive in small pockets of wilderness, hiding in the hills by day and creeping down to villages to steal scraps at night.

Wild Dogs of Desert and Grassland

Wild dogs inhabit open country, as well as forests. Deserts are one of the harshest environments for wild dogs. In these barren places, the sun beats down mercilessly by day, but at night the temperature plummets. Coyotes, dingoes and foxes survive in these barren places. They can live for long periods with little water, and derive most of the liquid they need from their food. Desert foxes keep cool during the hot days by hiding under rocks or in dark burrows, emerging to hunt only at night.

Many species of wild dog live on the world's grasslands, including African hunting dogs, maned wolves and jackals.

▲ CHANGE OF COLOUR
Wolves are found in deserts and dry areas in Mexico, Iran and Arabia. With little vegetation to provide cover, they stalk prey by hiding behind boulders or rocky outcrops. Desert wolves often have pale or sandy fur, to blend in with their surroundings.

▲ GIVING OFF HEAT
This jackal lives in the desert. Its large ears contain a network of fine veins. Blood flowing through these veins gives off heat, keeping the animal cool.

◄ HUNTERS OF THE OUTBACK
A pair of dingoes wait at a rabbit warren. Dingoes are descended from domestic dogs, but have lived wild in central Australia for more than 8,000 years. Their reddish-brown coats, with paler fur on their legs and bellies, are perfect desert camouflage.

▲ ADAPTING TO THE WILD
Feral dogs are the descendants of domestic dogs that have become wild. In Asia they are known as pariah (outcast) dogs. Feral dogs are very adaptable and change their behaviour to suit any situation. In India, pariah dogs hang around villages and sneak in to scavenge scraps.

▲ AVOIDING THE HEAT
A pack of African hunting dogs tears a carcass apart. These dogs live on the open grasslands of Africa, which have scorching daytime temperatures. The dogs tend to hunt in the early morning or late evening, when it is cooler, to avoid overheating. Gazelles and zebras are their main prey.

▲ SLY MARSHLAND HUNTER
A maned wolf hunts in Argentinian marshland. Its long legs help it to see over the tall grass, but it is not a fast runner. It also lacks the stamina needed to chase prey over great distances. Instead, it stalks animals such as rodents by slowly sneaking up on them before making a sudden pounce.

The Jackal-headed God

In ancient Egypt, Anubis, the god of the dead, was shown with a human body and the head of a jackal. This god was believed to be responsible for the process of embalming, which preserved the bodies of the dead. Anubis often appears in wall paintings and sculptures found in burial places. Here he is shown embalming the body of an Egyptian king.

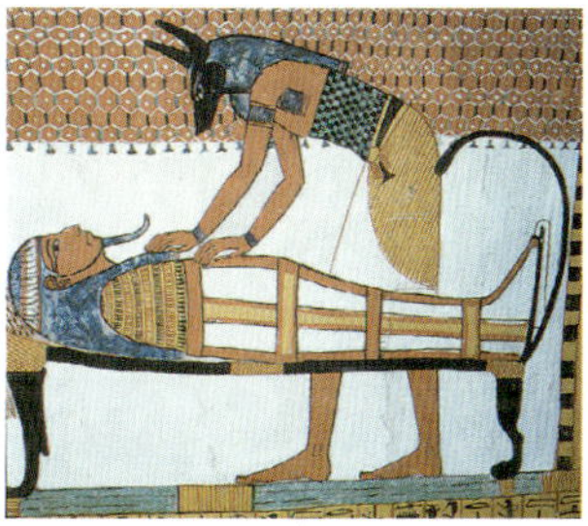

Forest Apes

There are five species of apes: chimpanzees, bonobos, gorillas, gibbons and orang-utans. They all live in Africa or South-east Asia. Most apes inhabit tropical rainforests, but chimpanzees can be found in more open, deciduous woodlands and in wooded grasslands, and some gorillas prefer mountain forests with their lush vegetation and misty atmosphere. Gibbons sometimes live in deciduous forests, too.

All the apes used to be more widespread, but they are being gradually squeezed into smaller and smaller areas as people hunt them and destroy their habitats.

▲ **VANISHING APE**
In the dark and dappled rainforest where orang-utans live, their shaggy, orange hair blends in with the tangle of forest plants. This makes them surprisingly difficult to see.

gorilla nest

droppings

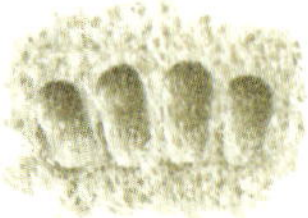

knuckle prints

flattened plants

food remains

► **FOREST DETECTIVES**
It is often hard for scientists to watch gorillas in their wooded habitats. Instead, they study the signs left behind by the gorillas as they move about the forest.

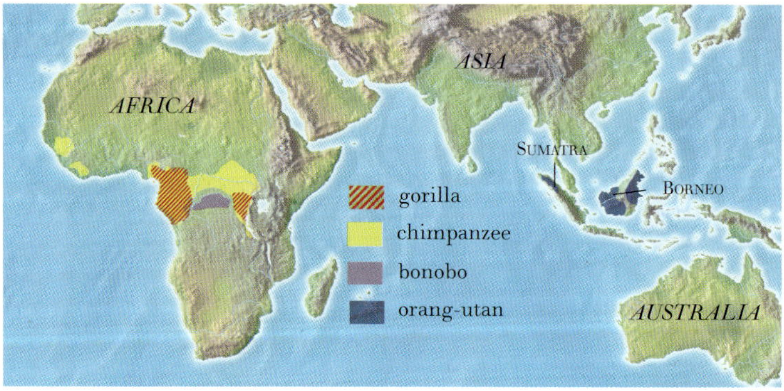

◄ **WHERE APES LIVE**
Gorillas, chimpanzees and bonobos live in Africa and orang-utans live only on the islands of Borneo and Sumatra. However, orang-utans once lived in parts of mainland South-east Asia. Some people believe that they were hunted out by poachers.

▲ TREETOP HABITAT
Gibbons are totally at home in the tops of the trees and hardly ever go down to the ground. They are the only apes that do not build nests. Gibbons sleep sitting up in the forks of branches, resting on tough sitting pads. These pads act like built-in cushions for the gibbon.

▼ MAKING A COSY NEST
This chimpanzee is making a nest to sleep in. Every night, adult apes (apart from gibbons) make nests in the trees or on the ground. They bend and weave together leafy branches and pile more leaves and branches on top. This makes a warm, springy nest to keep out the cold.

▲ LOCAL ROUTE MAP
Chimpanzees travel around their own neighbourhoods on the ground, following a network of paths. They use a mental map in their heads to decide where to go. Each day they work out where to get a good meal, climbing trees to find fruit and leaves, or to chase prey.

▲ MOUNTAIN HOMES
Dense, misty forests up to about 3,500m above sea level are the home of mountain gorillas. At night, the temperature sometimes drops to below freezing but the long hair of the gorillas helps them to keep warm.

chimpanzee
(Pan troglodytes)

Lowland and

It's 6.30 in the morning. A group of mountain gorillas is waking up. They are hungry after their night-time fast and reach out to pick a leafy breakfast in bed. Then the gorillas move off through the forest, feeding as they go. After a morning spent munching plants, they build day nests on the ground and take a rest for a couple of hours. This gives them time to digest their food and socialize. These gorillas live amid the beautiful and misty volcanic Virunga Mountains in Africa. They have lowland cousins who live in the tropical rainforests of eastern and western Central Africa.

CAREFUL CLIMBERS
Adult gorillas climb with great care and feel most secure when all four limbs are in contact with a branch. Young gorillas (*above*) are lighter and often play by hanging from a branch or swinging from tree to tree.

MOUNTAIN REFUGE
In 1925, the home of the mountain gorilla on the slopes of the Virunga volcanoes was declared Africa's first national park. The word virunga comes from a local expression meaning 'isolated mountains that reach the clouds.' The Virunga Mountains include both active and dormant volcanoes, but the gorillas live only on the dormant volcanoes.

SNACK IN A SWAMP
Travelling through the Odzala Forest at about 3–4 km per hour, these western lowland gorillas feed in a swampy glade. Like all gorillas, they walk on all fours.

Mountain Gorillas

GORILLA CHAMPION
From her hut on Mount Visoke, Dian Fossey devoted herself to studying and protecting mountain gorillas. She began her work in 1967, winning the trust of the gorillas, studying their family relationships and making discoveries about their behaviour.

LIVING IN THE MIST
Mists often swirl around the forests where the mountain gorillas live, so they are called cloud forests. Mosses and lichens grow well in the cool, damp air, and hang on the branches like untidy green hair.

LOWLAND FORESTS
Eastern lowland gorillas live in the rainforests of eastern Congo. It is more difficult for people to study lowland gorillas because the rainforests are less open than the mountain gorillas' habitat.

FOOD FOR FREE
On the rainy slopes where they live, the mountain gorillas have a wide variety of food, such as wild celery, bedstraw, bamboo shoots, thistles, brambles and nettles.

Mammals of the Open Sea

Whales and dolphins are mammals. Like all mammals, they breathe air and feed their young on milk. Their ancestors evolved on land, and so whales and dolphins have had to make many adaptations to live in a watery environment. They have a layer of fatty blubber beneath their skin to keep them warm, and can hold their breath for many minutes before needing to surface.

Whales and dolphins are found in all the world's oceans. Each species has a unique survival strategy to take advantage of its habitat.

◄ **OCEAN WANDERER**
Humpback whales migrate vast distances to find the perfect conditions for hunting and breeding.

▲ **IN THE MUD**
Like other dolphins that live in rivers rather than the sea, the Amazon river dolphin has a long jaw, or beak, to help it catch its prey. Its flexible neck helps it to manoeuvre around submerged trees and tangled vegetation in the muddy waters where it lives.

◄ **WORLDWIDE KILLER**
Among ice floes in the Arctic Ocean, a killer whale hunts for prey. Killer whales are found in all the oceans of the world. They live in coastal areas but may venture out to the open ocean. They also swim close to the shore, and may deliberately run aground to snatch a seal as their prey before letting the next wave wash them back to sea.

FAR NORTH ▶
A group of beluga whales swims in Hudson Bay, Canada. Belugas live around coasts in the far north of the world. In winter they hunt for fish under the Arctic pack ice. Belugas have a thick layer of blubber that protects them from the cold.

◀ WARM WATERS
These melon-headed whales prefer warm waters and are found in subtropical and tropical regions in both the northern and southern hemispheres. Melon-headed whales feed on a whole range of fish and squid, which they generally catch in deep water, well away from land.

WIDE RANGER ▶
The bottlenose dolphin is one of the most wide-ranging dolphin species, found in temperate and tropical waters in both the northern and southern hemispheres. It is also found in enclosed seas such as the Mediterranean and Red Sea. When bottlenose dolphins migrate to warmer areas, they lose weight. When they return to colder climes, their blubber increases again to protect them against the cold.

Shark Habitats

Each one of the world's oceans and seas is home to at least one species of shark. Often there are many species, living at different depths and hunting different prey. Some sharks, like bull sharks, even swim in rivers and lakes. Whale, reef and nurse sharks are all tropical species that prefer warm waters. Temperate-water sharks, such as the mako, horn and basking sharks, live in water with a temperature of 10–20°C. Cold-water sharks often live in deep water. The Portuguese shark, frilled shark, and goblin shark are all cold-water sharks. A few species will swim in extremely cold waters, such as the Greenland shark which lives around the Arctic Circle.

► SWIMMING POOLS
This map shows the main parts of the world's seas in which different kinds of sharks live. The key beneath the map shows which sharks live where.

LOOKING FOR FOOD ►
The oceanic whitetip shark lives in tropical and subtropical waters. It is one of the first sharks to appear at shipwrecks, perhaps because shipwrecks shelter lots of other fish for the whitetip to eat.

◄ ISLAND LIVING
The Galapagos shark swims in the waters of the Galapagos Islands, on the Equator. It also swims around other tropical islands in the Pacific, Atlantic and Indian oceans.

◄ **UNDER THE ICE**

The Greenland shark lives in deep water, and is the only shark known to survive under polar ice in the North Atlantic seas. It has a luminous parasite attached to each eye that attracts prey to the area around its mouth.

▲ **FEARSOME KILLER**

The great white shark lives in temperate, tropical and sub-tropical seas. It grows to over 6m long and is the largest hunting fish in the seas. Its powerful jaws can bite a fully grown elephant seal (which is about 4m long) in half. It has strong, triangular teeth that can slice through flesh, blubber and even bone.

▲ **TIGER OF THE SEAS**

The tiger shark has a long, rounded shape, typical of hunting sharks. It swims mainly in tropical and warm temperate waters, both in the open ocean, and close to shore.

◄ **REEF PATROL**

The blacktip reef shark patrols reefs in the Indian and Pacific oceans. It also lives in shallow waters in the Red Sea and the Mediterranean, as far west as the waters off Tunisia, in North Africa.

Amazing Animals

Every animal is stalked, chased or attacked at some point in its life by another animal. This section shows how a balance between instinct and learning helps it to survive those incidents, and reveals that some animals go to extraordinary extremes to outwit their aggressors.

Insect Defences

The naturalist Charles Darwin's theory of evolution explains how only the best-adapted animals survive to breed and pass on their characteristics to the next generation. The key to survival is escaping danger. Beetles and bugs have many enemies in the natural world. They also have many ways of avoiding attack. Many species run, fly, hop or swim away, but some species are also armed with weapons. Some bugs and beetles can bite or use sharp spines for protection. Others are armed with poisonous fluids or taste nasty. These insects are often brightly coloured, which tells predators such as birds to stay away.

▲ **PRICKLY CUSTOMER**
This weevil from the island of Madagascar has an impressive array of sharp spines on its back. Few predators will try such a prickly morsel – if they do, the pain may make them drop their meal!

▲ **READY TO SHOOT**
Desert skunk beetles defend themselves by shooting a foul-smelling spray from their abdomens. This beetle has taken up a defensive posture by balancing on its head with its abdomen raised in the air. It is ready to fire its spray if an intruder comes close. Most predators will back away.

▼ **LITTLE STINKER**
Squash bugs are also known as stink bugs because of the smelly liquid they produce to ward off enemies. Like other insects, squash bugs do not actively *decide* to defend themselves. Instead, they instinctively react when their sense organs tell them that danger is near.

Blistering Attack

The blister beetle gives off a chemical that causes human and animal skin to blister. Centuries ago, the chemical was thought to cure warts. Doctors applied blister beetles to the skin of patients suffering from the infection. The 'cure' was probably painful and did not work.

▼ TRICKY BEETLE

The devil's coach-horse beetle has several ways of defending itself from attack. First, it raises its tail in a pose that mimics a stinging scorpion (below). This defence is a trick, for the beetle cannot sting. If the trick does not work, the beetle gives off an unpleasant smell to send its enemies reeling. If all else fails, it delivers a painful bite with its large jaws.

devil's coach-horse beetle
(Staphylinus olens)

◀ PLAYING DEAD

This beetle from East Africa is trying to fool an enemy by playing dead. It drops to the ground and lies on its back with its legs curled in a lifeless position. This defence works well on enemies that eat only live prey. However, it does not work on the many predators that are not fussy whether their victims are alive or dead.

WARNING COLOURS ▶

The cardinal beetle's body contains chemicals that have a terrible taste to predators. The beetle's blood-red colour helps to warn its enemies away. This colour coding will only work if the predator has tried to eat another beetle of the same species. If so, it will recognize the species by its colour and leave it alone.

cardinal beetle
(Pyrochroa coccinea)

Focus on

FIREFLY BY DAY
Fireflies are flat and slender. Most are dark brown or black, with orange or yellow markings. The light organs are found in their abdomens. Most firefly species have two pairs of wings.

At nightfall in warm countries, the darkness may be lit up by hundreds of tiny, flashing yellow-green lights. The lights are produced by insects called fireflies. There are over 1,000 different types of firefly, but not all species glow in the dark. The light is produced by special organs in the insects' abdomens. Fireflies are nocturnal (night-active) beetles. Some species, known as glow-worms, produce a continuous greenish glow, while others flash their lights on and off. These signals are all designed for one purpose – to attract a mate in the darkness.

PRODUCING LIGHT
A male firefly flashes his light to females nearby. He produces light when chemicals mix in his abdomen, causing a reaction that releases energy in the form of light. In deep oceans many sea creatures, such as fish and squid, produce light in a similar way.

CODED SIGNALS
A female firefly climbs on to a grass stem to signal with her glowing tail. Each species of firefly has its own sequence of flashes, which serves as a private mating code. On warm summer evenings, the wingless females send this code to the flashing males that fly above.

Fireflies

FALSE CODE FOR HUNTING
Most adult fireflies feed on flower nectar or do not eat at all. However, the female of this North American species is a meat-eater – and her prey is other fireflies. When the flightless female sees a male firefly of a different species circling overhead, she flashes his response code to attract him to the ground. When he lands nearby, she pounces and eats him. She also flashes to males of her own species to attract them to her for mating.

LIT UP LIKE A CHRISTMAS TREE
A group of fireflies light up a tree by a bridge as they signal to one another. In parts of Asia, some species of fireflies gather in large groups on trees. When one insect, called the pacemaker, flashes its light, all of the other fireflies on the tree begin to flash their lights at the same time and to the same pattern. When this happens, the whole tree can be seen to glow and pulse with brilliant flashes of light.

YOUNG FIREFLY
Like the adults, firefly larvae also make light although their lamps are not usually very bright. Young fireflies hatch from eggs laid in moist places by the females. Unlike most of their parents, all firefly larvae are meat-eaters. They kill slugs and snails by injecting them with powerful digestive juices. These dissolve the flesh and the firefly larvae suck up the resulting solution through their hollow jaws. The young fireflies never have wings.

Six Lively Legs

Not all insects can fly, but they can all move around and even climb trees using their six legs. Social insects, such as wasps and bees, use their legs to groom (clean) their bodies as well.

All insects belong to a larger group of animals called arthropods, which means 'jointed legs'. True to this name, adult insects have legs with many joints in them. An insect's legs have four main sections – the coxa, femur, tibia and tarsus. The coxa is the top part of the leg, joined to the thorax. The femur corresponds to the thigh, and the tibia is the lower leg. The tarsus, or foot, is made up of several smaller sections. Insects' legs do not have bones. Instead, they are supported by hard outer cases, like hollow tubes.

Did you know? Adult insects have six legs, but young bees, wasps and ants have no legs at all.

▲ **GRIPPING STUFF**
This magnified photograph of a bee's foot shows clearly the tiny claws on the end of its foot. Claws help insects to grip smooth surfaces such as shiny leaves, stems and branches, and stop them from slipping. Ants can walk along the underside of leaves with the help of their claws.

STILT WALKER ►
Like other ants, this Australian bulldog ant has legs made up of several long, thin sections. In the hot, dry areas of Australia, the ant's stilt-like legs raise her high above the hot, dusty ground, helping to keep her cool. As well as walking, climbing and running, insects' legs have other uses. Some ants and termites use their legs to dig underground burrows. Bees carry food home on their hind legs.

▲ **MULTI-PURPOSE LEGS**
Bees use their legs to grip on to flowers and also to walk, carry nesting materials and clean their furry bodies. Their front legs have special notches to clean their antennae. They use their hind legs to carry pollen back to the nest.

▲ **ON THE MOVE**
Army ants spend their whole lives on the move. Instead of building permanent nests as other ants do, they march through the forest in search of prey, attacking any creature they find and scavenging from dead carcasses.

▼ **EXPERT CLIMBERS**
Termites swarm along a tree branch in Malaysia, South-east Asia. Many termites nest underground, but some build their nests high in trees. They climb vertical tree trunks by digging their claws into the bark

▲ **THREE-LEGGED RACE**
A running ant keeps three of her legs (shown in black) on the ground at the same time, but does not move all the legs on one side together. The front and hind legs touch the ground at the same time as the middle leg on the opposite side, helping to keep the ant steady.

Chemical Warfare

African euchromia moth *(Euchromia lethe)*

Most butterflies and moths escape their enemies by avoiding being spotted. However, some use other tricks. They cannot sting or bite like bees or wasps, but many caterpillars have different ways of using toxic chemicals to poison their attackers, or at least make themselves unpleasant to taste or smell. For example, the caterpillar of the brown-tail moth has barbed hairs tipped with a poison that can cause a severe skin rash even in humans. A cinnabar moth cannot poison a predator, but it tastes foul if eaten. Usually, caterpillars that are unpalatable to predators are brightly coloured to let potential attackers know that they should be avoided.

▲ BRIGHT AND DEADLY
The brilliant colours of the African euchromia moth warn any would-be predators that it is poisonous. It also has an awful smell. Some moths manufacture their own poisons, but others are toxic because their caterpillars eat poisonous plants. The poisons do not hurt the insects, but make them harmful to their enemies.

▲ HAIRY MOUTHFUL
The caterpillar of the sycamore moth is bright yellow. It is not poisonous like some of the other brightly coloured caterpillars, but its masses of long, hairy tufts make it distinctly unpleasant to eat.

▼ THREATENING DISPLAY
The caterpillar of the puss moth may look clown-like and harmless, but by caterpillar standards it is quite fearsome. When threatened, its slender whip-like tails are thrust forwards and it may squirt a jet of harmful formic acid from a gland near its mouth. It also uses red markings and false eye spots on its head to create an aggressive display.

puss moth caterpillar *(Cerura vinula)*

◄ **POISONOUS MILK**

A Monarch butterfly caterpillar feeds on various kinds of milkweed, which contain a powerful poison. This chemical is harmful to many small creatures. The poison stays in the Monarch's body throughout its life. This may be why Monarchs show less fear of predators than other butterflies.

► **RED ALERT**

The striking red, white and black colours of the spurge hawk moth caterpillar tell that it is poisonous. Unpalatable insects often display conspicuous colours such as reds, yellows, black and white. These insects do not need to protect themselves by blending into their background. This caterpillar acquires its poison from a plant called spurge, which it feeds on.

spurge hawk moth caterpillar
(Hyles euphorbiae)

Did you know? Many harmless butterflies mimic poisonous species so well that enemies dare not touch them.

▼ **SMELLY CATERPILLAR**

The swallowtail caterpillar produces an odour that is strong enough to ward off parasites. It comes from a scent-gland called the osmeterium situated just behind its head. This gland suddenly erupts and oozes acid when the caterpillar is threatened.

▲ **DEFENSIVE FROTH**

Rhodogastria moths of Australasia and Africa often have a bright red abdomen to warn enemies that they carry a deadly poison. When the moth is threatened, this poison oozes out from a gland on the back of its neck.

swallowtail caterpillar
(Papilio machaon)

Fabulous

1 Hawk moths begin life as eggs laid on the leaves of a food-plant. The round eggs are a distinctive shiny green. They are laid singly or in small batches and hatch a week or two afterwards.

2 The elephant hawk moth's name comes from the ability of its caterpillar to stretch out its front segments like an elephant's trunk. It takes about six weeks to grow fully and, like most hawk moths, it passes the winter in the pupal stage.

Hawk moths are perhaps the most distinctive and easily recognized of all the moth families. Their bodies are unusually large and they are strong fliers. Hawk moths can fly at speeds of up to 50km an hour, and many hover like hummingbirds while feeding from flowers. Many hawk moths have very long tongues that enable them to sip nectar from even the deepest flowers. When these moths come to rest, their wings usually angle back like the wings of a jet plane. Hawk moth caterpillars nearly all have a pointed horn on the end of their bodies.

3 The adult elephant hawk moth is one of the prettiest of all moths. It flies for a few weeks in the summer. Its candy-pink wings are a perfect match for the pink garden fuchsias and wild willow-herbs on which it lays its eggs.

Hawk Moths

GOING HUNGRY

During nights in late spring and summer, poplar hawk moths can often be seen flying towards lighted shop windows in European towns. These moths have a short tongue and do not feed as adults. Unusually for hawk moths, when they are resting by day, their hindwings are pushed in front of the forewings.

poplar hawk moth
(Laothoe populi)

HONEY LOVER

The death's head hawk moth is named for the skull-like markings near the back of its head. Its proboscis is too short to sip nectar. Instead, it sometimes enters beehives and sucks honey from the combs.

MASTER OF DISGUISE

The broad-bordered bee hawk moth resembles a bumblebee. It has a fat, brown and yellow body and clear, glassy wings. This disguise helps to protect it from predators as it flies during the day.

Spinning Spiders

All spiders make silk. They pull the silk out of spinnerets on their abdomens, usually with their legs. The silk is a syrupy liquid when it first comes out, but pulling makes it harden. The more silk is pulled, the stronger it becomes. Some spider silk is stronger than steel wire of the same thickness. As well as being very strong, silk is incredibly thin, has more stretch than rubber and is stickier than sticky tape. Spiders make up to six different types of silk in different glands in the abdomen. Each type of silk is used for a different purpose, from making webs to wrapping prey. Female spiders produce a special silk to wrap up eggs.

An *Agroeca* spider hangs its cocoon from a grass stem. It will plaster the cocoon with mud to form a hard protective coating.

▲ **EGG PARCELS**
Female spiders have an extra silk gland for making egg cases called cocoons. These protect the developing eggs.

The Industrious Spider
Spiders have been admired for their tireless spinning for centuries. This picture was painted by the Italian artist Veronese in the 1500s. He wanted to depict the virtues of the great city of Venice, whose wealth was based on trade. To represent hard work and industry he painted this figure of a woman holding up a spider in its web.

▲ **A SILKEN RETREAT**
Many spiders build silk shelters or nests. The tube-web spider occupies a hole in the bark of a tree. Its tube-shaped retreat has a number of trip lines radiating out like the spokes of a wheel. If an insect trips over a line, the spider rushes out to grab and eat it.

▲ STICKY SILK
Silk oozes out through a spider's spinnerets. Two or more kinds of silk can be spun at the same time. Orb-web spiders produce gummy silk to make their webs sticky.

▲ FOOD PARCEL
A garden spider (*Araneus*) stops a grasshopper from escaping by wrapping it in silk. The prey is also paralysed by the spider's poisonous bite. Most spiders make silk for wrapping prey.

SPINNERETS ►
A spider's spinnerets have many fine tubes on the end. The smaller tubes, or spools, produce finer silk for wrapping prey. Larger tubes, called spigots, produce coarser strands for webs.

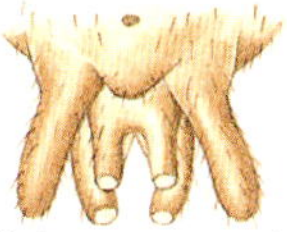

Spinnerets vary in size and number.

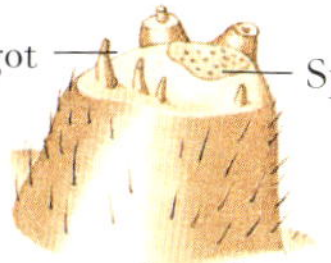

Close up of a spinneret.

▲ COMBING OUT SILK
This lace-weaver spider is using its back legs to comb out a special silk. It has an extra spinning organ (the cribellum) in front of its spinnerets that produces very fine silk.

▲ VELCRO SILK
The lacy webs made by cribellate spiders contain tiny loops, like velcro, that catch on the hairs and bristles of insect prey. Combined in bands with normal silk, the fluffy-looking cribellate silk stops insect prey from escaping.

Venom Injection

Nearly all spiders use poison for defence and to kill or paralyse their prey. Spider poison is called venom. It is injected into prey through needle-like jaws called fangs. There are two main kinds of venom that can have serious effects. Most dangerous spiders, such as widow spiders, produce nerve poison to paralyse victims quickly. The other kind of venom works more slowly, destroying tissues and causing ulcers and gangrene. It is made by the recluse spiders. Spider venom is intended to kill insects and small prey – only about 30 spider species are dangerous to people.

▲ **VIOLIN SPIDER**
This small brown spider is one of the recluse spiders. It lives in people's homes and may crawl into clothes and bedding. Bites from recluse spiders in America have caused ulcers, especially near the wound, and even death in humans.

▲ **WANDERING KILLER**
The Brazilian wandering spider is a large hunting spider that produces one of the most toxic venoms of all spiders. If disturbed it raises its front legs to expose its threatening jaws. It has the largest venom glands of any spider (up to 10mm long), which hold enough venom to kill 225 mice. Several people have died from this spider's bite.

The Spider Dance
In the Middle Ages people from Taranto in southern Italy called the large wolf spider (Lycosa narbonensis) *the tarantula. They believed the venom of this spider's bite could only be flushed from the body by doing the tarantella, a lively dance. However,* Lycosa's *bite is not serious. An epidemic of dangerous spider bites at the time was probably caused by the malmignatte spider.*

▲ **SUDDEN DEATH**

Crab spiders do not spin webs so they need to kill their prey quickly. They usually inject their venom into the main nerve cords in the neck where the poison will get to work most rapidly. They are able to kill insects much larger than themselves, such as bees.

WIDOW SPIDER ►

The Australian red-back spider is one of the world's most deadly widow spiders. Widow spiders are named after the female's habit of eating the male after mating. Only female widow spiders are dangerous to people – the much smaller male's fangs are far too tiny to break through human skin.

Did you know? A black widow's venom is 15 times more poisonous than a rattlesnake's.

▲ **GENTLE GIANT**

Tarantulas look very dangerous and have huge fangs, but at worst their bite is no more painful than a wasp sting. They have small venom glands and are unlikely to bite unless handled roughly. They use venom to digest their prey.

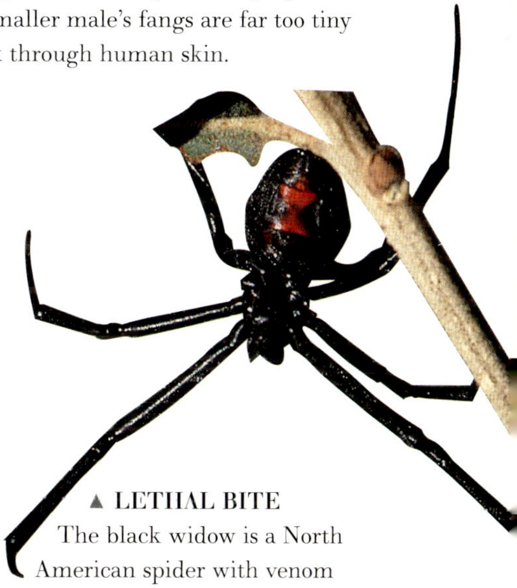

▲ **LETHAL BITE**

The black widow is a North American spider with venom powerful enough to kill a person (although medicines can now prevent this happening). These shy spiders hide away if disturbed, but like to live near people. One of the main ingredients in their venom knocks out insects and another paralyses mammals and birds by damaging their nervous systems.

American racer
(Coluber constrictor)

Stranglers and Poisoners

Most snakes kill their prey before eating it. Snakes kill by using poison or by squeezing their prey to death. Snakes that squeeze are called constrictors and they stop their prey from breathing. Victims die from suffocation or shock. To swallow living or dead prey, a snake opens its jaws wide. Lots of slimy saliva helps the meal to slide down. After eating, a snake yawns widely to put its jaws back into place. Digestion can take several days, or even weeks.

▲ **BIG MOUTHFUL**
This American racer is trying to swallow a living frog. The frog has puffed up its body with air to make it more difficult for the snake to swallow.

▲ **AT FULL STRETCH**
This fer-de-lance snake is at full stretch to swallow its huge meal. It is a large pit viper that kills with poison.

▲ **SWALLOWING A MEAL**
The copperhead, a poisonous snake from North America, holds on to a dead mouse.

▲ KILLING TIME
A crocodile is slowly squeezed to death by a rock python. The time it takes for a constricting snake to kill its prey depends on the size of the prey and how strong it is.

Spotted python
(Liasis maculosus)

► COILED KILLER
The spotted python sinks its teeth into its victim. It throws coils around the victim's body, and tightens its grip until the animal cannot breathe.

Did you know? King cobras sometimes kill Indian elephants by biting them on the trunk.

▲ HEAD-FIRST
A whiptail wallaby's legs disappear inside a carpet python's body. Snakes usually try to swallow their prey head-first so that legs, wings or scales fold back. This helps the victim to slide into the snake's stomach more easily.

▼ BREATHING TUBE
An African python shows its breathing tube. As the snake eats, the windpipe moves to the front of the mouth so that air can get to and from the lungs.

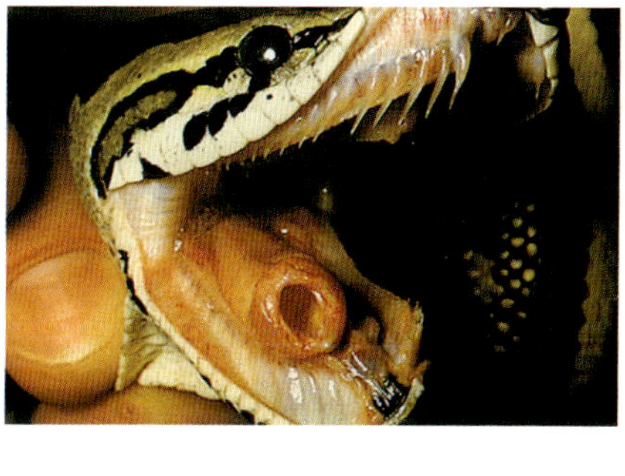

Slithering Scales

▼ POINTED SNOUT

As its name suggests, the European nose-horned viper has a strange horn on its nose. The horn is made up of small scales that lie over a bony or fleshy lump sticking out at the end of the nose.

A snake's scales are extra-thick pieces of skin. Like a suit of armour, the scales protect the snake from knocks and scrapes as it moves. The scales also allow the skin to stretch when the snake moves or feeds. Scales are usually made of a horny substance, called keratin. Every part of a snake's body is covered in scales, even the eyes. Every so often a snake grows a new skin underneath its old one. Then it wriggles out of the dead skin.

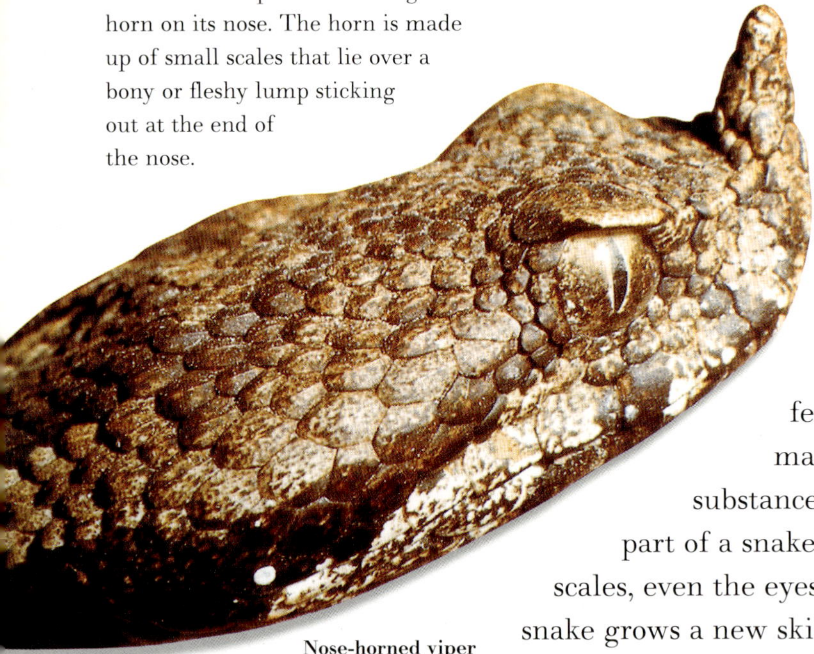

Nose-horned viper
(Vipera ammodytes)

▼ SCUTES

Most snakes have a row of broad scales, called scutes, underneath their bodies. The scutes go across a snake's body from side to side, and end where the tail starts. Scutes help snakes to grip the ground.

Corn snake's scutes

▼ WARNING RATTLE

The rattlesnake has a number of hollow tail-tips that make a buzzing sound when shaken. The snake uses this sound to warn other animals. When it sheds its skin, a section at the end of the tail is left, adding another piece to the rattle.

Rattlesnak rattle

▸ SKIN SCALES

When a snake's skin is stretched, the scales pull apart so that you can see the skin between them. The scales grow out of the top layer of the skin, called the epidermis. There are different kinds of scales. Smooth scales make it easier for the snake to squeeze through tight spaces.

Corn snake's scales

Look closely at the rough scales of the puff adder (left) and you will see a raised ridge, or keel, sticking up in the middle of each one.

Did you know? Most snakes get their colours from pigments in the scales.

The wart snake (right) uses its scales to grip its food. Its rough scales help the snake to keep a firm hold on slippery fish until it can swallow them. The snake's scales do not overlap.

The green scales and stretched blue skin (left) belong to a boa. These smooth scales help the boa to slide over leafy branches. Burrowing snakes have smooth scales so that they can slip through soil.

Did you know? The hairy bush viper has pointed scales with curled tips, making it look hairy.

Eternal Youth

A poem written in the Middle East about 3,700 years ago tells a story about why snakes can shed their skins. The hero of the poem is Gilgamesh (shown here holding a captured lion). He finds a magic plant that will make a person young again. While he is washing at a pool, a snake eats the plant. Since then, snakes have been able to shed their skins and become young again. But people have never found the plant – which is why they always grow old and die.

Mighty Bites

The huge jaws of a crocodile and its impressive spiky teeth are lethal weapons for catching prey. Crocodiles and their relatives (crocodilians) have two or three times as many teeth as a human. They have sharp, pointed teeth at the front of the mouth that are used to pierce and grip prey. The force of the jaws closing drives these teeth, like a row of knives, deep into a victim's flesh. The short, blunt teeth at the back of the mouth are used for crushing prey. Crocodilian teeth are no good for chewing food, and the jaws cannot be moved sideways to chew either. Food has to be swallowed whole, or torn into chunks. The teeth are constantly growing. If a tooth falls out, a new one grows through to replace it.

▲ **MEGA JAWS**
The jaws of a Nile crocodile close with tremendous force. They sink into their prey with many tonnes of crushing pressure, but the muscles that open the jaws are weak. A thick elastic band over the snout can easily hold a crocodile's jaws shut.

◄ **NEW TEETH FOR OLD**
Each tooth is set in a socket and held in place by a connecting layer of tissue. Throughout a crocodile's life, the old teeth fall out and new teeth underneath take their place. Teeth last up to two years before falling out. Alternate teeth are replaced together, so that not all the teeth in one part of the mouth are lost at once.

◄ LOTS OF TEETH

The gharial has more teeth than any other crocodilian, around 110. Its teeth are also smaller than those of other crocodilians and are all the same size. The narrow, beak-like snout and long, thin teeth of the gharial are geared to grabbing fish with a sweeping sideways movement of the head. The sharp teeth interlock to trap and impale the slippery prey.

▲ BABY TEETH

A baby American alligator is born with a full set of 80 teeth when it hatches from its egg. Baby teeth are not as sharp as adult teeth and are more fragile. They are like tiny needles. In young crocodiles, the teeth at the back of the mouth usually fall out first. In adults it is the teeth at the front that fall out more often.

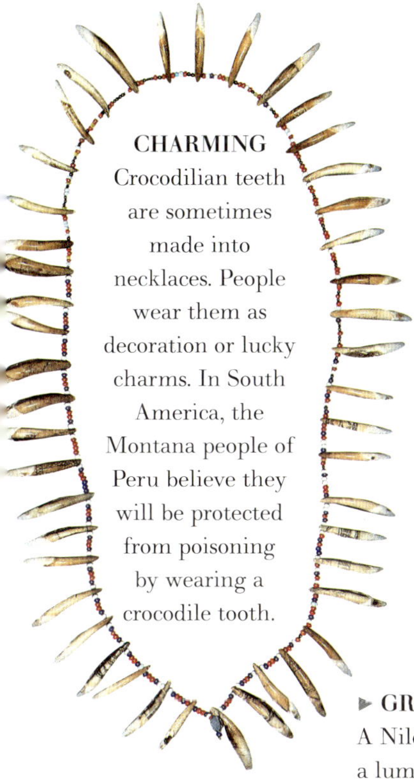

CHARMING

Crocodilian teeth are sometimes made into necklaces. People wear them as decoration or lucky charms. In South America, the Montana people of Peru believe they will be protected from poisoning by wearing a crocodile tooth.

► GRABBING TEETH

A Nile crocodile grasps a lump of prey ready for swallowing. If prey is too large to swallow whole, the crocodile grips the food firmly in its teeth and shakes its head hard so that any unwanted pieces are shaken off.

A Nile crocodile has 68 teeth lining its huge jaws.

Did you know? A Nile crocodile may use 45 sets of teeth by the time it is 4m long.

Cold-blooded Killers

Soon after the sun rises, the first alligators heave themselves out of the river and flop down on the bank. The banks fill up quickly as more alligators join the first, warming their scaly bodies in the sun's rays. As the hours go by and the day gets hotter, the alligators open their toothy jaws wide to cool down. Later in the day, they may go for a swim or crawl into the shade to cool off. As the air chills at night, the alligators slip back into the water again. This is because water stays warmer for longer at night than the land.

Crocodiles and their relatives (crocodilians) are cold-blooded, which means that their body temperature varies with outside temperatures. To warm up or cool down, they move to warm or cool places. Their ideal body temperature is between 30 and 35°C.

▲ **MUD PACK**
A spectacled caiman is buried deep in the mud to keep cool during the hot, dry season. Mud is like water and does not get as hot or as cold as dry land. It also helps to keep the caiman's scaly skin free from bloodsucking parasites.

◄ **SOLAR PANELS**
The crested scutes on the tail of a crocodilian are like the bony plates on armoured dinosaurs. They act like solar panels, picking up heat when the animal basks in the sun. The scutes can also move apart fractionally to let as much heat as possible escape from the body to cool it down.

◄ **UNDER THE ICE**
An alligator can survive under ice if it keeps a breathing hole open. Of all crocodilians, only alligators stay active at temperatures as low as 12 or 15°C. They do not eat, however, because the temperature is too low for their digestions to work.

▼ **OPEN WIDE**
While a Nile crocodile suns itself on a rock it also opens its mouth in a wide gape. Gaping helps to prevent the crocodile becoming too hot. The breeze flowing over the wide, wet surfaces of the mouth and tongue dries its moisture and, in turn, cools off its blood. If you lick your finger and blow on it softly, you will notice that it feels a lot cooler.

▲ **ALLIGATOR DAYS**
Alligators follow a distinct daily routine when the weather is good, moving in and out of the water at regular intervals. If they are disturbed they will also go into the water. In winter, alligators retreat into dens and become sleepy because their blood cools and slows them down.

LESS NEED TO FEED ►
Being cold-blooded can be quite useful. These alligators can bask in the sun without having to eat very much or very often. Warm-blooded animals such as mammals have to eat regularly. They need to eat about five times as much food as crocodilians to keep their bodies warm.

Flying South

Every bird of prey maintains a territory in which it can feed and breed. There is usually no room for the parents' offspring, so they have to forge a new territory themselves. The parents may stay in their breeding area all year long if there is enough food. If not, they may migrate (move away) to somewhere warmer in winter, because sometimes their prey have themselves migrated. For example, peregrines that bred on the tundra in northern Europe fly some 14,000 kilometres to spend winter in South Africa.

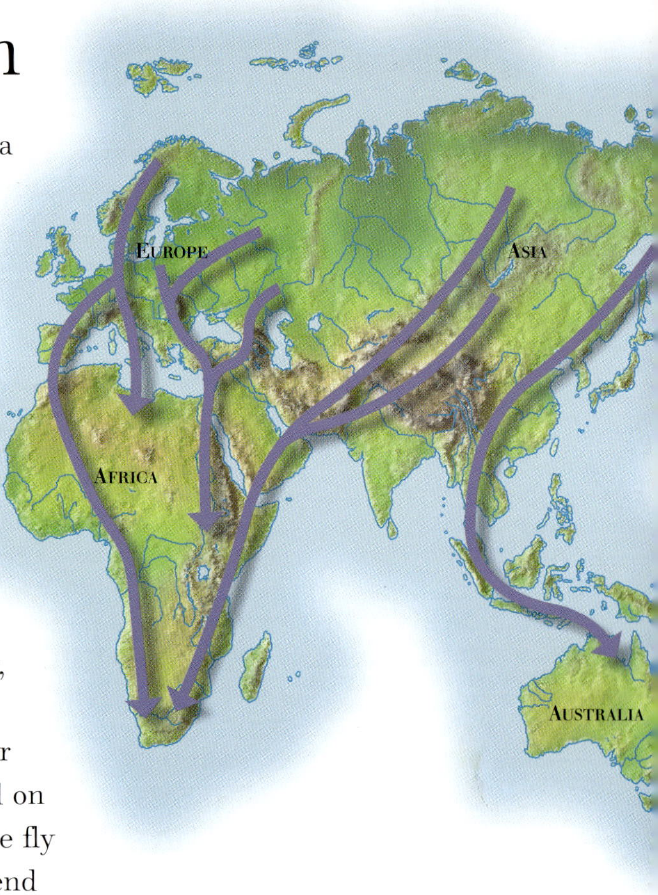

▲ **FLIGHT PATHS**
Birds avoid migrating over large stretches of water. There are fewer uplifting air currents over water than there are over land. So, many migration routes pass through regions where there is a convenient land bridge or a short sea crossing. Panama, in Central America, is one such area. Gibraltar, in southern Europe, is another.

◀ **SOON TIME TO LEAVE**
The rough-legged buzzard is slightly larger than its close relative, the common buzzard. It breeds in far northern regions of the world in the spring, both on the treeless tundra and the forested taiga. In the autumn, it migrates south to escape the freezing temperatures of the Arctic winter.

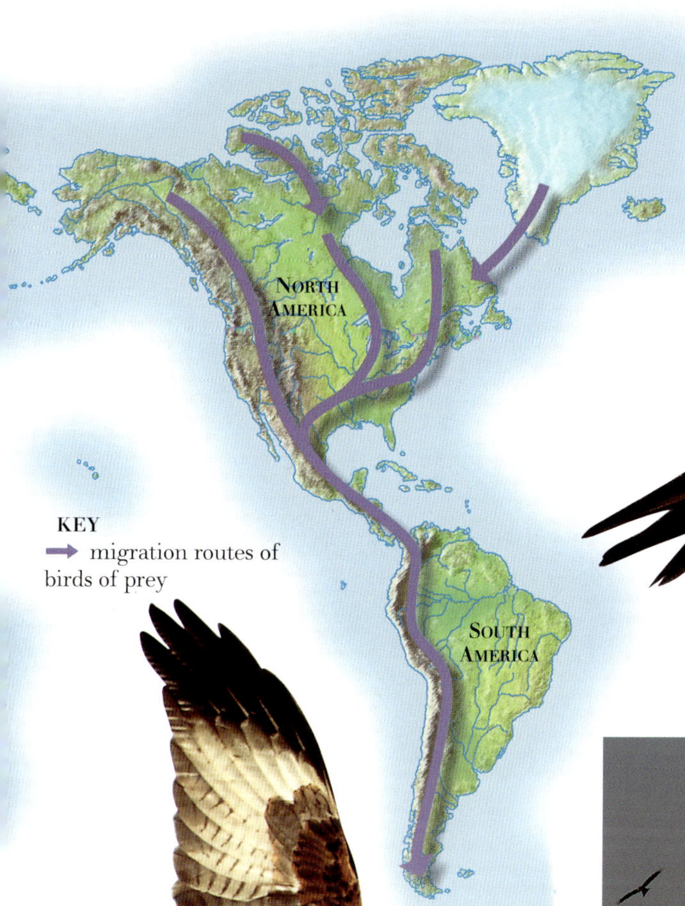

▼ JUST PASSING THROUGH

This sooty falcon was spotted on its way south to the island of Madagascar, where it spends the winter. In spring, it will return to north-east Africa or Israel to breed.

sooty falcon (*Falco concolor*)

▲ KITE FLYING

The red kite is unmistakable, with its rust-brown belly and white wing patches. There are about 100 red kites in Wales. Unlike many of their European cousins, those that breed in Wales do not usually migrate south in winter.

▲ LONG DISTANCE TRAVELLERS

Graceful kites fly over an Indian village during their annual migration from Asia to warmer winter quarters in southern Africa. They will cover hundreds of kilometres a day.

Night Birds

Owls are supreme night hunters with bodies perfectly adapted for hunting in the dark. For one thing, they fly silently. The flight feathers on their wings are covered with a fine down to muffle the sound of air passing over them. Owls' eyes are particularly adapted for night vision. They contain many more rods than the eyes of other bird species. Rods are the structures that make eyes sensitive to light. An owl's hearing is superb too. The rings of fine feathers owls have around their eyes help to channel sounds into the ears. The ears themselves are surrounded by flaps of skin, which can be moved to pinpoint the sources of sounds precisely.

A few other meat-eating birds also hunt after sundown. They include the bat hawk of Africa and Asia, which catches and eats bats and insects while on the wing.

▲ **GETTING A GRIP**
Like all owls, the barn owl has powerful claws for attacking and gripping prey. The outer toe can be moved backwards and forwards to change grip.

▲ **GHOSTLY FACE**
Of all the owls, the barn owl has the most prominent round face – this is called a facial disc. This gives it a rather ghostly appearance. The disc is formed of short, stiff feathers.

Wise Owls
For centuries, owls have had a reputation for being wise birds. This came about because in Greek mythology, the little owl was the sacred bird of the goddess of wisdom, Athena. She gave her name to Greece's capital city, Athens. The best-known coin of the ancient Greek world was issued in Athens and featured an owl.

▲ **THE WORLD'S LARGEST OWL**

A European eagle owl stands over a red fox left out for it as bait. It looks around warily before beginning to eat. The eagle owl is a fierce predator, and will hunt prey as big as a young roe deer. It is a large bird, growing up to 70 cm long, is powerfully built, and has long ear tufts.

▼ **TAKEAWAY MEAL**

A barn owl holds on to a mouse it has just caught. Owls usually carry prey in their hooked bills, unlike other birds of prey, which carry it in their claws. Barn owls are found throughout most of the world and in various habitats – moorland, desert, forest and farmland.

barn owl
(*Tyto alba*)

► **OFTEN HEARD, RARELY SEEN**

A mouse is carried off by a tawny owl. The long, hooting, 'twit-twoo' call of this owl can be heard in woods, parks and gardens across Europe.

▲ **PEEKABOO**

A burrowing owl peers out of its nest hole. These small, long-legged birds live in the prairies and grasslands of the New World, from Canada to the tip of South America. They often take over the abandoned holes of other burrowers, such as prairie dogs.

Africa's Striped

1 From July to September, hundreds of thousands of animals follow the rains from the Serengeti in Tanzania towards the Masai Mara in Kenya. They move in long columns, following the same, well-worn paths every year.

Vast herds of zebras, gazelles and wildebeest roam the open plains of south and east Africa. They are constantly on the move, searching for better areas of grazing. The herds migrate from the acacia thorn forests in the north-west to the grasslands in the south-east, and back again. Their circular trip takes a year.

Zebras can sense a rainstorm from up to 100km away. They gather into large herds to watch for rain clouds and listen for thunder. The rain fills waterholes and ensures the growth of plenty of fresh, new grass. Zebras are the first to arrive in these areas. They feed on the toughest parts of the vigorous new vegetation, paving the way for the more delicate grazers that follow.

2 One of the major obstacles on the great migration is the Mara River. No animal wants to take the plunge and cross first, as the river is filled with crocodiles. Enormous numbers of zebras and their travelling companions, wildebeest and gazelles, build up on the riverbank.

Migrators

3 When one animal starts to cross, the rest follow quickly. If the river is swollen by the rains, the animals must swim. Some are swept away in the torrent. Smaller members of the herd are pulled down and drowned by crocodiles. If the river is low, the zebras can wade across. They are quite capable of kicking an attacking crocodile with their hind feet and escaping.

4 Lionesses from a resident pride watch and wait among zebra and topi that have crossed the river. They will pounce on any floundering animal. The migrating animals offer a seasonal glut of food as they pass through the lions' territory.

5 The zebras have panicked at the scent of lions nearby and they abandon their river crossing. They will head back on to the plains, regroup and return to the river to try again. Somehow the zebras must cross to get to the new grass on the other side.

6 A lioness chases a scattered herd of zebra and antelope. The pride has fanned out and encircled the herd, chasing them towards an ambush. The migrating animals are followed by hyenas and nomadic lions on the lookout for stragglers and unprotected youngsters.

Trunk Tales

Imagine what it would be like if your nose and top lip were joined together and stretched into a long, bendy tube hanging down from your face. This is what an elephant's trunk must feel like. It can do everything that your nose, lips, hand and arm can do – and more besides. An elephant uses its trunk to breathe, eat, drink, pick things up, throw things, feel, smell, fight and play, squirt water, mud and dust, greet and touch other elephants and make sounds. Not surprisingly, a baby elephant takes a long time to learn all these ways to use its trunk.

▲ **DRINKING STRAW**
An elephant cannot lower its head down to the ground to drink so it sucks up water with its trunk. Baby elephants drink with their mouths until they learn to use their trunks to squirt water into their mouths.

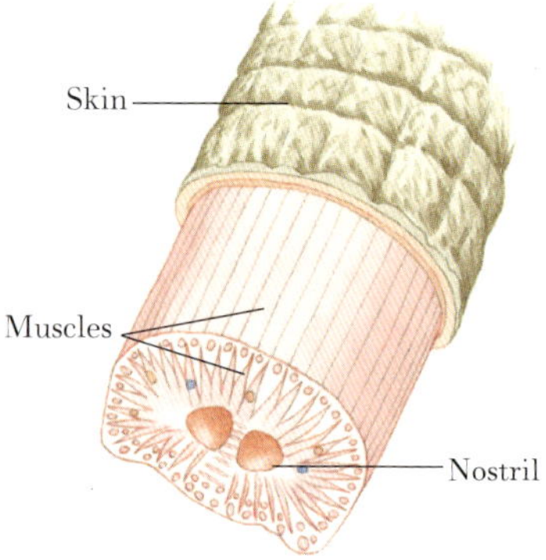

▲ **A CLOSER LOOK**
The two holes in the centre of the trunk are nostrils, through which the elephant breathes. Thousands of muscles pull against each other in different directions to move the trunk.

▲ **WEIGHT LIFTER**
An African elephant coils its trunk around a branch to lift it off the ground. Elephants can lift whole tree trunks in this way. The powerful trunk has more than 100,000 muscles, which enable an elephant to lift large, heavy objects easily.

▲ **TAKING A SHOWER**

An elephant does not need to stand under a shower to be sprayed with water, mud or dust. Its trunk is like a built-in shower, able to cover almost its whole body as it reaches backwards over the head. Showering cools the elephant down and gets rid of insects.

▲ **BENDY APPENDAGE**

Elephants sometimes double up their trunks and rest them on their tusks. They can do this because the trunk has no bones inside it, just muscles, which makes it very flexible.

► **TALL ORDER**

African elephants use their long, stretchy trunks to pull leaves off the branches of tall acacia trees. The highest leaves are the most juicy. The trunk is slightly telescopic, which means that, if necessary, it can be stretched out even longer than usual. The trunk can also be pushed into small holes or gaps between rocks to find hidden pools of water

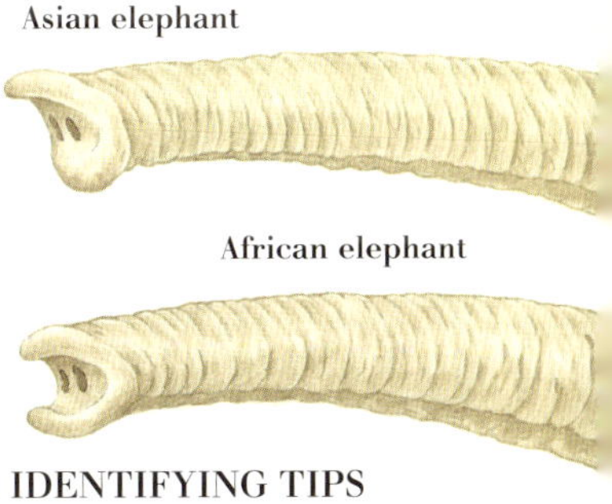

▲ **IDENTIFYING TIPS**

The trunk of an African elephant has two fingers at the tip, while the Asian elephant has only one. These fingers can pick up an object as small as a leaf or a coin.

Jumbo

Elephants love water. They drink lots of it and enjoy going into lakes and rivers to play and splash around. Elephants are good swimmers and can easily cross rivers or swim out to sea to reach islands with fresh food. They drink at least once a day, or more often when water is available. When water is hard to find in the wild, elephants can be very sneaky, drinking from taps, pipes or water tanks. This usually causes damaged or broken pipes. Elephants can go without water for up to two weeks.

SPLASHING ABOUT
Elephants spray each other with water, wrestle with their trunks and flop sideways with great splashes. Sometimes they turn upside down and poke the soles of their feet out of the water. All this play strengthens the bonds between individuals and keeps groups together.

LIQUID REFRESHMENT
These two elephants are refreshing themselves at a waterhole. Elephants drink by sucking in water through their trunk. They seal off the end with the finger or fingers at the end of the trunk. Then they lift the trunk to the mouth and squirt in the water.

CHAMPION SWIMMERS
Elephants are good at swimming even though they are so big. When an elephant swims underwater, it pokes its trunk above the water and uses it like a snorkel to breathe through.

Water Babies

KEEPING CLEAN
Frequent bathing washes the build-up of mud and dust out of the cracks in an elephant's thick skin. Disease-carrying insects and parasites that feed off the elephant's skin are also washed off in the water.

HOLDING ON TIGHT
In the water, baby elephants often hold on to the tail of the elephant in front for safety. They can easily be swept away by fast-flowing rivers. Baby elephants are also vulnerable to attack from crocodiles.

THIRST QUENCHER
An elephant needs to drink 70–90 litres of water a day. A full trunk of water holds about 5–10 litres. Incredibly, a very thirsty adult elephant can drink about 100 litres of water in 5 minutes.

Great Navigators

Bears have an uncanny knack of finding their way home even in unfamiliar territory. How they do this is only just beginning to be understood. For long distances, they rely on an ability to detect the Earth's magnetic field. This provides them with a magnetic map of their world and a compass to find their way around. When closer to home, they recognize familiar landmarks. In fact, bears have extraordinary memories, especially where food is involved. For example, a mother and her cubs are known to have trekked 32km to a favourite oak tree to feast on acorns. Five years later, the same cubs (now adults) were reported to have been seen at the same tree.

Stars in the Sky

The Great Bear constellation in the northern hemisphere is known to astronomers as Ursa Major. In Greek mythology, it was said to have been made in the shape of a she-bear and placed in the heavens by Zeus. The Great Bear is also worshipped in Hindu mythology as the power that keeps the heavens turning. The Inuit believe these stars represent a bear being continually chased by dogs.

▲ ARCTIC NOMADS

Polar bears are capable of swimming long distances between ice floes, at speeds of up to 10km/h. They may travel thousands of kilometres across the frozen Arctic Ocean and the surrounding lands in search of prey.

▲ BAD BEAR

A sedated polar bear is transported a safe distance out of town. Nuisance bears are often moved this way but they unerringly find their way back.

◄ TO AND FROM THE FOREST

The polar bears of Hudson Bay, Canada, migrate to the forests in summer and return to hunt on the sea ice in winter. On their return journey, they sometimes stop off at the town of Churchill. They gather at the rubbish tip there to feed on leftovers, while they wait for ice to reform.

KEY

- Bears return to ice in winter
- Bears come ashore in June and July
- Bears walk north in autumn

▲ REGULAR ROUTES

Polar bears move quickly even on fast, shifting ice floes. A bear moving north, for example, against the southward-drifting ice in the Greenland Sea, can travel up to 80km in a day.

▲ RELYING ON MEMORY

Male brown bears live in large home ranges covering several hundred square kilometres. They must remember the locations of food and the different times of year it is available.

The Big Sleep

Black bears, brown bears and pregnant female polar bears sleep during the winter months. They do this because food is scarce, not because of the cold. Scientists have argued for years about whether bears truly hibernate or merely doze during the winter months and this argument still goes on today. During this sleep, or hibernation, a brown bear's heart rate drops to about 10 beats per minute. American black bears reduce their blood temperature by at least one degree. They do not eat or drink for up to four months. Bears survive only on the fat that they have stored during the summer months. A bear might lose up to half its body-weight before it awakes at the end of the winter.

▲ **FAT BEAR**
Before the winter sleep a bear can become quite tubby. Fat reserves make up more than half of this black bear's body-weight. It needs this bulk to make sure that it has enough fat on its body to survive the winter fast. In the weeks leading up to the winter, a bear must consume large quantities of energy-rich foods, such as salmon.

Did you know? Some hibernating bears sleep for 5½ months non-stop.

◀ **HOME COMFORTS**
A brown bear pulls in grass and leaves to cushion its winter den. American black bears and brown bears sleep in small, specially dug dens. These are usually found on the sunny, south-facing slopes of mountains.

▲ FOREST REFUGE
A hole dug by a brown bear serves as its winter den in this Swedish forest. Bears spend winter in much stranger places, such as under cabins occupied by people, beneath bridges or beside busy roads.

▲ SNOW HOUSE
Female polar bears leave the drifting ice floes in early winter and head inland to excavate a nursery den. They dig deep down into the snow and ice, tunnelling for about 5m to make the den. Here they will give birth to their cubs. In severe weather, male polar bears rest by lying down and allowing themselves to be covered over by an insulating layer of snow.

▲ READY FOR ACTION
If disturbed, a bear wakes easily from its winter sleep. Although it is dormant, a bear's body is ready to be active. It is able to defend itself immediately against predators, such as a hungry wolf pack.

▲ WINTER NURSERY
In the early winter, one bear enters a den, but three might emerge in spring. Female polar bears, like most bears, give birth while hidden away in their dens. The tiny cubs (usually twins) are born in the middle of winter, in December or January.

Camouflaged Cats

A cat's fur coat protects its skin and keeps it warm. The coat's colours and patterns help to camouflage (hide) the cat as it hunts prey. Wild cats' coats have two layers – an undercoat of short soft fur and an outercoat of tougher, longer hairs, called guard hairs. Together these two layers insulate the cat from extreme cold or extreme heat. Some guard hairs are sensitive and help a cat to feel its way. Cats have loose skin, making it hard for an attacker to get a good grip and helping to prevent injury. The colours and patterns of a wild cat's coat depend on where it lives.

▲ **TIGER IN THE GRASS**
The stripes of a tiger's coat are the perfect camouflage for an animal that needs to prowl around in long grass. The colours and patterns help to make the cat almost invisible as it stalks its prey. These markings are also very effective in a leafy jungle where the dappled light makes stripes of light and shade.

Did you know? Domestic cats have a wider range of colours and markings than wild cats.

◄ **KING OF THE HILL**
King cheetahs were once thought to be different from other cheetahs. They have longer fur, darker colours and spots on their backs that join up to form stripes. Even so, they are the same species. All cheetahs have distinctive tear stripes running from the corners of their eyes down beside their muzzles.

▲ **NON-IDENTICAL TWINS**

Many big cats of the same species come in variations of colour, depending on where they live. These two leopard cubs are twins, but one has a much darker, blackish coat. Black leopards are called panthers. (Black jaguars and even pumas are sometimes called panthers.) Some leopards live deep in the shadows of the forest, where darker colouring allows them to hide more easily. Panthers are most common in Asia.

▼ **SPOT THE DIFFERENCE**

Spots, stripes or blotches break up the outline of a cat's body. This helps it to blend in with the shadows made by the leaves of bushes and trees, or the lines of tall grass. In the dappled light of a forest or in the long grass of the savanna, cats are very well hidden indeed.

A leopard's spots are in fact small rosettes.

The tiger has distinctive black stripes.

A jaguar has rosettes with a central spot of colour.

The cheetah has lots of spots and no rosettes.

A snow leopard's pale, thick coat has dark irregular spots and streaks. This helps the cat to hide between the rocks and snow.

◀ **MOUNTAIN DWELLER**

A snow leopard has a shaggy, off-white coat with darker spots. This colouring helps the snow leopard to stay well hidden in the rocky, mountainous terrain where it lives. It moves around early in the morning or late in the afternoon, blending with its habitat as it looks for prey.

Fur Coats

black-backed jackal
(Canis mesomelas)

Wolves and other members of the dog family have thick fur coats. This dense layer of hair helps to protect the animal's body from injury and keeps it warm in cold weather. Wolves and other dogs that live in cold places have extra-thick fur. Dingoes, jackals and wild dogs that live in warm countries close to the equator have sparser fur. The fur is made up of two layers. Short dense underfur helps to keep the animal warm. Long guard hairs on top have natural oils that repel snow and rain to keep the underfur dry. A wild dog's fur coat is usually black, white or tan, or a mixture of these. Markings and patterns on the fur act as camouflage to disguise these animals, so they can sneak up on their prey.

▲ DISTINCTIVE OUTFIT
The three species of jackal can be distinguished by their different markings. As its name suggests, the black-backed jackal has a dark patch on its back as well as brown flanks and a pale belly. The golden jackal is sandy brown all over. The side-striped jackal is so named because of the light and dark stripes that run along its sides.

◄ WRAPPED UP WARM
Two raccoon dogs shelter under a bush at the end of winter. Raccoon dogs are the only dogs in the world to hibernate. Their thick fur helps them survive through their long winter sleep. Originally from east Asia, raccoon dogs were brought to western Russia by fur farmers in the 1920s. Some escaped and they can now be found in eastern Europe.

◀ MANES AND RUFFS

The maned wolf gets its name from the ruff of long hairs on its neck. This may be dark or reddish brown in colour. Wolves also have a ruff of longer hairs that they raise when threatened, to make themselves look larger.

▲ HANDSOME CAMOUFLAGE

African hunting dogs have beautiful markings, with tan and dark grey patches on their bodies, and paler, mottled fur on their heads and legs. The patterns work to break up the outline of their bodies as they hunt in the dappled light of the bush.

Arctic wolf *(Canis lupus tundrarum)*

▲ ICE WHITE

The Arctic wolf has very thick fur to keep it warm in icy temperatures. Its winter coat is pure white so that it blends in with the snow. In spring, the thick fur drops out and the wolf grows a thinner coat for summer. This coat is usually darker to match the earth without its covering of snow.

grey wolf *(Canis lupus)*

VARYING COLOURS ▶

Grey wolves vary greatly in colour, from pale silver to buff, sandy, red-brown or almost black. Even very dark wolves usually have some pale fur, often a white patch on the chest.

Snow Dogs

Wolves were once widespread throughout the northern hemisphere. As human settlements have expanded, so wolves have been confined to more remote areas such as the far north. The Arctic is a frozen wilderness where very few people live. Wolves and Arctic foxes are found here. On the barren, treeless plains known as the tundra, harsh, freezing winter weather lasts for nine months of the year. Both land and sea are buried beneath a thick layer of snow and ice. Few animals are active in winter, so prey is scarce. During the brief summer, the ice and snow melt, flowers bloom and birds, insects and animals flourish, so prey is abundant. Arctic wolves and foxes rear their cubs in this time of plenty. Another harsh, remote habitat, the windswept grass steppes of Asia, is home to the small steppe wolf.

Arctic Legend

Native Americans named natural phenomena after the animals that lived around them. The Blackfoot people called the Milky Way the Wolf Trail. In Canada, the Cree believed the Northern Lights, shown below, shone when heavenly wolves visited the Earth. In fact these spectacular light shows in the Arctic are caused by particles from the Sun striking the Earth's atmosphere.

◀ POLAR GIANT
Arctic wolves are larger than most other wolves. They scrape under the snow to nibble plant buds and lichen if they are desperate for food.

Arctic wolf
(Canis lupus tundrarum)

Did you know? The largest Arctic wolf territories cover 13,000 sq km—an area about the same size as Northern Ireland.

▲ COSY HOOD
This Inuit girl is wearing a hood trimmed with wolf fur. The fur is warm and sheds the ice that forms on the hood's edge as the wearer breathes. The Inuit and other peoples of the far north traditionally dressed in the skins of Arctic animals. Animal skins make the warmest clothing and help to camouflage the wearer when hunting.

▲ NORTHERN HUNTER
A grey wolf feeds hungrily on a caribou carcass. In the icy north, wolves need very large territories to find enough prey. They will follow deer for hundreds of kilometres as the herds move south for the winter.

◄ ARCTIC HELPERS
One crack of a whip brings a team of huskies under control. Tough and hardy huskies, with their thick fur coats, are working dogs of the far north. They are used by the Inuit and other Arctic peoples to pull sleds and to help in hunting.

SNOWY BED ►
A grey wolf shelters in a snowy hollow to escape a howling blizzard. With its thick fur, it can sleep out in the open in temperatures as low as -46°C. Snow drifting over its body forms a protective blanket.

Monkey Magic

Primates are the most versatile movers of the animal world. Many can walk and run, climb and swim. Small monkeys and the larger lemurs can leap between branches. This method is risky for larger animals, in case a branch breaks beneath their weight. Heavier primates play safe by walking along branches on all fours and avoid jumping if possible.

When branches are bendy, climbers move with caution. They may use their weight to swing from one handhold to the next, but they do not let go of one handhold until the other is in place. Tree-climbing monkeys have long fingers to curl around branches and help them to grip.

Monkeys that live on the ground use their hands as well as their feet to propel themselves along.

Did you know? A spider monkey's tail is so strong it can support the monkey's entire weight.

spider monkey
(*Ateles geoffroyanus*)

◄ HANGING AROUND
New World monkeys rarely move at ground level. Most swing from tree to tree, stop and whip their tail around a branch, let go with both hands and grab something to eat. Old World monkeys do not have a prehensile (grasping) tail. Many have very short tails or no tail at all.

◄ PADDED MITTS
The palm of a sifaka lemur is one of the features that makes it a star jumper. The wrinkles and fleshy pads are like a baseball glove, giving extra holding power. Sifakas can push off with their long hind legs to leap up to 5m high. Their arms are short, making it impossible to walk on all fours. Instead, sifakas hop on both feet.

◄ **BABOONS ON THE MOVE**
A troop of baboons makes its way down a track in the African savanna. They are strong and tough because they have to walk long distances to find enough food to feed the troop. Baboons and other monkeys that walk on the ground, such as mandrills, geladas and macaques, put their weight on the fingertips and palms of their hands and feet. This is different from apes, such as gorillas and chimpanzees, who walk on their knuckles.

▲ **SLOW AND STEADY**
Lorises from Sri Lanka and southern India are known for their slow, deliberate movements. They have long, thin arms and legs with very flexible ankles and wrists. A loris can wriggle its way through, and get a grip on, dense twigs and small branches. Due to its strange appearance, some people describe the animal as a banana on stilts.

LIGHT AS AIR ►
A pygmy marmoset can perch on the flimsiest of twigs. It has to be small, light and quick to catch the insects that it eats. Marmosets scurry along branches rather like squirrels, and for this reason are the only primates to have claws instead of nails. They are also able to sit up on their hind legs to free their hands for collecting food as well as for feeding.

Hands and Feet

Can you imagine how difficult it would be to pick something up if your arms ended in paws, hooves or flippers? It would be impossible to grip any object and you could not turn it around, carry it, throw it, pull it apart or put it together. An ape's hands and feet are remarkable. They are very adaptable, and the opposable thumb or big toe enables them to grasp firmly or hold delicately. Ape hands and feet are strong and flexible, allowing apes to climb, swing and jump through the treetops. They also allow apes to reach food, investigate their surroundings, groom their family and friends and build nests. In most apes, the feet look very much like hands, but in humans, the feet look different. This is because human feet are adapted for walking rather than climbing.

▲ **SMILE PLEASE**
Grasping a delicate camera lens, a gorilla demonstrates how it can pick up fragile objects without breaking them. A gorilla has thicker, sturdier hands than a person, with fingers the size of bananas and a smaller thumb. Its hands have to be strong so that they can support the weight of the gorilla's body when it walks around on all fours.

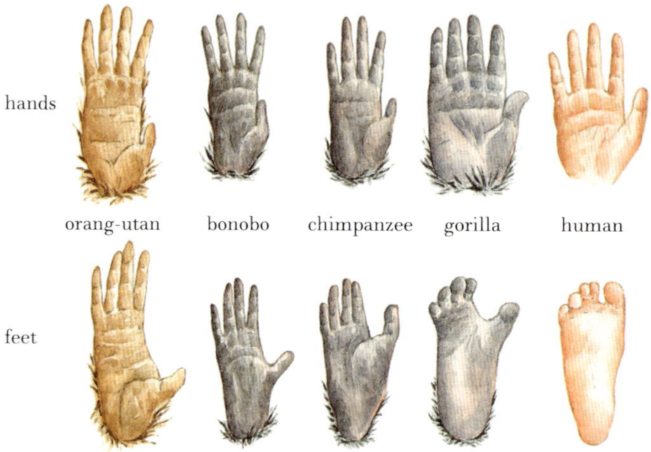

◄ **LOOK-ALIKE HANDS**
The hands of the great apes have several features in common, such as nails and long, sensitive fingers. The thumb on a great ape's hand goes off at an angle and can press against each finger. The big toe on an ape's foot can also do this, except in humans. Bonobos have a unique feature not shared by the other apes – webbing between the second and third toes.

▲ OPPOSABLE THUMB

Since a great ape's thumb can easily touch, or oppose, its fingers, it is called an opposable thumb. This special thumb gives an ape's hand a precise pincer grip, allowing it to pick up objects as small as berries.

Did you know? Humans have over 5 million hairs on their bodies.

orang-utan *(Pongo pygmaeus)*

▲ GRAPPLING IRONS

An orang-utan's arms and legs end in huge hands and feet that work like powerful clamps. Just one hand or foot can take the entire weight of the ape.

▲ HAND-FOOT

Unlike a human, a chimp can use its feet rather like hands, to hold and investigate things. The opposable big toe stretches out around one side of a branch while the other toes reach around the other side, giving a very strong grip.

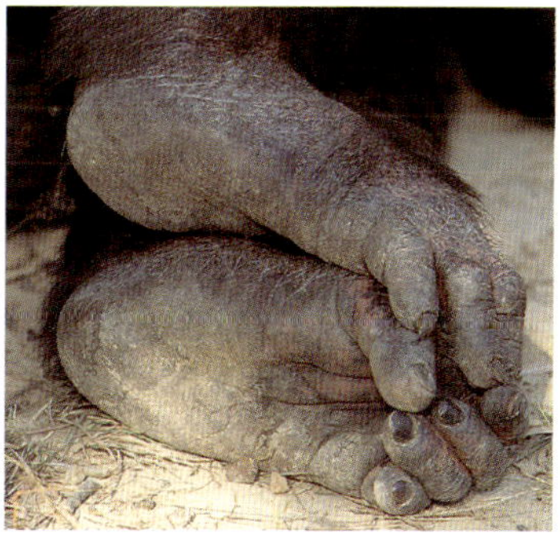

▲ FLAT FEET

Chimpanzees are flat-footed, with tough, hairless soles and long toes. When upright, their feet have to take all of the body weight.

Chimps

MAKING A TOOL
This chimpanzee is shaping a stick to help her dig for food. Chimpanzees have invented several clever ways to use sticks.

Humans were once thought to be the only animals clever enough to use tools. Now we know that a handful of other animals, such as Galapagos finches and sea otters, use them too. However, these animals are only beginners compared to chimpanzees. A chimp chooses its tools, changes them to make them better and uses them over and over again. Chimps plan ahead, collecting sticks or stones on their way to a source of food. Their nimble fingers and creative minds help them to invent and use tools. Adult chimps are good at concentrating, sometimes spending hours using their tools.

TASTY SNACKS
An intelligent chimp can shape and manipulate a grass stem to form a useful tool for fishing out termites from a mound. Scientists who have tried to copy the chimps have found that termite fishing is much, much harder than it looks.

FISHING FOR FOOD
This captive chimp is using a stick, in the same way as a chimp in the wild would use a grass stem, to fish in a termite mound. However, the termite mound in the zoo probably has yogurt or honey inside it, rather than termites.

That Use Tools

LEAF SPONGE

A wodge of leaves makes a useful sponge to soak up rainwater from tree holes. Chewing the leaf first breaks up its waterproof coating, so that it soaks up more water. Leaves may also be used as toilet paper, to wipe blood from wounds and to scrape up sticky food.

HANDY WEAPON

Wild chimps can only make tools from objects in their environment, which is why sticks are so important. Sticks make good weapons for attack and defence. They can also be used as levers, and thin sticks make a natural dental floss.

CRACKING PERFORMANCE

In West Africa, chimps use hammers and anvils to crack open the hard shells of nuts. Hammers are made from logs or stones, anvils from stones or tree roots. Hammer stones can weigh as much as 20kg. A skilled adult can crack a shell with just a few blows.

Underwater Voices

Sounds travel easily in water. Whales use sounds to communicate with one another and to find their food. The baleen (filter-feeding) whales use low-pitched sounds, which have been picked up by underwater microphones as moans, grunts and snores. Dolphins and most other toothed whales communicate and hunt using higher-pitched clicks. They send out beams of sounds, which are reflected by objects, such as fish. The dolphin picks up the reflected sound, or echo, and can work out where the object is. This is called echo-location.

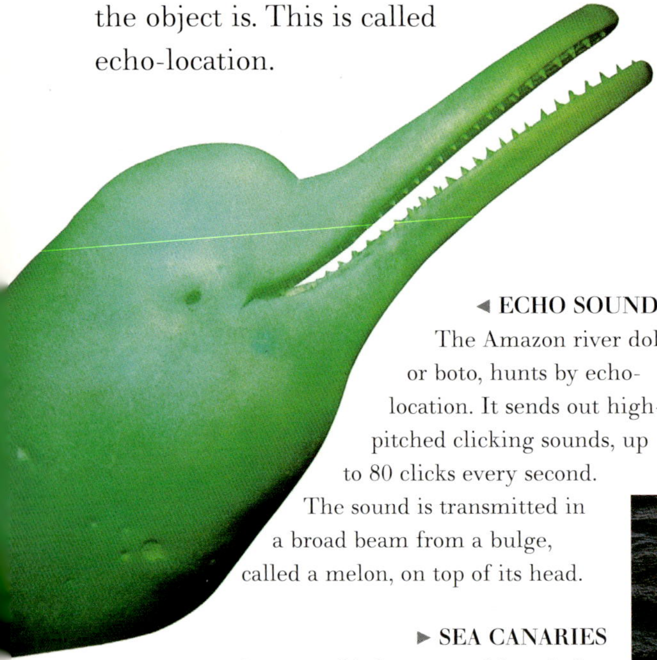

◄ **ECHO SOUNDINGS**
The Amazon river dolphin, or boto, hunts by echo-location. It sends out high-pitched clicking sounds, up to 80 clicks every second. The sound is transmitted in a broad beam from a bulge, called a melon, on top of its head.

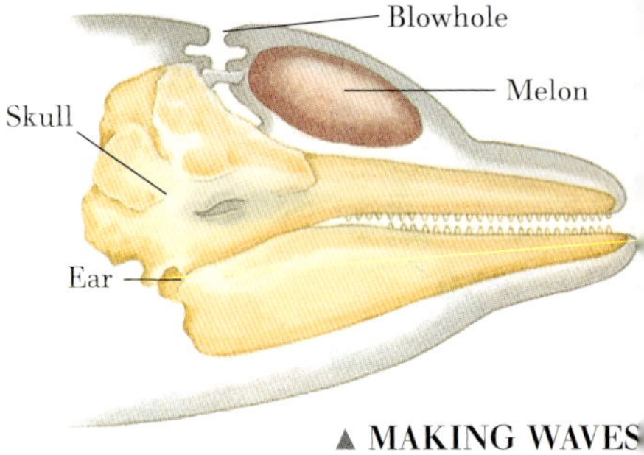

▲ **MAKING WAVES**
A dolphin makes high-pitched sound waves by vibrating the air in the passages in its nose. The waves are focused into a beam by the melon. The sound is transmitted into the water

► **SEA CANARIES**
A group of belugas, or white whales, swims in a bay in Canada. Belugas' voices can clearly be heard above the surface. This is why they are known as sea canaries. They also produce high-pitched sounds we cannot hear, which they use for echo-location.

◄ **SUPER SONGSTER**

This male humpback whale is heading for the breeding grounds where the females are gathering. The male starts singing long and complicated songs. This may be to attract a mate or to warn other males off its patch. The sound can carry for 30km or more.

▼ **WATER MUSIC**

This is a voice print of a humpback whale's song, picked up by an underwater microphone. It shows complex musical phrases and melodies. Humpback whales often continue singing for a day or more, repeating the same song.

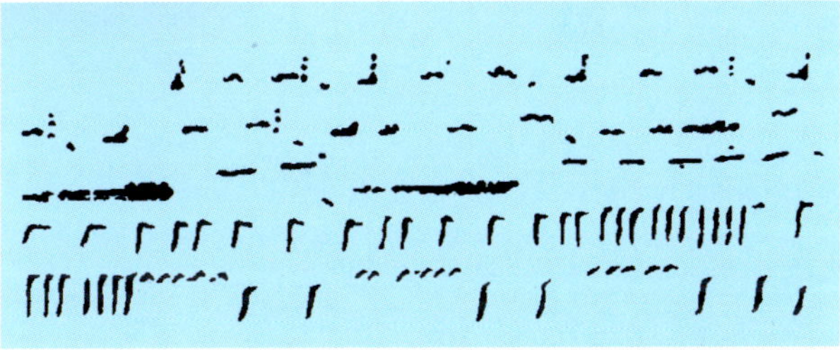

▼ **SOUND ECHOES**

A sperm whale can locate a giant squid more than a kilometre away by transmitting pulses of sound waves into the water and listening. The echo is picked up by the teeth in its lower jaw and the vibrations are sent along the jaw to the ear.

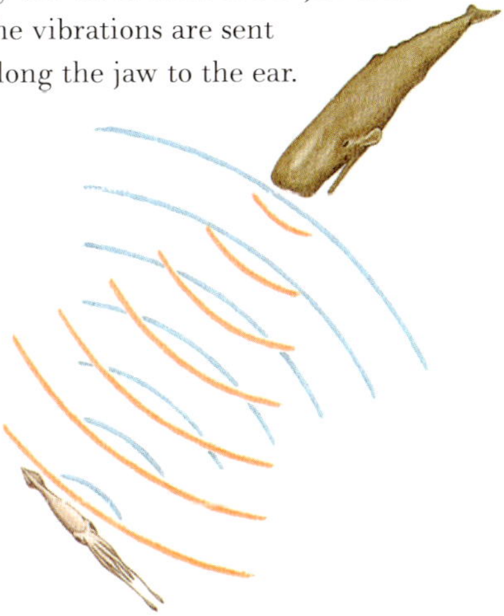

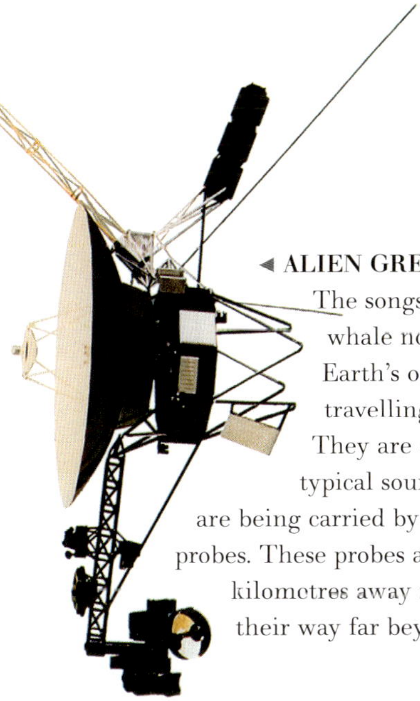

Did you know? A dolphin picks up sounds through its lower jaw.

◄ **ALIEN GREETINGS**

The songs of the humpback whale not only travel through Earth's oceans, but they are also travelling far out into Space. They are among the recorded typical sounds of our world that are being carried by the two Voyager space probes. These probes are now millions of kilometres away from Earth and are on their way far beyond our solar system.

Deep-sea Sharks

frilled shark
(Chlamydoselachus anguineus)

Many sharks are rarely seen because they live in the darkness of the deep. Catsharks and dogfish live in these gloomy waters, glowing in the dark with a luminous green-blue or white light. Some of these species travel and hunt in packs, following their prey to the surface at night and returning into the depths by day. Most of the world's smallest sharks live in the deep sea. Pygmy and dwarf sharks no bigger than a cigar travel for several kilometres through the ocean each day. On the deep-sea floor are enormous sharks such as the sixgill, sevengill and sleeper sharks. These eat the remains of dead animals that sink down from the sea's surface. Many deep-sea sharks look primitive, but strangest of all are the frilled and horned goblin sharks. These look like the fossilized sharks that swam the seas 150 million years ago.

▲ LIVING FOSSIL
The frilled shark is the only shark shaped like an eel. It has six feathery gill slits, 300 tiny, three-pointed teeth and a large pair of eyes. Like all sharks, it has a skeleton of flexible cartilage. These features show that the frilled shark resembles fossilized species that lived in the oceans millions of years ago.

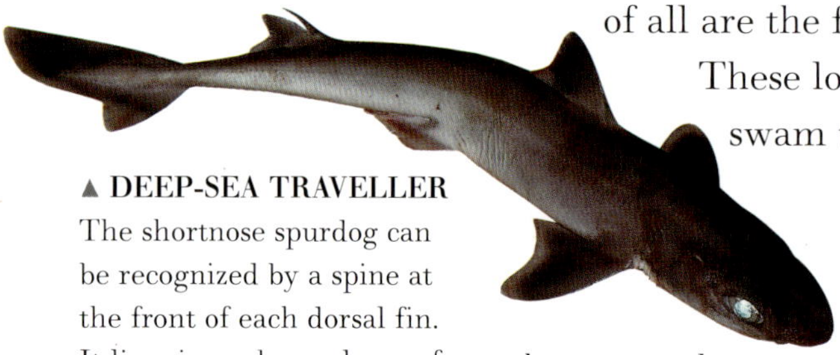

shortnose spurdog
(Squalus megalops)

▲ DEEP-SEA TRAVELLER
The shortnose spurdog can be recognized by a spine at the front of each dorsal fin. It lives in packs made up of thousands of sharks. It swims at depths of 800m in the northern waters of the Pacific and Atlantic oceans. At certain times of the year, the packs make a daily migration, from north to south and from coastal to deeper waters.

▼ DEEPEST OF THE DEEP
The Portuguese dogfish holds the shark record for living in the deepest waters. One was caught 2,718m below the sea's surface. At this depth, the water temperature is no higher than a chilly 5–6°C.

Portuguese dogfish
(Centroscymnus coelolepis)

◄ SIX GILL SLITS

Most modern sharks have five gill slits, but primitive sharks, such as this bluntnose sixgill shark, have more. These species are found at huge depths around the world. They have evolved (developed) slowly, and still have the features of sharks that lived millions of years ago.

▼ SEVEN GILL SLITS

Broadnose sevengill sharks have seven gill slits. They have primitive, sharp teeth that look like tiny combs. They use these to slice up ratfish, small sharks and mackerel. Because some of their prey live near the surface, sevengill sharks travel up to the sea's surface to hunt at night.

broadnose sevengill shark
(Notorynchus cepedianus)

Did you know? Many deep-sea sharks have light organs on their bodies.

velvet belly
(Etmopterus spinax)

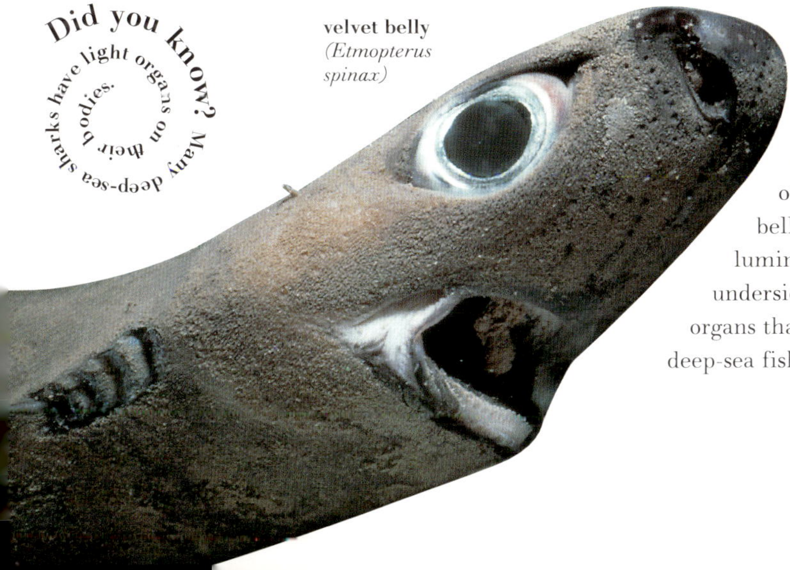

◄ SLIMY COAT

The velvet belly is 66cm long. It lives in the Atlantic and Mediterranean at depths of 70–2,000m. The velvet belly is covered with luminous slime, and the underside of its body has special organs that give out light. It eats deep-sea fish and shrimps.

Attack of

1 Huge groups of albatrosses nest on the ground close to the shore of Hawaiian islands, including the island of Laysan. The birds in each group breed, nest, and hatch their babies at the same time. When it is time, the young birds all take their first flight within days of each other.

Sharks can be found wherever there is food in or near the sea. Tiger sharks are rarely seen around some of the Hawaiian islands in the Pacific Ocean, but when the islands' young seabirds start to fly the sharks arrive suddenly. Any birds that fall into the sea are quickly eaten. The waters are too shallow for the tiger sharks to attack from behind and below as most sharks do. Instead, the sharks leap clear of the surface then drag the birds underwater to drown and eat them. Sharks arrive for their island feast at the same time each year. How they remember to do so is yet to be explained.

2 When ready to fly, a baby albatross practises by flapping its wings in the face of the islands' fierce winds. Eventually, the baby must make its first real flight over the ocean. When it does so, the tiger sharks are waiting in the water below.

3 Tiger sharks patrol the clear, shallow waters close to the albatross nests. Their dark shapes can be seen clearly against the sandy sea floor. Every now and again, a tiger shark's triangular dorsal fin and the tip of its tail can be seen breaking the water's surface.

the Tiger Sharks

4 Any baby bird that dips into the sea is prey for the waiting tiger shark. At first, the shark tries its usual attack, from below and behind. However, in the shallow waters the shark cannot make a full attack. Rather than hitting its prey at force, the shark just pushes the bird away on the wave made by its snout.

5 After failing to catch a meal, the shark soon realizes its mistake and tries another approach. Its next style of attack is to shoot across the surface of the water, slamming into its target with its mouth wide open. This technique seems to be more successful, and the shark usually catches the bird.

6 The shark then attempts to drag the bird below the surface, to drown it. If a bird is pushed ahead on the shark's bow wave, it will bravely peck at its attacker's broad snout and sometimes may even escape. Some birds also manage to wriggle free as the shark grapples with them underwater.

7 Many albatross babies do not manage to escape a shark attack. They are grabbed by the sharks and drowned. Inside the tiger shark's jaws are rows of sharp teeth that can slice into a bird's body like a saw. Sometimes the tiger shark tears off the bird's wings and leaves them aside to eat the body whole.

Animal Survival

Animals living in the wild are faced with many challenges and they must be constantly aware of their surroundings if they are to survive. The key thing about animals (unlike plants) is that they are able to change their behaviour immediately in response to changes in their environment. In this section we see how they do it … and survive.

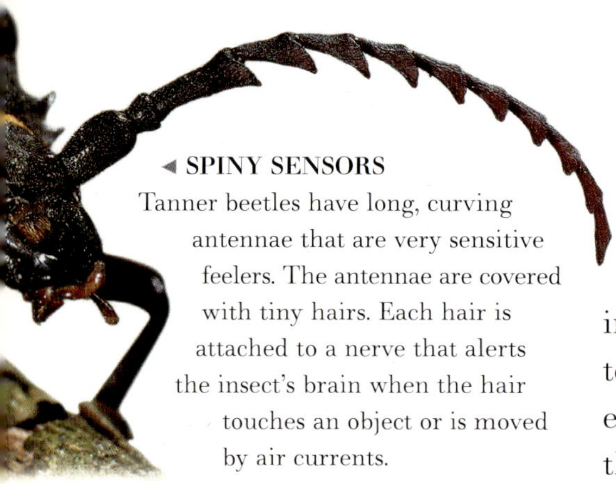

◄ **SPINY SENSORS**
Tanner beetles have long, curving antennae that are very sensitive feelers. The antennae are covered with tiny hairs. Each hair is attached to a nerve that alerts the insect's brain when the hair touches an object or is moved by air currents.

Insect Senses

Most insects have keen senses, but they do not sense the world in the same way that humans do. The main sense organs are on the head, but many types of insects use other parts of their body to tell them about their surroundings. For example, many crickets have ears on their forelegs, while flies taste their food with their hairy feet.

Insect eyes are very different from our own. Most insects have compound eyes, which are made up of many tiny lenses. These are particularly good at sensing movement, but cannot make sharp images. Several insects, such as fleas and some beetles and bugs, have very simple eyes that only detect light or dark.

An insect's antennae are its main sense tools. Most are used for smelling and feeling, and in some species for hearing and tasting, too. Sensitive hairs all over the insects' bodies pick up tiny currents in the air, which may alert them to nearby enemies.

▲ **BRANCHING ANTENNAE**
This unusual beetle from Central America has branched antennae that look like the antlers of a stag. The branches are usually held closed, but the insect can fan them out to detect chemicals carried on the wind, such as the scent of a faraway mate. Smells such as these would be far too faint for humans to detect.

SMELL AND TOUCH ►
Longhorn beetles are named for their long antennae. Some kinds have antennae that are twice as long as their bodies. An insect's antennae are sometimes called its 'feelers'. The term is rather misleading – the antennae are used for feeling, but their main function is to pick up scents.

◄ ELBOW-SHAPED
The weevil's antennae are attached to its long snout. Many weevils have jointed antennae, which bend in the middle like a human arm at the elbow. Some have special organs at the base of their antennae, which vibrate to sound and act as ears. This brush-snouted weevil has a bushy 'beard' of long, sensitive hairs on its snout.

COMPOUND EYES ►
The huge eyes of the harlequin beetle cover the front of its head. Only the area from which its antennae sprout remains uncovered. Each compound eye is made up of hundreds of tiny lenses, each one of which works in the same way as a human eye. Scientists believe that the signals from each lens build up to create one large picture.

◄ TINY LENSES
A close-up of a beetle's compound eye shows that it is made up of many tiny facets, each of which points in a slightly different direction. Each is made up of a lens at the surface and a second lens inside. The lenses focus light down a central structure inside the eye, called the rhabdome, on to a bundle of nerve fibres, which are behind the eye. The nerve fibres then send messages to the brain. The hundreds of tiny lenses probably do not create the detailed, focused image produced by the human eye. However, they can pick up colours and shapes and are very good at detecting tiny movements.

Focus on

SUN LOVERS
Butterflies and moths can only fly if their body temperature reaches at least 25–30°C. If they are too cold, the muscles powering the wings do not work. To warm up, butterflies bask in the sun, so that the wing scales soak up sunlight like solar panels. Night-flying moths shiver their wings to warm them instead.

Most adult insects have one or two pairs of wings. They fly by simply beating their wings very rapidly to move through the air. This sort of flight takes a lot of energy and can only be used for short journeys. Butterflies and moths, however, fly in a different way that is closer to birds' flight than that of other insects. They save energy by rippling their wings slowly up and down. Some, such as the white admiral, can even glide on currents of air with just an occasional flap to keep them aloft. This enables them to fly amazing distances. Smaller moths and butterflies beat their wings faster than larger species (kinds). Skipper butterflies have the fastest wingbeats of all. Hawk moths are the fastest-flying insects. Their narrow wings beat rapidly to keep them aloft. Birdwing butterflies have the largest wings, which can be 30cm across.

TWISTERS
To the human eye, the wings of butterflies and moths appear simply to flap. However, freeze-frame photography reveals that the bases of the wings twist as they move up and down, so that the wing tips move in a figure of eight.

DODGING DANGER
Butterflies look like clumsy fliers, but their acrobatic twists and turns enable them to escape sparrows and other predatory birds. Some moths can fly at up to 48km/h when frightened.

Flight

WING FLEXIBILITY

The base and front edge of each wing is stiff, but the rest of the wing is flexible. The stiff front edge of the wing produces a lifting force, like the wings of an aircraft, as it flies through the air. The bending of the rest of the wing pushes air backwards and drives the butterfly forwards.

FANCY FLIERS

Butterflies such as this painted lady are very efficient fliers. They tend to flap their wings only occasionally when in flight. They prefer to glide gracefully from flower to flower, with just the odd beat of their wings.

Spider Senses

Most spiders have poor eyesight and rely mainly on scents and vibrations to give them information about their surroundings. Even spiders with good eyesight, such as the jumping spiders, can see only up to 30cm away. Most spiders have eight eyes arranged in two or three rows. The eyes are pearly or dark and are usually protected by several bristles. Spider eyes are called ocelli and are of two types. Main eyes produce a focused image and help in judging distances. Secondary eyes are smaller and have light-sensitive cells to pick up motion.

▲ **NO EYES**
This cave spider has no need for eyes, because there is no light in the cave for the spider to see. Like many animals that live in the dark it relies on other senses. It especially uses many sensitive hairs to find its way around, taste its prey and sense the movements of its enemies.

◂ **BIG EYES**
A spider's main eyes are always the middle pair of eyes in the front row. In most spiders even the main eyes are small, but this jumping spider has very well developed main eyes, as this enlarged picture shows. They work rather like a telephoto lens on a camera. Inside, the large lens focuses light on to four layers of sensitive cells. The main eyes see clearly over a small area a few centimetres away and let the spider stalk and pounce when it gets close to its prey.

Did you know? A jumping spider's two big eyes together are bigger than its brain.

▲ SHORT SIGHT

Spiders that spend much of their time under stones or in burrows usually have small eyes. This trapdoor spider has eight tiny eyes in a close group. Spiders that catch their prey in webs also have very poor eyesight. These spiders rely much more on their sense of touch than their eyesight. They use their legs to taste objects around them.

▲ HUNTSMAN SPIDER

The giant huntsman is an agile, night-time hunter. Most hunting spiders have fairly large front eyes to help them find and pounce on prey in the dark. Secondary eyes help the hunters see in three dimensions over a wider area. They detect changes in light and dark.

▲ EYES FOR HUNTING

The spiders with the best eyesight are active daylight hunters such as this jumping spider. A jumping spider's eight eyes are arranged in three rows with four in the front, two in the middle and two at the back of the head. Lynx spiders and wolf spiders also have good eyesight.

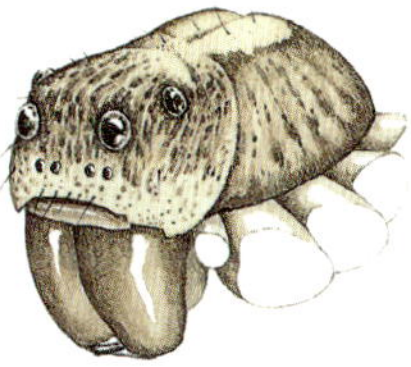

A large-eyed wolf spider

The small eyes of an orb-weaver

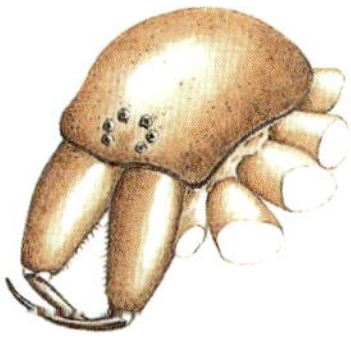

A six-eyed woodlouse spider

A jumping spider

▲ ALL KINDS OF EYES

The position and arrangement of a spider's eyes can help us to determine what type of spider it is and how it catches food. A small number of spiders only have six eyes or fewer. Many male money spiders have eyes on top of little lobes or turrets sticking up from the head.

Crawling Creatures

Have you ever seen a spider scuttle swiftly away? Spiders sometimes move quickly, but cannot keep going for long. Their breathing system is not very efficient, so they soon run out of puff.

Spiders can walk, run, jump, climb and hang upside down. Each spider's leg has seven sections. The legs are moved by sets of muscles and by pumping blood into them. At the end of each leg are two or three sharp claws for gripping surfaces. Spiders that spin webs cling to strands of silk with their claws. Hunting spiders have dense tufts of hair between the claws for gripping smooth surfaces and for holding prey.

▲ **AERONAUT**
Many young or small spiders drift through the air on strands of silk. Spiders carried away on warm air currents use this method to find new places to live.

▲ **WATER WALKER**
The fishing spider is also called the raft or swamp spider. It stands on the surface skin of water. Its long legs spread its weight over the surface so it does not fall through. Little dips form in the stretchy skin of the water around each leg tip.

▲ **SAFETY LINE**
This garden spider is climbing up a silk dragline. Spiders drop down these lines if they are disturbed. They pay out the line as they go, moving very quickly. As they fall, spiders pull in their legs, making them harder to see.

▲ **SPIDER LEGS**

Muscles in the legs of this trapdoor spider bend the joints rather like we bend our knees. To stretch out the legs, however, the spider has to pump blood into them. If a spider is hurt and blood leaks out, it cannot escape from enemies.

▲ **CHAMPION JUMPERS**

Jumping spiders are champions of the long jump. They secure themselves with a safety line before they leap. Some species can leap more than 40 times the length of their own bodies.

▼ **CLAWED FEET**

Two toothed claws on the ends of a spider's feet enable it to grip surfaces as it walks. Web-building spiders have a third, middle claw that hooks over the silk lines of the web and holds the silk against barbed hairs. This allows the spider to grip the smooth, dry silk of its web without falling or slipping.

▲ **HAIRY FEET**

Many hunting spiders have dense tufts of short hairs called scopulae between the claws. The end of each hair is split into many tiny hairs a bit like a brush. These hairs pull up some of the moisture coating most surfaces, gluing the spider's leg down. Spiders with these feet can climb up smooth surfaces such as glass.

▲ **EYESIGHT**
Snakes have no eyelids to cover their eyes. The snakes with the best eyesight are tree snakes, such as this green mamba.

Snake Senses

To find prey and avoid enemies, snakes rely more on their senses of smell, taste and touch than on sight and hearing. Snakes have no eardrums, so cannot hear sounds in the normal way. But their jawbones pick up sound vibrations travelling through the ground and pass them to a bone connected to the inner ear. As well as ordinary senses, snakes also have some special ones. They are among the few animals that smell with their tongues.

▲ **NIGHT HUNTER**
The horned viper's eyes open wide at night (*above*). During the day, its pupils close to narrow slits (*below*).

Heat pits

▲ **SENSING HEAT**
The green tree python has heat-sensitive pits on its face that pick up the warmth of its prey.

◄ **THE FORKED TONGUE**
This black-tailed rattlesnake is flicking its tongue to taste the air. The forked tongue picks up tiny chemical particles of scent.

▲ **HEARING**
As it has no ears, the cobra cannot hear the music played by the snake charmer. It follows the movements of the pipe, which resembles a snake, and rises up as it prepares to defend itself.

► **JACOBSON'S ORGAN**
As a snake draws its tongue back into its mouth, it presses the forked tip into the two openings of the Jacobson's organ. This organ is in the roof of the mouth and it identifies scents picked up by the tongue.

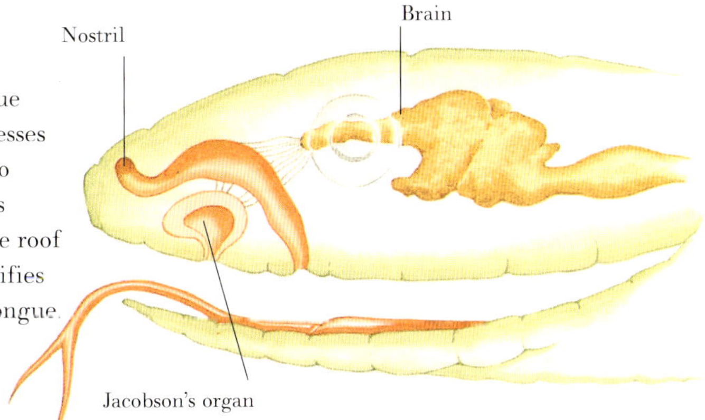

Slither and Slide

For animals without legs, snakes move around very well. They can glide over or under the ground, climb trees and swim through water. A few snakes can even parachute through the air. Snakes are not speedy – most move at about 3km/h. With their bendy backbones, snakes wriggle their bodies in the shape of a wave. They push themselves along using muscles joined to their ribs. The scales on their skin also grip the ground to help with movement.

Did you know? A person can walk faster than most snakes can move.

Corn snake
(Elaphe guttata)

► S-SHAPED MOVER
Most snakes move in an S-shaped path, pushing the side curves of their bodies backwards against the surface they are travelling on or through. The muscular waves of the snake's body push against surrounding objects and the body is pushed forward.

▲ SWIMMING SNAKE
The banded sea snake's stripes stand out as it glides through the water. Snakes swim using S-shaped movements. A sea snake's tail is flattened from side to side to give it extra power, like the oar of a rowing boat.

▼ SKINNY SNAKE
The green whip snake lives in the flimsy branches of forest trees. It curves its thin body into wide loops that spread the snake's weight over several branches.

▶ **SIDEWINDING**

The way snakes that live on loose sand move along is called sidewinding. The snake anchors its head and tail in the sand and throws the middle part of its body sideways.

Did you know? The fastest land snake is the black mamba, moving at up to 11 km/h.

▼ **HOW SNAKES MOVE**

Most land snakes move in four different ways, depending on the type of ground they are crossing and the type of snake.

1 S-shaped movement: the snake wriggles from side to side.

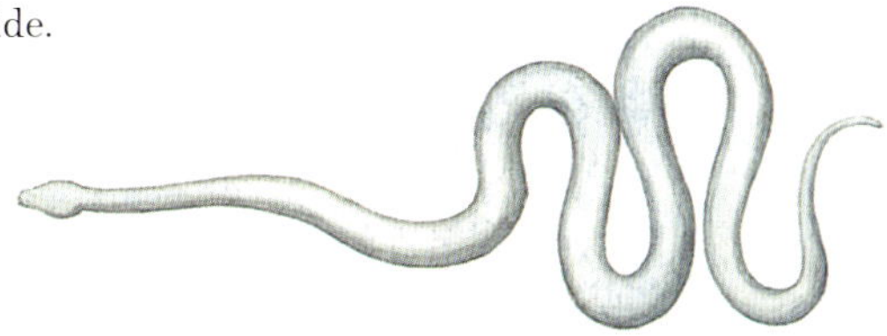

2 Concertina movement: the snake pulls one half of its body along first, then the other half.

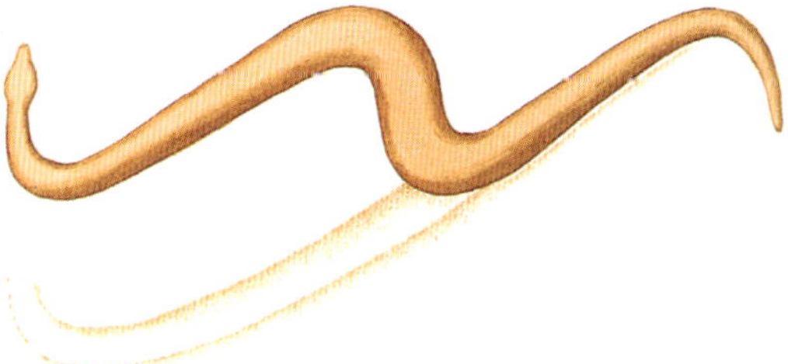

3 Sidewinding movement: the snake throws the middle part of its body sideways, keeping the head and tail on the ground.

4 Caterpillar movement: the snake uses its belly scales to pull itself along in a straight line.

Crocodilian Senses

The senses of sight, hearing, smell, taste and touch are much more powerful in a crocodilian than in other living reptiles. They have good eyesight and can see in colour. Their eyes are also adapted to seeing well in the dark, which is useful because they hunt mainly at night. Crocodilians also have sharp hearing. They sense the sounds of danger or prey moving nearby and listen for the barks, coughs and roars of their own species at mating time. Crocodilians also have sensitive scales along the sides of their jaws, which help to feel and capture prey underwater.

▲ **NOISY GATORS**
An American alligator bellows loudly to attract mates. Noises such as hissing or snarling are made at enemies. Young alligators call for help from adults. Small ear slits behind the eyes are kept open when the animal is out of the water. Flaps close to protect the ears when the animal submerges.

▲ **SMELL DETECTORS**
A Nile crocodile picks up chemical signals through the nostrils at the tip of its snout. These smelly messages help it to detect prey and others of its kind. Crocodiles can smell food over long distances. They are known to have come from as far away as 3km to feed together on the carcass of a large animal.

Did you know? Crocodiles shake their ear flaps up and down when they are angry.

Crocodile Tears
According to legend, crocodiles cry to make people feel so sorry for them that they come near enough for the crocodiles to catch them. Crocodiles are also supposed to shed tears of remorse before finishing their meal. It is said that people cry crocodile tears when they seem to be sorry for something, but really are not. Real-life crocodiles cannot cry but sometimes look as if they are.

▸ TASTY TONGUE

Inside the gaping mouth of this American crocodile is a wide, fleshy tongue. It is joined to the bottom of the mouth and does not move, so it plays no part in catching prey. We know that crocodilians have taste buds lining their mouths because some prefer one type of food to another. They can tell the difference between sweet and sour tastes. They also have salt glands on their tongues that get rid of excess salt. Salt builds up in the body over time if the animal lives in the sea or a very dry environment.

◂ GLOW-IN-THE-DARK EYES

A torch shone into a crocodile farm at night makes the dark glow eerily with a thousand living lights. The scientific explanation is that a special layer at the back of the eye reflects light back into the front of the eye. This makes sure that the eye catches as much light as possible. Above water, crocodilians see well and are able to spot prey up to 90m away. Underwater, an inner, transparent lid covers the eye. This makes their eyesight foggy, rather like looking through thick goggles.

▸ A PREDATOR'S EYE

The eye of a spectacled caiman, like all crocodilians, has both upper and lower lids. A third eyelid at the side, called a nictitating (blinking) membrane, moves across to clean the eye's surface. The dark, vertical pupil narrows to a slit to stop bright light damaging the inside. At night, the pupil opens wide to let any available light into the eye. A round pupil, such as a human's, cannot open as wide.

Land and Water

Have you ever seen a film of an alligator gliding through the water with slow, S-shaped sweeps of its powerful tail? Crocodilians move gracefully and easily in the water. They use very little energy to do this and keep most of their body hidden under the surface. Their legs lie close alongside their body to make them streamlined and to cut down drag from the water. Legs may also be used as rudders to change course. With their short legs, crocodilians appear to lumber along clumsily on land, dragging their tail behind them. However, they can move fast if they need to. Some can gallop at 17km/h when running over short distances of up to 100m. Crocodilians also sometimes drag themselves along in what is called a belly slide. With side-to-side twists of the body, the animal uses its legs to push along on its belly. This tobogganing movement is used to slip quietly into the water.

▲ **BEST FOOT FORWARD**
The tracks of a saltwater crocodile in the mud show how its legs move in sequence. The right front leg goes forward first, then the back left leg. The front left leg goes forward next, and finally the right back leg moves. The tail snakes along the ground between the footprints.

▼ **THE HIGH WALK**
To move on land, crocodilians hold their legs underneath their body, lifting most of the tail off the ground. This is called the high walk. It is very different from the walk of a lizard, which keeps its legs sprawled out at the sides of its body. The tail is dragged behind the body in the high walk, but if the animal starts to run, the tail swings from side to side. A special ankle joint lets crocodilians twist and turn their legs in the high walk.

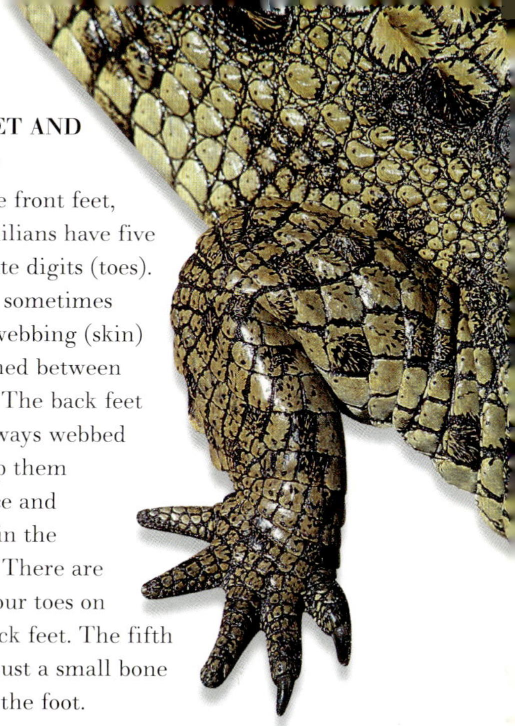

▸ **FEET AND TOES**

On the front feet, crocodilians have five separate digits (toes). These sometimes have webbing (skin) stretched between them. The back feet are always webbed to help them balance and move in the water. There are only four toes on the back feet. The fifth toe is just a small bone inside the foot.

▴ **FLOATING AROUND**

This Nile crocodile is floating near the surface of Lake Tanganyika, Tanzania, Africa. It is holding its feet out to the sides for balance. The toes and the webbing between them are spread out for extra stability. When the crocodile floats, its tail hangs down, but when it swims its body becomes horizontal.

▸ **TAIL WALKING**

Some crocodilians can leap straight up out of the water. They seem to be walking on their tails in the same way that a dolphin can travel backwards on its strong tail. This movement is, however, unusual. Large crocodiles will also spring upwards, propelled by their back legs, to grab prey unawares.

▴ **THE GALLOP**

The fastest way for a crocodilian to move on land is to gallop. Only a few crocodilians, such as the Johnston's crocodile shown above, make a habit of moving like this. In a gallop, the back legs push the crocodilian forward in a leap, and the front legs stretch out to catch the body as it lands at the end of the leap. Then the back legs swing forward to push the animal forward again.

Eagle Eyes and Ears

Common buzzard (*Buteo buteo*)

Humans rely on five senses to find out about the world. They are sight, hearing, smell, taste and touch. However, most birds use just the two senses of sight and hearing. In birds of prey, sight is by far the most important sense for finding and hunting the prey they need to survive. Their eyes are exceptionally large in relation to the size of their head, and they are set in the skull so that they look forwards. This binocular (two-eyed) forward vision enables them to judge distances accurately when hunting. Owls have particularly large eyes that are well adapted for seeing in dim light. These birds are equally dependent on hearing to find prey in the dark. Some harriers and hawks use their keen sense of hearing to hunt, too. Birds' ear openings are quite small. They are set back from the eyes and cannot be seen because they are covered in feathers.

▲ OPEN WIDE
A common buzzard opens its beak wide to make its distinctive mewing call. This bird has extremely large eyes in relation to its body, so it has excellent eyesight. The forward-facing eyes give it good stereoscopic (3D) vision and the ability to pinpoint the exact position of a mouse in the grass 100m away.

◄ NOT TO BE SNIFFED AT
The turkey vulture of North and South America, like all New World vultures, has nostrils that you can see right through. Its nose is very sensitive. This enables the turkey vulture to sniff out dead animals on the ground while it is flying high above the forest.

Turkey vulture (*Cathartes aura*)

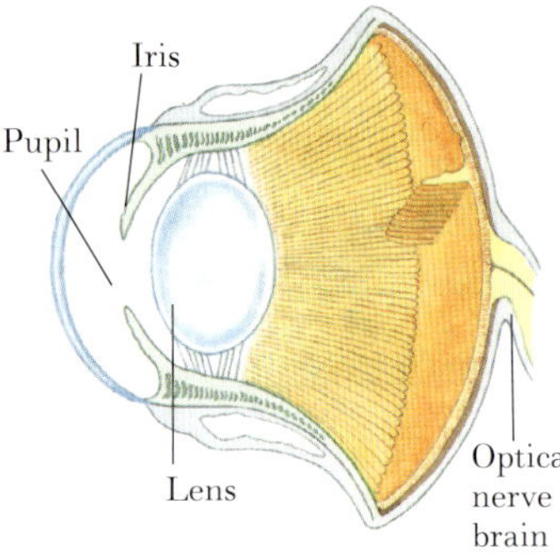

▲ OWL EYE
The owl has exceptional eyesight. Its unusual eye-shape, with a large lens, enables it to form a clear image even on a dark night.

Spotted eagle owl (*Bubo africanus*)

◄ **FORWARD FACE**

The African spotted eagle owl has big eyes. The pupil (centre) and lens are especially large to allow more light to enter and provide the owl with good night vision. The eyes are set in a flat facial disc. The earlike projections on top of the owl's head are actually ornamental tufts of feathers used for display. The true ears are hidden under stiff feathers at either side of the facial disc. The disc collects sounds like a satellite dish, directing them to the sensitive ears.

► **ON THE LOOKOUT**

This large falcon, called a lanner, is soaring high in the sky on outstretched wings, looking down with its sharp eyes on the scene below. If the lanner sees a flying bird, it will fold back its wings and dive on the unsuspecting bird. The lanner will hit the bird at high speed and usually break the bird's neck. Then it will either snatch the bird in mid-air or pick it up off the ground.

Montagu's harrier (*Circus pygargus*)

◄ **MONTAGU'S EYEBROW**

The Montagu's harrier is a slender, long-legged hawk with an owl-like facial ruff. The eyes are surrounded by a small bony ridge covered in feathers, called a supraorbital ridge. It probably helps protect the harrier's eyes from attack when the bird goes hunting, and may also act as a shield against the sun's rays when it is flying.

On the Wing

▲ **WING FINGERS**
An African fish eagle takes to the air. Like other eagles, it has broad wings and fingered wing tips, seen plainly here. The 'fingers' reduce air turbulence around the wings, giving better lift.

The wings of all birds work in the same way. Strong pectoral (chest) muscles make the wings flap and drive the bird through the air. As they move through the air, the wings produce a lift force, which supports the bird's weight. All birds have differently shaped wings that are adapted to their way of life. Large birds of prey (raptors), such as vultures, spend much of their time soaring high in the sky. These birds have long, broad wings that enable them to glide on air currents. The smaller hawks, such as the sparrowhawk, have short, rounded wings and a long tail for rapid, darting flight through woodland. A bird's tail is also important for flying. It acts much like a ship's rudder, steadying the bird's body and guiding it through the air. It can be fanned out to give extra lift and also helps the bird to slow down.

Mauritius kestrel
(*Falco punctatus*)

◄ **AGILE BIRD**
The Mauritius kestrel has a broad tail and, for a raptor, fairly short wings. These two features help it to manoeuvre well in the woodland habitat in which it lives. It lives on the island of Mauritius, in the Indian Ocean.

▲ **DROPPING IN**
A sparrowhawk's large tail enables it to twist and turn effortlessly in and out of cover as it hunts for prey. This sparrowhawk's wings beat rapidly and provide enough speed for it to surprise its unsuspecting prey.

Eagle of the Gods

In Greek mythology, the eagle was the favoured bird of the mighty Zeus. Zeus was god of the sky, lord of the winds and rains, and king among the gods. He is often depicted holding a thunderbolt in his right hand, with an eagle standing at his feet. Here we see him riding in a chariot, drawn by a pair of his sacred birds.

▼ LIKE AN ARROW

Lanner falcon
(Falco biarmicus)

The sharply pointed wings tell us that this bird is a falcon. In fact, it is a lanner falcon. A bird can fly extremely fast with pointed wings because the wings cut through the air and offer little wind resistance. Lanner falcons hunt over open ground and use pure speed to catch slower-flying birds.

▲ BUILT TO SOAR

A white-backed vulture soars high in the sky with its broad wings fully outstretched, on the lookout for carcasses on the ground. Using air currents, a vulture can remain in the air for a long time, because its wings provide plenty of lift.

► READY, STEADY, GO

A young male kestrel takes off in a multiple-exposure photograph. First the bird thrusts its body forwards and raises its wings. Its wings extend and beat downwards, pushing slightly backwards. As the air is forced back, the bird is driven forwards. At the same time, air moving over the wings gives the bird the lift it needs to keep itself airborne.

Sensing the World

Horses have relatively large brains that interpret information from their well-developed senses. As a result, horses and their relatives have excellent memories, a brilliant sense of direction and an extraordinary ability to sense danger. The senses work together in other ways, too. Eyes are set well back on each side of the skull, giving almost all-round vision. But there is a blind spot directly behind the head. To cover this, the horse swivels its ears right around and uses its sense of hearing to check behind itself. When both the horse's eyes look straight ahead they operate together to produce clear three-dimensional images. This enables horses to judge distances well, which is important when they are jumping obstacles.

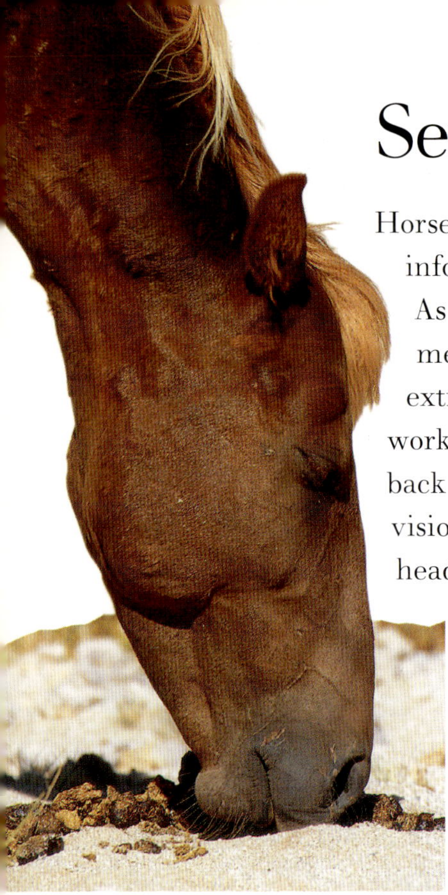

▲ CHECK IT OUT
A stallion (male horse) uses its good sense of smell to investigate piles of dung and urine from another herd. He will find out how recently the other herd passed by, if it contains a mare (female) ready to mate and if the herd is led by another stallion.

GATHERING SMELLS ▶
Curling back its lips in this way is a horse's reaction to unfamiliar smells. It is known as the flehmen reaction and is also used to find mares that are ready to breed. With its acute sense of smell, a horse can be alerted to predators and sniff out fresh grass and water.

▲ THE TASTE TEST
Little is known about a horse's sense of taste, although it is likely to be fairly sensitive. This can be seen from the way it grazes, pushing aside some plants to reach others. Taste may also be involved when horses groom each other.

▲ CLEVER HORSE
Memory is important for survival. Remembering where water or food can be found and which plants are good to eat may be a matter of life or death for a wild horse. Horses do well in intelligence and memory tests. In one test, horses were taught to recognize patterns. When they were tested a year later they could remember almost all of them, scoring better than most humans would.

▼ SHARP EYES
A horse can see objects clearly at short and long distances at the same time because images form on different areas of the eye. This is useful for keeping watch for predators while grazing. (Human eyes have variable focus that automatically adjusts to distances.) A horse can see better than a cat or a dog during daylight, and its night-time vision is also very good.

◄ ALERT EARS
All horses have ears that behave rather like radar dishes. They can turn in the direction of a sound quite independently of each other, while the rest of the body remains still. The rotating action is operated by no fewer than 16 muscles. This, together with the large size of the outer ear, means that a horse's sense of hearing is far more acute than a human's.

Running Like the Wind

▲ **THE TROT**
Once a horse reaches a certain walking speed, it becomes more energy-efficient to trot. In order to go faster, the feet leave the ground to incorporate little springs forward into the movement. Top trotting speed is about 14km/h for the average horse.

The way in which a horse moves makes the most of its energy reserves. The main thrust comes from the hind legs. The forelegs cushion jolts during running and jumping. Horses, zebras and donkeys (equids) have four ways of moving – walking, trotting, cantering and galloping. Each is designed to conserve energy at different speeds.

The hooves of wild and domestic horses are broad. This spreads weight over a wide area so that the hoof does not dig into the ground. Equids that live in rocky or mountainous areas, such as the Asiatic wild horse and the mountain zebra, have narrower hooves that are better for crossing rough ground.

▲ **THE CANTER**
A cantering horse has a rocking action and moves at 15–20km/h. The legs move one after the other, making a smoother action than the trot. Horses canter to cover distances quickly, perhaps when moving to a waterhole.

▲ **THE GALLOP**
The gallop is a horse's fastest way of moving, used when escaping predators. Horses and asses can gallop up to speeds of 50km/h. The gallop is designed for stability and best use of energy. The animal stretches its limbs to their limits, making a smooth action that reduces the shock of hitting the ground at speed.

▶ **SWIMMING**
A herd of semi-wild horses in Portugal wades and swims across a wide river. All equids can swim. Even foals can swim from very early days, though they keep close to protective mares.

◀ **NURSERY NAP**
A foal rests on its side with its limbs extended. Foals lie down more frequently than adults. Horses usually rest standing up as their heart and lungs have to work harder when they are lying down.

▼ **BEDTIME**
This herd of Przewalski's horses is fast asleep. In any 24-hour period, a horse is alert for about 19 hours, drowsy for two and asleep for three. Sleep is taken in short bursts. Horses do not sleep for long periods as they need to be alert to predators.

Rakahsh

The legendary Persian hero Rustam had a horse called Rakahsh, who was renowned for his speed and strength. Their adventures are told in the Book of Kings, *an 11th-century epic poem. Among many stories of the horse's bravery is the tale of a lion attacking the Persian camp. Rakahsh killed the lion and saved the day.*

Elephant Senses

Elephants use the five senses to learn about their surroundings – hearing, sight, smell, touch and taste. The most important sense is smell, which they rely on more than any other. Elephants smell through the trunk, using it as a directional nose. The trunk is also particularly sensitive to touch and has short hairs that help the elephant feel things. The tip of the trunk is used to investigate food, water and other objects. It can tell whether something is hot, cold, sharp or smooth. Elephants communicate with each other largely by sound. They make rumbling sounds, most of which are too low for humans to hear. Touch is also crucial for communication. When two elephants meet, each places the tip of its trunk in the other's mouth as a greeting.

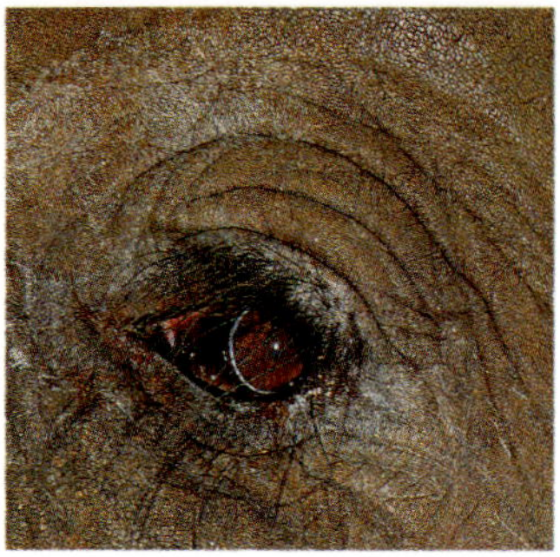

▲ **ELEPHANT EYES**
All elephants' eyes are brown with long lashes. They are small in relation to the huge head. Elephants are colour blind and do not see well in direct, strong sunlight. Their eyesight is better in darker, forest conditions.

Did you know? An African elephant's ear is as big as a single bed sheet and can weigh as much as a person.

◀ **SMELL**
An elephant raises its trunk like a periscope at the slightest scent of danger. It can tell who or what is coming towards it just from the smells picked up by the sensitive trunk. The sense of smell is so powerful that an elephant can pick up the scent of a human being from more than 1.5km away.

◀ **USING EARS**
An elephant strains to hear a distant noise by putting its ears forward to catch the sound. It also does this when it is curious about a certain noise. Elephants have a well-developed sense of hearing. Their enormous ears can pick up the rumble of other elephants up to about 8km away. Male elephants also flap their ears to spread a special scent that lets other elephants know they are there.

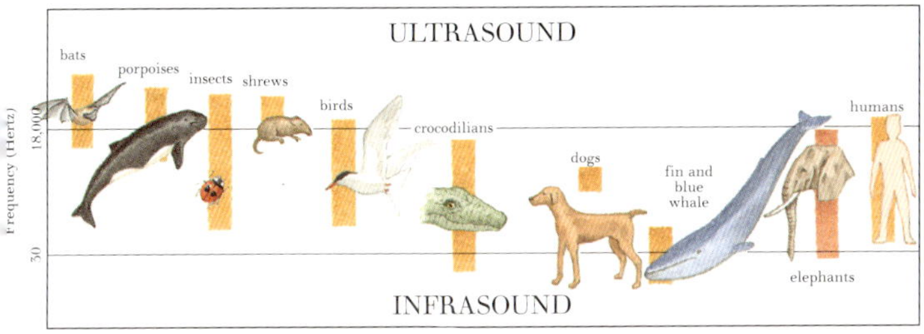

◀ **HEARING RANGE**
Elephants can hear low sounds called infrasound. Human beings cannot hear infrasound although we can sometimes feel it. Some animals, such as bats and mice, can hear very high sounds called ultrasound.

▲ **SENSE OF TOUCH**
A young elephant is touched by its mother or another close relative every few seconds. This constant reassurance keeps it from being frightened. Elephants also touch each other when they meet. They often stand resting with their bodies touching.

▲ **QUICK LEARNERS**
Some young working elephants learn to stop their bells ringing by pushing mud inside them. This allows the clever animals to steal food from farmers' fields without being heard.

On the Move

An elephant looks like a noisy, clumsy animal. In fact, it moves about quietly and is surprisingly agile. Forest elephants can quickly disappear into the trees like silent, grey ghosts. The secret of the elephant's silent movement is the way its foot is made. A fatty pad inside the foot cushions the impact of the foot on the ground. The sole then spreads out to take the weight of each step. Elephants usually walk slowly, at a rate of about 6km/h. They can run at more than 40km/h when angry or frightened, but only for a short distance. Elephants swim well, too, and they often reach islands in lakes or off the coast. Ridged soles grip the ground well and enable the animals to climb steep slopes. However, elephants cannot jump. They would crush their legs on impact.

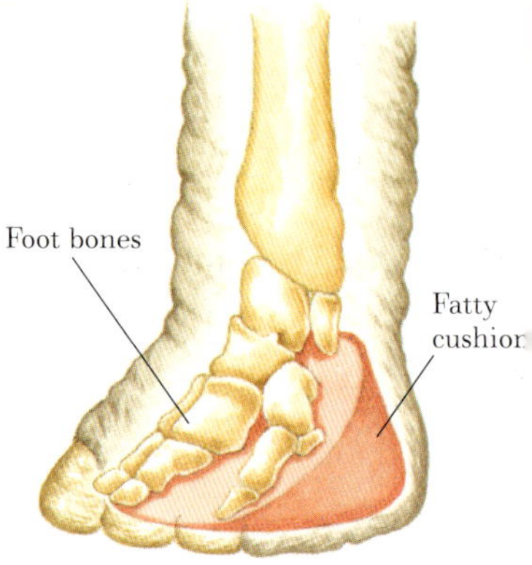

▲ **FATTY FOOT**
An elephant's enormous weight rests on the tips of its toes and on a fatty cushion that works like a giant shock absorber. This shock absorber spreads out as the elephant puts its foot down and contracts as the foot is lifted off the ground. On firm ground, the elephant leaves only faint footprints.

Did you know? An elephant's foot measures up to 1.5m around.

◀ **ELEPHANT WALK**
An elephant walks and runs with shuffling steps. It cannot trot, canter or gallop. Occasionally, elephants walk backwards. They sometimes find this easier than turning around, which can be a difficult manoeuvre for an elephant.

◄ **GRIPPING SOLES**
The skin on the sole of an elephant's foot is thick and covered in cracks and deep ridges. These help it to grip the ground effectively, rather like the treads on tyres or hiking boots.

Did you know? Elephants can swim for six hours without a break.

Royal Hunts
An Indian mythical story tells of King Khusraw, who was killed by his son Shirvieh. In the scene shown here, Shirvieh travels by elephant to the Royal Palace. Here he becomes caught up in a royal hunt. In India, people often rode elephants to hunt.

◄ **FOOTCARE**
An elephant has a thorn removed from its foot. Elephants in captivity move about less than they do in the wild. As a result, their feet are less tough and need to be looked after. Toenails are not worn away either, so they have to be trimmed.

► **ON THE MARCH**
A line of elephants crosses the savanna in Kenya. They sometimes march along with each elephant holding the tail of the one in front. They usually walk about 25km a day, but in the hot deserts of Namibia in southwest Africa they have been known to walk up to 195km a day in search of water.

Bear Brain and Senses

All bears are very intelligent. Size for size, they have larger brains than dogs and cats. They can remember sources of food and are very curious. Bears use their brains to find food or a mate, and to stay out of trouble. Although closely related to the meat-eating mammals (carnivores) most bears are mainly plant-eaters, so they have no need of hunting tactics. They rely on smell to find their food and the part of the brain that analyses scent is larger than in any of the meat-eaters. Their eyes and ears are small compared to their head size. Bears cannot see distant objects very clearly, but they have colour vision to recognize edible fruits and nuts. Bears often do not see or hear people approaching and may attack in self-defence.

▼ **SCENT MARKING**
An American black bear cub practises marking a tree by scratching. When it is older, the bear will leave a scent mark to indicate to other bears that the territory is occupied.

◄ **TEMPER TANTRUM**
A threatened brown bear puts on a fierce display. First it beats the ground or vegetation with its front feet. Then it stands up on its back legs to look larger. This is accompanied by a high-pitched snorting through open lips or a series of hoarse barks. The display of aggression finishes with snapping the jaws together.

▲ **FOLLOW YOUR NOSE**

A brown bear relies more on smell than sight. It often raises its head and sniffs the air to check out who or what is about. It can detect the faintest trace of a smell, searching for others of its kind.

▼ **GETTING TO KNOW YOU**

Polar bear cubs rub against their mother to spread her scent over themselves. Smell allows a mother and cubs to recognize each other. They also communicate with sounds. Distressed cubs make low-pitched snores that develop into high whines.

Bruno the Bear

Aesop's Fables are a set of tales written by the ancient Greek writer Aesop. One fable features Bruno the Bear. He is shown as stupid and easily deceived. Bears were considered slow-witted because they sleep a lot. But Bruno was kind, unlike the cunning Reynard the Fox. Bruno cared about others and forgave those who played pranks on him. Bruno was the forerunner of characters such as Winnie-the-Pooh.

▲ **SNOWY SCENT TRAIL**

Even in the Arctic, polar bears can pick up the trails of other bears and follow them. There are few objects around to use as scent posts for polar bears, so trails may be marked with dribbles of smelly urine.

Tree Climbers

Trees provide food for some bears and a place of safety for others. Sun bears, sloth bears and spectacled bears climb trees regularly in search of food, such as fruits, seeds and nuts, as well as birds' eggs. Black bears are also agile tree-climbers. Polar bears very rarely encounter trees, although a few come into forested areas during the summer, where they rest in hollows dug among tree roots to avoid the heat. Brown bear cubs climb trees to escape danger, but adult brown bears are too heavy to be good climbers. A female sloth bear will carry her small cubs into a tree on her back, unless she is escaping from a leopard since they can also climb trees! Most bears also use trees to mark their territory. They scratch the bark and rub on scents to tell other bears they are there.

▶ **BEAR DANGER**
A mother American black bear sends her cubs up into a tree while she stands guard at its base. If the danger is from an adult brown bear, the female will flee and return later for her cubs when the bear has gone.

◀ **TREE-TOP HOME**
The sun bear seeks out the nests of termites and bees, and will rip away bark to get at insects hidden underneath. Although the sun bear feeds mainly on insects it also eats ripe fruit and preys on small rodents, birds and lizards.

▲ **BELOW THE BARK**
An adult, cinnamon-coloured Asian black bear is able to climb into a tree with ease using its short but sturdy claws. It can also lift bark to lick out insects with a long tongue.

▲ **UP A TREE**

Giant pandas stay mainly on the ground, but they climb trees occasionally. They do so to sun themselves or to rest. Female pandas sometimes head up a tree to escape males, while males climb trees to advertise their presence.

▼ **SAFE HAVEN**

Black bears are normally found in forested areas. They have favourite trees located along trails where bears and other animals regularly pass. The bear marks the tree with its scent and climbs into the branches where it is safe from larger brown bears.

Short, sturdy claws on a black bear's feet make tree climbing easy.

▲ **HIGH SCHOOL**

Black bear cubs stay close to their mother both on the ground and in a tree. They watch and learn from her how to climb and find food among the branches.

▼ **TREE HOUSE**

Spectacled bears pull branches together to make a feeding platform. From here the bears feed on mainly tough plants called bromeliads. They also eat fruits, nuts and honey, and may take mice, forest rabbits and insects on to the platform to eat.

Watching Out

To hunt well and not be seen or heard by prey or enemies, cats use their senses of sight and hearing. Cats' eyesight is excellent. Their eyes are adapted for night vision, but they can also see well in the day. Cats' eyes are big compared to the size of their heads. Their eyes work as a pair (binocular vision), which allows cats to accurately judge how far away objects are. At night, cats see in black and white. They can see colours in the day, but not as well as humans can. Cats have very good hearing, much better than a human's. They can hear small animals rustling through the grass or even moving around in their burrows underground.

▲ CAUGHT IN BRIGHT LIGHT
Cats' eyes are very sensitive to light. During the day in bright light, the pupils of the eyes close right down, letting in only as much light as is needed to see well. A domestic cat's pupils close down to slits, while most big cats' pupils close to tiny circles.

◄ GLOWING EYES
Like other cats, the leopard has a reflecti layer called the tapetum at the back c eye. This reflects light back into th giving the nerve cells extra stimu so that they send stronger sign the brain. The reflection cau eyes to glow when light sl into them at night.

Did you know? A cat's pupils open wide when it is frightened and close up when it is angry.

PREY IN SIGHT ▶
As it stalks through the long grass a lion must pounce at just the right moment if it is to catch its prey. Because a cat's eyes are set slightly apart at the front of the head, their field of view overlaps. This means the cat has binocular vision, which enables it to judge the exact position of its prey so it knows when to strike.

▲ ROUND-EYED
This puma's rounded pupils have closed down in daylight. In dim light, the pupils will expand wide to let in as much light as possible.

SHARP EARS ▶
Cats' ears are designed for them to hear very well. This Siberian lynx lives in snowy forests where the sound is often muffled. It has specially-shaped, big ears to catch as much sound as possible.

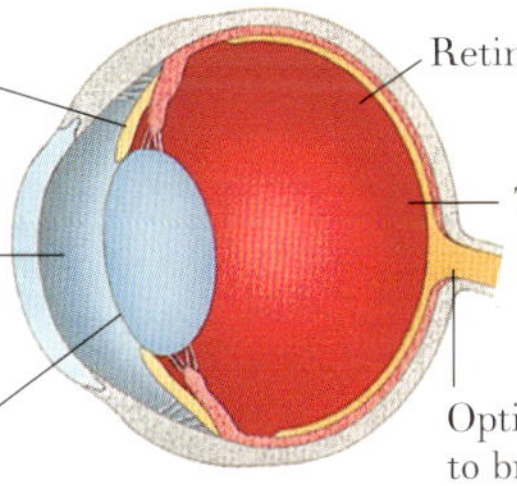

▲ INSIDE THE EYE
The lens focuses light rays to produce a sharp image on the retina. Impulses from the retina are carried to the brain by the optic nerve. Cats have a membrane that can be pulled over the surface of the eye to keep out dirt and dust.

Touching, Tasting and Smelling

Like all animals, cats can feel things by touching them with their skin, but they have another important touching tool – whiskers. These long, stiff hairs on the face have very sensitive nerve endings at their roots. Some whiskers are for protection. Anything brushing against the whiskers above a cat's eyes will make it blink. A cat's tongue is a useful tool and its nose is very sensitive. Cats use smell and taste to communicate with each other. Thin, curled bones in the nose carry scents inwards to smell receptors. Cats also have a chemical detector called a Jacobson's organ in the roof of the mouth to distinguish scents, especially those of other cats.

▲ TONGUE TOOL
A leopard curls the tip of its tongue like a spoon to lap up water. After several laps it will drink the water in one gulp. As well as drinking, the tongue is used for tasting, scraping meat off a carcass and grooming.

◀ ROUGH TONGUE
A tiger's bright pink tongue has a very rough surface. Cats' tongues are covered with small spikes called papillae. The papillae point backwards and are used by the cat, together with its teeth, to strip meat off bones. Around the edge and at the back of the tongue are taste buds. Cats cannot taste sweet things, but they can recognize pure water.

The tiger raises its head and grimaces to taste the air.

Cats twitch their tails from side to side as they concentrate. When angry, the tail lashes to and fro.

WHO PASSED BY? ►

By tasting the air a tiger uses its Jacobson's organ (the special scent centre in the roof of the mouth) to detect the scent left by another tiger. To get as much of the scent as it can, it wrinkles its nose, curls its lips upwards, bares its teeth and lifts its head. This action is known as flehmen. Males use it especially to locate females ready to mate.

Did you know? Hairballs coughed up by lions are worn as talismans in some parts of Africa.

▲ THE CAT'S WHISKERS

This snow leopard's face is surrounded by sensitive whiskers. Cats use their whiskers to sense nearby objects and air movements. The most important whiskers are on the sides of the face. These help a cat to feel its way in the dark, or when it is walking through tall grass.

▼ COAT CARE

The long, rough tongue of a lion makes a very good comb. It removes loose hairs and combs the fur flat and straight. Cats wipe their faces, coats and paws clean. They spend a lot of time looking after their fur. Hair swallowed during grooming is spat out as hairballs.

On the Prowl

Cats run and jump easily and gracefully. They have flexible spines and strong hind legs. With long, bouncy strides, they can cover the ground very quickly. Big cats are not good long-distance runners, but are great sprinters and pouncers. They use their long tails for balance when climbing trees and running fast. All cats can swim very well, but some prefer to avoid getting wet and will only swim to escape danger. Others, such as tigers and jaguars, live near water and often swim to hunt their prey.

▲ **THRILL OF THE CHASE**
A lion chases its prey through the scrub. When lions stalk, run and pounce, they make use of their flexible backs, strong back legs, powerful chests and cushioning pads under their paws. Cats' back legs are especially powerful. They provide the major thrust for running. Cats can outpace their prey over short distances before launching into a final jump.

◄ **TREE-CLIMBING CAT**
Leopards spend a lot of time in trees and are designed for climbing. They have very powerful chests and front legs. Their shoulder blades are positioned to the side to make them better climbers. A leopard can leap 3m without difficulty and, in exceptional circumstances, can leap over 6m.

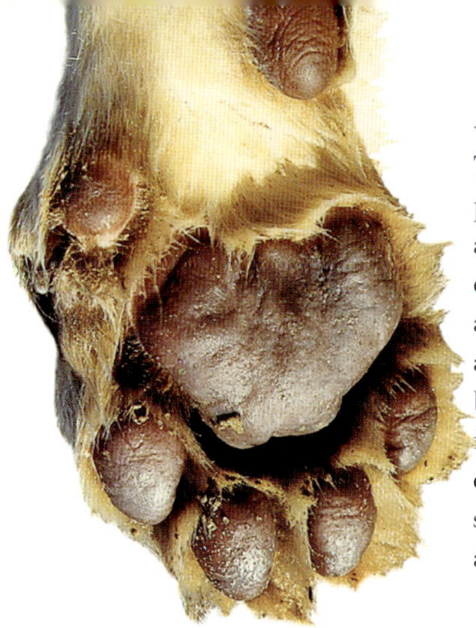

◄ SOFT PADDING

The thick pads under a lion's paw are like cushions. They allow the lion to move very quietly and also act as shock absorbers when running and jumping. Hidden between the pads and fur are the lion's claws, tucked away safely until they are needed.

Did you know? In the 1500s, rich people kept cheetahs as hunting animals like dogs.

GRACE AND AGILITY ►

A bobcat leaps with great agility off a rock. All cats have flexible backs and short collarbones to help make their bodies stronger for jumping and landing. Bobcats are similar to lynxes. Both cats have an extensive coating of fur on their feet to give them extra warmth. The fur also prevents them from slipping on icy rocks.

As it leaps, a bobcat pinpoints its landing position. The front feet land separately in quick succession.

◄ KEEPING COOL

A Bengal tiger swims gracefully across a river. Most tigers live in warm areas, such as India and South-east Asia. As well as swimming to get from one place to another, they often look for pools of water to bathe in during the heat of the day. They are one of the few cats that actively enjoy being in or near water. Tigers are excellent swimmers and can easily cross a lake 5km wide.

Eyes of the Wolf

Dogs have excellent hearing. They can hear the sound of a snapping twig over 3km away and are alert to the smallest noise that might give away the presence of potential prey. They also hear a wider range of sounds than humans. They can hear ultrasounds (very high-pitched sounds) that are too high for human ears to detect. This means they can track down mice and other rodents in the dark. Sight is less important than hearing for hunting. Wolves are good at spotting movement, even at a great distance, but find it harder to see objects that keep still. Wild dogs that hunt at night rely on sound and smell rather than sight. African hunting dogs and dholes (relations of the wolf), however, hunt by day, often in open country, and have keener sight.

▲ PRICKED EARS
Wolves cock (turn) their ears in different directions to pinpoint distant sounds. Even a tiny noise betrays the hiding place of a victim.

▲ LISTENING IN
An African hunting dog's large, rounded ears work like satellite dishes to gather sound. Keen hearing is vital in the hunt and allows pack members to keep in touch among the tall grass.

Coyote
(*Canis latrans*)

HOWLING HELLO ▶
Coyotes and other wild dogs keep in touch with distant members of their group by howling. The coyote call is actually a series of yelps that ends in a long wail.

Did you know? African hunting dogs chatter like monkeys as they play together.

◀ BARKING MAD

Some domestic dogs, such as this German shepherd, have been bred to bark loudly to warn their owners of approaching strangers. Wolves also bark if they meet an intruder near the den, but more quietly and less aggressively.

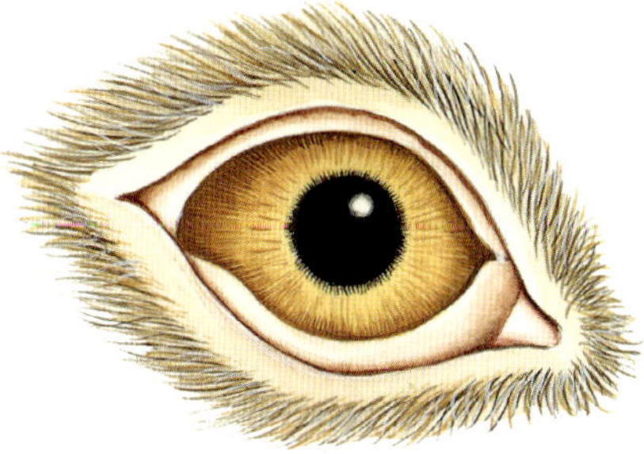

▲ A THIRD EYELID

Wolves' eyes have a third eyelid, called a nictitating (blinking) membrane. This membrane is inside their upper and lower eyelids, and sweeps over the surface of the eye when the wolf blinks. It protects the eyes from dust and dirt that might damage it otherwise.

◀ GLOWING EYES

Wolves have round, yellow eyes. As with cats, in dark conditions, a reflective layer at the back of the eye, the tapetum, intensifies what little light there is. This allows a wolf to see at night. If a strong light is shone into a wolf's eyes, the reflection gives the eyes an eerie glow.

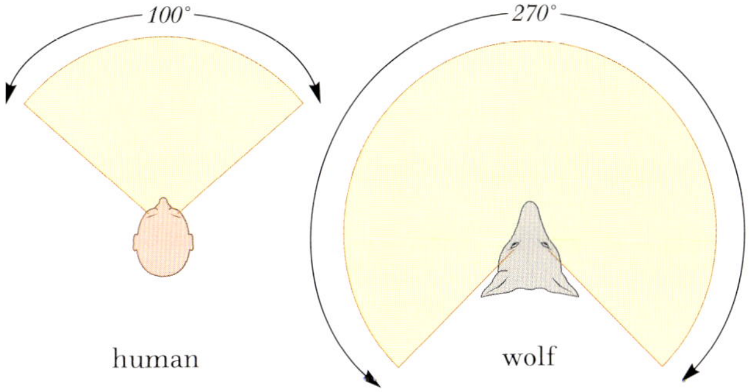

◀ WOLF VISION

Wide-set eyes in the front of its face give a wolf a very wide field of vision. As the view from each eye overlaps, binocular vision (using both eyes at the same time) allows a wolf to judge distances and locate its prey.

A Keen Sense of Smell

Of all the senses, smell is the most important for wolves and other wild dogs. These animals are constantly surrounded by different scents and their keen sense of smell can distinguish them all. They follow the scent trails left behind by other animals in their quest for food, and can pick up even faint whiffs of scent on the wind. This helps them to figure out the direction of distant prey. Wild dogs that hunt in packs use scent to identify and communicate with other pack members. They also communicate by sight and touch. Like other mammals, wolves and wild dogs have taste buds on their tongues to taste their food. They eat foods they find the tastiest first. The tongue is also used to lap up water.

▲ **TRACKING PREY**
Nose to the ground, a wolf follows a scent trail on the ground. From the scent a wolf can tell what type of animal left it, whether it is well or ill, how long ago it passed by and whether another wolf is following the trail.

► **ON THE SCENT**
Bloodhounds were specially bred as tracking dogs. They have a very acute sense of smell and can follow a scent that is several days old. They keep their noses very close to the ground. Their drooping ears help to channel scent into the nose.

▲ **PLEASED TO MEET YOU**
When two wolves meet they sniff the glands at the base of the tail. Pack members all have a familiar scent. Scent is also used to signal mood, such as contentment or fear, or if a female is ready to breed.

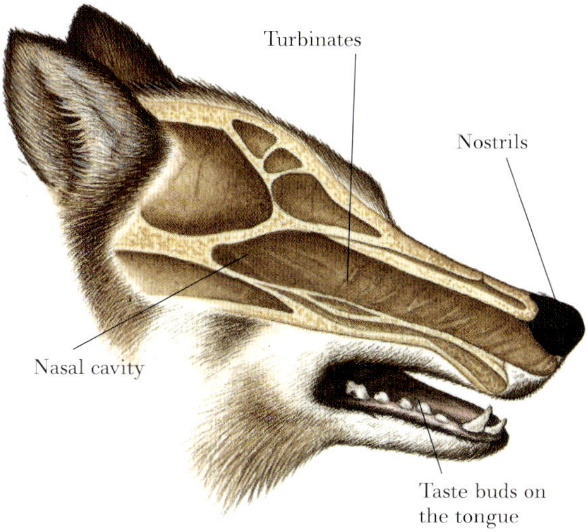

▲ **INSIDE THE SNOUT**

Inside a wolf's snout is a large nasal cavity used for smelling. Scent particles pass over tubes of very thin bone in the roof of the nasal cavity. These tubes, called turbinates, are connected to a nerve network that sends signals to the brain.

▲ **TOUCHY-FEELY**

Wolves use touch to bond with each other. They rub bodies, lick one another and thrust their noses into each other's fur when they meet. Pack members play-fight by wrestling with locked jaws, or chasing around in circles.

▼ **SENSITIVE NOSE**

The wolf's leathery outer nose is set right at the end of its snout. Two nostrils draw air laden with scents into the nasal cavity. The wolf may flare its nostrils to take in extra air. The animal may lick its nose before scenting, because a damp nose helps its sense of smell. Long, sensitive whiskers on either side of the snout are used for touching things at close range.

▲ **WELL GROOMED**

A wolf nibbles at the tufts of hair between its paw pads. It is removing ice that might cut and damage the paw. Wolves groom (clean) their fur to keep it in good condition. Licking and running fur through the teeth helps to remove dirt and dislodge fleas.

▲ **SPEEDING COYOTE**
Like wolves, coyotes are good long-distance runners. They run on their toes, like other dogs. This helps them to take long strides and so cover more ground. If necessary, coyotes can trot along for hours in search of food.

Running Wild

Wild dogs are tireless runners. Wolves can lope along for hours on end at a steady pace of 40km/h without resting. They have been known to cover an amazing 200km in a day searching for food. Compared to cheetahs, which can reach speeds of about 100km/h over short distances, wolves are not fast runners. They can, however, put on a burst of speed to overtake fleeing prey.

Wolves and most other dogs have four toes on their back feet and five toes on their front feet. The fifth toe on the front foot is called the dew claw, a small, functionless claw located a little way up on the back of each front leg. It is more like a pad than a claw. Dogs also have tough pads on the underside of their toes to help absorb the impact as their feet hit the ground.

Did you know? Studies of wolves in the U.S. show one pack travelled 1100km in 40 days.

Grey wolf
(Canis lupus)

◄ **IN MID-LEAP**
Strong leg muscles enable a wolf to leap long distances – up to 4.5m in a single bound. Wolves and other dogs are very agile and can leap upwards, sideways and even backwards. As the wolf lands, its toes splay out to support its weight and prevent it from slipping.

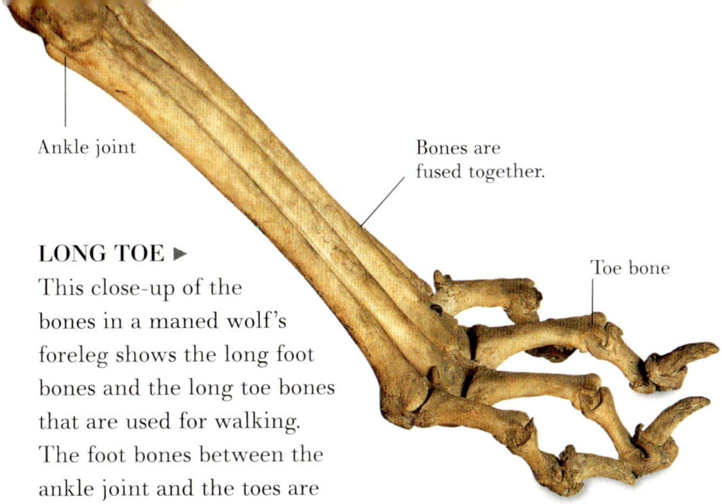

LONG TOE ▶
This close-up of the bones in a maned wolf's foreleg shows the long foot bones and the long toe bones that are used for walking. The foot bones between the ankle joint and the toes are fused together for greater strength.

▲ WOLF TRACK
Clawmarks show up clearly in a line of wolf prints in a snowy landscape. Unlike cats, wolves and other wild dogs cannot retract (draw in) their claws. When walking, the wolf places its paws almost in a straight line, to form a single track. The pawprints of a running wolf are more widely spaced.

IN THE WATER ▶
Bush dogs make their homes near streams and rivers and spend much of their lives in water. They are strong swimmers, and water creatures such as capybaras (a large type of rodent) form part of their diet. Wolves, dingoes and most other dogs can also swim well.

A KEEN CLIMBER ▶
Wolves and wild dogs are quick on the ground, but they cannot climb trees. Some foxes, however, climb well. The grey fox of North America is an expert climber. It scrambles up trees to steal birds' eggs and chicks. It also climbs to get a good view over surrounding countryside when searching for prey.

Grey fox
(Urocyon cinereoargenteus)

Apes on the Move

To an ape, the tangle of trunks, branches and vines in a forest is like a gigantic climbing frame that provides high-level walkways through the air. Gibbons, orang-utans and bonobos spend a lot of time in the trees. Large male orang-utans also travel on the ground some of the time because of their great weight. The true masters of treetop travel are the gibbons, able to leap and swing effortlessly across gaps at great speed and at great heights. Chimpanzees and gorillas are mainly ground-based creatures, although chimpanzees often climb trees to find food and may spend the night in the branches. Gorillas, even with their great bulk, sometimes venture into trees.

▲ KNUCKLE WALKING
On the ground, chimpanzees and gorillas rest their weight on pads of thick skin on their knuckles. This is called knuckle walking.

▲ CLIMBING CHIMP
Chimpanzees climb into the trees to find leaves or fruit to eat, to chase prey and to build sleeping nests. Their long fingers hook over the branches and give them a good grip for both climbing and swinging.

Tarzan of the Apes
American writer Edgar Rice Burroughs created the character Tarzan in a magazine story published in 1912. Tarzan is orphaned as a baby in the jungles of Africa. A tribe of apes takes care of him, teaching him how to survive in the jungle and swing through trees. He shares his later adventures with his wife Jane and their son Korak.

Orang-utans
(*Pongo pygmaeus*)

◄ FLEXIBLE APE

When climbing, the body weight of an orang-utan is evenly spread between its arms and legs. This helps the orang-utan to keep its balance. The shoulder and hip joints of an orang-utan are very supple, allowing it to stretch easily between branches. Orang-utans can even eat hanging upside-down. They will sway slender trees until they can reach far enough to catch a branch on the next tree. They often make a lot of noise.

Did you know? A gorilla can run at 25–33km/h over short distances.

◄ SWINGING GIBBONS

With their extraordinarily long arms, gibbons swing at breathtaking speed from branch to branch, often leaping huge distances. Special wrist bones allow a gibbon to turn its body as it swings without loosening its grip. This means it can swing hand-over-hand in a speedy swing, known as brachiating. Compared with the noisy crashings of monkeys leaping from tree to tree, gibbons are almost silent travellers.

▲ GRIPPING FEAT

Gorillas are wary tree climbers and rarely swing by their arms like orang-utans or gibbons. They climb down from a tree backwards, holding the trunk loosely with both feet in a controlled slide.

The Senses of Small Primates

Monkeys and apes are usually active in the daytime, and make the most of their excellent colour vision. Most other primates, known as prosimians, move around at night, and have eyes that can see in the dark. All primate eyes contain cone cells and rod cells, but monkeys have more colour-sensitive cone cells in their eyes. The eyes of prosimians have plenty of rod cells, that work in dim light. Their eyes glow in the dark because most prosimians' eyes are backed by a mirror-like layer that reflects the light.

Sight is very important to monkeys and apes, but other primates rely much more on smelling and hearing. The ears of prosimians are constantly on the alert. The slightest rustle in the dark could identify an insect snack or an approaching predator.

▲ **COLOUR SELECTION**
Thanks to its colour vision, a vervet monkey can select the tastiest flowers when they are at the peak of perfection. Many leaf-eating monkeys have eyes that are particularly sensitive to different shades of green. This means that they can easily identify the fresh green of tender young leaves which are good to eat.

▲ **EYES LIKE SAUCERS**
Unlike the eyes of many prosimians, tarsiers' eyes have no reflective layer, but their size means they catch as much light as possible. Like monkeys, their eyes have a sensitive area called the fovea, which picks out very sharp detail.

MIDNIGHT MONKEY ►
Douroucouli monkeys are the only nocturnal (night-active) monkeys. They live in South America where there are no other nocturnal primates to compete with. Their eyes are big to catch maximum light. They are able to pick up detail but not colour.

▼ A KEEN SENSE OF SMELL
An emperor tamarin monkey marks its territory with scent. American monkeys and most prosimians have a smelling organ in the roof of their mouths that monkeys from elsewhere do not have. They use their sense of smell to communicate with each other and to identify food that is good and ready to eat.

▲ WET-NOSED SMELLING AIDS
Look at the shiny nose of this ruffed lemur. It is more like that of a dog than a monkey. Most prosimians have this moist nostril and lip area, called the rhinarium. It gives them a better sense of smell. The nose has a layer of cells that detect chemicals in the air. The cells work better when they are wet.

▼ MUFFLED SENSE OF HEARING
The furry ears of squirrel monkeys probably muffle sound. But although these and other monkeys use sound to communicate with each other, hearing is not as important for them as keen eyesight. Nocturnal primates, however, have highly sensitive, delicate-skinned ears.

Brain Waves in the Sea

A whale controls its body through its nervous system. The brain is the control centre, carrying out many functions automatically, but also acting upon information supplied by the senses. The sizes of whale brains vary according to the animals' sizes. However, dolphins have much bigger brains for their size. Hearing is by far a whale's most important sense, it picks up sounds with tiny ears located just behind the eyes.

▲ **EYES**
Compared with its large body, a whale's eyes are tiny. It can see quite well when it is on the surface and often lifts its head out of the water to look around.

Did you know? A sperm whale's brain is five times the size of a human's.

◄ **CLOSE ENCOUNTERS**
A group of Atlantic spotted dolphins swim closely together in the seas around the Bahamas (Atlantic islands). Like most other whales, the dolphins nudge one another and stroke each other with their flippers and tail. Touch plays a very important part in dolphin society, especially in courtship.

◀ SLAP HAPPY
A humpback whale slapping its tail, or lob-tailing, a favourite pastime for large whales. Lob-tailing creates a noise like a gunshot in the air, but, more importantly, it will make a loud crash underwater. All the other whales in the area will be able to hear the noise.

Cupids and Dolphins
In this Roman mosaic, cupids and dolphins gambol together. In Roman mythology, Cupid was the god of love. Roman artists were inspired by the dolphin's intelligence and gentleness. They regarded them as sacred creatures.

◀ BRAINY DOLPHIN?
Some dolphins, such as the bottlenose, have a complex brain with many folds, much the same size as our own. However, scientists are still not sure how intelligent dolphins really are.

▶ IN TRAINING
A bottlenose dolphin is shown with its trainer. This species has a particularly large brain for its size. It can be easily trained and has a good memory. It can observe other animals and learn to mimic their behaviour in a short space of time. It is also good at solving problems, something we consider a sign of intelligence.

▲ **STEERING**
Among whales, the humpback has by far the longest front flippers. As well as for steering, it uses its flippers for slapping the water. Flipper-slapping seems to be a form of communication.

Swim and Splash

All whales are superb swimmers. All parts of the whale's body help it move through the water. The driving force comes from tail fins, or flukes. Using very powerful muscles in the rear third of its body, the whale beats its tail up and down and the whole body bends. It uses its pectoral fins, or flippers, near the front of the body to steer with. The body itself is almost hairless to make it streamlined and smooth so it can slip through the water easily. The body can change shape slightly to keep the water flowing smoothly around it.

◀ **TAIL POWER**
The tail flukes of a grey whale rise into the air before it dives. Whales move their broad tails up and down to drive themselves through the water.

▼ **MASSIVE FIN**
The dorsal fin of a killer whale (orca) projects high into the air. The animal is a swift swimmer, and the fin helps keep its body well balanced. The killer whale has such a large dorsal fin that some experts believe it may help to regulate its body temperature, or even be used in courtship. Many whales and dolphins have a dorsal fin, and others only have a raised hump.

Did you know? A killer whale can swim up to 65km/h.

◄ STREAMLINING
Atlantic spotted dolphins' bodies are beautifully streamlined – shaped so that they slip easily through the water when they move. The dolphin's body is long and rounded, broad in front and becoming narrower towards the tail. Apart from the dorsal fin and flippers, nothing projects from its body. It has no external ears or rear limbs.

▼ HOW A DOLPHIN SWIMS
Dolphins beat their tail flukes up and down by means of the powerful muscles near the tail. The flukes force the water backwards at each stroke. As the water is forced back, the dolphin's body is forced forwards. Its other fins help guide it through the water. They do not provide propulsion.

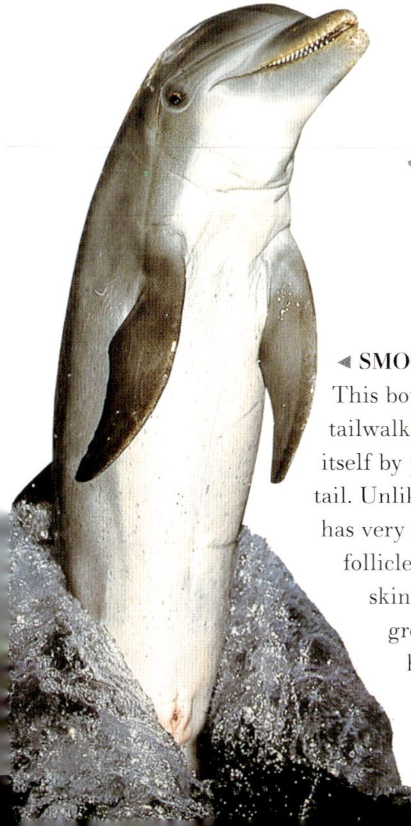

◄ SMOOTH-SKINNED
This bottlenose dolphin is tailwalking – supporting itself by powerful thrusts of its tail. Unlike most mammals, it has very few hairs or hair follicles – the dimples in the skin from which the hair grows. Its smooth skin helps the dolphin's body slip through the water.

▼ HOW A FISH SWIMS
It is mainly the tail that provides the power for a fish to swim. The tail has vertical fins, unlike a dolphin's horizontal flukes. It swims by beating its tail and body from side to side.

The Senses of a Killer

A shark's brain is small for its size, but its senses are highly developed. Sharks see well, and see in colour. They can also recognize shapes. Just as amazing are a different range of senses that allow sharks to pick up sounds and vibrations from great distances. They can detect changes in the ocean currents, recognize smells and follow the trail of a smell right back to its source. Some species have shiny plates at the backs of their eyes that collect light to help them see as they dive to deep, dark water. They also have dark-coloured membranes that they draw across the shiny plates to avoid being dazzled by the light when they return to the surface. Sharks even have special nerves in their noses that can detect minute electrical fields, such as those produced by the muscles of their fish prey.

▲ **ELECTRICAL SENSE**
Like all sharks, sandtiger sharks have tiny pits in their snouts, known as the ampullae of Lorenzini. Inside these pits are special nerves. These help the shark to find food by detecting minute electrical fields in the muscles of its prey.

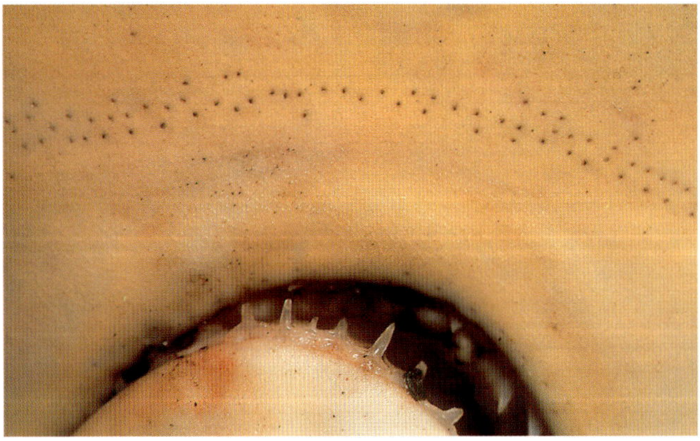

◄ **PREY DETECTOR**
In a hammerhead shark the special pits that can sense electrical fields in its prey are spread across the hammer of the shark's head, helping it to scan for prey across a wide area. The hammerhead searches for food by sweeping its head from side to side, rather as if using a metal detector. It can find any prey buried in the sand below.

Scalloped hammerhead shark
(*Sphyrna lewini*)

◀ SIGHT, SMELL AND SOUND

The nostrils of the hammerhead shark are positioned wide apart on its head. This gives the shark 'stereo smelling' with which it can more easily track odours to their source. But, because its eyes are at the ends of its hammer, it must turn its head from side to side in order to see forwards.

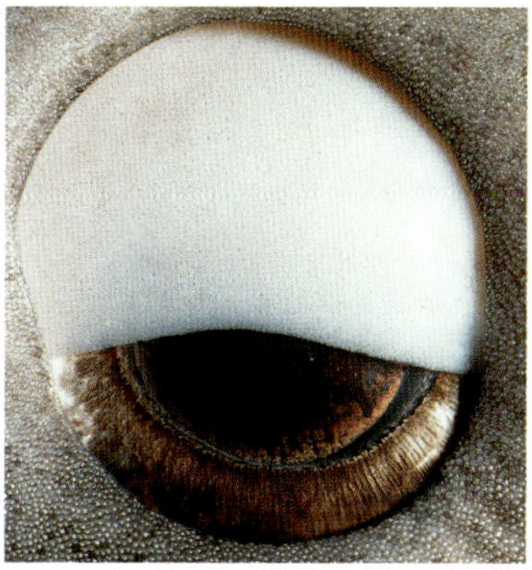

▲ EYE PROTECTION

When a shark bites, its eyes can easily be injured by the victim's teeth, spines or claws. To prevent this, sharks such as this tiger shark have a special membrane (sheath) that slides down across the eye during the attack.

Eye of blacktip reef shark

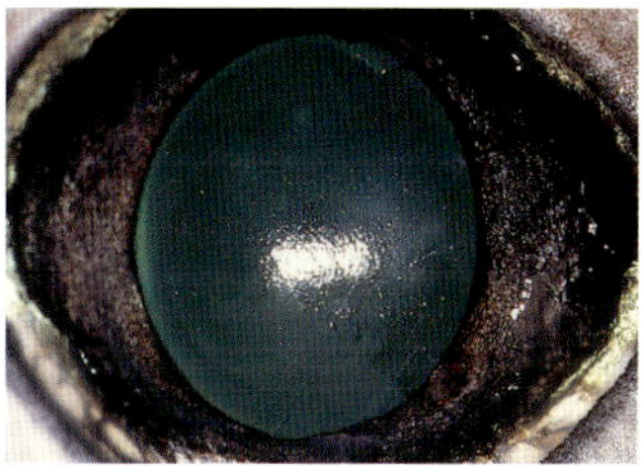

Eye of bluntnose sixgill shark

◀ DEEP AND SHALLOW

The blacktip reef shark has a small eye with a narrow, vertical slit. This type of eye is often found in shallow-water sharks. Sharks that swim in deeper waters, such as the sixgill shark, tend to have large, round pupils.

Did you know? Sharks find their way through mazes as fast as rabbits.

Shark Callers

On the islands of the south-west Pacific, sharks are the islanders' gods. To test their manhood, young shark callers attract sharks by shaking a coconut rattle under the water. Sensing the vibrations, a shark will swim close to the canoe. It is then wrestled into the boat, and its meat divided among the villagers as a gift from the gods.

The Hunt for Food

There are fundamental physical differences between animals that eat meat and those that feed on plants. This section focuses on the special adaptations that animals have made in order to take advantage of one particular food, and it explores their similarities and differences.

The Diet of Animals

Pandas have given up regular hunting in favour of a diet of bamboo.

All living things need food of some kind or another. Food provides them with the energy needed to move about and to power all of life's other activities. Food also provides the 'building bricks' needed for growth. Plants use the energy in sunlight to make their own food by a process called photosynthesis, but animals all have to find and eat 'ready-made' food in the form of plants or other animals. Animals that feed on plants are called herbivores. Those that eat meat or flesh are called carnivores and those that regularly eat both plants and other animals are called omnivores. We are omnivores, and so are chimpanzees and most bears.

Sensing food

Herbivorous animals generally track down tasty foods by using their eyes and sense of smell. Nectar-seeking butterflies, for example, home in on flowers by picking up their colours and scents, and grazing mammals can smell fresh grass from many miles away. Carnivores use their eyes, their sense of smell and also their ears to find food. Many snakes track down their prey by flicking out their tongues to pick up traces of scent on the ground or in the air. Rattlesnakes have heat-sensitive pits on their snouts that tell them when warm-blooded prey is near. This is particularly useful at night. Hearing is also important for animals that hunt at night. Owls have excellent hearing as well as superb eyesight. Their ears pick up the slightest rustle in the grass below and enable the owls to home in on their prey with amazing accuracy. Soft-edged feathers enable the owls to fly very quietly, so the prey does not hear them coming.

Snakes use their senses to detect other animals and, instead of hunting, many snakes simply lie in wait for their prey to come to them.

To chase or to lie in wait?

Meat-eaters have two main ways of getting their food. They can chase after their prey, or they can hide and lie in wait for it. Wolves and other dogs are chasers, often hunting in packs to catch prey much larger than themselves. The chase can last for hours, with the dogs taking turns at the front. Lions and other cats also chase their prey, but their chases are much shorter. Leopards sometimes lie in wait for their prey, often sitting on a branch or a rock and dropping on anything that passes beneath. Some crab spiders lurk in flowers and often blend so well with the petals that they are very hard to see. Insects visiting the flowers for a drink are quickly grabbed by the spiders. Many spiders make sticky webs to trap their prey but some rely on sensing the vibrations when prey walk over or near their webs.

Most big cats are only too happy to eat someone else's meal and steal kills from other animals whenever they can. Cheetahs are an exception, and eat only animals they have killed themselves.

Teeth and claws

Most predators use their claws or teeth to catch and kill their prey. Cats, for example, use their powerful claws to bring down their victims, and then kill them either by biting through the neck or by gripping the throat until their prey suffocates. Birds of prey usually use their talons to snatch and kill their victims. The birds then use their hooked beaks to tear up the flesh, although owls usually swallow their prey whole. Mammalian teeth vary with the animals' diets. Grass-eaters have big grinding teeth to crush grass and release as much of the goodness from it as possible. Meat-eaters have sharp-edged cheek teeth for slicing through the flesh of their prey. Insect jaws are on the outside of the body and they cut or crush the food before pushing it into their mouth. Bugs feed on liquids by piercing plants or other animals with sharp, tubular beaks. Butterflies suck up nectar with slender 'drinking straws'.

Eagles attack with their talons. They are so long, sharp and deeply curved that one swipe is usually enough to kill their prey.

All depend on plants

Whatever they eat, all animals depend on plants for their food. Lions eat zebras and antelopes but the nutrition provided by the meat of these grazing animals comes from their diet of grass and other plants. Even sharks depend on plants as the fish that they eat feed on plants floating near the surface of the sea.

A swallowtail butterfly uses its long tongue to suck up nectar.

Insect Plant-eaters

Many insect species are herbivores (plant-eaters), including caterpillars, most bugs and some beetles. Different insects specialize in eating particular parts of plants – the leaves, buds, seeds, roots or bark. Many plant-eating insects become pests when they feed on cultivated plants or crops. Other pests nibble things that humans would not consider edible, such as clothes, carpets and wooden furniture.

Beetles and bugs do not always eat the same food throughout their lives. Rose chafer beetles, for example, nibble petals and pollen, but their larvae (young) feed on rotting wood. Some adult beetles and bugs do not feed at all. Instead, they put all their energy into finding a mate and reproducing.

▲ **TUNNEL-BORERS**
Female bark beetles lay their eggs under the tree's bark. When the young hatch, each one eats its way through the soft wood just under the bark, creating a long, narrow tunnel just wide enough to squeeze through.

Did you know? Wood boring beetle grubs may eat for 7 years before they reach full size.

squash bug
(Coreus marginatus)

◄ **SQUASH-LOVERS**
Squash bugs are named after their favourite food. The squash-plant family includes courgettes and pumpkins. This bug is about to pierce a courgette flower bud and suck out its sap. Most squash bugs are green or brown. They feed on leaves, flowers and seeds. The insects are serious pests in North America.

▲ A PLAGUE OF APHIDS
Aphids are small, soft-bodied bugs. They use their sharp, beak-like mouths to pierce plant leaves and stems and suck out the life-giving sap that is found inside. Aphids reproduce so quickly in warm weather that they can cover a plant within a few hours – and suck it dry.

▲ BEETLE ATTACK
Colorado beetles are high on the list of dangerous insects in many countries. The beetles originally came from the western USA, where they ate the leaves of local plants. When European settlers came and cultivated potatoes, the beetles ate the crop and did great damage. Colorado beetles later spread to become a major pest in Europe, but are now controlled by pesticides.

▲ SCALY FEEDERS
Most female scale insects have neither legs nor wings, but they can be identified as bugs as they have sucking mouthparts (beetles have biting jaws). Scale insects are usually hidden under waxy or horny scales, as shown here. The insects are piercing the skin of a juicy melon and sucking its juices.

▲ THE EVIL WEEVIL
These grains of wheat have been infested by a type of beetle called the grain weevil. The adult weevils bore through the grain's hard case with their long snouts to reach the soft kernel inside. Females lay their eggs inside the kernels. Then, when the young hatch, they can feed in safety.

Beetle and Bug Attack

ground beetle
(Loricera pilicornis)

▲ SPEEDY HUNTER
A ground beetle feeds on a juicy worm it has caught. Ground beetles are a large family of over 20,000 species. Many species cannot fly, hence their name. However, most ground beetles are fast runners. The beetle uses its speed to overtake a fleeing victim. Once trapped, the victim is firmly grabbed in the attacker's powerful jaws.

Some insects eat only vegetable matter, others are carnivores (meat-eaters). Some of the carnivorous species hunt and kill live prey, while others are scavengers and feed on dead animals. There are also parasitic insects that live on larger animals and eat their flesh or suck their blood, without killing them. Most insect predators feed on insects of around their own size. Some, however tackle larger game, such as frogs, fish, tadpoles, snails and worms. Insects are adapted in different ways to catch and overpower their prey.

All beetles have jaws, which are used by the carnivorous species to seize and crush or crunch up their victims. Bugs have jointed mouthparts made for sucking living victims' juices from their bodies.

◄ GONE FISHING
Great diving beetles are fierce aquatic hunters. They hunt fish, tadpoles, newts and minibeasts that live in ponds and streams. This beetle has caught a stickleback. It grabs the fish in its jaws, then injects it with digestive juices that dissolve the fish's flesh. When the victim finally stops struggling and dies, the beetle begins to feed.

Famous Victim
Charles Darwin (1809–1882), the British naturalist who first developed the theory of evolution, is thought by some to have been bitten by a South American assassin bug. Darwin had gone to South America to study wildlife. On his return to Britain, he fell victim to a mysterious illness, which weakened him for the rest of his life. Some historians believe that when the assassin bug bit into Darwin for a blood snack, it transmitted a dangerous disease.

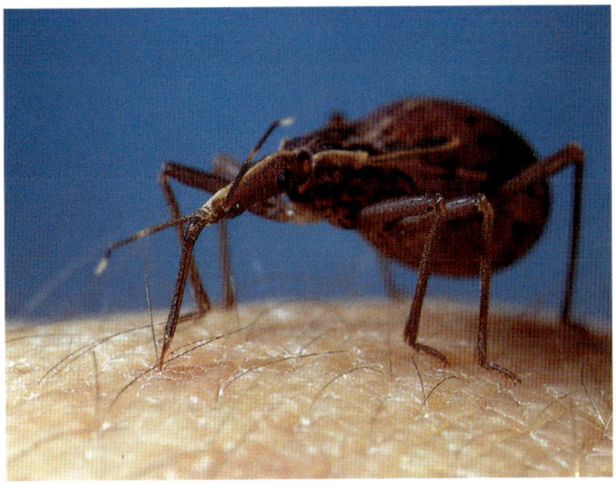

▲ VAMPIRE BEETLE
The person on which this assassin bug has landed will not feel a thing, as the bug has injected a pain killer. These bugs are found world wide, especially in the tropics. Most of them hunt minibeasts and suck their juices dry.

EATEN ALIVE ▸
Although most shield bugs are plant-eaters, this one is not. Some species start their lives as herbivores and move on to a mixed diet later. This one has caught a caterpillar, and uses its curving mouthparts to suck its prey dry. The bugs use their front legs to hold their victims steady while they feast on them.

shield bug
(Palomena prasina)

Did you know? Bedbugs check the smell and temperature of hosts before feeding on them.

◂ NO ESCAPE
When attacked, snails withdraw into their shells and seal them with slime, but this is no defence against a snail-hunting beetle, which squirts liquid into the shell to dissolve the slime and kill the snail. The snail-hunters usually have narrow heads that they can push right inside the shells.

Hungry Caterpillars

▲ **LEAF MINING**
Many tiny caterpillars eat their way through the inside of a leaf instead of crawling across the surface. This activity is known as leaf mining. Often, their progress is revealed by a pale tunnel beneath the leaf surface.

Caterpillars are streamlined eating machines. They must store enough energy to turn into adult moths or butterflies. Their bodies are like expandable sacks, fitted with strong mandibles (jaws) that are edged with teeth or blunt grinding plates. Caterpillars munch through several times their own body weight of food in a single day, and grow incredibly fast.

A caterpillar's first meal is usually the eggshell from which it has hatched. It then moves on to the next food source. Some species eat unhatched eggs or even other caterpillars. Most feed on the leaves and stems of a particular food plant – which is usually the one on which they hatched. The caterpillar stage lasts for at least two weeks, and sometimes much longer.

swallowtail butterfly caterpillar
(Papilio machaon)

▲ **FEEDING HABITS**
Caterpillars eat different food plants from those visited by adult insects. Swallowtail butterfly caterpillars feed on fennel, carrots and milk-parsley. The adult butterflies drink the nectar of many different flowers.

IDENTIFYING FOOD ▶
The head end of a privet hawk moth caterpillar is shown in close-up here. A caterpillar probably identifies food using sensitive organs called palps which are just in front of the mouth.

◄ **FAST EATERS**
Cabbages are the main food of the large white caterpillar. These insects can strip a field of leaves in a few nights. Many farmers and gardeners kill caterpillars with pesticides. The caterpillar population may also be kept down by parasitic wasps that attack the caterpillars.

▲ **PICKY EATER**
Many caterpillars feed on trees. Some, such as the gypsy moth caterpillars, feed on almost any tree, but others are more fussy. This cecropia moth caterpillar feeds only on willow trees.

Alice in Wonderland
In Lewis Carroll's story Alice in Wonderland, *a pipe-smoking caterpillar discusses with Alice what it is like to change size. Carroll was probably thinking of how fast caterpillars grow as a result of their non-stop eating.*

▲ **PROCESSIONARY CATERPILLARS**
The caterpillars of processionary moths rest together in silken nests, and travel to their feeding areas in long lines. These insects are poisonous and do not hide from predators.

Butterfly Food

postman butterfly
(Heliconius)

Many flowers produce a sugary fluid called nectar. This attracts insects in search of a meal, including butterflies and bees. Butterflies and moths do not have jaws and teeth, as they did in the caterpillar stage of their development. Instead, they suck up fluids through long, tongue-like proboscises, which act like drinking straws. Most butterflies survive exclusively on nectar. They spend most of their brief lives flitting from flower to flower in search of this juice. Some woodland species extract sweet liquids from other sources, such as rotting fruit and sap oozing from wounds in trees. A few species even suck on dung. Butterflies rarely live for more than a few days, as none of their foods are very nutritious.

▲ POISONOUS PLANTS
The larvae of *Heliconius* butterflies feed on passion flowers in the rain forests of South America. They absorb the plant's poison. It does not hurt them, but makes them unpalatable to birds. The adult butterflies also feed on the plant. They can detoxify the poison.

▲ FRUIT EATERS
The first generation of comma butterflies appears each year in early summer. These insects feed on the delicate white blossoms of blackberries, because the fruit has not ripened at this time. The second generation appears in autumn, and feeds on the ripe blackberry fruits.

red admiral butterfly
(Vanessa atalanta)

▼ CIDER DRINKING
In autumn, butterflies such as the red admiral and the Camberwell beauty often feed on rotting fruit. Sometimes the juice has fermented to alcohol, and the red admiral may be seen reeling around as if drunk.

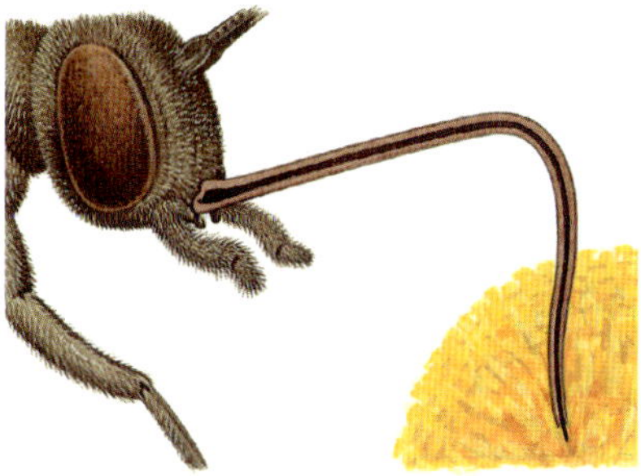

◄ DRINKING STRAW

Many flowers have nectaries inside the blooms to draw insects on to their pollen sacs. The insects carry pollen on to other flowers as they feed, and pollinate them. Some butterflies have very long proboscises to reach deep stores of nectar.

Did you know? The purple emperor butterfly often survives by sucking juices from the rotting bodies of dead animals.

▲ HOVERING HAWK MOTHS

The day-flying hummingbird hawk moth gets its name from its habit of hovering in front of flowers like a hummingbird. It sips nectar from this mid-flight position, rather than landing on the flower. Hawk moths have the longest proboscises of all butterflies and moths. The proboscis of the Darwin's hawk moth is 30–35cm long, which is about three times the length of its body.

▲ NIGHT FEEDER

Noctuid moths often sip nectar from ragworts in meadows by moonlight. In temperate countries, these moths mostly feed on warm summer nights. They get their name from the Latin word *noctuis*, which means night.

► WOODLAND VARIETY

Many woodland butterflies extract juices from a variety of sources. The speckled wood butterfly sometimes sips nectar from bluebells. However, it feeds mainly on honeydew, the sugary secretion of tiny insects called aphids. The leaves of flowers are often coated with honeydew.

speckled wood butterfly
(Pararge aegeria)

Spider Traps

Many spiders catch their prey on a sticky web, but this is only one of many quite different hunting methods. Some set traps for their prey. They lurk inside hidden tubes of silk or underground burrows and wait patiently. Silk threads around the entrance trip up passing insects and other small creatures. Inside the burrow, the spider feels the tug on its trip lines, giving it time to rush out and pounce on the prey before it can escape. Lie-in-wait spiders include trapdoor spiders, which have special spines on their fangs to rake away the soil as they dig their burrows.

▲ **SILK DOORS**
The lid of a trapdoor spider's burrow is made of silk and soil. The door fits tightly into the burrow opening and may be camouflaged with twigs and leaves. In areas liable to flooding, walls or turrets are built around the entrance to keep out the water.

▲ **A SILKEN TUBE**
This purse-web spider has emerged from its burrow. It usually lies in wait for prey inside its tubular purse of densely woven silk. The tube is about 45cm long and about the thickness of a finger. Part of it sticks out of the ground or from a tree trunk, and is well camouflaged with debris.

a spider waits for an insect to land on its tube-like web

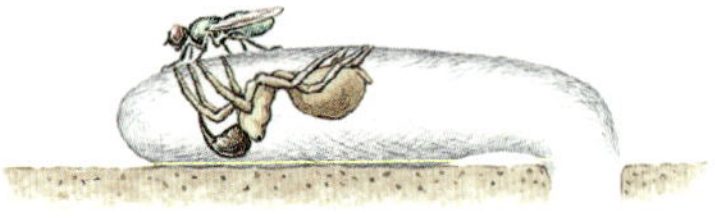

an insect is speared by the spider's sharp jaws

▲ **INSIDE A PURSE-WEB**
The spider waits inside its silken purse for an insect to walk over the tube. It spears the insect through the tube with its sharp jaws and drags the prey inside.

▲ **FUNNEL-WEB SPIDERS**
The Sydney funnel-web is one of the deadliest spiders in the world. It lives in an underground burrow lined with silk. Leading from the mouth of the burrow is a funnel that can be up to 1m across. Trip wires are also strung from the funnel, so that when an insect hits one, the spider is alerted. The spider can dig its own burrow with its fangs, but prefers to use existing holes and cracks. Funnel-web spiders eat beetles, snails and other small animals.

▲ **TRIP WIRES**
The giant trapdoor spider may place silken trip lines around the entrance to its burrow to detect the movements of a passing meal. If it does not have trip lines, the spider relies on feeling the vibrations of prey through the ground. If it senses a meal is nearby, it rushes from the burrow to grab the prey in its jaws.

Did you know? Trapdoor spiders may live up to 20 years in their burrows.

▲ **ODD SPIDER OUT**
A tiger wolf spider has dug out soil with its fangs and lined the walls of its burrow with silk. Most wolf spiders do not burrow. Instead, they chase their food, using their sharp vision and fangs to capture live insect prey.

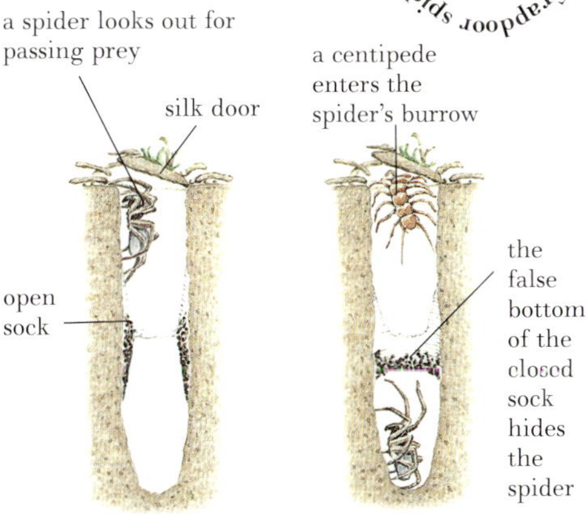

▲ **ALL KINDS OF TRAPS**
Trapdoor spider burrows range from simple tubes to elaborate lairs with hidden doors and escape tunnels. The burrow of *Anidiops villosus* has a collapsible sock. The spider pulls it down to form a false bottom, hiding it from predators.

The Hunt of the

The salticid jumping spiders are a huge spider family of about 5,000 species. They are found all over the world, and most are squat, hairy, and dull in colour, although some tropical species have splashes of brilliant, iridescent colour. All jumping spiders, however, have big, bulging eyes – all the better to hunt with! (If a human looks at a jumping spider, it will turn its tiny head to peer back.) As a family, salticids have the sharpest eyesight of any spider. Most species are constantly darting along jerkily, on the lookout for prey. They see in colour and form clear images of their victims, stalking as a cat stalks a mouse, crouching before the final pounce.

SIGN LANGUAGE
A male jumping spider's front legs are longer and thicker than a female's. He waves them about in courtship dances, like a sign language.

PREPARATION
Before it takes off, a jumping spider anchors itself firmly to a surface with a silk safety line. It pushes off with its four back legs and leaps on to the target. The Australian flying spider has wing-like flaps that enable it to glide.

STURDY LEGS
This female heavy jumper is feeding on a leaf-hopper. A jumping spider's legs do not seem to be specially adapted for jumping. Their small size (less than 15mm long) and light weight probably help them to make amazing leaps.

Jumping Spider

THE BIG LEAP

A jumping spider's strong front legs are often raised before a jump. They stretch forwards in the air, and grip fast on the prey when the spider lands. Hairy tufts on the feet help jumping spiders to grip surfaces that are smooth and vertical. They can even leap away from a vertical surface to seize a flying insect.

JUMPING CANNIBALS

This female two-striped jumping spider is feeding on another member of the salticid family. Some *Portia* jumping spiders vibrate the webs of orb-weaving spiders, imitating the movement of an insect struggling to escape. When the orb-weaver comes to investigate, the *Portia* spider pounces on it.

A Snake's Rare Meal

Snakes are all predators, but different species eat different foods and hunt in different ways. Some snakes eat a wide variety of prey, while others have a more specialized diet. Snakes have to make the most of each meal because they move fairly slowly and may not catch prey very often. A snake's body works at a slow rate, which means that it can go for months without eating.

▲ TREE HUNTERS
A rat snake, from North America, grasps a baby bluebird in its jaws and begins the process of digestion. Rat snakes often slither up trees in search of baby birds, eggs or squirrels.

rat snake
(Elaphe)

▲ FISHY SNACKS
The tentacled snake of southern Asia lives on fish. It hides among plants in the water and ambushes passing prey.

▼ TRICKY LURE
The Australasian death adder's colourful tail tip looks like a worm. The adder wriggles the 'worm' to lure birds and small mammals.

◀ **EGG-EATERS**

The African egg-eater snake checks an egg with its tongue to make sure it is fresh. Then it swallows the egg whole. It uses the pointed ends of the bones in its backbone to crack the eggshell. It eats the egg and then coughs up the crushed shell.

SURPRISE ATTACK ▶

Lunch for this gaboon viper is a mouse. The viper hides among dry leaves on the forest floors of West and Central Africa. Its colouring and markings camouflage it well. It waits for a small animal to pass, then grabs hold of it in a surprise attack. Many other snakes that hunt by day also ambush their prey.

Did you know? Sometimes a snake coughs up its prey – alive!

smooth snake
(Coronella austriaca)

◀ **SNAKE SNACK**

This smooth snake is eating an asp viper. The viper fits neatly inside the body of the smooth snake. This makes it easier to swallow than animals that are a different shape.

1 Rat snakes feed on rats, mice, voles, lizards, birds and eggs. Many of them hunt at night. They are good climbers and can even go up tree trunks with smooth bark and no branches. The snakes find their prey by following a scent trail or waiting to ambush an animal.

A Rat Snake's Lunch

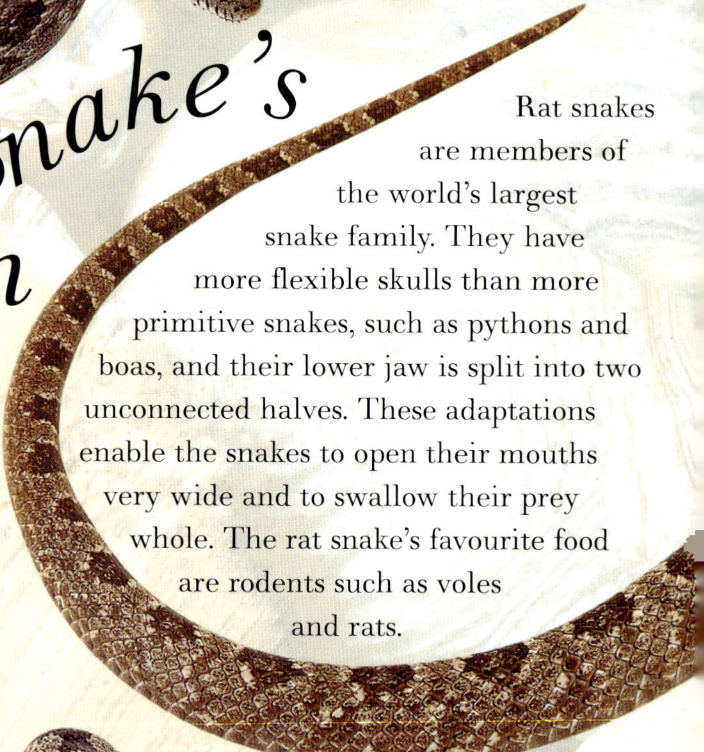

Rat snakes are members of the world's largest snake family. They have more flexible skulls than more primitive snakes, such as pythons and boas, and their lower jaw is split into two unconnected halves. These adaptations enable the snakes to open their mouths very wide and to swallow their prey whole. The rat snake's favourite food are rodents such as voles and rats.

2 When the rat snake is near enough to its prey, it strikes quickly. Its sharp teeth sink into the victim's body to stop it running or flying away. The snake then loops its coils around the victim as fast as possible, before the animal can bite or scratch to defend itself.

3 Each time the vole breathes out, the rat snake squeezes around the victim's rib cage to stop it breathing in again. Breathing becomes impossible, and the victim soon dies from suffocation.

4 Once the victim is dead, the rat snake loosens its coils and begins the process of swallowing. It unhinges its jaws and 'walks' its mouth over its meal. The loose lower jaw stretches sideways to fit around the shape of the dead prey.

5 The rat snake swallows its meal head-first. As the vole moves down the snake's throat, its legs fold back against the sides of its body. The way the fur lies makes it easier to swallow the vole. The snake's skin stretches as the meal moves down its body.

6 As the vole moves farther down inside the snake's body, the skin stretches more. The ribs move apart at the front to make space for the vole's body. The snake pushes its windpipe to the front of its mouth, so that it can use it like a snorkel for breathing. It may take only one or two gulps for a snake to swallow a small animal whole.

Crocodile Snacks

A big crocodile can survive for up to two years between meals. It lives off fat stored in its tail and other parts of its body. Generally, though, crocodilians (crocodiles, alligators and caimans) eat a lot of fish, although their strong jaws may snap up anything that wanders too close. Young crocodilians eat small animals such as insects, snails and frogs, while adults feed on birds, turtles and mammals. Big Nile crocodiles tackle large animals such as zebras and wildebeest when they visit the rivers to drink. Crocodiles cannot chew and have to tear large prey apart before swallowing it. They eat small prey whole, bones and all. Crocodiles also scavenge on dead animals.

Most crocodilians hunt at night and save energy by sitting and waiting for their food to pass their way. They may stalk prey, lunging forward or leaping out of the water to capture it. In water, a crocodile may sweep its open jaws from side to side to catch its next meal.

▲ **SURPRISE ATTACK**
A Nile crocodile lunges from the water at an incredible speed to grab a wildebeest in its powerful jaws. It is difficult for the wildebeest to jump back as the river bank slopes steeply into the water. The crocodile will plunge back into the water, dragging its prey with it in order to drown it.

▼ **CHEEKY BIRDS**
Large crocodiles feed on wading birds such as this saddlebill stork. Birds, however, often seem to know when they are in no danger from a crocodile. Plovers have been seen standing on the gums of crocodiles and even pecking at the fearsome teeth for leftovers. A marabou stork was once seen stealing a fish right out of a crocodile's mouth.

▶ **SMALLER PREY**

This dwarf caiman, hiding in floating debris, has just snapped up a tasty bullfrog. Caimans and other small crocodilians eat lots of frogs and toads, and also catch fish. The slim, pointed teeth of the Indian gharial are ideal for grasping any slippery fish that is within range, but its jaws are not strong enough to tackle anything bigger.

crocodilians have varied diets and will eat any animal they can catch

◀ **SWALLOWING PREY**

A crocodile raises its head and grips a crab firmly at the back of its throat. After several jerky head movements the crab is correctly positioned to be eaten whole. High levels of acid in the crocodile's stomach help it break down the crab's hard shell so that every part is digested.

Did you know? A Nile crocodile has a stomach that is about the size of a basketball!

▶ **FISHY FOOD**

A Nile crocodile swallows a fish head first so that the fish's spines do not stick in its throat. Fish make up about 70 per cent of the diet of most crocodilians, especially the narrow snouted species, such as the gharial of northern India and the African slender-snouted crocodile. The narrowness of the snout offers little water resistance in the sideways sweeping movement used to catch fish.

Ambush on

1 A Nile crocodile is nearly invisible as it lies almost submerged in wait for its prey. Only eyes, ears and nostrils are showing. The crocodile lurks in places where it knows prey will regularly visit the river. The dark olive of its skin is well camouflaged against the murky water. It may disappear completely beneath the water. Some crocodilians can hold their breath for more than an hour while they are submerged.

A crocodile quietly drifting near the shore looks just like a harmless, floating log. This is just a disguise as it waits for an unsuspecting animal to come down to the river to drink. The crocodile is in luck. A herd of zebras come to cross the river. The crocodile launches its attack with astonishing speed. Shooting forwards, it snaps shut its powerful jaws and sharp teeth like a vice around a zebra's leg or muzzle. The stunned zebra is pulled into deeper water to be drowned. Other crocodiles are attracted to the large kill. They gather round to bite into the carcass, rotating in the water to twist off large chunks of flesh. Grazing animals constantly risk death-by-crocodile to drink or cross water. There is little they can do to defend themselves from the attack of such a large predator.

2 The crocodile erupts from the water, taking the zebras by surprise. It lunges at its victim with a fast burst of energy. The crocodile must overcome its prey quickly as it cannot chase a zebra overland. It is also easily exhausted and takes a long time to recover from exercise of any kind.

the River Nile

3 The crocodile seizes, pulls and shakes the zebra in its powerful jaws. The victim's neck is sometimes broken in the attack and it dies quickly. More often the shocked animal is dragged into the water, struggling feebly against its attacker.

4 The crocodile drags the zebra into deeper water and holds it down to drown it. It may also spin round in a roll, until the prey stops breathing. The crocodile twists or rolls around over and over again, with the animal clamped in its jaws, until the prey is dead.

5 A freshly killed zebra attracts Nile crocodiles from all around. A large kill is too difficult for one crocodile to defend on its own. Several crocodiles take it in turns to share the feast and may help each other to tear the carcass apart. They fasten their jaws on to a part of the body and turn over and over in the water until a chunk of meat is twisted loose and can be swallowed whole.

A Swift Attack from Above

sparrowhawk
(Accipiter nisus)

Birds of prey hunt in different ways. A raptor, which is another name for any bird of prey, may sit on a perch and simply wait for a meal to appear on the ground or fly past. This technique is called 'still-hunting'. Other birds search for prey by flying low over open ground, or darting in and out of cover such as a clump of trees. Kestrels are among the raptors that hover in the air while looking for prey, and then swoop down suddenly on it. Peregrines are noted for their spectacular dives, or stoops. With wings almost folded, they dive on their prey from a great height, accelerating up to perhaps 300 kilometres an hour. Their aim is to strike the prey at high speed to kill it instantly. Peregrines either snatch prey from the air, or pick it off the ground.

▲ **SURPRISE, SURPRISE**
The sparrowhawk uses surprise and speed to make a kill. It flies under cover until it spots a potential meal, then dashes out into the open to snatch its unsuspecting prey at speed.

◄ **PLUCKY EAGLE**
An American bald eagle plucks a cattle egret it has just killed. The bird makes a change from the eagle's usual diet of fish. Most birds of prey pluck the feathers from birds they have caught before eating, as they cannot digest them. Owls are the only raptors to swallow their prey whole.

bald eagle
(Haliaeetus leucocephalus)

buzzard
(Buteo buteo)

◂ RABBIT RELISH

A common buzzard stands guard over the rabbit it has just killed. Over grassland, the buzzard hunts on the wing, sometimes hovering like a kestrel. Where there are trees or rocks, it may perch on a high point until it sights prey. The buzzard then swoops in for the kill.

▴ IN HOT PURSUIT

An African harrier hawk chases doves along the riverbank. Such chases more often than not end in failure. This hawk is about the same size as a typical harrier, but it has longer wings.

▾ IT'S A COVER-UP

A kestrel spreads its wings in an attempt to cover up the mouse it is preparing to eat on its feeding post. This behaviour is known as mantling, and is common among birds of prey. They do it to hide their food from other hungry birds that may try to rob them.

▾ MAKING A MEAL OF IT

A kestrel tucks into its kill on its favourite feeding post. The bird holds the prey with its feet and tears the flesh into small pieces with its sharp bill. It swallows small bones, but often discards big ones. Later, as with most raptors, it regurgitates pellets containing fur and other indigestible parts of its prey.

kestrel
(Falco tinnunculus)

Raptor Food

Birds of prey hunt all kinds of animals. Many attack other birds, such as sparrows, starlings and pigeons, which are usually taken in the air. Some raptors hunt small mammals, such as rabbits, rats, mice and voles. Large species of eagle may tackle even larger mammals. The Philippine eagle, and the harpy eagle of South America, for example, pluck monkeys from the rainforest canopy. Both species are massive birds, with bodies a metre long. Serpent eagles and secretary birds feast on snakes and other reptiles. Small birds of prey often feed on insects and worms. Most species will also supplement their diet by scavenging on carrion (the meat of dead animals) whenever they find it.

▲ **INSECT INSIDE**
A lesser kestrel prepares to eat a grasshopper it has just caught on a rooftop in Spain. This kestrel lives mainly on insects. It catches grasshoppers and beetles on the ground, and all kinds of flying insects while on the wing. When there are plenty of insects, flocks of lesser kestrels feed together. Unlike the larger common kestrel, the lesser kestrel does not hover when hunting.

golden eagle
(Aquila chrysaetos)

◄ **GOLDEN HUNTER**
A golden eagle stands guard over the squirrel it has just caught. This eagle usually hunts at low levels. It flushes out prey – mainly rabbits, hares and grouse – which it catches and kills on the ground. Whenever they get the chance, golden eagles also eat carrion.

martial eagle
(Polemaetus bellicosus)

▲ REPTILIAN SNACK
A martial eagle stands over its lizard kill in the Kruger National Park, South Africa. This is Africa's biggest eagle, and it is capable of taking prey as big as a small antelope.

The Fabulous Roc

In the tales of The Arabian Nights, *Sinbad the Sailor encountered enormous birds called rocs. They looked like eagles, but were gigantic in size, and preyed on elephants and other large beasts. In this picture, the fearsome rocs are dropping huge boulders on Sinbad's ship in an attempt to finally destroy him.*

Did you know? 12 species of birds of prey eat only insects.

▼ SNAIL SPECIALIST
A snail kite eyes its next meal. This is the most specialized feeder among birds of prey, eating only freshwater snails. It breeds in the Everglades National Park, Florida, USA.

▲ COBRA KILLER
A pale chanting goshawk has caught and killed a yellow cobra. The chanting goshawks earned their name because of their noisy calls in the breeding season. The African plains are the hunting grounds of both the pale and the dark chanting goshawks, which feed mainly on lizards and snakes but also eat small mammals.

snail kite
(Rostrhamus sociabilis)

The Barn Owl's

1 An owl waits for a rustle in the undergrowth. Suddenly it hears something. It swivels its head, and its sensitive ears pinpoint exactly where the sound is coming from. The owl then spots its prey – a mouse rummaging among the leaf litter on the ground.

2 Keeping its eyes glued on its potential meal, the owl launches into the air. It brings its body forwards, pushes off the post with its feet and opens its wings. The mouse is just a few metres away. It is busy searching for grubs and insects, and does not hear the swift, silent swoop.

The barn owl is found on all continents except Antarctica. It is easily recognizable because of its white, heart-shaped facial disc. Its eyes are relatively small for an owl, but it can still see well at night. The barn owl tracks its prey as much by ear as by eye. Its hearing is particularly keen, because the feathers on its facial disc channel sounds into its ears with great precision. The owl featured here is 'still-hunting' – the tactic of watching for prey from a favourite perch. However, barn owls also often hunt on the wing. They cruise slowly and silently back and forth over their feeding grounds until they hear or spy prey, then swoop down silently for the kill.

Silent Strike

3 The owl makes a beeline for its prey with powerful beats of its wings. Even though it is travelling quite fast, it still makes no sound. Dense, soft feathers cover its wings and legs and muffle the sound of air flowing over them. Its noiseless flight allows the owl to concentrate on the sounds that the mouse is making and so keep track of its prey.

5 Now only a few centimetres above the ground, the owl thrusts its feet forwards, claws spread wide, and drops on the prey. At the same time, it spreads its wings and tail to slow down the approach. The hunter's aim is deadly. Its talons close round the mouse and crush it to death. Then the owl transfers the dead mouse to its beak and returns to its perch. The owl will swallow the mouse head-first.

4 The mouse at last begins to sense that something is wrong. For an instant it is glued to the spot in fear. Then it starts to run for its life. However, the owl is more than a match for it. By making use of its rounded wings and broad tail, the bird can twist and turn easily in the air, following the scuttling mouse at every change of direction.

Eating on the Hoof

The world's most successful herbivores (plant-eaters) are animals with hoofs, such as horses, cattle, deer and sheep. They use speed, endurance and sure-footedness to escape predators, and have digestive systems that make the most of vegetable diets. To convert low-quality food such as grass into body-building energy, an animal's digestive system has to break down tough cellulose fibre. One group of animals, which includes cattle, deer and sheep, do this by ruminating – they eat then later regurgitate the food, and chew it again slowly to draw as much goodness out of it as possible. Horses have a less efficient digestive system and have to spend more time eating than other grazers.

▲ **RIVER HORSE**
Hippopotamuses graze for a few hours each night, delicately plucking grasses with their broad, horny lips. Although they are huge animals, they can manage on about 40kg of grass each night because they rest in the water all day.

▶ **HIGH LIVING**
In Africa's open woodland savanna, giraffes browse the tops of trees that are out of reach to other herbivores. Their prehensile (grasping) lips and long, flexible tongues can pick out the most digestible and tasty leaves. Giraffes eat in the cool parts of the day and chew the cud while resting in the hot mid-day.

▲ **TINY PUDU**
The pudu of South America is the world's smallest deer. It lives in beech forests, feeding on flowers, fruit, bark and other vegetation. Like other deer and cattle, it spends a lot of its time resting and chewing the cud.

▲ **TRAVELLING COMPANIONS**
The wildebeest, or gnu, are grazers of the African plains. Every dry season, when their food supply is exhausted, these big antelopes move to fresh pastures with permanent water and shade. They travel in vast herds along well-worn routes, joined by zebra and other grazing animals.

▲ **VARIED DIET**
Warthogs feed almost entirely on grasses. After the rains, they pluck the growing tips with their incisor teeth or their lips. At the end of the rains they eat grass seeds, and in the dry season they use the hard upper edge of their nose to dig up roots.

▼ **HIGH-SPEED GAZELLE**
Thomson's gazelles use the same food-plants as other grazers of the African plains, but each animal eats a different part of the plant. Zebras tackle the tough woody bits, wildebeest eat the leaves, and gazelles nibble at the new growth beneath.

▼ **FIGHTING HORNS**
Male bighorn sheep, like other ruminants, make use of their horns when defending their territory or their females. Bighorn sheep have adapted to a wide range of habitats in North America, from desert to chilly alpine areas. They establish seasonal pathways to fresh grazing grounds when food runs out in the harsh winters. As they bound over rocky ground, their padded feet grip and absorb the shock of impact.

Horse Power

Cows and other ruminants have an extra chance to chew every bit of goodness from their vegetable diet. Horses, however, have to gain their nutrients by eating more, but are able to survive and thrive on grass, the most nutrient-poor diet of all.

The horse's digestive system processes large quantities of food in order to extract enough energy. They have an extra-long digestive system – of around 30m – to push as much food as they can through their bodies and convert it quickly to energy. Horses run on a virtually non-stop cycle of eating, digesting and producing waste. In the wild, they graze for about 16 hours a day, from early in the morning until around midnight. Horses can survive on poor vegetation as long as there is plenty of it. Cattle can manage with less food, as long as it is of a reasonable quality.

▲ **CHEWING STYLE**
A horse's slow, deliberate style of eating ensures that food is thoroughly ground down. Horses nibble vegetation with their front incisor teeth, then grind it down with their molars before swallowing. They chew slowly and wash the food down with plenty of saliva to aid digestion.

◄ **HARD TIMES**
Cold weather has made the ground hard, and snow covers the scant winter vegetation. These horses must paw at the ground to uncover the grass and dig up roots. They may even eat tree bark. Weak horses may not survive a hard winter.

STRESS IN THE STABLE ►

When domestic horses are brought into stables they are fed well but often only three times a day. This is very different from a horse's natural feeding pattern, which is continuous and varied grazing. Bored stabled horses sometimes develop 'vices', such as crib-chewing, tongue swallowing and rug-chewing. Although a domesticated horse may be given nutritious fodder, it is starved of its natural behaviour.

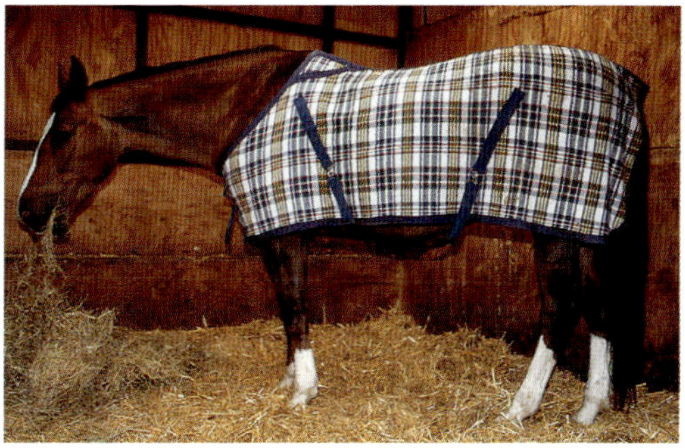

◄ SURVIVAL IN DRY LAND

Grevy's zebras live in dry thornbush country on the African plains. If water is scarce, they migrate to the highlands. They can survive, however, on grasses, or even bushes, that are too tough for other herbivores to eat. They also dig waterholes – and defend them fiercely.

▲ ALTERNATIVE FOODS

A horse from the New Forest, England, uses its flexible lips to pick some gorse flowers. Horses often choose more interesting foods than grass when they are available. They push out unwanted bits with their tongue.

▲ WATERHOLE

Wild horses drink daily, although they can go without water for long periods of time. Most animals only drink fresh water. Wild asses and some species of zebra can tolerate brackish (stale, salty) water. This gives them a better chance of surviving droughts than fellow grazers, such as antelope.

Elephant Appetites

As herbivores, elephants only eat plants. Their diet is much more varied than that of horses, however, as it is made up of more than 100 different kinds of plants. Elephants eat leaves, flowers, fruit, seeds, roots, bark and even thorns, but still need huge quantities to gain enough nutrients to survive. They spend about 16 hours a day picking and eating their food. As with cattle and horses, millions of microscopic organisms live inside an elephant's gut, which help it to digest food. Even with the help of these organisms, half the food eaten by an elephant is not digested when it leaves the body.

▲ **STRIPPING BARK**
An elephant munches on tree bark, which provides it with essential minerals and fibre. The elephant pushes its tusks under the bark to pull it away from the tree trunk. Then it peels off a strip by pulling with its trunk.

◀ **EATING THORNS**
Elephants do not mind swallowing a mouthful of thorns – as long as there are some tasty leaves attached. Leaves and thorns are an important part of an elephant's diet as they stay green in the dry season long after the grasses have dried up. This is because trees and bushes have long roots to reach water deep underground.

▼ **GRASSY DIET**
Marshes are packed full of juicy grasses. About 30–60 per cent of an elephant's diet is grass. On dry land, an elephant may beat grass against its leg to remove the soil before feeding.

Did you know? Elephants can become drunk by eating overripe fruit.

BABY FOOD ►
Young elephants often feed on the dung of adult elephants. They do this to pick up microscopic organisms that will live inside their gut and help them digest food. Youngsters learn what is good to eat by copying their mothers and other adults. They are also curious and like to try new types of food.

◄ DUNG FOOD
Elephant dung provides a feast for dung beetles and thousands of other insects. They lay their eggs in the dung, and the young feed on it when they hatch. Certain seeds only sprout in dung after having first passed through an elephant.

EATING IN CAPTIVITY ►
Meals for captive elephants include grasses and molasses (a type of sugar). Zoo elephants eat hay, bread, nuts, fruit, leaves, bark and vegetables. They need huge amounts. In the wild, elephants eat 100–200kg of plants every day – that equates to about 1–2,000 carrots!

Food in Season

Although bears are classified as meat-eating animals (carnivores), most of them eat whatever is available at different times of the year. They have binges and put on fat in times of plenty, then fast when food is scarce. Brown bears are typical of most bears in that they eat an enormous variety of food, from grasses, herbs and berries to ants and other insects. They also catch salmon, rodents, and birds, and on rare occasions hunt bigger game, such as caribou and seals. Only polar bears eat almost entirely meat – usually young seals. In summer, however, they supplement their diet with grasses and berries. All bears, even bamboo-loving pandas, scavenge on the carcasses of prey left by other animals. To track down their food, bears rely mainly on their keen sense of smell. Their snouts are well-developed in relation to their small ears and eyes.

Goldilocks
Bears are often featured in children's stories, such as Goldilocks and the three bears. They are regularly portrayed as friendly animals, however bears are not always so friendly, they plot to ambush their prey and use their size to overcome them.

American black bear
(Ursus americanus)

▸ **HUNTING DOWN A MEAL**
This American black bear has caught a white-tailed deer fawn. Both black and brown bears are successful hunters. They are able to ambush large animals and kill them by using their considerable bulk, strong paws and jaws. The size of the bear determines the size of its prey. Large brown bears may prey on moose, caribou, bison, musk ox, seals and stranded whales. The smaller black bears take smaller prey, such as deer fawns, lemmings and hares. Roots, fruit, seeds and nuts, however, form up to 80 per cent of the diet of both species.

WALRUS CITY ▸
Polar bears arrive on the northern coast of Russia each summer to hunt walruses that have gone there to breed. Enormous adult walruses shrug off attacks, but the young walrus pups are more vulnerable.

▲ BEACHCOMBING
Brown bears visit rivers and estuaries, hoping for a fishy meal. They overturn stones to find crabs and crayfish underneath. Bears are also attracted to rubbish on beaches and campsites.

▲ FRUIT LOVERS
An American black bear snacks on the ripe berries of a mountain ash tree. It carefully uses its incisors (front teeth) to strip the berries from their woody stem.

▲ INSECT EATERS
Two sloth bear cubs from southern Asia learn to dig up termites. Sloth bears use their sickle-shaped claws to break open ant hills, bees' nests and termite mounds. They have developed an ingenious way of collecting their insect food. First they blow away any dust. Then they form a suction tube with mouth and tongue, through which they vacuum up their food.

Fishing Match

Brown and black bears sometimes overcome their reluctance to be with other bears when there is plenty of food available. This often happens on the rivers of the northwest coast of North America. Thousands of salmon come in from the sea and head upriver to spawn (lay their eggs). The bears fish alongside each other at sites such as rapids where the water is shallower and the salmon are easier to see. An uneasy truce exists between the bears, although isolated fights do occur. The salmon runs take place at different times of the year, but the most important are those in the months leading up to winter. The bears catch the oil-rich salmon to get the extra fat they need to see them through the long winter ahead.

▲ **STRIPPED TO THE BONE**
Having caught a fish, the bear holds it firmly in its forepaws. Then it strips the skin and flesh from the bones.

▲ **EASY MEAL**
Salmon sometimes jump right into a bear's mouth. The bear stands at the edge of a small waterfall. Here the salmon must leap clear of the water to continue their journey upriver. All the bear needs to do is open its mouth.

◀ **FIGHT FOR SPACE**
Sometimes the uncertain truce between bears breaks down and they fight for the best fishing sites in the river. Young bears playfight, but older ones fight for real. An open mouth, showing the long canine teeth, is a warning to an opponent. If the intruder fails to back down it is attacked. Fights are often soon over, because the bears are keen to return to their abundant source of fish.

▲ **FISHING LESSON**
Bear cubs watch closely as their mother catches a salmon. The cubs learn by example and will eventually try it themselves. It will be a long time before they are as skilful as their mother.

▲ **A SLOUTHE OF BEERYS**
A group of bears is called a sloth. Brown bears on a salmon river are 'a sloth of grizzlies'. The term 'a slouthe of beerys' was used in the Middle Ages. It came from the word 'sloth' (laziness) as people thought bears were slow and lazy.

Wild Cat Feasts

All big cats are carnivores (meat-eaters). In the wild, they hunt and kill their own food, and also steal kills from other animals. Cheetahs, however, only eat animals they have killed themselves. They patrol their neighbourhoods, stalking prey. Other cats, such as jaguars, hide in wait before ambushing their victims. Many cats, including leopards, employ both tactics. In either case, camouflage is vital. Many of their prey can outpace them over distances, so big cats have to creep close to their victims unnoticed before going in for the kill.

King Solomon

Solomon ruled Israel in the 900s BC and was reputed to be very wise. His throne was carved with lions because of his admiration for these big cats who killed only out of necessity. In law, if a missing person was said to have fallen into a lion's den, it meant that there was no proof of his or her death.

◀ **THE MAIN COURSE**
A lion can kill large, powerful animals such as buffalo. A big cat usually attacks from behind, or from the side. The prey may be too big to kill right away. If so, the cat knocks it off balance, takes a grip and bites into its neck.

CHOOSING A MEAL ▶
A herd of grazing antelope and zebra keeps watch on a lioness crouched in the grass. The lioness lies as close to the ground as possible, waiting to pounce. When she has focused on a victim, she draws back her hind legs and springs forwards.

▲ CAT AND MOUSE
A recently killed capybara (a large rodent) makes a tasty meal for a jaguar. Jaguars often catch prey such as fish and turtles in water. On land they hunt armadillos, deer, opossums, skunks, snakes, squirrels, tortoises and monkeys.

▲ WARTHOG SPECIAL
Four cheetahs surround an injured warthog. The mother cheetah is teaching her three cubs hunting techniques. The cheetah on the right is trying a left paw side swipe, while another uses its claws. Cheetahs love to eat warthogs but also catch antelope and smaller animals such as hares.

Did you know? Cheetahs will only chase prey if it runs. If it stops, so does the cheetah.

SLOW FOOD ►
If a lion has not been able to hunt successfully for a while, it will eat small creatures such as this tortoise. Lions usually hunt big animals such as antelope, wildebeest, warthogs, buffalo, bush pigs and baboons. They work together in a group to hunt large prey.

Cats Go in for the Kill

Did you know? Lions try to flip porcupines on to their backs to avoid the sharp spines.

The way a wild cat kills its prey depends on the size of both predator and prey. If the prey is small with a bite-sized neck, it is killed with a bite through the spinal cord. Alternatively, a cat can crush the back of a small skull in its powerful jaws. Large prey is gripped by the throat so that it suffocates.

Cats stalk silently, their acute senses of sight, smell and hearing on the alert. Their ears are shaped and move to capture even the slightest of sounds.

lion
(Panthera leo)

▼ PAST ITS BEST
When big cats get old or injured it is very difficult for them to hunt. They eventually die from starvation. This lion from the Kalahari Desert in South Africa is old and thin. It has been weakened by hunger.

◄ FAIR GAME
A warthog is a delicious meal for a cheetah. Because the cheetah is quite a light cat, it must first knock over warthog-sized prey. It then bites the windpipe so that the victim cannot breathe.

▲ A DEADLY EMBRACE
A lioness immobilizes a struggling wildebeest by biting its windpipe and suffocating it. Lions are very strong. A lion weighing 150–250kg can kill a buffalo more than twice its weight. Lions live in groups called prides and the females do most of the hunting.

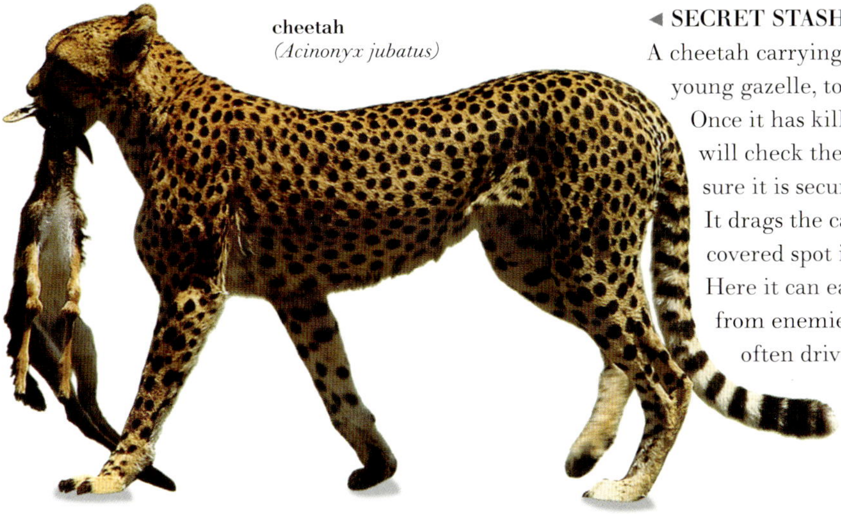
cheetah
(Acinonyx jubatus)

◀ **SECRET STASH**

A cheetah carrying off its prey, a young gazelle, to a safe place. Once it has killed, a cheetah will check the area to make sure it is secure before feeding. It drags the carcass to a covered spot in the bushes. Here it can eat its meal hidden from enemies. Cheetahs are often driven off and robbed of their kills by hyenas and jackals or even other big cats.

A SOLID MEAL ▶

These cheetahs will devour as much of this antelope as they can. Big cats lie on the ground and hold their food with their forepaws when they eat. When they have satisfied their hunger, cheetahs cover up or hide the carcass with grass, leaves or whatever is available in order to save it for later.

▶ **LIONS' FEAST**

A pride of lions gathers around its kill. Lions often combine forces to kill large prey. One lion grabs the prey's throat, while the others attack from behind. The cats eat quickly before scavengers move in. Each has to wait its turn to eat. The dominant male usually eats first.

High-speed Cats

A cheetah is the world's fastest land animal. It can run at 115km/hour – the equivalent of a car being driven at high speed – but only over short distances. The cheetah's body is fine-tuned for short bursts of speed, with wide nostrils to breathe in as much oxygen as possible and specially adapted paws. Today, most cheetahs are found in east and southern Africa, with small populations in Iran and Pakistan. They live in many different kinds of habitats, from open grassland to thick bush, or even near-desert environments.

1 A pair of cheetahs creep up stealthily on a herd of antelope. Cheetahs hunt their prey by slinking slowly towards it, holding their heads low. They are not pouncing killers, like other big cats. Instead, they pull down their prey after a very fast chase. In order to waste as little energy as possible, cheetahs plan their attack first. They pick out their target before starting the chase.

2 The cheetah begins its chase as the herd of antelope starts to move. It can accelerate from walking pace to around 70km/hour in two seconds. Cheetahs have retractable claws (they can draw them in). However, unlike the claws of other cats, they have no protective sheaths. When drawn, the exposed claws act like the spikes on the bottom of track shoes. This, combined with ridges on the paw pads, help cheetahs to grip when running.

3 At top speed a cheetah makes full use of its flexible spine and lean, supple physique. Its legs are very long and slender compared to its body. The cat can cover several metres in a single bound.

of the Plains

4 As the cheetah closes in on the herd, the antelope spring in all directions. The big cat changes direction at full speed. If it does not catch its prey within about 400m, it has to give up, as it can only keep up speed over short distances. Cheetahs usually hunt in the morning or late in the afternoon, when it is not too hot. Their life expectancy is short because their speed and hunting ability decline with age.

5 As the cheetah may have to make several sharp turns as it closes in on its prey. Its long tail gives it excellent balance as it turns. The cheetah knocks its victim off balance with a swipe of a front paw. Most chases last no more than about 30 seconds.

6 Once the prey animal is down, the cheetah grabs the victim's throat. A sharp bite suffocates the antelope. Cheetahs are not strong enough to kill by biting through the spinal cord in the prey's neck like other cats. They just hang on to the victim's throat until the animal is dead.

Hungry Canines

Wolves and other wild dogs are carnivores. They kill prey for fresh meat, but also eat carrion (dead animals). When no meat is available, they will eat fruit and berries, and also grass to aid digestion. As good long-distance runners, wild dogs can range over large territories in search of food. Packs of wolves target large herd animals such as moose, deer and caribou. They swim well and chase fish, frogs and crabs, but still spend much of their lives with empty bellies. When food is scarce, they sometimes rifle through rubbish near human settlements, or kill domestic animals such as sheep and cattle.

Most wild dogs have long, fang-like canine teeth to stab or pierce their prey. At the back of the mouth they have sharp-edged teeth for slicing through the flesh.

▲ NOT-SO-FUSSY FEEDERS
Raccoon dogs of eastern Asia eat all kinds of different foods, including rodents, fruit and acorns. Raccoon dogs also catch fish, frogs and water beetles and scavenge carrion and scraps from people's rubbish tips.

▼ CAUGHT BY COYOTES
Three coyotes tear at the carcass of a moose. These North American dogs usually hunt small prey such as mice. Sometimes they band together to go after larger creatures, or to gang up on other predators and steal their kills.

◄ FAST FOOD

A pack of dholes (an Asian species of wild dog) makes quick work of a deer carcass. Each dog eats fast to get its share – it may eat up to 4kg of meat in an hour. Dholes mainly eat mammals, but if meat is scarce they will also eat berries, lizards and insects.

▲ LONE HUNTER

A maned wolf is searching for food. Without a pack to help it hunt, this South American wolf looks for easy prey in open country, including armadillos and small rodents. It also eats birds, reptiles, insects, fruit and sugar cane.

▲ BEACH SQUABBLE

Two black-backed jackals squabble over the carcass of a seal pup. Jackals eat almost anything – fruit, frogs, reptiles and a wide range of mammals, from gazelles to mice. Jackals also scavenge kills from other hunters.

HIDDEN TREASURE ►

A wolf looks for a suitable spot in the snow to bury a freshly caught hare. After a pack has killed a large beast, or when a lone hunter has eaten its fill, it hides the remains of its food. Then, when food is scarce, the wolf can return to the hidden cache and retrieve its kill.

grey wolf
(Canis lupus)

Did you know? All canids are quick feeders, but dholes in particular consume their food at a great rate.

Wild Dog Hunt

The smaller species of wild dog, such as foxes and jackals, tend to hunt small prey such as rodents, alone or in pairs. Some, including the solitary maned wolf, the bush dogs of the Americas and raccoon dogs, are mainly nocturnal (active at night). They rely on smell and hearing to find prey.

Dholes and African hunting dogs hunt in packs by day. They track prey by sight, smell and sound. Wolves hunt at any time of day or night. Hunting in packs means that larger prey can be tackled – ideally large enough to feed the whole pack. The size of a pack depends on the amount of food available in the area. Members of a pack work together like a sports team, with individuals providing particular strengths. Some may be good trackers, while others are fast or powerful. A hunt may last for several hours, but many are unsuccessful.

Little Red Riding Hood
In the story of Little Red Riding Hood, *a cunning wolf eats Red Riding Hood's grandmother. The wolf then steals the old woman's clothes to prey on the little girl. Fortunately a wood cutter rescues Red Riding Hood in the nick of time. After he kills the wolf, the grandmother emerges alive from inside its stomach.*

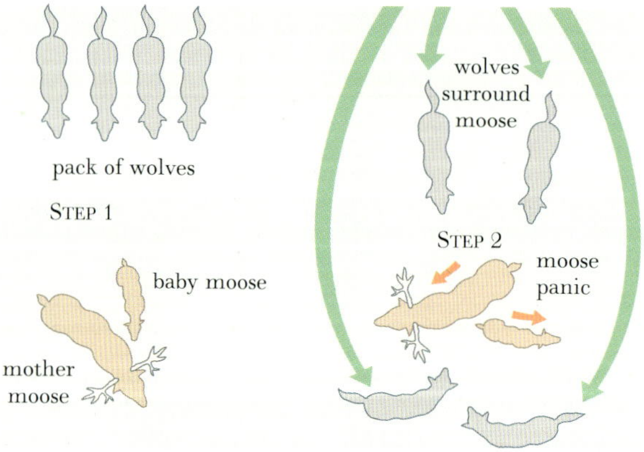

◄ WOLF PACK IN ACTION
Wolves use skill as well as strength to hunt large creatures such as moose. A calf is an easier target than an adult but will provide less meat. The wolves stalk their prey, then fan out and run ahead to surround the victim. Pack members dash forward to panic the animals and separate the mother from her baby. Once the young calf is alone, the wolves run it down and kill it by biting its neck.

DINGO KILL ▶
Two dingoes have just caught a kangaroo. In the Australian outback, dingoes hunt a wide range of creatures, from tiny grasshoppers and lizards to large prey such as wild pigs and kangaroos. Sheep, introduced by settlers in the 1800s, are a favourite target.

◀ GROUP HUNTING
A large pack of wolves has killed a white-tailed deer. This amount of meat will not satisfy the group for long. Where food is scarce, a pack has to range over a much larger territory to find enough food. A pack will always hunt the largest game it can find.

coyote
(Canis latrans)

Did you know To be in peak condition, a wolf needs to eat 4kg of meat a day.

CLEVER TACTICS ▶
A coyote plays with a mouse it has surprised in the snow. Coyotes often hunt mice. They leap high in the air to pounce on their victims. Coyotes have a more varied diet than wolves, feeding on fruit, grass, berries and insects, as well as mammals such as rabbits, deer and rodents. They take to the water to catch fish and frogs, and also steal sheep and chickens – which makes them unpopular with farmers.

▲ TEAMWORK
Working as a team, dholes hunt large prey such as sambar (a type of deer). Dholes whistle to keep in touch with one another as they surround their prey. Teamwork also helps the pack to defend the kill from scavengers such as vultures.

Hunting Dogs of

African hunting dogs eat more meat than any other wild dog. One in every three of their hunts ends in a kill, which is a very high success rate. They live on the savanna (grassy plains) of central and southern Africa, which is also home to vast herds of grazing animals such as wildebeest, gazelle and other antelopes. The pack wanders freely over a huge area, looking for herd animals to prey on. They rely on sight to find their quarry, so they hunt during daylight hours or on bright moonlit nights. They hunt mainly at dusk or dawn, when the air is coolest, and rest in the shade during the hottest time of day.

1 A pack of African hunting dogs begins to run down its quarry, a powerful wildebeest. On the open plains of the Serengeti in East Africa, there is little cover that would enable the dogs to sneak up on their prey. The hunt is often a straightforward chase. The hunt may be led by a junior dog at the start of the pursuit.

2 The dogs run along at an easy lope at first. They have tested out the wildebeest herd to find an easy target. They look for weak, injured, or young and inexperienced animals that will make suitable victims. This wildebeest is an older animal whose strength may be failing.

the African Plains

3 A hunting dog tries to seize the wildebeest's tail. Members of the pack with different strengths and skills take on particular roles during the hunt. The lead dogs are in excellent condition and strong. They dodge out of the way if the wildebeest turns to defend itself with its sharp hooves and horns. Fast runners spread out to surround the victim and cut off its escape.

4 As the wildebeest tires, two dogs grip its snout and tail, pinning it down. Hunting dogs can run at 50km/hour for quite a distance, but their prey is much quicker. While the lead dogs follow the fleeing animal's twists and turns, backmarkers take a more direct line to save their strength. The rear dogs take over the chase as the leaders tire.

5 More dogs arrive and the strongest move in for the kill. While some dogs hold their victim by the snout and flanks, others jump up to knock it off balance. The dogs attack their victim's sides and rump and soon the animal is bleeding freely. It begins to weaken through shock and loss of blood.

6 The wildebeest crashes to the ground and the dogs rip at its underparts to kill it There is little snapping and snarling as they eat, but the kill is fiercely defended if a scavenger such as a jackal comes close. Half-grown cubs feed first, then the carcass is ripped apart and bones, skin and all are eaten. Back at the den, meat is regurgitated to feed the cubs.

Forest Food for Apes

Apes live in the rainforests of Africa and Asia and feed on fruit and leaves. They also eat a small amount of animal food, such as insects. Chimpanzees have a more varied diet than other apes and occasionally eat red meat from birds and mammals, such as monkeys and young antelopes. Orang-utans have also been seen eating young birds and squirrels.

Apes spend a lot of time travelling all over the forest to find their food. If they stayed in one place, they would quickly use up all the food. They remember the locations of the best fruit trees in their area, and know when they will bear fruit. Apes have to eat a lot because a diet that consists mainly of plant food is often low in nutrients. As they cannot digest the tough fibres (cellulose) in the stems and leaves, much of what they eat passes through their gut undigested.

▲ **HUNGRY GIBBON**
Gibbons, from South-east Asia, are mainly frugivores (fruit eaters) but they also eat leaves and occasionally insects and eggs. They are so light and have such long arms that they can hang from thin branches and pick the ripest fruit growing right at the ends.

► **BANANA BONANZA**
Orang-utans live in the forest canopies of South-east Asia. Fruit forms about 65 per cent of their diet. The apes spread the seeds over a wide area by passing them in their droppings far from the parent tree. This female has found some bananas, but the football-sized fruit of the durian tree is another orang-utan favourite. It contains a sweet-tasting but foul-smelling flesh, which they adore.

▲ **MASSIVE MEALS**
Gorillas are mainly herbivores, munching their way through 20–30kg of greens (equal to 40 cabbages) every day. They smack their lips a lot and make other appreciative noises. Gorillas are careful eaters, often preparing their food by folding leaves into a roll, or peeling off inedible layers. They drop any unwanted stalks, in a neat pile.

▲ **RAIDING PARTY**
Chimpanzees live in communities in West and Central Africa. They eat both meat and vegetable matter and may band together to form a raiding party to hunt small animals such as monkeys and bush pigs. A hunt may last up to two hours, involving high-speed chases and ambushes.

▲ **FOOD ALL AROUND**
The upland rainforests of Central and eastern Africa are full of plant food for the mountain gorillas that live there. They eat leaves, roots and fruit, soft bark and fungi. The gorillas need to eat a lot of food, so meals last two to four hours at a time. They have big stomachs to store the food while it is being digested. Gorilla days are mainly spent walking and eating food, then resting between meals to digest it.

▼ **CHIMP FEASTS**
Chimpanzees spend about six hours a day feeding, mostly just after sunrise and just before sunset. They eat a lot of fruit, which makes up about 68 per cent of their diet, but they also eat leaves and other plant matter, as well as meat and insects.

chimpanzee
(Pan troglodytes)

▲ **CRUNCHY KRILL**
These tiny shrimp-like creatures known as krill form the diet of many baleen whales. Measuring up to 75mm long, they swim in vast shoals, often covering areas of several square kilometres. Most krill are found in Antarctic waters.

Whale Feeding

About 90 per cent of whales have pointed teeth that are ideal for grasping slippery fish. The other ten percent, known as baleen whales, do not have any teeth. Brush-like plates of horny baleen hang from the upper jaw. A baleen whale takes a mouthful of seawater and sieves it out through the baleen plates. Food such as fish, algae and krill, is held back in the baleen, and then swallowed. Toothed whales catch single fish, while baleen whales eat a mass in one go.

◄ **PLOUGHING**
A grey whale ploughs into the seabed, stirring up sand and ooze. It dislodges tiny crustaceans, called amphipods, and gulps them down. Grey whales feed mostly in summer in the Arctic before they migrate south.

southern right whale
(Euhalaena australis)

◄ **SKIM FEEDING**
With its mouth open, a southern right whale filters crustaceans, called copepods, out of the water with its baleen. The whale is huge, up to 80 tonnes, and it needs to eat up to two tonnes of the copepods daily. Usually, right whales feed alone, but if food is plentiful, several feed as they cruise side by side.

◄ **SUCCULENT SQUID**

Squid is the sperm whale's favourite food and is eaten by other toothed whales and dolphins as well. Squid are molluscs, in the same animal order as snails and octopuses. They have eight arms and two tentacles, and are called decapods (meaning ten feet). Squid swim together in dense shoals, many thousand strong.

Did you know? A blue whale eats nearly 1,000kg of krill in a single meal.

◄ **TOOTHY SMILE**

A Ganges river dolphin has more than 100 teeth. The front ones are very long. Ganges river dolphins eat mainly fish, and also take shrimps and crabs. They usually feed at night and find their prey by echo-location.

Ganges river dolphin
(Platanista gangetica)

► **SUCKING UP A MEAL**

Belugas feed on squid, small fish and crustaceans. Unlike common dolphins, belugas do not have many teeth. They suck prey into their mouths and then crush it with their teeth. Beaked whales also suck in their prey – mainly deep-sea squid – as their teeth are not suitable for grasping hold of fish.

▲ **HUNT THE SQUID**

The sperm whale is the largest toothed whale, notable for its huge head and tiny lower jaw. It hunts the giant squid that live in waters around 2,000m deep. At that depth, in total darkness, it hunts its prey by echo-location.

A Killer Whale

1 A killer whale hunts by itself if it chances upon a likely victim, such as a lone sea lion. This hungry whale has spotted a sea lion splashing in the surf at the water's edge. With powerful strokes of its tail, it surges towards its prey. The whale's tall dorsal fin shows that it is a fully-grown male.

Among the toothed whales, the killer whale, or orca, is the master predator. It bites and tears its prey to pieces with its fearsome teeth and may also batter them with its powerful tail. It is the only whale to take warm-blooded prey. Fortunately, there is no record of a killer whale ever attacking human beings. As well as fish and squid, a killer whale will hunt seals, penguins, dolphins and porpoises. It may even attack a large baleen whale many times its size. Killer whales live in family groups called pods. They often go hunting together, which greatly improves the chance of success.

2 The sea lion seems totally unaware of what is happening but, in any case, it is nearly helpless in the shallow water. The belly of the killer whale is scraping the shore as it homes in for the kill.

on a Seal Hunt

3 Suddenly the killer's head bursts out of the water, and its jaws gape open. Vicious teeth, curving inwards and backwards, are exposed. It is ready to sink them into its sea lion prey. The killer whale has fewer teeth than most toothed whales, but they are large and very strong.

4 Now the killer snaps its jaws shut, clamping the sea lion in a vice-like grip. With its prey struggling helplessly, it slides back into deep water to eat its fill. Killer whales are in danger of stranding themselves on the beach when they lunge after prey. They usually manage to wriggle their way back into the sea with the help of the surf.

Sea Hunters

Most sharks are fearsome carnivores and streamlined swimmers with an amazing sense of smell. Some make the most of their powerful, torpedo-shaped bodies to chase or pounce suddenly upon their prey. Others can be more leisurely, as they have special tracking and hunting adaptations. The lantern shark has organs on its skin that produce light and lure prey to certain death. The wide-spaced eyes of the hammerhead give it a wide field of vision to spot its favourite food of sting rays. The shortfin mako is one of the world's fastest sharks and can leap high above the water's surface. The white shark can leap, too, and has an awesome set of razor-sharp teeth to rip into large prey such as seals and dolphins.

▲ **FEEDING FRENZY**
Large quantities of food will excite grey reef sharks, sending them into a feeding frenzy. If divers hand out food, the sharks will circle with interest, until one darts forward for the first bite. Other sharks quickly follow, grabbing at the food until they seem out of control.

▲ **FOREVER EATING**
A large shoal of mating squid provides a great feast for blue sharks. The sharks feed until full, then empty their stomachs to start again!

▲ **FISH BALL**
A group of sharks can herd shoals of fish into a tight ball. The sharks will then pick off fish from the outside of the ball, one by one.

▶ NOT POWERFUL ENOUGH

The black-tipped shark is generally a powerful swimmer, but this one was caught by a larger relative, the bull shark. Black-tipped sharks hunt in the shallow waters of tropical seas, using their amazing sense of smell. Small fish hide out of reach in rocky crevices to escape.

Did you know? The great white shark sometimes eats crabs and lobsters.

◀ OCEAN DUSTBIN

Most sharks will eat anything that swims into their territory, and many are scavengers. Tiger sharks, though, are notorious for the variety of their diet. They have been known to eat coal, rubber tyres, clothes – and humans – and they move into coastal waters at night to feed. They are found all over the world and grow to a length of 5.5m.

▼ BITESIZE CHUNKS

The cookie-cutter shark feeds by cutting chunks out of whales and dolphins, such as this spinner dolphin. The shark uses its mouth like a clamp, attaching itself to its victim. It then bites with its razor-sharp teeth and swivels to twist off a circle of flesh.

spinner dolphin
(Stenella longirostris)

▲ OPPORTUNISTS

Sharks will often follow fishing boats, looking for a free meal. This silvertip shark is eating pieces of tuna fish that have been thrown overboard.

New Life

Wild animals have developed a whole range of strategies to ensure their offspring reach maturity and can breed themselves. Young animals face danger from predators, the weather and starvation. This section begins with pregnant mothers and follows the offspring through to adulthood.

How Life Continues

The swallowtail butterfly does not stay with its young, but it ensures they have the best possible start in life. The eggs are well disguised and laid on a suitable food source, ready for when the caterpillars hatch out.

The aim of all living things is to reproduce more of their own kind. Most animals do this by sexual reproduction, and their young are a unique mix of their male and female parents. Sexual reproduction is successful because some of the young will combine the best elements of both their mother and father. These animals are better adapted to their environment and have the greatest chance of surviving.

Male and female animals

Most animals have two separate sexes – males and females. Males are often bigger than females, and male butterflies often have brighter colours than females. But the really important differences are in the internal organs. Males have testes that produce microscopic sperms, while the females have ovaries that produce eggs. A sperm and an egg join together in a process called fertilization to form a new animal.

Eggs or babies?

Most reptiles and birds form protective shells around their fertilized eggs and lay them as soon as possible. This means that the female is not burdened with a family of babies growing inside her. Female birds would find it impossible to fly if they gave birth to live young. On the other hand, the female has to provide each egg with a lot of food, in the form of a yolk, and this uses up a lot of her energy. Some snakes do give birth to live young, but their babies develop in a similar way, taking nourishment from the yolk of an egg. These snakes have decided that the safest nest site for their eggs is inside the mother's body.

Mammals have a different way of producing their young. Their eggs have no shells, and they grow into babies inside the female's body. The babies absorb food from their mother's blood. Carrying

This bear cub is a unique mix of its parents' genes. With any luck, it will have inherited the best characteristics from each. This will help it survive to produce cubs of its own – passing on the features that help it to survive in its environment.

Two female Atlantic spotted dolphins swim with their young. Dolphins are very sociable animals, and mothers and their young evidently enjoy each other's company.

babies inside the mother's body is a good way to protect them from danger, and it also means that the mother does not have to provide a lot of food at once. Only a few babies can be born at a time, but the mammals care for their young after birth so that they have the best possible chance of surviving to become new adults.

Parental care

Many animals abandon their eggs as soon as they have laid them. Predators eat a lot of these eggs and the newly hatched young, but parents make up for it by producing huge numbers of eggs. An insect may lay hundreds or even thousands of eggs. Animals that take good care of their eggs and their young lay far fewer eggs. Some insects and spiders, and all crocodiles, make good parents, finding food for their young or coming to their defence if danger threatens.

Baby mammals feed on milk from their mother's bodies for weeks, months or even years after birth. Many babies are naked and helpless when they are born, and they are fed and kept warm in a nest or den for several weeks. Horses and other grazing animals, however, give birth to well-developed babies that can get up and walk about immediately. These animals are always on the move, and a baby must be able to keep up with its mother. Mammals that give birth to large babies have one or perhaps two babies at a time, because of the limited room in a female's body.

A young chimpanzee is fully at home in the treetops. With attentive care from its mother and protection from its group, this young ape should survive to have offspring of its own.

The new generation

Each species of animal uses a slightly different strategy to ensure that at least some of their young survive. This book examines some of those strategies. You will discover how each animal tries to ensure its genes continue, so that at least one of its offspring goes on to breed itself.

Lions are fearsome predators, but, when they are young, they are in danger from other predators, such as hyenas and crocodiles. A cub's mother will guard it fiercely until it is large enough to defend itself.

The Transformation of a Beetle

▲ LAYING EGGS
A cardinal beetle lays her eggs in dead wood. The hard tip of the beetle's abdomen pierces the wood to lay the eggs inside. When the eggs hatch, the log provides the larvae with a hiding place from predators. They feast on wood-eating insects until they are fully grown.

Almost all insects start their lives as eggs. They go through dramatic life changes to become fully formed adults. When beetle larvae (grubs) hatch, they look nothing like their parents. Many resemble pale worms although some have legs. They often live in different places from adult beetles and may eat quite different food.

Larvae put most of their energy into finding food, and they eat constantly. They grow bigger but do not change form. When the larva is fully grown, it changes into a pupa. Inside the pupa, the grub's body dissolves and then rebuilds in a completely different shape. It emerges from the pupa stage as an adult beetle. This amazing four-stage process of change is called complete metamorphosis. The adult beetle is now ready to look for a mate, breed and create young.

◄ ALL CHANGE
The ladybird's life cycle shows the four stages of complete metamorphosis. The adult lays eggs (1) and these hatch out into larvae or grubs (2). When fully grown, the larvae become pupae (3) before emerging as adult ladybirds (4). At each stage, the ladybird's appearance is totally different from the last, almost as if it were several animals in one.

◀ HIDDEN EGGS

These ladybird eggs have been glued on to a leaf so that they stand on end. Beetle eggs are generally round or oval, and they are usually yellow, green or black for camouflage. Eggs are usually laid in spring or summer, and most hatch between one and four weeks later. However, some eggs are laid in autumn and hatch the following spring, when there is plenty of food and conditions are warmer.

WRIGGLY LARVA ▶

A cockchafer larva has a long, fat body that is very different from the adult's rounded shape. The larva does not have the long antennae or wings of the adult either, but unlike many beetle grubs, it does have legs. It moves about by wriggling its way through the soil.

◀ UNDER COVER

When a beetle grub is fully grown, it attaches itself to a plant stem or hides underground. Then it becomes a pupa, often with a tough outer skin. Unlike the grub, the pupa doesn't feed or move much. It looks dead, but inside an amazing change is taking place. The insect's body breaks down into a thick, soup-like liquid, and is then reshaped into an adult beetle.

PERFECTLY FORMED ADULT ▶

A seven-spot ladybird struggles out of its pupa case. Like most adult beetles, it has wings, antennae and jointed legs. This ladybird's yellow wing cases will develop spots after just a few hours. Some beetles spend only a week as pupae before emerging as fully grown adults. Others pass the whole winter in the resting stage, waiting to emerge.

Caterpillar Survival

Like beetles, butterflies and moths go through a complete metamorphosis. They begin life as eggs, and hatch out into caterpillars. At this stage they eat as much as possible, chomping their way through leaves, fruits and stems. They grow rapidly, shedding their skin several times as they swell. A caterpillar may grow to its full size within a month. Not all caterpillars reach the stage of becoming a chrysalis. Many are eaten by predators or killed by diseases. Caterpillars hide among vegetation and crevices in bark, often feeding at night to try to avoid danger.

◀ CATERPILLAR PARTS
Caterpillars have big heads with strong jaws for snipping off food. Their long, soft bodies are divided into 13 segments. The front three segments become the thorax in the adult insect and the rear segments become the abdomen.

FALSE LEGS ▶
The caterpillar of an emperor gum moth has five pairs of prolegs (false legs) on its abdomen. All caterpillars have these prolegs, which help them cling on to plants. They lose the prolegs as an adult. Caterpillars also have three pairs of true legs, which become the legs of the adult.

▲ BREATHING HOLES

A caterpillar does not have lungs for breathing like humans. Instead, it has tiny holes called spiracles which draw oxygen into the body tissues. There are several spiracles on each side of the caterpillar.

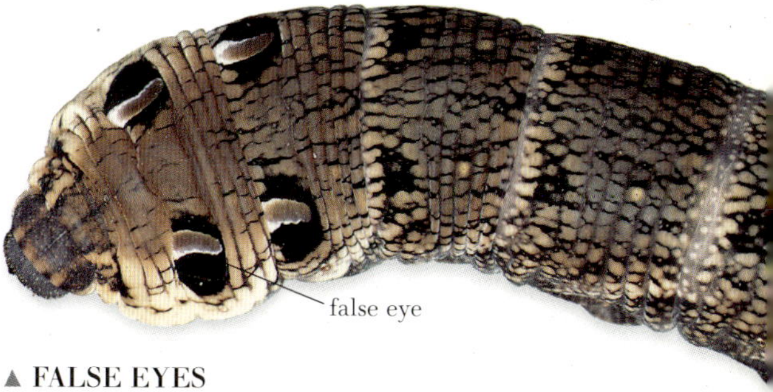

▲ FALSE EYES

The large eye shapes behind the head of an elephant hawkmoth caterpillar are actually false eyes for scaring predators. In fact, caterpillars can barely see at all. They possess six small eyes that can only distinguish between dark and light.

Did you know? Caterpillars can close up their spiracles and survive underwater for hours.

◀ CHANGING SKIN

Every week or so, the skin of a growing caterpillar grows too tight. It splits down the back to reveal a new skin underneath. At first, the new skin is soft and stretchy. As the caterpillar sheds its old skin, it swells the new one by swallowing air. It lies still for a few hours while the new large skin hardens. This skin changing process is called moulting.

◀ FLY ATTACK

A puss moth caterpillar can defend itself against predators. It puffs up its front and whips its tail like a tiny dragon, before spraying a jet of poison over its foe.

SILK MAKERS ▶

Peacock butterfly caterpillars live and feed in web-like tents. They spin these tents from silken thread. All caterpillars can produce this thread from a device called a spinneret under their mouth. The silk helps them to hold on to surfaces as they move.

The Birth

Once a caterpillar reaches its full size it is ready for the next stage in its metamorphosis, and it turns into a pupa or chrysalis. The caterpillars of many moths spin a silken cocoon around themselves before turning into pupae. Inside the chrysalis, the body parts of the caterpillar gradually dissolve. New features grow in their place, including a totally different head and body, and two pairs of wings. This whole process can take less than a week. When the changes are complete, almost magically, a fully-formed adult emerges from the chrysalis.

1 The monarch butterfly caterpillar spins a silken pad on to a plant stem and grips it firmly with its rear claspers. It then sheds its skin to reveal the chrysalis (pupa), which clings to the silken pad with tiny hooks.

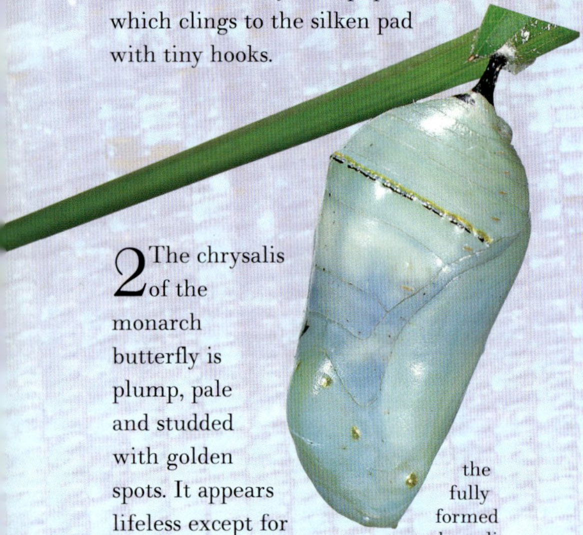

2 The chrysalis of the monarch butterfly is plump, pale and studded with golden spots. It appears lifeless except for the occasional twitch. However, changes can sometimes be vaguely seen through the skin.

3 The chrysalis grows dark and the wing pattern becomes visible just before the adult butterfly emerges. Inside, the insect pumps body fluids to its head and thorax (upper body). The chrysalis then cracks open behind the head and along the front of the wing.

# of a Butterfly

4 The butterfly swallows air to make itself swell up, which splits the chrysalis even more. The insect emerges shakily and clings tightly to the chrysalis skin.

the butterfly's wings are soft and crumpled at first

5 The newly emerged adult slowly pumps blood into the veins in its wings, which begin to straighten out. The insect hangs with its head up so that the force of gravity helps to stretch its wings. After about half an hour, the wings reach their full size.

split skin of the chrysalis

wing veins with blood pumping into them

6 The butterfly basks in the sun for an hour or two while its wings dry out and harden. After a few trial flaps of its wings, it is ready to fly away and begin life as an adult butterfly.

the bright colour of the monarch butterfly warns predators that it is poisonous

monarch butterfly
(Danaus plexippus)

Spider Eggs

Female spiders are usually larger than males because they need to carry a lot of eggs inside their bodies. The eggs are usually laid a week or two after mating, although some species wait several months. Many spiders lay several batches of eggs, usually at night when they are less likely to be seen by predators. There may be from one to over 1,000 eggs per batch. Most spiders lay their eggs on a circular pad of silk, and the female then covers them with more silk to form a protective cocoon known as the egg sac.

◄ **IN DISGUISE**
To hide their eggs from predators, spiders may camouflage the egg cases with plant material, insect bodies, mud or sand. This scorpion spider hangs her cocoon from a web like a string of rubbish, then poses as a dead leaf beneath them. Other species of spider hide their egg cases under stones or bark, or fix leaves around them like a purse.

Ananse the Spider Man
In West Africa and the Caribbean, the hero of many folk tales is Ananse. He is both a spider and a man. When things are going well Ananse is a man, but in times of danger he becomes a spider. Ananse likes to trick the other animals and get the better of those who are much bigger than himself. He may be greedy and selfish, but he is also funny. He is a hero because he brought the gift of telling stories to people.

▲ **SPINNING THE COCOON**
A *Nephila edulis* spider spins a cocoon. She uses special strong, loopy silk that traps a lot of air and helps to stop the eggs drying out. Her eggs are covered with a sticky coating to fix them to the silk. The final protective blanket of yellow silk will turn green, camouflaging the cocoon.

◄ FLIMSY EGG CASE

The daddy-longlegs spider uses hardly any silk for her egg case. Just a few strands hold the eggs loosely together. Producing a large egg case uses up a lot of silk so females with large egg cases often have shrunken bodies. The daddy-longlegs spider carries the eggs in her jaws, and so she cannot feed until the eggs have hatched.

SILK NEST ►

The woodlouse spider lays her eggs in a silken cell under the ground. She also lives in this shelter to hide from her enemies. At night, the spider emerges from its silken house to look for woodlice, which it kills with its enormous fangs.

◄ CAREFUL MOTHER

A green lynx spider protects her egg case on a cactus. She fixes the case with silk lines, like a tent's guy ropes, and attempts to drive off any enemies. If the predator persists, she cuts the silk lines and lets the cocoon swing in mid-air, balancing on top like a trapeze artist. If a female green lynx spider has to move her eggs to a safer place, she drags the case behind her with silk threads.

Did you know? A female garden spider can lay over 1,000 eggs in under ten minutes.

GUARD DUTY ►

Many female spiders carry their eggs around with them. This rusty wandering spider carries her egg case attached to her spinnerets (the organs at the back of the body that produce silk). Spiders that carry their eggs like this often sunbathe to warm them and so speed up their development.

Spiderlings

Most spider eggs hatch within a few days or weeks of being laid. The spiderlings (baby spiders) feed on egg yolk that is stored in their bodies, and they grow fast. Like insects, spiders moult to grow bigger. They shed their old skin and reveal a new, bigger skin that slowly hardens. Spiders moult several times. At first, spiderlings do not usually have any hairs, claws or colour but after the first moult, the young spiders resemble tiny versions of their parents.

Most spiderlings look after themselves from the moment of hatching, but some mothers feed and guard their young until they leave the nest. Male spiders do not look after their young at all.

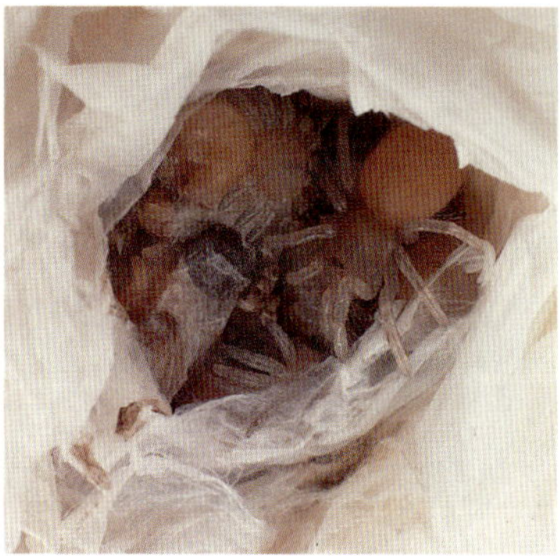

▲ **HATCHING OUT**
These spiderlings are emerging from their egg case. They may have stayed inside the case for some time after hatching. Some spiders have an egg tooth to help break them out of the egg, but mother spiders may also help their young to hatch. Spiderlings from very different species look similar.

◄ **NURSERY WEB**
Female nursery-web spiders build a silk tent for their egg cases close to the time that they are ready to hatch. The mother sits on the tent and guards the eggs and hatchlings when they emerge, for a week or so. The baby spiders moult once and then gradually leave the nest to start life on their own.

▲ **A SPIDER BALL**
Garden spiderlings stay together for several days after hatching. They form small gold and black balls that break apart if threatened by a predator, but re-form when the danger has passed.

◂ BABY BODIES

A female crab spider watches over her young as they hatch. Spider eggs contain a lot of yolk, which provides a good supply of energy for the baby spiders. All spiderlings are well developed when they hatch out, with the same body shape and number of legs as adults. Spiderlings, however, cannot produce silk or venom until after their first moult.

spotted wolf spider
(Pardosa amentata)

BABY CARRIER ▸

Pardosa wolf spiders carry their egg cases around with them. When the eggs are ready to hatch, the mother tears open the case and the babies climb on to her back. If the spiderlings fall off, they can find their way back by following silk lines that the mother trails behind her.

▴ FOOD FROM MUM

The mothercare spider feeds her young on food brought up from her stomach, made of digested insects and the cells that line her gut. The babies shake her legs to beg for food. They grow faster than the young of species that have to feed themselves.

Did you know? When their mother dies, many young spiders eat her body.

▴ BALLOON FLIGHT

Many spiderlings take to the air to find new places to live or to avoid being eaten by their brothers and sisters. On a warm day with light winds, they float through the air on strands of silk they have made. This is called ballooning.

Nesting Birds of Prey

Most bird species have a different mate every year, staying together only long enough to raise their young. However, birds of prey (also known as raptors) tend to stay with one mate for life. As with all birds, courting still takes place every year to help the pair to strengthen their bond and to establish their hunting territory.

Within their territory, raptors build a nest in which the female lays her eggs. Birds of prey usually nest far apart from each other because they need a large hunting area. However, some species, such as griffon vultures and lesser kestrels, nest in colonies.

The nests and nesting sites vary greatly, from species to species. Nests may be an elaborate structure of branches and twigs or no more than a simple bare patch of soil on a ledge. Many pairs of raptors return to the same nest every year, adding to it until it becomes a massive structure.

▲ FEED ME
This female hen harrier is brooding (sitting on her eggs). Like several other raptors, male hen harriers often catch prey for their mate while she is unable to hunt for herself. Hen harriers nest on the ground, and so they need to be well camouflaged. Both the birds and the nest are hard to spot.

Bonelli's eagle
(Hieraaetus fasciatus)

◄ SETTING UP HOME
A Bonelli's eagle repairs her clifftop perch, keeping a careful watch over her young chick. If there are no cliffs in her territory, the female builds her nest at the top of a tall tree. The nests measure up to 2m across and are used year after year. Scientists have ringed this chick's leg so that its movements can be traced throughout its life.

GO AWAY! ▶

By spreading his wings to make himself look bigger, a barn owl adopts a threatening pose to protect his nest. The female has already laid several eggs, which she will incubate (sit on to keep warm) for just over a month. During this time, the male feeds her, usually with rats, mice or voles, but sometimes with insects and small birds. If food is plentiful, the pair may raise two broods a year.

◀ IN A SCRAPE

This peregrine falcon has made a nest on a cliff ledge by simply clearing a small patch of ground. This type of nest is called a scrape. Many peregrines use traditional nesting sites, where birds have made their homes for centuries. Others have adapted to life in the city, making their scrapes on the ledges of skyscrapers, office buildings or churches.

◀ FULL UP

A secretary bird comes in to land on the huge tree-top nest of a flock of weaver birds in search of its own nesting site. As the tree is full, the secretary bird will have to choose another site in which to nest. It prefers low thorny trees such as acacia. Its nest is made from sticks, lined with soft grass.

secretary bird
(Sagittarius serpentarius)

▲ SECOND-HAND NEST

A disused raven's nest has been adopted by this peregrine falcon. Peregrines often lay their eggs in nests abandoned by other birds. Female peregrines usually lay 3–4 eggs, and both parents take it in turns to incubate them. It takes about 30 days for the eggs to hatch.

Young Birds of Prey

▲ **TAKING OFF**
A young kestrel launches itself into the air. It is fully grown but still has juvenile plumage. Other adults recognize the plumage and do not drive the young bird away.

Birds of prey chicks remain in the nest for different periods, depending on the species. The chicks of small raptors, such as merlins, are nest-bound for only about eight weeks, while the offspring of larger species, such as the golden eagle, stay in their nests for more than three months. Young vultures may stay for more than five months.

As raptor chicks grow, their thick down moults to reveal proper feathers. The chicks become stronger, and start to exercise their wings by standing up and flapping them. Eventually they are ready to make their first flight. This greatest step in the life of a young bird is called fledging. It takes weeks or even months before the young birds learn all of the flying and hunting skills they need to catch prey. Until then, they are still dependent on their parents for all their food.

▼ **GROWING UP**
As a tawny owl grows, its appearance changes dramatically. At four weeks old, the chick is a fluffy ball of down. Three weeks later, it is quite well feathered. At three months, the young owl is fully feathered and can fly.

4 weeks old

7 weeks old

12 weeks old

adult pygmy falcon

uvenile pygmy falcon
(Poliohierax semitorquatus)

◂ BIG PYGMY

This pygmy falcon is still feeding its offspring, even though the chick is as big as its parent. In the early stages of the chick's life, the male pygmy falcon supplies all the food, while the female keeps the chick warm in the nest. Then both adults feed the fledgling, until the young bird learns to catch insects for itself. This skill can take up to two months to master.

▸ KESTREL COMPANY

A pair of month-old kestrels huddle together near their nest in an old farm building. They are fully feathered and almost ready to take their first flight. However, it will probably be another month before they learn to hunt.

tawny owl
(Strix aluco)

◂ JUST PRACTISING

This young tawny owl is still unable to fly. It is flapping its wings up and down to exercise and strengthen the pectoral (chest) muscles that will enable it to fly. As the muscles get stronger, the young bird will sometimes lift off its perch. Eventually, often on a windy day, the owl will find itself flying in the air. On this first flight, it will not travel far, but within days, it will be flying as well as its parents.

Crocodile Eggs

All crocodilians (crocodiles, alligators and gharials) lay eggs. The number of eggs laid by one female at a time ranges from about 10 to 90, depending on the species and the age of the mother. Older females lay more eggs. The length of time it takes for the eggs to hatch varies with the species and the temperature, and takes from 50 to 110 days. During this incubation period, bad weather can damage the babies developing inside the eggs. Too much rain may cause water to seep through the shells and drown the babies before they are born. Hot weather may make the inside of the egg overheat and harden the yolk, which means the baby cannot absorb the yolk and it starves to death. Another danger is that eggs laid by one female may be accidentally dug up and destroyed by another female digging a nest in the same place.

▲ **EGGS FOR SALE**
In many countries, people eat crocodilian eggs. They are harvested from nests and sold at local markets. This person is holding the eggs of a gharial. Each egg weighs about 100g. The mother gharial lays about 40 eggs in a hole in the sand. She lays them in two tiers, separated from each other by a fairly thick layer of sand, and may spend several hours covering her nest.

► **NEST-SITTING**
The mugger crocodile of India digs a sandy pit about 50cm deep in a river bank and lays between 10 and 50 eggs inside. She lays her eggs in layers and then covers them with a mound of twigs, leaves, soil and sand. During the 50–75 day incubation period, the female spends most of her time close to the nest. Female muggers are usually quite placid when they lay their eggs, and researchers have even been able to catch the eggs as they are laid.

▶ INSIDE VIEW

Curled tightly inside its egg, this alligator has its head and tail wrapped around its belly. Next to the developing baby is a supply of yolk, which provides it with food during incubation. Researchers have removed the top third of the shell to study the stages of growth. The baby will develop normally even though some of the shell is missing. As the eggs develop, they give off carbon dioxide gas. This reacts with moisture in the nest chamber and may make the shell thinner to let in more oxygen.

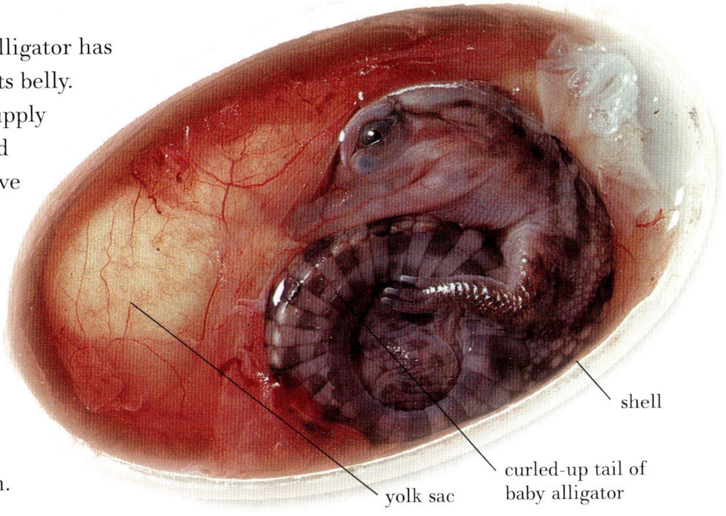

◀ CRACKING EGGS

A mother crocodile sometimes helps her eggs to hatch. When she hears the baby calling inside, she picks up the egg in her mouth. She rolls it to and fro against the roof of her mouth, pressing gently to crack the shell. The mother may have to do this for about 20 minutes before the baby breaks free from the egg.

EGGS IN THE NEST ▶

All crocodilian eggs are white and oval-shaped, with hard shells like a bird's eggs. This is the nest of a saltwater crocodile, and the eggs are twice the size of chickens' eggs. It takes a female saltwater crocodile about 15 minutes to lay between 20 and 90 eggs. The eggs take up to 90 days to hatch.

Crocodiles

1 A female Nile crocodile has heard her babies calling from inside their eggs, so she knows it is time to help them escape from the nest. She scrapes away the soil and sand with her front feet and may use her teeth to cut through any roots that have grown between the eggs. Her help is very important as the soil has hardened during incubation. The hatchlings would find it difficult to dig their way up to the surface without her help.

Baby crocodilians make yelping, croaking and grunting noises from inside their eggs when it is time to hatch. The mother hears the noise and digs the eggs from the nest. The babies struggle free of their eggshells, sometimes with help from their mother. During this time, the mother is in a very aggressive mood and will attack any animal that comes near. Nile crocodile hatchlings are about 28cm long, lively and very agile. They can give a human finger a painful nip with their sharp teeth. Their mother carries them gently in her mouth down to the water. She opens her jaws and waggles her head from side to side to wash the babies out of her mouth.

the hatchling punches a hole in its hard shell with a forward-pointing egg tooth

2 This baby Nile crocodile has just broken through its eggshell. It used a horny tip on the snout, called the egg tooth, to break through. The egg tooth is the size of a grain of sand and disappears after about a week. The egg has become thinner during the long incubation, which makes it easier for the baby to break free.

Hatching Out

3 Struggling out of an egg is a long, exhausting process. When the hatchlings are half out of their eggs, they sometimes take a break so they can rest before completely leaving their shells. After all the babies have hatched, the mother crushes or swallows the rotten eggs that are left.

4 Even though they are fierce predators crocodilians make caring parents. The mother Nile crocodile lowers her head into the nest and delicately picks up the hatchlings and any unhatched eggs between her sharp teeth. She gulps them into her mouth. The weight of all the babies and eggs pushes down on her tongue to form a pouch that holds up to 20 eggs and live young. Male mugger crocodiles also carry the young like this and help hatchlings to escape from their eggs.

5 A young crocodilian's belly looks fat when it hatches. This is because it contains the remains of the yolk sac, which nourished it through the incubation period. The hatchling can swim and catch its own food straight away, but it continues to feed on the yolk sac for up to two weeks. In Africa, baby Nile crocodiles usually hatch just before the rainy season. The wet weather brings an abundance of food, such as insects, tadpoles and frogs for the hatchlings. Baby crocodilians are very vulnerable to predators and are guarded by their mother for at least the first few weeks of life.

Young Crocodilians

Life is full of danger for juvenile (young) crocodilians. They are too small to defend themselves easily, despite their sharp teeth. All sorts of predators lurk in the water and on the shore, from birds of prey and pelicans, to monitor lizards, otters, tiger fish and even other crocodilians. Crocodilians lay many eggs, but not all of their young survive to hatch out, and many that do, do not survive for long. Only one in ten alligators lives to the end of its first year. Juveniles often stay together in groups during the first weeks of life, yelping to each other if one gets separated. They also call loudly to the adults for help if they are in danger. By the time the juveniles are four years old, they stop making distress calls and start responding to the calls of other young individuals.

▲ INSECT DIET
A spiky-jawed Johnston's crocodile is about to snap up a damselfly. Young crocodiles mainly eat insects. As they grow, they take larger prey, such as snails, shrimps, crabs and small fish. Their snouts gradually strengthen, so that they are able to catch bigger fish, which are the main food of this small Australian crocodile.

Did you know? 15 per cent of baby saltwater crocodiles do not survive a month.

◄ FAST FOOD
These juvenile alligators are in captivity and will grow twice as fast as they would in the wild. This is because they are fed at regular times and do not have to wait until they can catch a meal for themselves. It is also because they are kept in warm water – alligators stop feeding in cooler water. The best temperature for alligator growth is 30–32°C.

SMALL BUT SAFE ▶

Juveniles stay close to their mother for the first few weeks, resting on her back. No predator would dare to attack them there. Baby alligators are only about 25cm long when they leave their eggs, but grow very quickly. When they have enough food to eat, male alligators grow about 30cm a year until they are about ten years old.

▲ CROC CRECHE

A group of crocodilian young is called a pod. Here, a Nile crocodile guards her pod as they bask in the sun. At the first sign of danger, the mother rapidly vibrates her muscles and the young immediately dive underwater. A pod may stay in the same area for as long as two years.

▲ TOO MANY ENEMIES

The list of land predators that attack juvenile crocodilians includes big cats such as this leopard. Large wading birds, such as ground hornbills, marabou storks and herons, spear them with their sharp beaks in shallow water, while in deeper water, catfish, otters and turtles all enjoy a young crocodilian as a snack. Only about two per cent of all the eggs laid each year survive to hatch and grow into adults.

NOISY POD ▶

These crocodilians are caimans. A pod of juveniles, like this group, is a noisy bunch. By chirping and yelping for help, a juvenile warns its brothers and sisters that there is a predator nearby. The siblings quickly dive for shelter and hope that an adult will come to protect them. If a young Nile crocodile strays from its pod, it makes loud distress calls. Its mother, or any other female nearby, will pick up the youngster in her jaws and carry it back to the group.

Some species of snake give birth to live young, like mammals. Others lay eggs, like birds. Most egg-laying species abandon their eggs after laying them. However, some cobras and most pythons guard their eggs from predators and the weather.

Inside the egg, the baby snake feeds on the yolk. Once this has been used up the snake is fully developed and ready to hatch. All the eggs in a clutch tend to hatch at the same time.

1 As rat snakes develop inside the egg, they feed on the yolk. About eight weeks after being laid, the eggs begin to hatch.

Baby Snake Breakthroug

2 The baby snake is now fully developed and has become restless, twisting in its shell. It cannot get enough oxygen through the egg. The shell of a snake's egg is almost watertight, although water and gases, such as oxygen, pass in and out of it through tiny pores (holes). The baby snake cuts a slit in the shell with a sharp egg tooth on its snout. This egg tooth drops off a few hours after hatching.

3 After it has broken through the stretchy, leathery shell, the baby snake has a rest. It pokes its nose through the slit in the egg to breathe the air and takes a first look at the strange and exciting world outside.

4 All the eggs in this clutch have hatched at the same time. The baby snakes will not crawl out of their shells straight away. They poke their heads out of their eggs to taste the air with their forked tongues. If they are disturbed, they will slide back inside the shells where they feel safe. They may stay inside the shells for a few days.

Did you know? The mud snake lays over 100 eggs at a time.

5 Eventually, the baby snake slithers out of the egg. It may be as much as seven times longer than the egg because it was coiled up inside. It wriggles away to start a life on its own. It has to survive without any help from its parents.

rat snake
(Ptyas mucosus)

pope's tree viper *(Trimeresurus popeorum)*

Snakes That Give Birth

▲ TREE BIRTH
Tree snakes often give birth in the branches of trees. The membrane around each baby snake sticks to the leaves and helps stop the baby from falling out of the branches to the ground.

▲ BIRTH PLACE
The female sand viper chooses a quiet, remote spot to give birth to her young. Snakes usually give birth in a hidden place, where the young are safe from enemies.

Instead of laying eggs, some snakes give birth to fully developed, live young. Snakes that do this include adders, boas and rattlesnakes. The young develop in an egg inside the mother's body. The surface of the egg is a thin protective membrane instead of a shell. The baby snake gets its food from yolk inside the egg. Anything from six to 50 babies are born at a time, depending on the species. The baby snakes are still inside their membranes when they are born.

Did you know? An anaconda may have 100 babies at a time.

BABY BAGS ►
These red-tailed boas have just been born. They are still inside their tough membranes, which are made of a thin, see-through material, rather like the one inside the shell of a hen's egg.

BREAKING FREE ▸

A baby rainbow boa has just pushed its head through the membrane that surrounds it. Snakes have to break free on their own. Each baby has an egg tooth to cut a slit in the membrane so that it can wriggle out. They usually do this a few seconds after birth.

◂ NEW BABY

A red-tailed boa has broken free of its membrane, the remains of which can be seen around the body. Some newborn snakes crawl off straight away, while others stay with their mother for a few days.

◂ COLOUR CHANGE

Emerald tree boas are bright red when they are born. It takes a year for them to turn the vivid green of their parents.

emerald tree boa
(Epicrates cenchria)

Did you know? Baby boa constrictors grow from 50cm to 100cm in their first year.

▲ **EGG WITH A TWIST**
The egg case of a horn shark has a spiral-shaped ridge. The mother shark uses her mouth like a screwdriver to twist the case round and fix it firmly into gaps in rocks.

Egg-laying Sharks

Sharks are fish, not mammals, and so their young do not suckle from their mother or need to breathe air. Sharks bring their young into the world in two ways. In most species, eggs grow into baby sharks inside the mother's body. The mother gives birth to active young called pups. In other species, the female shark lays eggs, each enclosed in a tough case or capsule. Young catsharks grow in cases like this. Each mating season, catsharks lay up to 20 cases and fix them to seaweed. A single pup develops inside each capsule. Catsharks do not guard or look after their egg cases in any way. Instead, they rely on the tough, leathery case to protect the pup inside.

▲ **TIME TO LEAVE**
When it is ready to leave its egg, the baby horn shark uses special scales on its snout and fins to cut its way out of the tough egg case. The dorsal fins on its back have tough spines that protect it from the moment it emerges.

Mermaid's Purses
The mermaid is a mythical undersea creature with a woman's body and a fish's tail. In legends, mermaids lured men to their deaths with beautiful songs. Catshark egg cases, which are sometimes washed up on beaches, look like pouches, and are often called mermaid's purses.

50 days 100 days 150 days 200 days

◄ ▲ IN THE SAC

In the earliest stages of development, the catshark pup is tiny, about the size of a pea. It is attached to a huge, yellow yolk sac from which it takes its food. Inside the egg case, the growing pup makes swimming movements, which keep the egg fluids and the supply of oxygen fresh. After nine months, the catshark pup breaks free of the case.

► SWELL SHARK

The length of time it takes the swell shark pup to grow and hatch out of its case depends on the temperature of the sea water around it. In warm water, it can take just seven months. In cold water, it might take ten months. The pup has special skin teeth to tear its capsule open.

The Birth of a

A year after mating, pregnant lemon sharks arrive at Bimini Island, off the coast of Miami, in the Atlantic Ocean. Here, they give birth to their pups in a shallow lagoon where males do not enter. An adult male is quite likely to eat a smaller shark, even one of its own kind. In many species of shark, pregnant females leave the males and swim to safer nursery areas to give birth. Some scientists even believe that females lose their appetite at pupping time, to avoid them eating their own young. After birth, the lemon shark pups live on their own.

1 By pumping sea water over her gills, a pregnant lemon shark can breathe while resting on the seabed. She gives birth on the sandy lagoon floor to the pups that have developed inside her for a year.

2 Baby lemon sharks are born tail first. Female sharks give birth to 5–17 pups at one time. Each pup is about 60cm long. After her pups are born, a female lemon shark will not be able to mate again straight away. Instead, she will rest for a year.

Lemon Shark Pup

3 A lemon shark gives birth to her pups in the shallows. The pups are still attached to the umbilical cord when born, but a sharp tug soon frees them. The small remora fish that follow the shark everywhere will feast on the discarded umbilical cord.

4 After birth, a baby lemon shark makes for safety in the shallow, muddy waters at the edge of the lagoon. It spends the first few years of its life among the tangled roots of the mangrove trees that grow there. The pup feeds on small fish, worms and shellfish. It must be wary of sharks larger than itself, which may try to eat it.

5 To avoid being eaten, young lemon sharks gather with others of the same size. Each group patrols its own section of the lagoon at Bimini. This young lemon shark is about one year old. When it is seven or eight, it will leave the safety of the lagoon and head for the open reefs outside.

The Birth

Horses belong to the large group of animals called mammals. Like almost all mammals, the babies grow inside their mother, taking their nourishment from her rather than the yolk of an egg. This means the young can be born fairly well developed. All mammals feed their young on milk.

In the wild, horses, zebras and asses give birth when there is plenty of food and water around and weather is not too extreme. The breeding season is usually brief so that all the foals in one area will be born at about the same time. They have a greater chance of survival from predators if all of the foals are the same age, rather than being born in ones or twos throughout the year.

1 Some mares lie on their side during foaling, while others remain standing. The foal emerges head first, with its forelegs extended. It only takes a few minutes for it to be born. At first, it is still enclosed in the membrane in which it developed in the womb, but it soon breaks free by shaking itself or standing up.

2 The placenta, through which the foal received nutrients when it was still in the womb, comes out immediately after the birth. The mother might chew on this, but she does not eat it.

3 The mother licks the newborn foal all over to establish her bond with the baby. From now on, she will be able to recognize her foal from all others. It will take about a week, however, for the foal to know its mother.

# of a Baby Horse

4 The newborn foal struggles to its feet. It will stand up within ten minutes of birth, and will soon be able to canter. The foal's first few days of life are taken up with feeding, practising using its legs and napping. Feeds last for a few minutes each, and a rest may be between 20 minutes and one hour long.

5 The mother is very aggressive at this time. She chases other horses away and may even bite them. This ensures that the foal will imprint on her (recognize her as its source of food and protection) rather than any other animal in the herd. After about a week, the mare calms down, and the foal is allowed to meet with others of its own kind.

LOOKING FOR FOOD
Instinct tells this plains zebra foal that its mother's teats are found between the legs and the belly, but it might search between the forelegs before finding the right spot.

TWO YEARS UNTIL INDEPENDENCE
This wild ass foal will stay with its mother for two years. Asses usually foal every two years, but horses and zebras sometimes have one foal a year, if conditions are good.

Elephant Calves

▲ **BIRTH TIME**
A baby elephant emerges from its mother in a protective membrane called a birth sac. The other females in the group sniff the newcomer and softly touch it all over, while rumbling with excitement.

Female elephants live in family groups with their mothers, sisters, daughters and their offspring. Like horses, females often have babies at about the same time, at the time of year that food is most plentiful.

An elephant's pregnancy lasts for nearly two years, and females only have one calf every four to six years. A female elephant may have her first calf at the age of 10 and her last when she is 50. She has between five and 12 babies in a lifetime.

Young elephant calves are highly vulnerable, and about a third do not survive to reach adulthood. Some are taken by predators, such as crocodiles, lions and tigers. Others drown or are crushed by falling trees. All the elephants in the group try to keep the calves safe.

a baby elephant practises using its trunk

▲ **TRUNK TRICKS**
Baby elephants are curious and inquisitive. They want to touch and feel everything with their trunk. At first, they cannot control their long, wobbly nose. They trip over it or suck on it – just as human babies suck their thumbs. It takes them months of practice to learn how to use their trunks.

► **THIRSTY CHILD**
A calf sucks milk from its mother's breasts with its mouth. The milk is thin and watery, but very nourishing. Babies put on weight at a rate of 10–20 kg per month.

◄ LEARNING FAST

A young elephant has to master the technique of giving itself a dust bath. It must also learn to pick up and carry things with its trunk, drink, feed and have a mudbath. If a young elephant cannot reach water, the mother sucks up water in her trunk and squirts it down her baby's throat.

Did you know? A newborn baby elephant weighs more than an average adult human.

GUIDING TRUNK ►

At first, a baby elephant sticks close to its mother night and day. It is always within reach of a comforting touch from her strong, guiding trunk. The mother encourages her baby, helps it to keep up with other members of the herd and often pulls it back if it starts to stray. Baby elephants will die quickly if they are left on their own.

▲ PROPER FOOD

After a few months, calves begin to eat plants. A calf may put its trunk into its mother's mouth to taste her food and learn which plants are edible.

▲ HELPFUL RELATIVES

The survival of both mothers and calves depends greatly on the support of the family group. Each member of the group takes part in bringing up the babies. This helps the mother, and allows young female elephants to learn how to care for calves.

Caring Elephant Families

A baby elephant is brought up by its family in a fun-loving, easy-going and caring environment. At first, a calf spends a lot of time with its mother, but as it grows older and stronger, it begins to explore and make friends with other calves. Young elephants spend a lot of time playing together. They can do this because they feed on their mother's milk and so they do not have to spend all day finding food. Gradually, the calf learns all the skills it will need as an adult.

▲ **BROTHERS AND SISTERS**
A female elephant may have a calf every five years, but elephants do not become adults until they are about ten years old. Usually, just when the first calf can feed itself, another one arrives. The older calf still spends a lot of time with its mother.

Did you know? Female elephants become adult in nine or ten years but males mature a few years later.

◀ **MOTHER'S MILK**
A calf drinks its mother's milk until it is between four and six years old. By then, the mother usually needs her milk for the next baby. Even so, calves as old as eight have been known to push a younger brother or sister out of the way to steal a drink.

◀ PLAYTIME

A growing elephant learns a lot simply by playing. Male elephants push and shove each other to test their strength. Females play games with lots of chasing, such as tag. Both males and females like to mess about in mud, dust and water.

▲ PROTECTING THE YOUNG

All the adults in a family are protective of the young. They shade calves from the sun and stand guard over them while they sleep. Small calves are vulnerable to attack from many other animals, including poisonous snakes.

Ganesh

In the Hindu religion of India, Ganesh is the elephant-headed god of wisdom and the remover of obstacles. Ganesh's father, the god Siva, is said to have cut off Ganesh's head. His mother, the goddess Parvati, was so angry that she forced Siva to give her son a new head. This new head turned out to be that of an elephant. Hindus seek good luck from Ganesh before the start of important business.

◀ LOTS OF MOTHERS

Allomothers are female elephants in the group that take a special interest in the upbringing of calves. They wake up the calf when it is time to travel, help it if it gets stuck in mud and protect it from danger.

Baby Great Apes

▲ **NEWBORN GORILLA**
This day-old gorilla is tiny and helpless as it clings to its mother's fur. Its wrinkled face is a pinkish colour and its big ears stick out. Soon after birth, the baby's brown eyes open and peer curiously at its surroundings. Despite its long, skinny arms and legs, the baby gorilla is quite strong.

The great apes – gorillas, orangutans, chimpanzees, gibbons and bonobos – usually have one baby at a time and spend many years looking after their young, just as humans do. Most apes are pregnant for eight or nine months, although baby gibbons are born after seven or eight months.

Baby apes are much smaller than human babies and weigh only about half as much. This means that giving birth is easier for an ape than for a human mother. Both labour and birth are fairly swift and trouble-free. Newborn apes are almost helpless, but they have a very strong grip so that they can cling to their mother's hair. She feeds them on her milk and may carry them around for four or five years as they gradually grow up and become more independent.

Did you know? A gorilla usually gives birth in less than an hour.

◀ **MILK FROM MUM**
A newborn baby gorilla depends on its mother's milk for nourishment. After six to eight months, it gradually begins to try different bits of plant food, but it continues to drink its mother's milk for at least two years.

chimpanzees
(Pan troglodytes)

▲ **HITCHING A RIDE**
Very young chimpanzees are carried underneath their mother, clinging on to her fur with their tiny fists. By the age of five to six months, a baby chimp starts to ride on its mother's back. It is alert, looking around and touching things.

gorillas
(Gorilla gorilla)

PIGGY-BACK ►
Riding piggy-back on its mother's broad back, a baby gorilla watches the other gorillas and looks around its habitat as the group travels from place to place. This is the safest place for the young gorilla until it is strong enough to walk by itself.

◄ **GOOD PARENTS**
Baby gibbons depend on their mothers for warmth and milk. Gibbon fathers groom their babies and play with them. Siamang gibbon fathers look after their youngsters during the day.

▲ **CHIMP CHILDHOOD**
The bond between a mother chimpanzee and her baby is strong and lasts throughout their lives. A young chimp is completely dependent on its mother for the first five years. It stays close to its mother so that she can see and hear it.

The Life of a

MOTHER LOVE

There is a very strong bond between a mother orang-utan and her baby. When she is not moving through the trees or feeding, the mother may groom her baby or suckle it, although she doesn't often play with it. A baby orang-utan may scream and throw a tantrum to get its mother's attention.

Young orang-utans live a different life from gorilla and chimpanzee babies. Instead of being brought up in a group, the orang-utan's world is almost entirely filled by its mother. Most orang-utans live alone, but following the birth of a baby, a mother becomes even more shy than usual. She tries to avoid other orang-utans in order to protect her baby.

For the first year of its life, a baby orang-utan is entirely dependent on its mother, and she cares for it without any help. A young orang-utan stays with its mother for seven to nine years, gradually learning what to eat, where to find food, how to climb and swing through the trees safely, and how to make a nest to sleep in.

MOTHER'S MILK

For the first year of its life, a baby orang-utan drinks its mother's milk and clings to her chest or back. After a year, it starts to eat solid food but it continues to suck for another three to five years. Like most baby mammals, orang-utans are keen to take their mother's milk for as long as possible.

Young Orang-utan

NEST-BUILDING
Orang-utans sleep in nests made with leafy branches. During their second year, young orang-utans experiment with making their own nests.

PLAYTIME
Although they are usually solitary, on the rare occasions young orang-utans meet they wrestle and play together in the forest. They may get so carried away that they do not notice when their mother leaves. Then they have to hurry after her, screaming angrily as they go.

SOLID FOOD
To start her baby on solid food, a mother orang-utan partly chews up bits of food and then presses them into the baby's mouth. Young orang-utans eagerly take the solid food.

A NEW BABY
When an orang-utan is between five and eight years old, its mother may give birth again. The new baby takes most of the mother's attention, and the young orang-utan becomes more independent. Even so, it may stay with its mother for a year or more after the new baby is born.

Great Ape Childhood

orang-utans
(Pongo pygmaeus)

Apes spend a long time growing up. As well as learning how to move, feed and defend themselves, they have to know how to behave with others of their own kind. This is especially important for chimpanzees and gorillas because they live in large groups. Young apes do not become independent of their mothers until they are aged about eight. Female orang-utans and gorillas will not have babies of their own until they are about ten years old, and female chimps not until they are 14. Male orang-utans and gorillas will not have offspring until they are about 15 years of age. When they are grown-up, orang-utans and gibbons leave their parents to start a life of their own. Most gorillas and female chimps also leave the group they were born into.

▲ **MOTHER AND BABY**
Female orang-utans spend most of their adult lives caring for their offspring. An orang-utan may have only four young in her lifetime.

▲ **APE EXPLORER**
Young chimps love to explore, moving farther away from their mothers as they test their climbing skills. At the first sign of danger, though, they run back to their mothers.

▲ **SPEEDY GORILLAS**
Baby gorillas develop through the same stages of movement as human babies, only much faster. They can crawl at nine weeks of age and walk by nine months – an age when most human babies have only just started to crawl.

▲ **FOOD FROM MOTHER**
A chimpanzee watches its mother and other chimps to find out what is good to eat. Young chimps chew the other end of whatever food their mother is eating.

◄ **PLAYING THE GAME**
Little chimps have a lot of free time, which they spend at play. Young females spend much of their time playing with the babies in their group. Through playing, the chimps learn the rules of chimpanzee society.

chimpanzee
(Pan troglodytes)

Did you know? Young gorillas have a white tuft on their rear to help their mothers find them.

AT PLAY ►
Young gorillas wrestle, chase, playfight and climb and slide all over the adults. This helps them to test their strength, build up their muscles and learn how to get along with other gorillas.

Inside a Bear Den

Bear cubs are born naked and helpless at the harshest time of year. They are absolutely tiny compared to the size of an adult bear and need to be protected from the cold weather as well as from predators. A den, hidden away from the outside world, makes a perfect home. The den can be in a cave, a hollow tree or a self-made hollow.

The female bear does not leave the den for the first few months. She does not hunt, but relies on her fat reserves to survive. Producing enough milk to nourish her cubs takes a lot of energy, and a mother bear is only able to feed them if she has eaten enough food in the months before.

▲ **BLIND AND HELPLESS**
Ten-day-old brown bear cubs nestle into their mother's fur for warmth. With their eyes and ears tightly closed shut, they are totally dependent on her. The cubs remain in the den until May or June when they are about four months old.

Did you know? Polar bear cubs are no bigger than guinea pigs when they are born.

◀ **POLAR TWINS**
A polar bear mother tends her two young. The family leaves its den between late February and April depending on where it lives. The farther north the bears are, the later in the year they emerge.

polar bear
(Ursus maritimus)

▲ **TRIPLE TROUBLE**
This American black bear has given birth to three healthy cubs. Females may have up to four cubs at one time. Newborn black bear cubs are about the size of a rat, but they grow quickly. They leave the den in April or May.

▲ **PANDA BABY**
At Wolong breeding station in Sichuan, China, a baby giant panda is put in a box to be weighed. Giant pandas give birth to one or two cubs in a cave or tree hollow. If twins are born, the mother often rears only one, leaving the other to die.

◀ **MOTHER'S MILK**
Three-month-old polar bear cubs feed on their mother's milk. Unlike most bear cubs, polar bears are born covered with fine hair to help keep them warm in the bitter Arctic weather.

IN THE DEN ▶
Newborn American black bears weigh less than 300g, which is about the same as a can of fizzy drink. Their small size and lack of fur makes them vulnerable to the cold. The mother cleans and dries the cubs, then cuddles them close. The den is lined with branches, leaves, herbs and grasses to make a warm blanket. The mother spends a lot of time grooming her cubs and keeps the den scrupulously clean by eating their droppings

Snow Den

1 A bank of snow makes an ideal site for a polar bear's winter den. The pregnant female bear digs about 5m into the south side of the snowdrift. The wind in the Arctic blows mainly from the north, so the snow piles up on the other side.

From late October, a pregnant female polar bear digs a snow den. Usually it is some distance from the sea, on a slope facing south. This means the den's entrance and exit hole faces towards the sun, which is low on the horizon in early spring. The sun's rays help to warm the den.

The mother bear gives birth during the harshest part of winter, when permanent night covers the Arctic. The den is kept warm and snug with heat from her body. A tunnel to the nursery chamber slopes upwards so that warm air rises and collects in the chamber, which can be 20°C warmer than outside.

2 This picture is an artist's impression of the inside of a polar bear's den. The cubs are about three months old and they are almost ready to leave their snow home for the first time. Polar bear cubs are born between late November and early January, but don't leave the den until the spring.

3 The female polar bear emerges from her winter home. She drives two holes through the walls of the den and helps the cubs make their first journey outside. The family remains near the den site for a few days so that the cubs become used to the cold.

for Polar Bears

4 Sitting upright in a snow hollow, a female polar bear nurses her cubs. She differs from other female bears in that she has four working nipples rather than six. Her cubs stay with her for three years, which is a year longer than the average for bears. During the years they spend with her, the cubs will learn how to survive in the cold Arctic conditions and also how to hunt seals for food.

5 The cubs play outside in the snow during the short days, and shelter in the den at night and during storms. Soon the family leave the den altogether and head towards the sea where the mother can hunt and feed.

6 The cubs' first journey is often a long one. They may have to walk up to 22km to reach the sea ice where they will see their first seal hunt. The mother takes great care to avoid danger on the journey. She looks out for adult male polar bears who might try to kill her cubs.

Bear Cubs

Young bears spend their first 18 months to three years with their mother. If she dies, they may be adopted by another mother with cubs the same age. The cubs learn everything from their mother. She teaches them how to recognize the best food and where and when to find it. The cubs must also learn how to escape danger and how to find a winter den or shelter in a storm. Without this schooling, the young bears would not survive. Mothers and cubs communicate by calling, particularly if they become separated from each other.

During their development, cubs must keep out of the way of large male bears who might attack and kill them.

▲ **SAFE IN THE BRANCHES**
Black bear cubs instinctively know that they should head for the nearest tree when danger threatens. It is easier for a mother to defend a single tree than a scattered family.

▼ **FEEDING TIME**
A mother brown bear suckles her twins. Her milk is thick and rich in fats and proteins, but low in sugars. It has three times the energy content of human or cow milk. The milk also contains antibodies, which help protect the cubs from disease.

brown bear
(Ursus arctos)

◄ LEAVING THE FAMILY

Young bears on their own, such as this brown bear, often become thin and scrawny. Despite being taught by their mothers where and how to feed, they are not always successful. At popular feeding sites, such as fishing points, they may be chased off by larger bears. When the time comes for young bears to look after themselves, the mother either chases them away or is simply not there when they return to look for her.

A LONG APPRENTICESHIP ►

Polar bear cubs are cared for by their mother for much longer than other bear cubs. They need to master the many different hunting strategies used by their mother to catch seals. These are not something that the cubs know instinctively, but skills that they must learn.

polar bear
(Ursus maritimus)

Did you know? Giant panda cubs are the first bears to leave their mother at 18 months old.

◄ FAMILY TRAGEDY

This polar bear cub is the victim in a tragic tug-of-war. A male bear has attacked the cub and its mother is trying to save it. Female bears fight ferociously to protect their young, but are often unsuccessful against the larger males. About 70 per cent of polar bear cubs do not live to their first birthday. Attacks by adult male bears, starvation, disease and the cold are the usual causes of death.

Big Cat Babies

The cubs (babies) of a big cat are usually born with spotted fur and closed eyes. They are completely helpless. The mother cat looks after them on her own with no help from the father. She gives birth in a safe place called a den. For the first few days after birth, she stays very close to her cubs so that they can feed on her milk. She keeps them warm and cleans the cubs by licking them all over. The cubs grow quickly. They can crawl even before their eyes open, and they soon learn to hiss to defend themselves.

▲ SNOW CUB
Snow leopard cubs have white fur with dark spots, and they are always born in the spring. The cubs begin to follow their mothers around when they are about three months old. By winter, they will be almost grown up.

MOTHERLY LOVE ▶
Tiger cubs are capable killers by the time they are 11 months old. They stay with their mothers, however, until they are two or even three years of age. A female tiger does all she can to protect her young, but often at least half of the litter dies. Predators may kill the cubs, or sometimes they starve to death if the mother cannot catch enough food.

cheetah cub
(Acinonyx jubatus)

IN DISGUISE ▶

A cheetah cub is covered in long, woolly fur. This makes it look similar to the African honey badger, a very fierce animal, which may help to discourage predators. The mother cheetah does not raise her cubs in a den, but moves them around every few days.

▲ BRINGING UP BABY

Female pumas give birth to up to six kittens at a time. The mother has several pairs of teats for the kittens to suckle from. Each baby has its own teat and will use no other. They will take their mother's milk for at least three months, and from about six weeks they will also eat meat.

▲ ON GUARD

Two lionesses guard the entrance to their den. Lions are social cats and share the responsibility of keeping guard. Dens are kept very clean so that there are no smells to attract predators.

▲ MOVING TO SAFETY

If at any time a mother cat thinks her cubs are in danger, she will move them to a new den. She carries the cubs one by one, gently grasping the loose skin at their necks between her teeth.

Cubs Growing Up

Young cubs have to learn all about life as an adult big cat so that they can eventually look after themselves. Their mother teaches them as much as she can, and the rest they learn through play. As cubs play, they learn how to judge distances and when to strike to kill prey quickly, without getting injured or killed themselves. The exact games cubs play vary from one species of cat to another, because each has different hunting techniques to learn. Cheetahs, for instance, playfight using their paws to knock each other over. Lions play by biting each other's throats.

Mothers and cubs generally use very high-pitched sounds to communicate, but if the mother senses danger, she growls at her cubs to tell them to hide.

▲ **PRACTICE MAKES PERFECT**
These cheetah cubs are learning to kill a Thomson's gazelle. When the cubs are about 12 weeks old, a mother cheetah brings back live injured prey for them to kill. They instinctively know how to do so, but need practice to get it right.

▼ **FOLLOW MY LEADER**
Curious cheetah cubs watch an object intently, safe beside their mother. At about six weeks, the cubs start to go on hunting trips with her. They are able to keep up by following her white-tipped tail through the tall grass.

cheetah
(Acinonyx jubatus)

THE CLASSROOM ▸

These lion cubs lounge on a fallen tree. From here they watch the adults hunt, as if in a big, open-air classroom. Females stay in the same pride (group) all their lives, but young males will leave at about three years old.

lion cubs
(Panthera leo)

◂ WHAT IS IT?

Three young lions sniff at the shell of a tortoise. Cubs learn to be cautious when dealing with unfamiliar objects. First, the object is tapped with a paw, before being explored further with the nose. Cubs' milk teeth are replaced with permanent canine teeth at about two years old. Not until then can they begin to hunt and kill big animals.

TAIL TOY ▸

A mother leopard's tail is a good thing for her cub to learn to pounce on. She twitches it so that the cub can develop accurate timing and coordination. As the cub grows, it practises on rodents and then bigger animals until it can hunt for itself. Once they leave their mothers, female cubs usually establish a territory close by, while males go farther away.

Newborn Wolves

Most wolf packs have between 8 and 24 members. Only the leaders will mate and have cubs, but every pack member then helps to bring up the cubs.

Newborn wolves are helpless. They cannot hear, their eyes are tightly closed and their legs are too weak to allow them to stand. The cubs squirm around and huddle close to their mother for warmth. Like all mammals, their first food is their mother's rich milk.

After one or two weeks, the cubs' eyes open and they begin to take notice of their surroundings. They take their first wobbly steps and scramble over each other in the den. At about five weeks, the cubs start to take solid food as well as milk. Half-chewed meat, stored in the stomach of an adult wolf, is brought to the den and regurgitated (coughed up) when the cubs beg for food.

▲ **AT THE DEN**
Wolf cubs take a first look at the big world outside their den. For nearly eight weeks, their only experience has been the burrow – a 4m-long tunnel dug in soft earth with room for an adult wolf to creep along. The cubs sleep in a cosy chamber at the end.

Did you know? The mother of the wolf cubs sleeps in a hollow near the entrance of the den.

NURSING MOTHER ►
Like bears, most wolves are born in a den, and the female stays with her cubs for the first few weeks. A wolf mother, however, does not have to rely on fat reserves as bears do. Her mate, and the rest of the pack, bring food so that she does not have to go hunting. She needs large quantities of food to produce enough milk for her cubs.

▼ CUBS IN DANGER

These wolf cubs are six or seven weeks old. Not all cubs are born in a den. Some are born in a sheltered hollow, or in a nest flattened in long grass. There are many dangers for cubs in the open, including being snatched by predators such as bears and eagles. Many do not survive to adulthood.

grey wolf cubs
(Canis lupus)

Romulus and Remus

According to ancient Roman legend, Romulus and Remus were twin brothers who were abandoned as babies on a remote hillside. A she-wolf found them and brought them up, feeding them on her milk. Both brothers survived, and Romulus went on to found the city of Rome.

▲ HUNGRY PUPPIES

An African hunting dog suckles her pups. They suck milk from two sets of nipples on her underside. Female hunting dogs often have more nipples than other canids, because they have the biggest litters and therefore the most mouths to feed. As the pups' sharp teeth begin to hurt, she will wean them on to meat.

▲ RARE CUBS

In the mountains of Ethiopia, a female Simien wolf guards her litter of five cubs. Simien wolves are much rarer than other wolves. These cubs look healthy, so have a good chance of surviving long enough to breed as adults.

Older Wolf Cubs

At eight weeks old, wolf cubs are very lively. Their snouts have grown longer, their ears stand up and they look much more like adult wolves. They bound about on long, strong legs. Now weaned off milk, they live on a diet of meat brought by the adults. As they leave the safety of the den, the other pack members gather round and take great interest in the cubs. The cubs' new playground is the rendezvous, the safe place at the heart of wolf-pack territory where the adults gather. This is usually a sheltered, grassy spot near a stream where the cubs can drink. Here they develop their hunting skills by pouncing on mice and insects. As they playfight, they establish a ranking order that mirrors the social order in the pack.

▲ **CARRIED AWAY**
A wolf carries a cub to safety by seizing the loose skin at the scruff of its neck in its teeth. This adult is most likely the cub's mother or father, but it may be another member of the pack. All the adult wolves are very tolerant of the youngsters to begin with. Later, as the cubs grow up, they may be punished with a well-placed nip if they are naughty.

Did you know? Father wolves make squeaking noises to call their cubs.

SHARING A MEAL ►
A young African hunting dog begs for food by whining, wagging its tail and licking the adult's mouth. The adult responds by arching its back and regurgitating a meal of half-digested meat from its stomach. The pups grow quickly on this diet. At the age of four months, they are strong enough to keep up with the pack when it goes hunting.

▼ PRACTICE MAKES PERFECT

Two Arctic fox cubs practise their hunting skills by pouncing on one another. Young cubs playfight to establish a ranking order. By the age of 12 weeks, one cub has managed to dominate the others. He or she may go on to become leader of a new pack.

▲ YOUTHFUL CURIOSITY

Young maned wolves investigate their surroundings. Females usually bear three cubs at most. Newborn young have grey-brown fur, short legs and snouts. Later they develop long legs and handsome red fur.

ALMOST GROWN ▶

These two young wolves are almost full grown. Cubs can feed themselves at about ten months, but remain with the pack to learn hunting skills. At about two or three years old, many are turned out. They wander alone or with brothers or sisters until they find mates and start new packs.

Wolfchild

Rudyard Kipling's Jungle Book, *which was published in 1894, is set in India. The book tells the story of Mowgli, a young boy who is abandoned and brought up by wolves in the jungle. When Mowgli becomes a man he fights his archenemy, the tiger Shere Khan. Kipling's tale was inspired by many true-life accounts of wolf-children who grew up in the wild in India during the 1800s.*

Baby Whales

BIRTH DAY
A bottlenose dolphin gives birth. The baby is born tail-first. This birth is taking place near the bottom of an aquarium. In the wild, birth takes place close to the surface so the baby can surface quickly and start breathing.

Although they live in the sea, whales are mammals, which means that they breathe air and the mother feeds her young with milk. Many whales are enormous, and so are their babies. A newborn blue whale can weigh up to 2.5 tonnes, which is twice as much as a family car.

The first thing a newborn whale must do is to take a breath. Its mother and perhaps another whale may help it up to the surface. After that, the calf can breathe and swim unaided. Baby whales feed on their mother's milk for several months until they learn to take solid food such as fish. Mother and calf may spend most of the time alone, or join nursery schools with other mothers and calves.

SUCKLING
A beluga mother suckles her young. Her fatty milk is very nutritious, and the calf grows rapidly. It will drink milk for up to two years. At birth the calf's body is dark grey, but it slowly lightens as the calf matures.

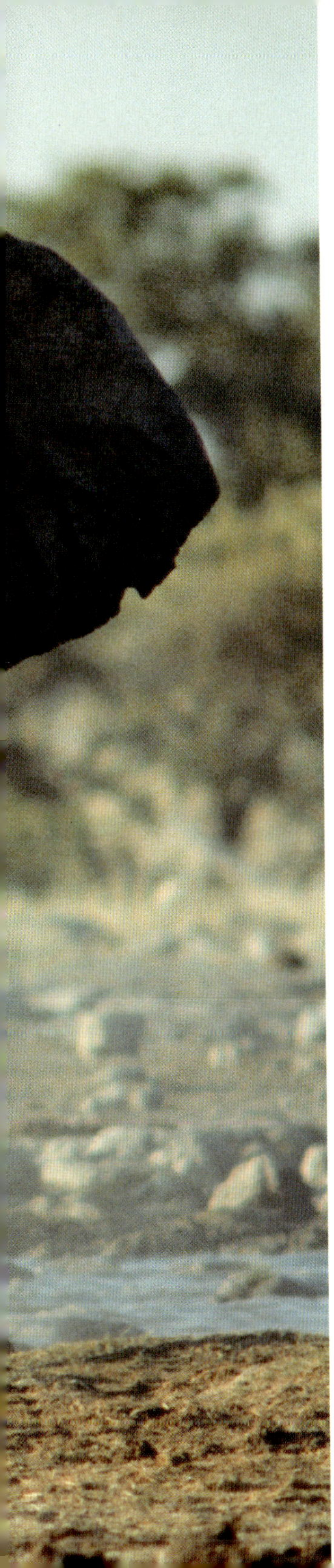

How Animals Communicate

The way that animals interact with each other can be a vital factor in their survival. Some animals live together in groups while others live alone. This section looks at some of the most social animals on earth, explaining how their communities work. It also looks at some of the animals that are usually solitary and explains why they find it better to live alone.

Communicating in the Wild

Animals 'talk' to each other in many different ways. Most forms of communication are with other individuals of the same kind, but many animals also send signals to other species. These signals are usually concerned with defence. Rattlesnakes, for example, rattle their tails to warn predators or any other large animals that they might get hurt if they get any closer. Many poisonous or distasteful insects, including the Monarch butterfly, are brightly coloured. Predators might try them once or twice, but they soon learn that brightly coloured insects taste bad and should be left alone. Some animals even give out signals to trick their prey. The snapper turtle, for example, attracts fishes to its mouth by waggling its worm-like tongue.

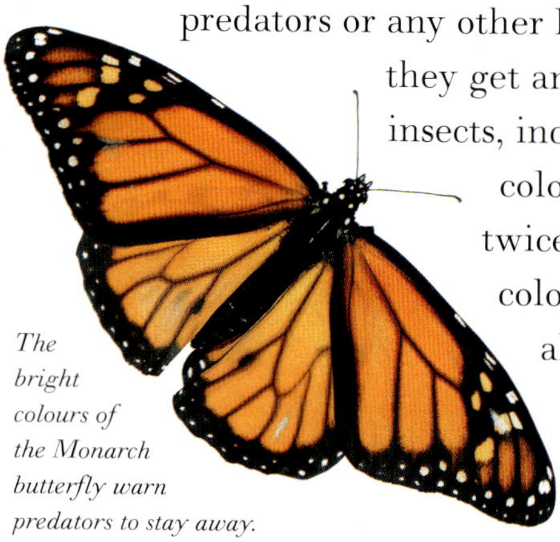

The bright colours of the Monarch butterfly warn predators to stay away.

Communicating with the neighbours

Nearly every species uses some kind of signal to attract mates. Male crickets and grasshoppers attract females with their chirpy 'songs'. Many birds also use songs, although others, including most birds of prey, rely more on spectacular aerial displays. Some male spiders also perform elaborate dances in front of the females. Scents – given out by one or both sexes – play a major role in the courtship and mating of most animals. Mating signals are the only forms of communication used by some solitary animals (those animals that live alone) but most species have a much more complex range of signals.

The most complex 'language' is found among the social animals – those that live in groups and co-operate with each other. They use sounds, visual signals, and scents to pass information to each other. Touching each other is also an important method of giving and receiving information. One of the most amazing forms of communication is the dance language of honeybees. A worker bee finding a good source of nectar returns to the hive and dances on the honey combs. Other workers join in the dance, and the direction and speed of the action tells them the direction and distance of the nectar. They then fly off to collect more of this important food.

Wolves are sociable animals and use touch to bond with each other. They rub bodies, lick each other, and nuzzle each other's fur when they meet.

and Dolphins

AT PLAY
A young Atlantic spotted dolphin and its mother play together, twisting, turning, rolling and touching each other with their flippers. During play, the young dolphin learns the skills it will need later in life when it has to fend for itself. The youngster is darker than its mother and has no spots. These do not start to appear until it is about a year old.

Did you know? Blue whales are born in tropical waters, but nine months later they are thousands of kilometres away in cold polar waters.

TOGETHERNESS
A humpback whale calf sticks closely to its mother as she swims slowly in Hawaiian waters. The slipstream (water flow, created by the mother's motion) helps pull it along. For the first few months of its life, the calf will not stray far from its mother's side.

Communicating by sound

The songs of many male birds attract mates, but they also help to defend a territory by telling other males to keep away. Gibbons and howler monkeys also use sounds to stake out their territories. Chimpanzees are very noisy and excitable animals and they use more than 30 different grunts, screams and hoots to talk to each other. Elephants also make a wide variety of calls, including strange tummy rumbles, some of which can be heard several kilometres away. Dolphins talk to each other by way of an amazing variety of clicks and whistles as they swim through the water.

Dolphins communicate by making high-pitched sound waves by vibrating the air in the passages in their nose. The waves are focused into a beam through the bulge on their head. This sound is then transmitted into the water.

Body language

Many social animals convey their moods and messages by the way they stand or move. Horses and elephants signal to other herd members by moving their ears. The members of a wolf pack all get on well together because each animal knows its place. A low-ranking wolf lowers its head and puts its tail between its legs when it meets a higher ranking individual, as if saying "You're the boss and I won't cause any trouble". A male gorilla makes sure that the other clan members know he is in charge by standing and thumping his chest. Chimpanzees pull faces to indicate their various moods, such as fear, anger, or playfulness. An angry chimp, for example, clenches his lips shut.

Gorillas communicate with a variety of sounds, facial expressions and gestures. They stand on their back legs and beat their chests rapidly with their hands. Gorillas very rarely fight with each other, and this is a display to scare away rivals.

Getting close

Chimpanzees, horses, wolves, lions and many other animals spend a lot of time nuzzling and licking each other. This is known as grooming and it helps to keep all the members of a group on good terms. Ants and other social insects also touch and feed each other. This helps to spread the pheromones (bodily scents) that keep the colonies running smoothly.

When members of a zebra herd meet up, they welcome each other with a series of greeting rituals which include touching and sniffing. Good friends sometimes lay their heads on each other's back.

Bee and Wasp Colonies

Social bee and wasp colonies work like miniature, smooth-running cities. Like good citizens, all the insects in the colony instinctively know their roles and carry out their tasks.

In a honeybee colony, the workers perform different tasks according to their age. The youngest workers stay in the nest and spend their first weeks cleaning out the brood cells. Later they feed the young. As the wax glands in their abdomen develop, they help build new cells. They also keep the nest at the right temperature. After about three weeks, the worker honeybees go outside to fetch nectar and pollen to store or to feed their sisters. The oldest, most-experienced workers act as guards and scouts. Many wasp colonies work in a similar way, with workers doing different jobs according to their age.

▲ **ADJUSTING THE HEAT**
Honeybees are very sensitive to tiny changes in temperature. The worker bees adjust the temperature around the brood cells to keep the air at a constant 34°C. In cold weather, they cluster together to keep the brood cells warm. In hot weather, they spread out to create cooling air channels.

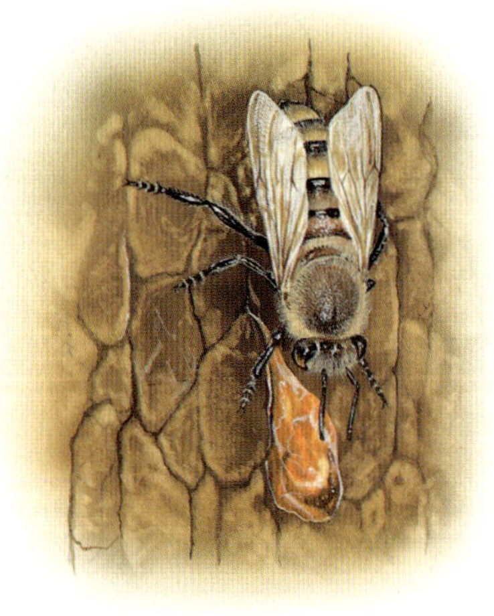

◀ **NEST REPAIRS**
Worker honeybees use a sticky tree resin to repair cracks in their nest. This gummy material is also known as propolis, or 'bee glue'. The bees carry it back to the nest in the pollen baskets on their hind legs. If there is no resin around, the bees may use tar from roads instead.

▲ **BUILDING NEW CELLS**
Honeybee cells are made by workers using wax from their abdomens. The bees use their antennae to check the dimensions of the cells as they must be the right size to fit the young.

◀ THREAT DISPLAY
Paper wasp workers from Equador in South America swarm over the outside of their nest to frighten off intruders. Like all wasp workers, one of their main roles is to defend the nest. If this display fails, the wasps will attack and sting their enemy. However, most animals will retreat as quickly as they can.

▲ PRECIOUS CARGO
A worker honeybee unloads her cargo of nectar. The bees use the nectar to make honey, which is a high-energy food. The honeybee workers eat the honey, which allows them to survive long, cold winters in temperate regions, when other worker bees and wasps die.

TENDING THE YOUNG ▶
A honeybee tends the larvae (young bees) in the nest cells. Honeybees feed their young on nectar and pollen from flowers. Wasp workers feed their larvae on balls of chewed-up insects. The young sister is allowed to feed for about ten seconds, then the worker remoulds the food ball and offers it to another larva. The adult may suck juices from the insect meat before offering it to the young.

◀ LITTLE BUMBLEBEE NESTS
Social bumblebees, shown here, live in much smaller colonies than honeybees. European bumblebee nests usually hold 20–150 insects, whereas a thriving honeybee colony may hold 60–80,000 insects. The queen bumblebee helps her workers with the day-to-day running of the nest as well as laying eggs.

Ant and Termite Societies

Like bee and wasp societies, ant colonies are all-female for much of the year. Males appear only in the breeding season to mate with the young queens. Ant colonies are tended by hundreds or thousands of sterile female workers. The worker ants also fight off enemies when danger threatens, repair and expand the nest, and adjust conditions there. Some ants use the workers from other species as 'slaves' to carry out these chores.

In most types of ants, the large queen is still nimble and active. However, the termite queen develops a huge body and becomes immobile. She relies on her workers to feed and care for her, while she produces masses of eggs.

▲ ON GUARD
These ants are guarding the cocoons of queens and workers, who will soon emerge. One of the workers' main tasks is to defend the colony. If you disturb an ants' nest, the workers will rush out with the cocoons of young ants and carry them to a new, safe site.

▼ RIVER OF ANTS
Safari ants march through the forest in long lines called columns. The workers, carrying the cocoons of young ants, travel in the middle of the column, where it is safer. They are flanked by a line of soldiers on each side. Resembling a river of tiny bodies, the column may stretch more than 100m.

▲ ANT RAIDERS
Slavemaker ants survive by raiding. Here an ant is carrying off a worker from another species. Some slavemakers, such as red Amazon ants, have sharp, pointed jaws that are good for fighting, but no use for other tasks. They rely on ant slaves to gather food and run the nest.

◄ TERMITE SKYSCRAPER
These African termite workers are building a new ventilation chimney for their nest. African termites build the tallest towers of any species, up to 6-7m high. If humans were to build a structure of the same height relative to our body size, we would have to build skyscrapers that were more than 9.5km high. The tallest skyscraper today is less than 500m tall.

FAMILY LIFE ►
A queen termite is flanked by the king (the large insect below her), workers and young termites. The king and queen live much longer than the workers – for 15 years or even more in some species. The queen may lay 30,000 eggs in a day – that is one every few seconds. The king stays at her side in the royal chamber and fertilizes all the eggs.

Did you know? A column of army ants on the march may contain 150,000 insects.

nasute termite
(*Nasutitermes* species)

◄ BLIND GUARD
A soldier termite displays its huge head, which is packed with muscles to move the curved jaws at the front. Being blind, the guard detects danger mainly through scent, taste and touch. Like termite workers, soldiers may be either male or female, but they do not breed. The arch-enemies of these plant-eating insects are meat-eating ants, which hunt them for food.

How Social Insects

THE QUEEN'S SCENT
Honeybee workers lick and stroke their queen to pick up her pheromones. If the queen is removed from the nest, her supply of pheromones stops. The workers rear new queens who will produce the vital scents.

Communication is the key to the smooth running of social insect colonies. Colony members interact using smell, taste, touch and sound. Social insects that can see also communicate through sight. Powerful scents called pheromones are the most important means of passing on information. These strong smells, given off by special glands, are used to send a wide range of messages that influence nestmates' behaviour. Workers release an alarm pheromone to rally their comrades to defend the colony. Ground-dwelling ants and termites smear a scent on the ground to mark the trail to food. Queens give off pheromones that tell the workers she is alive and well.

TERMITE PHEROMONES
A queen termite spends her life surrounded by workers who are attracted by her pheromones. The scents she releases cause her workers to fetch food, tend the young and enlarge or clean the nest.

FRIEND OR FOE?
Two black ants meet outside the nest and touch antennae to identify one another. They are checking for the particular scent given off by all colony members. Ants with the correct scent are greeted as nestmates. 'Foreign' ants will probably be attacked.

Communicate

THIS WAY, PLEASE

A honeybee worker exposes a scent gland in her abdomen to release a special scent that rallies her fellow workers. The scent from this gland, called the Nasonov gland, is used to mark sources of water. It is also used like a homing beacon to guide other bees during swarming, when the insects fly in search of a new nest.

ALARM CALL

These honeybees have come to the hive entrance to confront an enemy. When alarmed, honeybees acting as guards give off an alarm pheromone that smells like bananas. The scent tells the other bees to come to the aid of the guards against an enemy. In dangerous 'killer bee' species, the alarm pheromone prompts all hive members to attack, not just those guarding the nest.

SCENT TRAIL

This wood ant worker has captured a worm. The ant is probably strong enough to drag this small, helpless victim back to the nest herself. A worker that comes across larger prey returns to the nest to fetch her comrades, rubbing her abdomen along the ground to leave a scent trail as she does so. Her fellow workers simply follow the smelly trail to find the food. Ants can convey as many as 50 different messages by releasing pheromones and through other body language.

The Butterfly's Mating Quest

common blue butterfly
(Polyommatus icarus)

Butterflies are usually solitary insects. Although hundreds of thousands of them sometimes migrate together, this is not true social behaviour because they do not co-operate with each other. The butterflies don't work together as a group, or communicate. However, all butterflies do need to communicate with each other when looking for a mate.

Most males court females with elaborate flights and dances. Males and females are drawn to each other by the shape of each other's wings and by their colourful patterns. Both sexes also emit pheromones to encourage their mate. Courting butterflies circle each other, performing complicated dances.

▲ **COURTING BLUES**
When courting a female, a male butterfly often flutters its wings flamboyantly. It looks as if it is showing off, but it is really wafting around its pheromones (the scents from special scales on its forewings). Only if the female picks up these pheromones with her antennae will she be willing to mate.

Did you know? Some butterflies, pheromones are so strong they can be smelt by humans.

◄ **THE HAPPY COUPLE**
This pair of butterflies is about to mate. When she is ready, the female (right) flies away and lands with her wings half open. The male flutters down on top of her and begins to caress her abdomen with his rear end. The male then turns around to face the opposite way as they couple. The pair may remain joined for hours.

Madame Butterfly

One of the most famous operas is Puccini's Madame Butterfly, written in 1904. The opera is set in the 1800s in Osaka, Japan. It tells the story of an American officer, James Pinkerton, who falls in love with a beautiful young Japanese girl. His nickname for her is Butterfly. They have a child, but Pinkerton abandons Butterfly for his wife in America. The opera ends as Butterfly dies broken-hearted.

▼ SCENT POWER

A butterfly's scent plays a major role in attracting a mate. The scents come from glands on the abdomen of a female. On a male, the scents come from special wing scales called androconia. A male often rubs his wings over the female's antennae.

▼ COLOURS ATTRACT

Many male butterflies use bright colours to attract mates. This male orange-tip has a distinctive coloured tip to its wings. Females often lack bright colours so are less obvious.

male orange-tip butterfly
(Anthocharis cardamines)

▼ SINGLE MATE

Male butterflies mate several times in their lifetime. However a female butterfly usually mates just once and then concentrates on egg-laying. Once they have mated, many females release a special pheromone that deters other males.

female orange-tip butterfly
(Anthocharis cardamines)

▲ FLYING TOGETHER

Butterflies usually stay on the ground or on a plant while coupling. But, if they sense danger, they can fly off linked together, with one (the carrier) pulling the other backwards.

Spider

Although some spiders look after their young, most species only need to communicate with each other when they are ready to mate. Female spiders attract males by giving off pheromones. Each species has a different pheromone, to help the males find the right mate. Once he has found a female, the male has to give out the right signals so that the female realizes he is not a meal. These include special dances, drumming, buzzing, or plucking the female's web in a particular way. Some males distract the females with a gift of food.

NOISY COURTSHIP
The male buzzing spider beats his abdomen against a leaf to attract a mate. The sound is loud enough for people to hear. He often buzzes on the roof of the female's oak-leaf nest. Other male hunting spiders make courtship sounds by rubbing one part of their bodies against another.

MATING SUCCESS
The male grass funnel-weaver is almost as large as the female and can be quite aggressive. He taps his palps (leg-like feelers) on her funnel web to announce his arrival. If the female is ready to mate, she draws in her legs and collapses as if she is paralysed.

BEARING GIFTS
A male nursery-web spider presents an insect gift to the female. He has neatly gift-wrapped his present in a dense covering of very shiny white silk. Once the female has accepted his gift and is feeding, the male can mate with her in safety.

Courtship

DISTANT DANCE
Spiders that can see well at a distance often dance together before mating. This wolf spider waves his palps like semaphore flags to a female in the distance. Male spiders also strike special poses and use their long, stout front legs to make signalling more effective.

DANGEROUS LIAISONS
This male green orb-weaver has lost four of his legs in the process of courting a female. When the female attacked him, he swung down a silken dragline (escape line). He will climb back up again when it is safe.

A RISKY BUSINESS
Male garden spiders often have great difficulty courting a female. They are usually much smaller and lighter than the female and have to persuade her to move on to a special mating thread. The male joins the mating thread to the edge of the female's web. He then tweaks the silk strands of her web to lure the female towards him.

JUMPING SPIDERS
This pair of jumping spiders are ready to mate. Male jumping spiders impress females by twirling and waltzing, waving their legs, palps and abdomens. Females often attract more than one male and the males have to compete to mate with her. The female reaches out and touches the male when she is ready to mate.

Crocodile Talk

Most reptiles spend very little time with each other, but crocodiles, alligators and other crocodilians have a remarkably sociable life. Groups gather together for basking in the sun, sharing food, courting and nesting.

Crocodilians use sounds, body language, smells and touch to communicate. Adults are particularly sensitive to hatchling and juvenile distress calls and respond with threats or actual attacks. Sounds are made with the vocal cords and with other parts of the body, such as slapping the head against the surface of the water. Crocodilians also use visual communication. Body postures and special movements show which individuals are strong and dominant. Weaker animals signal to show that they recognize a dominant individual and in this way avoid fighting and injury.

▲ **HEAD BANGER**
A crocodile lifts its head out of the water, jaws open. The jaws slam shut just before they smack the surface of the water. This is called the head slap and makes a loud pop followed by a splash. Head slapping may be a sign of dominance and is often used during the breeding season.

▲ **GHARIAL MESSAGES**
The gharial does not head slap, but claps its jaws under water during the breeding season. Sound travels faster through water than air, so sound signals are very useful for aquatic life.

The Fox and the Crocodile
In this Aesop's fable, the fox and the crocodile met one day. The crocodile boasted at length about its cunning as a hunter. Then the fox said, "That's all very impressive, but tell me, what am I wearing on my feet?" The crocodile looked down and there, on the fox's feet, was a pair of shoes made from crocodile skin.

THE LOW SOUND ►

Some crocodilians make sounds by rapidly squeezing their torso muscles just beneath the surface of the water. The water bubbles up and bounces off the back. The sounds produced are at such a low level we can hardly hear them. At close range, they sound like distant thunder. Very low sounds, called infrasounds, travel quickly over long distances through the water. They may be part of courtship. Sometimes these sounds are produced before bellowing, roaring or head slaps.

Did you know? The bellow of an alligator can be heard at least 150m away.

◄ I AM THE GREATEST

Dominant animals are usually bigger and more aggressive than submissive ones. They show off their importance by swimming boldly at the surface or thrashing their tails from side to side on land. When threatened, weaker individuals usually only lift their heads out of the water and expose their vulnerable throats. This shows that they submit and do not want to fight.

GETTING TOGETHER ►

Caimans gather together at the start of the rainy season in Brazil. Crocodilians often come together in loose groups, for example when basking, nesting or sharing food. The largest, oldest crocodiles dominate the group. Scent glands on a crocodile's jaw and under its tail produce smells that tell the other crocodiles its place in the pecking order. The younger ones steer clear, resting at the fringes of the basking area and avoiding their elders when they are in the water.

Courting Crocodiles

Crocodilians are sociable animals throughout the year, but during the mating season, more communication than usual takes place. Males jostle to become the dominant animal in their stretch of river. They need to establish their social position because the dominant male will mate with most of the females in his territory. Females also need to indicate to the male that they wish to mate.

Courtship behaviour for both male and female crocodilians includes bellowing and grunting, rubbing heads and bodies, blowing bubbles, circling and riding on the partner's back.

▲ **POT NOSE**
Most male gharials have a strange bump, or pot, on the end of the snout near the nostrils. Females have flat snouts. No-one is quite sure what the pot is for, but it is probably used in courtship. It may help the male to change hissing sounds into buzzing sounds as air vibrates inside the hollow pot.

◄ **TOUCHING COUPLE**
Crocodilians touch each other a lot during courtship, especially around the head and neck. Males try to impress females by bubbling water from the nostrils and mouth. An interested female arches her back, then raises her head with her mouth open. The two may push each other under the water to see how big and strong their partner is.

◄ SWEET-SMELLING SCENT

Crocodilians have little bumps under their lower jaws. These are called musk glands. The musk is a sweet-smelling, greenish, oily perfume. It produces a scent that attracts the opposite sex. Musk glands are more noticeable in male crocodilians. During courtship, the male may rub his throat across the female's head and neck. This releases the scent from the musk glands and helps to prepare the female for mating.

FIGHTING MALES ►

Male crocodilians may fight each other for the chance to court and mate with females. They may spar with their jaws open or make themselves look bigger and more powerful by puffing up their bodies with air. Saltwater crocodiles are particularly violent and bash their heads together with a loud thud. These contests may go on for an hour or more but do not seem to cause much permanent damage.

◄ THE MATING GAME

A female crocodile often begins the courtship process. She approaches the male and raises her head, exposing her vulnerable throat to show she is no threat. She rubs against the male's head and neck, nudging and pushing him gently. Courtship can last for up to two hours before mating occurs. Both male and female crocodiles court and mate with several different partners.

Feuding Birds of Prey

Birds often squabble over food, and birds of prey (raptors) are no exception. Some birds of prey intimidate others that have already made a kill and try to force them to drop it. This behaviour is called piracy. Sometimes birds of prey are attacked by the birds that they prey on. A number of small birds may join forces against a larger adversary and give chase, usually calling loudly. This is known as mobbing and it generally serves to confuse and irritate the raptor and also warns other prey in the area.

Birds of prey must also defend their nests against predators. The eggs and chicks of ground-nesting raptors are especially vulnerable to attack. Nesting adults will often fly at intruders and try to chase them off.

▲ **SCRAP IN THE SNOW**

On the snowy shores of the Kamchatka Peninsula, in north-east Russia, these sea eagles are fighting over a fish. A Steller's sea eagle, the biggest of all sea eagles, is shown on the right, with its huge wings outstretched. Its opponents, struggling in the snow, are white-tailed eagles. The two kinds of sea eagles are bound to meet and fight, because they occupy a similar habitat and feed on similar prey – fish, birds and small mammals.

◀ **FISH FIGHT**

Two common buzzards fight over a dead fish they have both spotted. Buzzards do not go fishing themselves, but they will feed on any carrion they find.

common buzzards
(Buteo buteo)

UNDER THREAT ►
On the plains of Africa, a dead animal carcass attracts not only vultures, but other scavengers as well. Here, a jackal is trying to get a look-in, but a lappet-faced vulture is warning it off with outstretched wings.

Did you know? Hunters once used eagle owls as bait to attract mobbing birds into range.

jay
(Garrulus glandarius)

▲ CLEVER MIMIC
When a jay spots a predator, such as a bird of prey, it gives out an alarm call or mimics the predator's own call to warn other jays.

▲ IN HOT PURSUIT
An osprey has seen this pelican dive into the water and assumes that it now has a fish in its pouch. So it gives chase. Time and again, the osprey will fly straight at the pelican and scare it so much that it will finally release the fish from its pouch.

▼ MOB RULE
A number of crows have ganged up to mob a steppe eagle. They are bold enough to perch dangerously close to their enemy, calling loudly to persuade it to move on. Although the eagle would be more than a match for its tormentors, it might fly off just to escape aggravation.

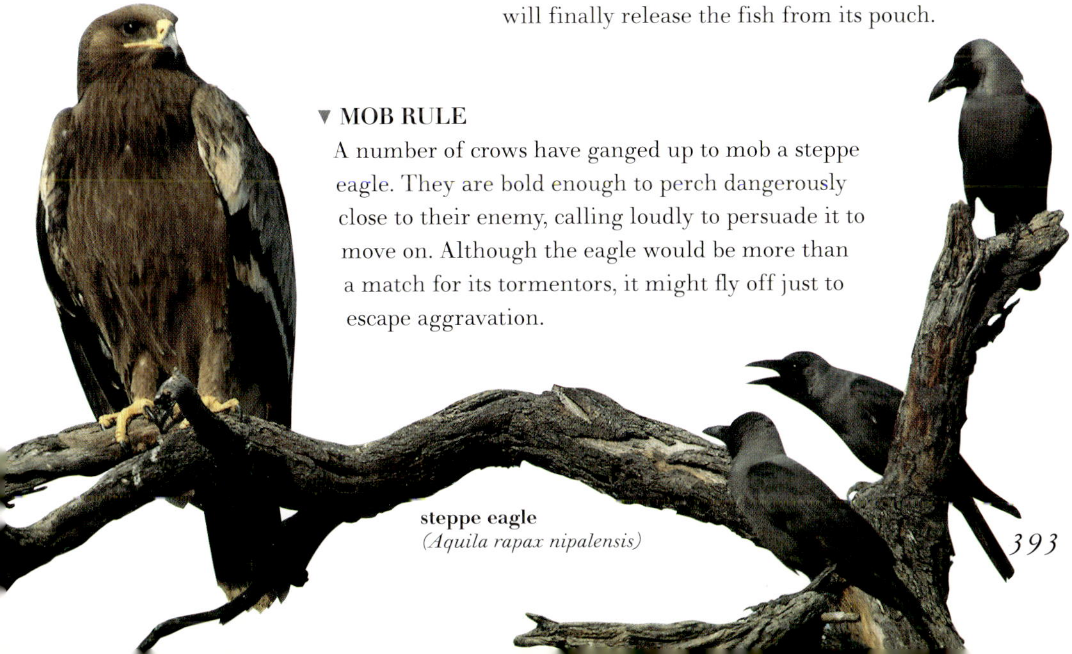

steppe eagle
(Aquila rapax nipalensis)

Close Raptor Couples

Most birds of prey stay with their mates for life. However, every year, during the breeding time, the pair strengthen their bonds with each other. This process is called courting.

In courtship displays there is usually a great deal of calling to each other, with the birds close together. The male may offer the female prey that he has caught. This shows her that he is an able hunter and can provide food for her when she is brooding (sitting on eggs) and also provide for their chicks.

Since most birds of prey are superb fliers, however, the most spectacular courtship displays take place in the air. The birds may perform acrobatic dances, or fly side by side, then swoop at each other and even clasp talons. The male may also drop prey whilst in flight for the female to dive and catch in an extravagant game of courtship feeding.

▲ **THE MARRIED COUPLE**
Like most birds of prey, American bald eagles usually mate for life. They occupy the same nest year after year, gradually adding to it each time they return to breed.

◄ **TOGETHERNESS**
Secretary birds become inseparable for life once they have paired up, rarely straying apart. Their courtship flights are most impressive, as they fly through the sky with their long tails streaming behind them. They also sleep side by side in their nest throughout the year, not just during the breeding season.

▲ **A MOUSE FOR A MATE**

A male barn owl has caught a mouse and takes it to his mate back in the nest. This behaviour is called courtship feeding. It helps strengthen the bond between the pair. It is also preparation for the time when the female is nest-bound and incubating their eggs.

▼ **BALANCING ACT**

A pair of ospreys struggle to keep their balance as they mate on a high perch. The male scrunches up his feet to avoid hurting the female with his talons. Ospreys generally pair for life, but if mating is unsuccessful, they will 'divorce'.

osprey
(Pandion haliaetus)

▲ **CARACARAS ON DISPLAY**

A pair of striated caracaras call to one another by their nest. They are no longer courting but are raising their young. Mated pairs display like this frequently in order to strengthen the bond between them.

Did you know? Peregrines spend hours performing an amazing courtship flight.

▲ **FACE TO FACE**

A pair of Egyptian vultures stand face to face on the ground as part of an elaborate courtship display. In addition to their ground-based performances, the pair will also perform spectacular aerial displays. They fly, climb and dive close together, often presenting their talons to each other.

Herds of Horses

Horses, like zebras and asses, are herd animals, and horses living in the wild form what is described as a 'stable' herd. Each member of the herd knows everyone else. The groups are strictly structured, with each animal knowing its place. Stable herds consist of a single stallion with a collection of mares and their foals. The group of mares is called a harem.

Wild asses and Grevy's zebras have a loose, or 'unstable' herd structure. They live in dry habitats where individual dominant males defend territories that contain water and food. Females live in unstable groups, usually with related animals. They enter the territories of resident males to feed and drink, and so the males will join their herds on a temporary basis.

▲ LEARNING BEHAVIOUR
A foal learns its first lessons on survival from its mother. In a process called imprinting, foals bond to the animal they see most often, which is usually their mother, within a few days of being born. They later learn from watching other members of the herd.

BACHELOR BOYS ►
These young males have been driven from their herd. At two to three years, they are old enough to form a threat to the reigning stallion. Lone male horses find survival difficult away from the herd. Like these three, they often form small herds called bachelor groups.

◄ SOCIAL RISE
Like horses, plains zebras live in a stable herd. Each zebra has its position in the pecking order. Zebras are very sociable animals. They groom one another by nuzzling each other's manes and withers (shoulders) with their front teeth.

▲ HERD ORDER
This group of wild horses is a typical herd, consisting of a dominant stallion, six mares and a foal. The foal will have the same social status as its mother until it grows up. It moves up the social ladder as it gains more experience.

FEMALE POWER ►
Mares and stallions take different roles in the herd. It is usually the dominant mare who decides where to graze and when to move on. The stallion keeps the group together and prevents mares from leaving the herd.

◄ SEASONAL CHANGE
Herds do not always remain the same size. These wild asses live in the desert. When food is scarce they live in small groups, but during the wet season they gather in larger groups of up to 50.

Horse Language

Because horses are sociable animals that live in herds, they need to communicate with each other. They have a wide range of expressive behaviour ranging from sounds and smells to a complex body language.

Animals recognize each other by their appearance and smell, and certain sounds are common to all equids. The short whinny is a warning call, while the long version is a sign of contentment. Other calls, such as greetings and aggressive threats, vary from species to species. Horses whinny, asses bray, mountain zebras whistle, and plains zebras bark. Horses, asses and zebras recognize and react to the calls of all other species of equids but do not respond to the calls of cattle or antelope.

▲ **BABY TALK**
Young horses show respect to their elders by holding their ears to the side, displaying their teeth and making chewing movements. This is not a sign that the foal might bite, but is rather like preparing for a mutual grooming session. It's a way of saying "I'm friendly".

▲ **ON YOUR GUARD!**
Horses need to work out where they fit in the social order of the herd. This horse has flattened its ears in a threatening posture – it is showing its dominance. Flattened ears can also indicate boredom or tiredness.

▲ **TAKING NOTE**
Horses are alert to the signals of others. If one horse is curious about something, its ears will prick forwards. The rest of the herd will look to see what has caught its interest.

◄ **MUTUAL GROOMING**
Horses, like all other equids, will nibble a favourite partner, grooming those places they cannot reach for themselves. The amount of time two horses spend grooming each other shows how friendly they are. Grooming helps to keep a herd together, and it occurs even when the horses' coats are in perfect condition.

FRIENDLY GREETING ►
When members of a herd meet up, they welcome each other with a series of greeting rituals. They may stretch heads, touch and sniff noses, push each other and then part. Good friends may lay their heads on each other's back.

◄ **WILD AT HEART**
Mares often develop personal bonds with other horses in the herd. These bonds can form between unrelated mares or with close relatives, such as sisters or adult daughters. The bonds are stronger in all-female herds. In groups led by a stallion, the mares make him their centre of attention. The stallion may have a favourite mare, which he spends a lot of time with.

Elephant Families

An elephant family group is made up of related females and their offspring. Each family is led by an older, dominant female known as the matriarch. She makes all the decisions for the group. Bulls (male elephants) leave their family group when they are between 10 and 16 years old. When they are adults, only the strongest males mate with the females. Bulls spend most of their lives in small, all-male groups or wander on their own. Each family group has close links with up to five other families in the same area. These linked groups make up a herd. An elephant's day follows a regular pattern of feeding, sleeping and travelling to new feeding areas. Meeting, greeting and communicating with other elephants is an important part of every day and interrupts other activities from time to time. Adult elephants co-operate with each other to protect and guide the young.

▲ KEEPING IN TOUCH
A group of elephants drink together. The calves stay close to the group, so that they are continually touched by their mothers, or other close relatives, for reassurance.

▼ FOLLOW MY LEADER
Touch is a vital tool in elephant communication. As the group moves together, they constantly touch each other. In this way, the matriarch controls when they eat, drink and rest. She also protects the group from dangers and controls family members who misbehave.

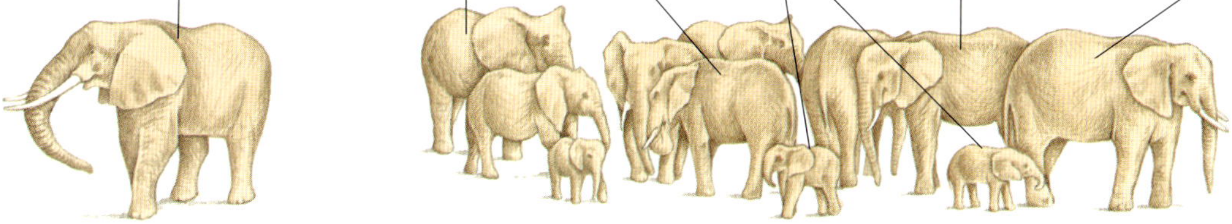

▲ AFRICAN ELEPHANTS
A family of African elephants usually consists of a matriarch, her adult daughters and sisters, their calves and a number of young males and females. Bulls may sometimes join the family for mating but they do not stay with it for long. They soon leave to resume their solitary lives.

◀ SMALL GROUPS
Elephants in Asia live in smaller groups than African elephants. Asian families have between four and eight members, although as many as 10–20 individuals may stay in touch.

◀ ALL ALONE
Male elephants do not form such strong social bonds with each other as the females in family groups do. As a result, some bulls lead entirely solitary lives. However, their calls carry over such a range that it seems likely that, even when out of each other's sight, most bull elephants remain in long-distance communication.

Communicating Elephants

Everyone knows the loud trumpeting sound that elephants make. They make this noise when they are excited, surprised, angry or lost. Elephants also make a wide range of low, rumbling sounds that carry for many kilometres through forests and grasslands. Different rumbles might mean "Where are you?" or "Let's go" or "I want to play". Females can signal when they are ready to mate, and family members can warn each other of danger.

But sound is just one way in which elephants can communicate with one another. They also touch, smell, give off chemical signals and perform visual displays, by altering the positions of the ears and the trunk. Their sense of smell can even tell them about another elephant's health.

▲ **ELEPHANT GREETING**
When elephants meet, they touch each other with their trunks, smell each other and rumble greeting sounds. Frightened elephants also touch others for reassurance.

BODY LANGUAGE ►
Elephants send visual signals by moving their ears and trunk. Spreading the ears wide makes the elephant look bigger. This sends a message to a potential attacker to stay away. The elephant also stands up extra tall to increase the threat, raising its tusks, shaking its head and flapping its ears.

Did you know? Humans can only hear about one-third of the sounds an elephant makes.

◄ TRUNK CALL

An elephant makes its familiar high-pitched trumpeting call. Elephants also make a variety of crying, bellowing, screaming, snorting and rumbling sounds. Asian elephants make sounds that African elephants do not, and many of their rumbles last for longer. There are over 20 different kinds of rumble, with females making many more rumbling sounds than males. Females sometimes make rumbling calls when they are together, but male elephants do not do this.

▲ ALARM SIGNALS

This nervous baby elephant is interested in the crocodiles lying on the river bank. It raises its ears, either in alarm or as a threat to the crocodiles. If a baby calls out in distress, its relatives rush to its side, with rumbles of reassurance and comforting touches with their trunks.

▲ TOUCH AND SMELL

An elephant's skin is very sensitive, and touch is an important way of communicating feelings in elephant society. Smells also pass on useful messages, such as when a female or male is ready to mate.

Babar

One of the most famous elephants in children's literature is Babar the elephant king. He was created by French writer Jean de Brunhoff. Babar rules over the Land of the Elephants with the help of his wife Queen Celeste and his old friend General Cornelius. He fights wars with the rhinos, escapes from the circus and has many other exciting adventures.

Bear Aggression

Adult bears are solitary animals. They prefer to wander alone and do not like other bears. When two animals do meet they need to establish which is the dominant one. This sometimes means a fight, but usually it is just a shouting match and display. If one bear can scare away the other without a fight, it means there is less chance of either animal being injured.

Some bears do congregate together in one area at certain times of year, but this is to take advantage of a plentiful food source. Brown bears tolerate each other at fishing rivers and polar bears scavenge together at whale carcasses and rubbish dumps. As soon as the food is gone, the bears resume their solitary life.

▲ STAND TALL
To show aggression, bears rear on their hind legs, as this American black bear is doing. This makes it look bigger and more frightening. The bear will also growl at its opponent and show its teeth.

◄ ICE DANCE
Like two ballet dancers, young male polar bears play at fighting. They use exaggerated lunges and swipes with their paws and jaws. They do not hurt each other, but they must learn to fight well. Later in life as fully grown adults they will compete with other males for females during the breeding season. Fights between well-matched individuals can be violent and often bloody.

The Jungle Book

Rudyard Kipling's famous story The Jungle Book *was first published in 1894. A young boy named Mowgli is brought up by wolves. He is befriended by Baloo the bear and Bagheera the panther who teach him the law of the jungle. The tiger Shere Khan plots to kill the man-cub.*

▲ FRIENDS AT THE FEAST

Brown bears gather to catch salmon in Alaska. They use body language, such as ears pointed forward or back, necks stretched or contracted, to avoid conflicts and establish the pecking order.

▲ TRAGEDY ON THE ICE

Adult male polar bears are cannibals. They will kill cubs and feed upon the body. Here a female has attacked and driven away the male, but her cub is unlikely to survive. Male bears are much bigger than females, but a female with cubs is a fierce opponent.

▲ FISHING BREAK

Young brown bears take a break from learning to fish and practise fighting instead. They fight by pushing and shoving at each other, using their enormous bulk to overcome their opponent. They also try to bite each other around the head and neck.

Big Cat Signals

Although most big cats are solitary, they do communicate with one another. They indicate how old they are, whether they are male or female, what mood they are in and where they live. Cats communicate by signals such as smells, scratches and sounds. The smells come from urine and from scent glands. Cats have scent glands on their heads and chins, between their toes and at the base of their tails. Every time they rub against something, they transfer their special smell. Cats make many different sounds. Scientists know that cats speak to each other, but still do not understand much about their language. Cats also communicate using body language. They use their ears to signal their mood and twitch their tails to show if they are excited or agitated.

▲ A MIGHTY ROAR
The lion's roar is the loudest sound cats make. It is loud enough for all the neighbourhood lions to hear. Lions roar after sunset, following a kill and when they have finished eating. Lions make at least nine different sounds. They also grunt to each other as they move around.

HISSING LEOPARD ►
An angry leopard hisses at an enemy. Cats hiss and spit when they feel threatened, or when they are fighting an enemy. The position of a cat's ears also signals its intentions. When a cat is about to attack, it flattens its ears back against its neck.

▲ EAR SIGNALS

Many wild cats, such as this tiger, have white markings on the back of their ears. They turn their ears to show the markings to an enemy when they are angry.

▲ MARKS FOR SHOW

Cats like to scratch things to clean their claws and stretch their limbs. At the same time they leave a scented mark for others to both see and smell. When this lioness scratches, she leaves her own personal scent from the glands between her toes on the scratch marks.

▲ CAT SPRAY

A king cheetah marks its territory by spraying urine at points along its trails. Scent marks left by a male tell other males to stay away. The scent left by a female will tell a nearby male if she is ready to mate.

Did you know? When they are close together, lions chirrup, meow and yowl to each other.

BABY TALK ►

Mothers talk to their cubs a lot. The sounds are quiet so that enemies do not hear. The softest and safest sound of all is purring.

Life in a

Lions live in family groups called prides. A pride may contain 30 or 40 animals consisting of up to 12 lionesses and their cubs and three or four adult males, but many prides may be much smaller. Each pride defends its territory and does not allow other lions to hunt there. Lionesses usually stay in the same pride until they die, but male cubs are driven out when they are about three years old. They roam in small groups called coalitions until they are fully grown. Each coalition attempts to take over an existing pride by killing or driving out the old males.

FATHER AND SON
Male lions are the only big cats that look different from the females. Their long, shaggy manes make them look larger and fiercer and protect their necks in a fight. A male cub starts to grow a mane at about the age of three, he is then driven out of the pride and must establish his own territory.

FAMILY MEETING
A large pride of lions rests near a waterhole. When members of the pride meet, they greet each other with soft moans, swinging their heads from side to side and holding their tails high. Then they head-butt.

Lion Pride

FIRST AT THE TABLE
Male lions usually eat first, even though the females do most of the hunting. Lions are the only cats that share their feast. All other cats kill prey and eat alone.

NURSERY SCHOOL
Young lions play tag to learn how to chase things and to defend their pride. The pride does not usually allow strange lions to join the family group. Young lions need to be prepared in case other lions come to fight with them.

CAT SCRAP
Two lionesses fight each other to decide who will be the first to eat. There is usually a dominant female in each pride, even when there are males around. This chief female rules the family.

MOTHER AND CUBS
Lionesses give birth to a litter of between one and six cubs. Males cubs stay with their mother for over two years and the females usually stay for a lifetime. The mother calls her cubs to her with a soft growl and they respond.

lionesses help to raise the young together and even suckle each other's cubs

Cat Communication

The social lions are the exception among big cats. Most cats lead solitary lives. They hunt alone and the females bring up their cubs alone. Big cats come together only when they want to mate. Their loner lifestyle has evolved because of their need to find food. There is usually not enough prey in one area for a large group of big cats to live on.

All wild cats have territories which they defend from other cats. These areas will include a hunting area, drinking places, lookout positions and (for females) a den where she brings up her young. Female cats have smaller territories than males. Males that have more than one mate have territories that overlap with two or more female territories.

Did you know? Big cats' territories range from a few kilometres to over 1,000 sq km.

▲ **BRINGING UP BABY**
Female snow leopards bring up their cubs on their own. They have up to five cubs who stay with their mother for at least a year. Although snow leopards are loners, they are not unsociable. They like to live near each other and let other snow leopards cross their territories.

◄ **THE LOOKOUT**
A puma keeps watch over its territory from a hill. Pumas are solitary and deliberately avoid each other except during courtship and mating. The first male puma to arrive in an area claims it as his territory. He chases out any other male that tries to live there.

▲ **A PRIDE OF LIONS**
The lions in a pride drink together, hunt together, eat together and play together. They try to avoid contact with other prides. To tell the others to keep out of its territory, the pride leaves scent markings on the edge of its range.

Daniel and the Lions' Den
A story in the Bible tells how Daniel was taken prisoner by Nebuchadnezzar, king of Babylon. When Daniel correctly interpreted the king's dreams he became the king's favourite. His enemies became jealous of his position and had him thrown into a lions' den, a common punishment for prisoners at the time. But instead of eating Daniel, the lions befriended him. They were tamed by his great faith in God.

▲ **FAMILY GROUPS**
A cheetah mother sits between her two cubs. The cubs will leave their mother at about 18 months old and the female then lives alone. Males, however, live in small groups and defend a territory. Male cheetahs are the only big cats apart from lions to live in groups.

▲ **WELL GROOMED**
Cats that live together groom each other. They do this to be friendly and to keep clean. Cats also groom to spread their scent on each other, so that they smell the same. This helps them to recognize each other and identify strangers.

The Communities of Wolves

Wolves are very social animals. A few may live alone, but most live in packs. Most wolf packs have between 8 and 24 members. The main purpose of living in a pack is to hunt. A team of wolves working together can hunt down and kill much larger and stronger prey than a solitary wolf could. Only the strongest, healthiest pair in the wolf pack will actually mate. Every pack member then helps to feed and bring up the cubs.

Other canids have a similar social structure. Bush dogs, dholes and African hunting dogs also live in packs, while jackals, and sometimes coyotes and raccoon dogs, live in smaller family groups. Maned wolves and foxes usually live alone and prey on smaller animals.

▲ TWO'S COMPANY
A pair of jackals drink from a water hole in South Africa. Most jackals pair up for life and co-operate over rearing their pups. Jackals also work together when hunting. They use yips, growls, hisses and howls to work together to hunt down their prey.

Did you know? Foxes produce alarming screams when looking for a mate.

ON PATROL ▶
A wolf pack is led by the strongest, most experienced animals. Every morning the pack patrols the edges of its territory, making fresh scent markings and checking for strange scents that will tell them if rival wolves have been there.

▲ **A FAMILY AFFAIR**
Dholes live in family packs of between five and twelve animals. Sometimes several families join together to form a large dhole pack called a clan. Hunting in a big group helps these relatively small wild dogs to tackle large prey such as wild cattle and buffalo.

maned wolf
(Chrysocyon brachyurus)

▲ **EACH FOR ITSELF**
The maned wolf is mostly solitary, living and hunting rodents on its own. It does not howl, but barks, whines and yaps like a domestic dog. It also growls when it is frightened or preparing to attack.

◄ **COYOTE COUPLE**
Most coyotes live and hunt alone, in pairs or in small family units. Coyotes mark their territory with urine or faeces. The smell warns intruders that another coyote is living here and to stay away.

DOG SOCIETY ►
African hunting dogs are the next most social canids after wolves, and hunt co-operatively. Unlike most other canids, however, African hunting dogs are not territorial and do not make scent markings with their urine.

Living in

A wolf pack has a strict social order and each member knows its place. The senior male and female, known as the alpha male and female, are the only animals to breed. The alpha male takes the lead in hunting, defends the pack members from enemies, and keeps the other animals in their place. In most packs, a second pair of wolves, called the beta male and female, come next in the ranking order. The other pack members are usually the offspring of the alpha pair, aged up to three years old.

LEADER OF THE PACK
An alpha male wolf greets a junior pack member. Wolves use different body positions and facial expressions to show rank. The leader stands upright with tail held high. The junior has his ears laid back and his tail tucked between his legs.

IT'S A PUSHOVER
A junior wolf rolls over on its back in a gesture of submission to a more dominant pack member. A junior wolf can also pacify a stronger animal by imitating cub behaviour, such as begging for food.

SHOWING WHO IS BOSS
A wolf crouches down to an alpha male. The young wolf whines as it cowers, as if to say, "You're the boss." The pack leader's confident stance makes him look as large as possible.

a Wolf Pack

"I GIVE UP"
A male grey wolf lays its ears back and sticks its tongue out. Taken together, these two gestures signal submission. A wolf with its tongue out, but its ears pricked, is sending a different message, showing it feels hostile and rebellious.

REJECTED BY THE PACK
Old, wounded or sickly wolves are often turned out of the pack to become lone wolves. Although pack members may be affectionate with each other, there is no room for sentiment. Young wolves may also leave to start their own packs. Lone wolves without the protection of a pack are much more vulnerable to attack and must be more cautious.

SCARY SNARL
A grey wolf bares its canine teeth in a snarl of aggression. Studies have shown that wolves use up to 20 different facial expressions. Junior wolves use snarling expressions to challenge the authority of their leaders. The alpha male may respond with an even more ferocious snarl. If it does so, the junior wolf is faced with a choice. It must back down, or risk being punished with a nip.

Primates Living Together

All primates communicate in some way with other members of their species, and most of them live in social groups. Community living has advantages. There are more eyes to spot predators, and several animals can work as a team to fight off attack or forage for food. As a community, they stand a better chance of survival if there is a problem with the food supply, during a drought, for instance. The leaders will feed themselves and their young first to make sure that they survive. Solitary animals may have a hard time finding a mate, but within a group, there's plenty of choice. And, when there are young to be cared for, a community can provide many willing helpers.

Nocturnal prosimians rely on being solitary and silent to avoid being noticed by predators. Among bush babies and lorises, even couples live independently of each other, but they occupy the same patch, and their paths often cross. Babies stay with their mother until they are old enough to live alone.

▲ **TREE-SHARING**
Sifakas work together in groups of about seven adults to defend their territory. They are generally led by the females, and males may swap between groups. These prosimians gather in the higher branches of the trees in western Madagascar. If danger threatens, they all start a hiccuping groan.

HAPPY COUPLE ►
In the jungles of South America, male and female sakis mate and usually live as a couple for a year. The female cares for the young. The father may not spend the day with his family, but does return to them at night. If there is plenty of food, families mingle with each other, forming large, loosely-knit groups.

◄ **FEMALE RULE**
A female is in charge of this troop of black tufted-ear marmosets. As with most other New World marmosets and tamarins, there may be several other females, but only the head female breeds. She mates with all the males to make sure her top-level genes are passed on. As none of the males knows who is the father, they all help rear and protect the young.

EQUAL SOCIETY ►
The relationship between a woolly monkey mother and her children can last for life. Woolly monkeys live in troops – there may be 20 to 50 of them, with roughly equal numbers of males and females. Adult males often cooperate, and all the males and females can mate with each other. Individual females care for their own young. Woolly monkey groups are bound by an intricate web of relationships between all members that is hard for outsiders to understand.

◄ **MALE POWER**
These female hamadryas baboons are just two in a harem of several females. A single, top male mates with all the females to make sure he fathers all the children. Males with no harem live in separate bachelor groups of two or three. They try to mate with a harem when the leader is not looking. When the leader gets old, a few young males will team up to depose him. Once he has been chased away, the victors fight for control of the harem.

▲ **DON'T HURT ME**
This toque macaque is showing by its posture and expression that it is no threat. If an adult monkey wants to make friends, it may make a sound like a human baby gurgling. The other monkey will usually respond gently.

Monkey Signals

Attracting attention in a noisy forest is a challenge. Groups of tree-living monkeys and prosimians lose sight of each other and keep in touch by calling. Nocturnal prosimians, however, need to keep a low profile, and so they leave scent messages that are easier to place accurately.

All prosimians and, to a lesser extent, monkeys, send messages of ownership, aggression or sexual readiness with strong-smelling urine, or scent from special glands. Monkeys can also express their feelings with facial expressions and gestures, and some use their ability to see in colour. African guenons, for example, have brightly coloured patches on their bodies that can be seen by their companions when they are hurtling through the trees. Even fur and tails can be useful. Ring-tailed lemurs swish their tails menacingly at rivals, and at the same time, fan evil smells over them.

Did you know? Monkeys have more face muscles than prosimians and pull more expressions.

PERSONAL PERFUME ▸
A black spider monkey smears a strong-smelling liquid on a branch. The liquid is produced by a gland on the monkey's chest. Its smell is unique to this monkey. When other monkeys smell it, they know that another of their kind has been there. If they meet the particular monkey that left the scent, they will recognize it.

◀ TELL-TAIL SIGNS
In complicated langur societies, high-ranking males hold their tails higher than lesser members of the group. Primates that live in complex social groups have a wider range of communication skills than solitary species. More information has to be passed around among a greater number of individuals.

▲ YOU SCRATCH MY BACK…
Grooming a fellow monkey not only gets rid of irritating fleas and ticks, but also forges a relationship. A lot of monkey communication is about preventing conflicts among group members. Forming strong personal bonds holds the troop together.

▲ BE CAREFUL
A mandrill has mobile face muscles to make different expressions. Here, he pulls back his gums and snarls. This makes him look very menacing to other males.

▲ I'M ANGRY
When a mandrill becomes angry, he opens his mouth in a wide yawn to show the size of his teeth and roars. Another monkey will hesitate before confronting this male.

LOOKING FIERCE ▶
This marmoset is literally bristling for a fight. Its fur stands on end like an angry cat's to make it look much bigger. It may scare its rival into withdrawing. Marmosets look cute, but they squabble a lot among themselves.

Ape Groups

▲ **GENTLE GIANTS**
Life in a gorilla group is generally friendly and there is seldom serious fighting within the group. The silverback (named for the white hair on its back) can stop most squabbles by strutting and glaring at the troublemakers. He is the group's leader, deciding where it will travel and where it will settle.

Of all the apes, chimpanzees live in the largest groups – up to about 100 individuals. The chimps constantly change their friends and often drop out altogether to spend time on their own. A chimpanzee group is based around the most important male chimps. Gorilla groups are similar but smaller, led by a strong adult male called a silverback. Bonobos live in smaller groups than chimpanzees, but their society is led by females rather than males. Orang-utans tend to live on their own, although females and their young spend a lot of time together while the youngster is growing up. Gibbons have a completely different social system from that of other apes – they live in family groups of a mother, father and their young.

Did you know? Bonobos can understand language as well as a human toddler.

bonobos
(Pan paniscus)

▼ **SOCIABLE SOCIETY**
Bonobos are very sociable creatures. Most of the time they live in large, loose groups, called communities, which are split up into smaller groups of 15 or less when foraging for food.

◄ HAPPY FAMILIES

Gorillas like to live in extended family groups, usually with between five and thirty members. A gorilla without a group will do its best to join one or start a new one. Each group is controlled and defended by a silverback.

LONE ORANG ►

Orang-utans spend most of their time alone. One reason for this may be that they need to eat a lot of fruit every day. If lots of orang-utans lived together, they would not be able to find enough fruit to eat. Even when they do meet, they often ignore each other.

▲ TREETOP SINGERS

Gibbons live in family groups and are the only apes to mate for life. A mated pair of gibbons 'sing' a loud duet to declare their territory to other gibbons in the forest. The male hoots, whoops and wails, while the female makes a rising twitter.

BEST FRIENDS ►

Females form the backbone of a bonobo group. Adult female bonobos form strong friendships, which are reinforced by grooming and hugging each other. This group of female bonobos have been raised in captivity. Boredom in captivity leads some apes to pluck out their hair.

bonobos
(Pan paniscus)

Great Ape Language

Although apes cannot speak, they communicate with a variety of sounds, facial expressions and gestures. Scientists have even learned some of this ape-speak in order to reassure the apes they are studying, and avoid frightening the animals away. Orang-utans and gibbons both call loudly to stake their claim to their territory, rather as we would put up a fence and a 'keep out' sign around our property. In chimp and gorilla societies, body positions and gestures show which animals are most important, or dominant, and which are least important, or submissive. Chimps and gorillas also communicate through a variety of sounds, especially chimps, who can be very noisy apes.

▼ GIBBON DUET
As well as warning other gibbons to stay out of their territories, the duet sung by gibbon pairs may also help to strengthen the bond between them. The pair will also use facial expressions to show feelings such as fear and excitement.

siamang gibbon *(Hylobates syndactylus)*

▲ PULLING FACES
Chimpanzees have a variety of different expressions for communication. A wide, open and relaxed mouth is a play face used to start, or during, a game. An angry chimp clenches its lips shut.

◄ A GAME OF BLUFF
Rising on his back legs, a male silverback gorilla slaps his cupped hands rapidly against his chest, making a 'pok-pok-pok' sound. Then he charges forwards, tearing up plants and slapping the ground. This display is really a bluff to scare away rivals. Gorillas hardly ever fight, and a male usually stops his charge at the last minute.

▲ GORILLA-SPEAK
Researchers observing gorillas in the wild have learned to make the same sounds and gestures as the gorillas. A content gorilla makes a rumbling belch sound. A sharp, pig-grunt noise means the gorilla is annoyed.

◄ KEEP OUT!
Fully grown male orang-utans usually keep to a particular area of forest – up to 10 sq km. This is called their home range. Every day, a male roars loudly to warn other orang-utans to stay away. This long call lasts for about two minutes. By calling, males avoid meetings that might end in a fight.

TOP CHIMP ►
The dominant chimpanzee in a group shows off occasionally by charging about, screaming and throwing branches. He also hunches his shoulders and makes his hair stand up on end.

▼ LOW RANK
To avoid fighting with important chimps, low-ranking chimps behave in a certain way. They flatten their hair, crouch down or bob up and down, and back towards the more important chimp, while pant-grunting.

The Close

All the chimpanzees in a community know each other well. Mothers have a very strong bond with their young, and many chimps who are not related form close friendships, especially males. Dominant males form the stable core of a chimpanzee group and they will attack and even kill males from other communities. Female chimps may emigrate to a neighbouring community. Members of a community will meet, spend time together and then separate throughout the day. In chimp society there is a hierarchy of importance, which is maintained by powerful males. The chimps jostle for position, constantly checking where they stand with each other and challenging their leaders.

YOU GROOM MY BACK

One of the most important activities in a chimpanzee group is grooming. It helps to keep the group together by allowing the chimps to strengthen friendships and patch up quarrels. High-ranking chimps are often groomed by low-ranking ones. It takes a young chimp about two years to learn how to groom properly.

MOTHERS AND BABIES

For the first three months of its life, a baby chimpanzee clings to its mother. By watching her face, it learns to copy her expressions of fear, anger and friendship. The bond between a mother chimpanzee and her young is very strong, and lasts for many years. In fact, the closest relationships within the family group are between a mother and her grown-up daughters.

Chimp Group

GANG WARFARE
A dominant male chimp often makes friends with two or three others, who spend time with him and back him up in fights. Powerful supporters enable a chimp to become a leader.

PLAYTIME
As young chimpanzees play, they get to know how to mix with the other chimps in a group. They learn how to greet others and which individuals are the most important.

FRIENDSHIP
To show their affection for one another, chimps hug, kiss and pat each other on the back. As males spend much more time together than females, this friendly contact is more common between males, although females strike up special friendships, too.

NOISY CHIMPS
Chimpanzees make more than 30 different sounds. When they are contented, they make soft 'hooing' noises, when they discover food they hoot, and when they are excited they scream.

Whale Life

Many toothed whales – which eat fish and squid – are sociable and live together. Sperm whales live in groups of up to about 50. A group may be a breeding school of females and young or a bachelor school of young males. Older male sperm whales usually live alone. Beluga whales often live in groups of several hundred.

Baleen whales are not as sociable and move singly or in small groups. This is probably because they filter huge amounts of small creatures out of the water as they swim – they could not find enough food if they lived close together.

▲ **HERD INSTINCT**
Beluga whales gather together in very large groups, or herds. They are noisy creatures whose voices can clearly be heard above the surface. This is why they are sometimes called sea canaries. Belugas have a wide range of facial expressions and often appear to be smiling.

Did you know? Dolphins will nudge a sick member of the group up to the surface, so it does not drown.

▼ **BONDED ORCAS**
Two killer whales, or orcas, rise out of Antarctic waters together, as if on a signal. They are members of the same pod, or group, which stay together all their lives. The bonds between the animals are very strong. This helps them co-ordinate their activities, especially when they are hunting for food.

Did you know? Male whales often try to help injured females. Females rarely try to help injured males.

◂ **STAYING CLOSE**
Two Atlantic spotted dolphins swim with their young. Mother and young often play together, turning, rolling, and touching each other with their flippers. During play, the young dolphins learn the skills they need in later life.

▾ **HUMAN CONTACT**
A bottlenose dolphin swims alongside a boy. These dolphins usually live in social groups but lone animals often approach humans.

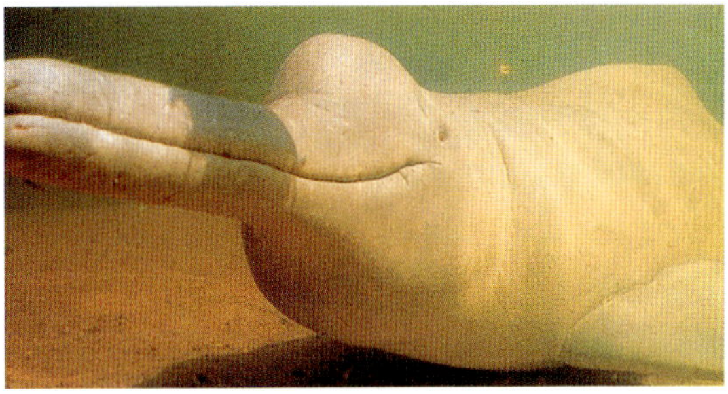

▴ **SOLITARY SWIMMER**
An Amazon river dolphin rests on the river bed. It spends most of its life alone, or with just one other. This solitary behaviour is typical of river dolphins, but untypical of most ocean dolphins and whales.

HELP AT HAND ▸
These long-finned pilot whales are stranded on a beach. Pilot whales usually live in large groups, with strong bonds between group members. One whale may strand itself on a beach. If others try to help they may also get stranded.

Dolphins at Play

Dolphins delight people with their acrobatic antics. They somersault, ride the bow waves of boats and go surfing. Dusky and spinner dolphins are particularly lively. In most animal species only the young play. In whale and dolphin society, adults play too. Often the animals seem to perform just for fun. But some antics have a purpose, such as sending signals to other dolphins.

Dolphins also use whistles and clicking sounds to communicate. Each dophin has a signature 'whistle' to identify it. As each dolphin 'talks' the other one listens.

▲ **PLAYFUL PAIR**
Two Atlantic spotted dolphins jostle as they play with a sea fan. Dolphins spend much of their time playing, especially the younger ones. They make up games, using anything they can find. Their games can last for many hours.

▼ **JUMPING FOR JOY**
A pair of bottlenose dolphins leap high, leaving the water together, as if they have rehearsed their act. They seem to jump for joy, but their behaviour may have a social function within their family group.

► PORPOISING ON PURPOSE

A group of long-snouted spinner dolphins go porpoising, taking long, low leaps as they swim. They churn the water behind them into a foam. Many dolphins practise porpoising, in order to travel fast on the surface.

Did you know? Killer whales like brushing against each other as they swim at high speed.

◄ RIDING THE WAKE

A Pacific white-sided dolphin surfs the waves. This is one of the most acrobatic of the dolphins, like other species of dolphins it likes to ride in the waves left in the wake of passing boats.

Did you know? The rough skin on a porpoise's back may be for giving calves piggy-back rides.

AQUATIC ACROBAT ►

This dusky dolphin is throwing itself high into the air. It twists and turns, spins and performs somersaults. This behaviour is like a roll call – to check that every dolphin in the group is present and ready to go hunting. The behaviour is repeated after hunting to gather the group together once more.

Did you know? A dolphin may play cat and mouse with its prey before eating it.

The Shark's Pecking Order

No shark is alone for very long. Sooner or later, one shark will come across another, including those of its own kind. In order to reduce the risk of fights and injury, sharks talk to each other, not with sound, but with body language. Sharks have a clear pecking order. The bigger the shark, the more important it is. Not surprisingly, small sharks tend to keep out of the way of larger ones. Many species use a sign that tells others to keep their distance. They arch their back, point their pectoral fins down and swim stiffly. If this doesn't work, the offending shark will be put in its place with a swift bite to the sides or head. Bite marks along its gill slits can be a sign that a shark has stepped out of line and been told firmly to watch out.

▲ **A COUPLE OF CHUMS**
Great white sharks were once thought to travel alone, but it is now known that some journey in pairs or small groups. Some sharks that have been identified by scientists will appear repeatedly at favourite sites, such as California's Farallon Islands, 42km off the coast of San Francisco. There they lie in wait for seals.

Did you know? Male sharks bite females to encourage them to mate.

◀ **BED FELLOWS**
Sharks, such as these whitetip reef sharks, will snooze alongside each other on the seabed. They search for a safe place to rest below overhanging rocks and coral, where, as fights rarely break out, they seem to tolerate each other. The sharks remain here until dusk, when they separate to hunt.

◄ **ATTACK MARKS**
This grey reef shark has swum too close to another, larger shark and has been bitten on its gill slits as a punishment. The marks on its skin show that its attacker raked the teeth of its lower jaw across the sensitive skin of the grey reef's gill slits. A shark's injuries heal rapidly, so this unfortunate victim will recover quickly from its wounds.

REEF SHARK GANGS ►
Sharks have their own personal space. When patrolling the edge of a reef, the blacktip reef sharks will tell others that they are too close by moving their jaw or opening their mouth. During feeding, order sometimes breaks down and a shark might be injured in the frenzy.

◄ **SHARK SCHOOL**
Every day schools of scalloped hammerhead sharks gather close to underwater mountains in the Pacific Ocean. They do not feed, even though they come across shoals of fish that would normally be food. Instead, they swim repeatedly up and down, as though taking a rest.

Schools for

By day scalloped hammerhead sharks swim in large groups called schools around underwater volcanoes in the Pacific, off the coast of Mexico, and the Cocos and Galapagos islands. This species of shark cannot stop swimming or it will drown, so schools are a safe resting place for them. Even sharks have enemies, such as other sharks and killer whales, and there is safety in numbers. In schools, scalloped hammerheads can also find a mate. At night, they separate to hunt. They swim to favourite feeding sites, they are thought to use their electric sensors to find their way.

BAD-TEMPERED SHARKS
The larger a female hammerhead becomes, the less likely she is to get on with her neighbours. Older and larger hammerhead sharks like more space than smaller, younger sharks. In hammerhead schools, the relationship between sharks seems to be controlled by constant displays of threat and small fights.

FEMALES ONLY
The sharks in this huge school of hammerheads are mainly females. The larger sharks swim in the centre and dominate the group, often butting one another to choose the best positions in which to swim. Not only is the middle safer, but it is also the place where the male sharks will be on the lookout for a mate.

Hammerheads

CLEAN UP OPERATION
At some gathering sites, such as Cocos Island in the eastern Pacific, sharks drop out of the school and swoop down to cleaning stations close to the reef. From the reef, butterfly fish dart out to eat the dead skin and irritating parasites that cling to the outside of the shark's body.

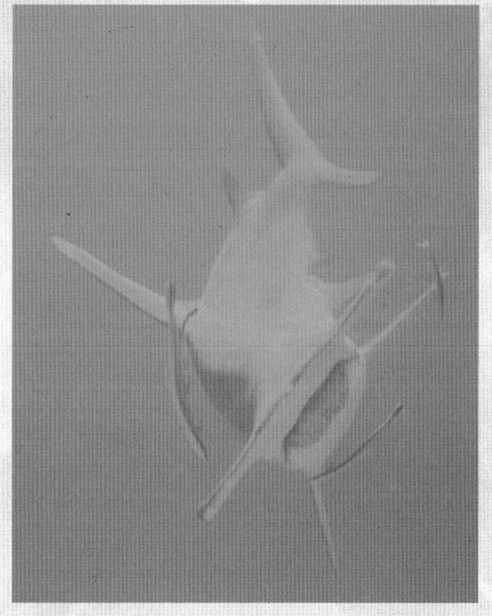

BODY LANGUAGE
Larger sharks within a school perform strange movements and dances to keep smaller sharks in their place. At the end of the movement, a large shark may nip a smaller one on the back of the head.

STRANGE HEAD
The scalloped hammerhead is so named because of the grooves along the front of its head, which gives it a scalloped (scooped out) appearance. The black tips on the underside of its pectoral fins are another way of identifying this shark.

Animals in Danger

Changes in climate or living conditions have caused some animal species to die out. More recently people have interfered with nature, endangering the future of many animals. This section examines why animals are in danger of becoming extinct and what is being done to protect them.

Facing Extinction

Over 6,000,000,000 people are living on the earth today, and numbers are growing at the rate of nearly 80,000,000 every year. Every day we take up more land for houses and crops as well as roads and factories, so there is less room for wildlife. The only animals that benefit from the human population explosion are things like cabbage white butterflies, grain weevils, and carpet beetles that have become pests on our crops and in our homes.

Habitat Destruction

The greatest threat to the world's wildlife is the loss of habitat. Rainforests are being destroyed at an alarming rate – in some parts of the world over 30 hectares are being cut down every minute – and with them go all the plants and animals that lived there. Scientists have estimated that about 50 species of rainforest plants and animals disappear every day. Thousands more species are in danger of becoming extinct in the next few years. They include the tiger, the Philippine eagle, and many beautiful butterflies. Elsewhere in the world, wetlands are being drained and grasslands are being ploughed up for crops or covered with concrete. Pollution of the air and the water harms many more animals, and so does the widespread use of insecticides and weedkillers.

Hunted for Food and Fun

People who traditionally hunted animals for food with bows and arrows did no harm to the wildlife populations. The invention of high-powered rifles, harpoons and other deadly weapons, however, meant that large numbers of animals could be killed for 'sport' and for skins, or simply because they competed with domestic livestock. Many animals then became rare and further hunting of them has put them in even greater danger.

Fishing is also a serious threat to some animals; the fishing nets that are now being used to catch tuna and other seawater fishes also kill large numbers of dolphins. The animals get tangled up in the nets and are unable to get to the surface to breathe. Conservationists are urging people not to buy the fish that are caught by these killer nets in an attempt to prevent the problem.

Dolphins and killer whales are always popular animals at aquariums, but it is not to their benefit to keep them in captivity.

The Remedies

The most obvious and important thing is to stop destroying wild habitats. Many animals are already protected in nature reserves, where the habitats are safe from destruction, but before creating reserves biologists need to know how much space the animals need and how far they travel in their search for food. Such information is often obtained by putting little radio transmitters on the animals and listening for the signals to find out where the animals go. This has been done with bears, wolves, and big cats.

Gorillas, orang-utans, chimpanzees and bonobos are all endangered species. To help them survive in the future, their habitat needs to be protected in national parks or reserves.

Many countries have laws that control hunting and prohibit the killing of rare and endangered animals, but it is not easy to enforce these laws because it is impossible to patrol vast areas of forest and savanna. Elephants and big cats are legally protected but poachers still kill them for their ivory and skins. The Convention on International Trade in Endangered Species (CITES) is dedicated to stopping all trade in endangered species and any article that comes from them – such as ivory, tortoiseshell, skins, fur and feathers. If the objects cannot be exported or sold, people will hopefully be less interested in killing the animals.

Re-introductions

Several species that have been threatened with extinction have been saved by being taken into zoos or wildlife parks and bred there in safety. When the population is big enough, it is sometimes possible to release the animals back into the wild – as long as suitable habitat remains or can be re-created. The Arabian oryx was the first large animal to be saved from extinction in this way. Other animals that have been successfully re-established in the wild include the Hawaiian goose, Przewalski's horse, and the golden lion tamarin.

Many species of wild horses and asses are a cause for concern as they live in isolated groups and are in great danger of becoming extinct.

A bright outlook?

The future for some wild animals depends on whether their habitat can remain, if they continue to be destroyed then the only place that these large and fascinating animals will be seen will be in the confined spaces of zoos.

Battling Beetles and Bugs

Beetles and bugs do many jobs that benefit people, either directly or indirectly. They pollinate plants and consume waste matter. They are also a valuable food source for other animals, including reptiles and birds.

However, most people regard these insects as pests because they can harm us or our lands and possessions. Aphids, chafers and weevils attack crop-fields, orchards, vegetable plots and gardens. Wood-boring beetles damage timber and furniture, and other beetles attack carpets and clothes. Blood-sucking bugs spread many human and livestock diseases, while sap-sucking bugs may carry plant diseases. People wage war against these pests – and many other harmless beetles and bugs. Some species are in danger of dying out altogether because people are killing them, or destroying the places in which they live.

▲ CARPET-CRUNCHER
A carpet beetle larva munches on a woollen carpet. These young beetles become pests when they hatch out on carpets and clothes. The larvae have spines on their bodies that protect them from enemies. A close relative, the museum beetle, also causes havoc. It eats its way through preserved animal specimens in museums.

COLLECTING INSECTS ►
If you are collecting insects, remember to handle them carefully so that you do not damage them. Always return insects to the place where you found them. Do not try to catch delicate insects such as dragonflies, or ones that could sting you, such as wasps.

▲ DUTCH ELM DISEASE
Elm bark beetles are wood-borers. The fungus they carry causes Dutch elm disease, which kills elm trees. During the 1970s, a major outbreak of the disease destroyed most of the elm trees in Britain.

Manna from Heaven
The Old Testament of the Bible tells how the ancient Israelites survived in the desert by eating 'manna'. After many centuries of debate, historians now believe this strange food may have been scale insects, living on tamarisk trees.

▲ WOODWORM DAMAGE
This chair has fallen prey to woodworm. These beetles can literally reduce wood to powder. Laid as eggs inside the timber, the young feed on the wood until they are ready to pupate. As winged adults, they quickly bore their way to freedom, leaving tell-tale exit holes in the wood.

▲ GARDENERS' FRIEND
These black bean aphids are infested with tiny parasitic wasps. The female wasp lays her eggs on the aphids. When the young hatch, they eat the bugs. Gardeners consider aphids to be pests and welcome the wasps in their gardens. Wasps are sometimes used in large numbers by gardeners to control pests.

Swarms and Armies

Social insects affect our lives and the world we live in. We think of some species as friends, others as enemies. Bees are important because they pollinate crops and wild plants. They also give us honey and several other products. We fear bees and wasps for their stings, which can kill if the victim has a strong allergic reaction. However, bee venom contains chemicals that are used in medicine. Wasps help us by killing huge numbers of pests that feed on farmers' crops.

Plant-eating ants damage gardens and orchards, and can spoil food stores. Some types of ants protect aphids, which are a pest in gardens, but other ants hunt and kill caterpillars and other crop-harming pests. In tropical countries, termites cause great damage in plantations and orchards and to wooden houses. However, even termites play an important role in the cycle of life in their natural habitats.

▲ **WONDERFUL WAX**
Bees are much more helpful than harmful to people. They do not just give us honey – they also produce beeswax, which is used to make polish and candles, like the ones shown here. Some people eat royal jelly, which young bees feed on, because it is healthy and nourishing.

Did you know? Termite control is a multi-billion dollar industry.

◄ **WASP SAVES CABBAGE**
This hornet is eating a cabbage white caterpillar, which feeds on cabbage plants and is a pest for farmers and gardeners. Hornets are among the many wasp species that help farmers and gardeners by killing large numbers of insects that harm crops and prize plants. Some people spray cabbages and other plants to keep caterpillars at bay but this kills all sorts of harmless insects too.

▲ **FRUIT FARMERS' ENEMY**
In warm parts of the USA, leafcutter ants can become a major pest in plantations and orchards. These insects need large quantities of leaves to feed the fungi in their fungus gardens. A large colony of leafcutters can strip a fruit tree bare of leaves in a single night.

▲ **NATURAL PEST CONTROL**
These weaver ants are being used to control pests in an orange orchard. In China, weaver ant nests have been sold for the last 2,000 years, making them the earliest-known form of natural pest control. Farmers hang the nests in their trees and the ants eat the harmful pests.

◀ **TASTY TERMITE**
This man from West Africa is eating a fat, juicy termite queen, which is considered to be a delicacy in that part of the world. Social insects, including adult termites and young wasps, bees and ants, are eaten in many parts of the world, including Australia. In Western countries, people are squeamish about eating insects, but in some developing countries, tasty and nourishing insects provide up to 10 per cent of the animal protein in people's diets.

EATING YOUR WORDS ▶
Wood-eating termites have damaged this book. Termites also cause major damage to timber structures in some parts of the world. Some species burrow under buildings, where they damage the wooden foundations. People often do not even know the termites are there until the damage is done and the wood is eaten away. When they are found in time, people try to kill them by using chemical insecticides.

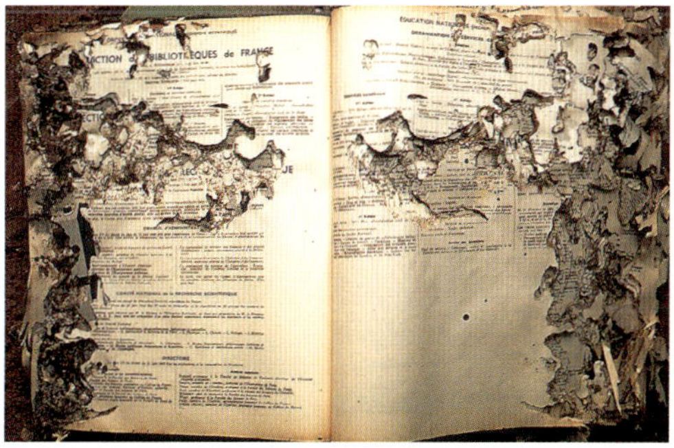

Insect Conservation

Just as insects affect our lives, so we affect the lives of insects. As human populations expand, we change the wild places where insects live. For example, large areas of tropical rainforest are being felled for timber or fuel, and to build settlements. This threatens the survival of the forest's plants and animals, including thousands of insect species. In developed countries all over the world, farms cover large areas that used to be wild. Crops are a feast for many insects, so their numbers multiply quickly and they become pests. Many farmers use chemical insecticides to protect their crops from the pests, but these chemicals kill 'helpful' insects along with the pests.

All over the world, conservationists fight to save rare animal species, such as tigers. It is important that we start to protect insects, too.

▲ **POISON SPRAY**
A tractor sprays insecticide over a field. The poisonous chemicals kill not only pests but also other insects such as bees, which pollinate flowers, and wasps, which prey on the pests. Some types of insecticide are now banned because they damage and pollute the natural world. Herbicides designed to control weeds also kill wild plants that insects feed on.

◄ **FOREST DESTRUCTION**
A forest is being felled for timber. The tropical rainforests contain over half of all known animal species, including thousands of insects. Destroying forests affects not only large animals but also tiny insects. Experts fear that some insects in these huge forests may become extinct before they have even been identified.

◄ **PROTECTED BY LAW**

In temperate forests, wood ant colonies do a vital job in preying on insects that harm the forest. In Aachen, Germany, in 1880, the wood ant became the first insect to be protected by a conservation law. It is now protected in several other European countries. Foresters also help to protect the insects by screening off their mounds to prevent people from stealing the young ants to use as fish food. Although one wood ants' nest may contain up to a million insects, including several hundred queens, it is still vulnerable to human destruction.

HELPING THE FOREST ►

Termites become our enemies when they move into our houses and eat wooden beams and furniture. People kill them using poisonous chemicals. In the wild, however, even these unpopular insects do a useful job. As they munch through leaves and wood, they help to break down plant matter so the goodness it contains returns to fertilize the soil.

◄ **RARE BEE**

A long-tongued bumblebee feeds from a field bean flower. This and several other crops can be pollinated only by bumblebees with long tongues. In some areas, however, domestic honeybees now thrive at the expense of the native long-tongued bees. When the long-tongued bees become scarce, the plants that depend on them for pollination are threatened too.

VITAL FOR POLLINATION ►

Many of the most popular fruits and vegetables are pollinated by honeybees. These include apples, pears, melons, onions, carrots and turnips. Honeybees also pollinate other important crops, such as cotton. Experts estimate that up to a third of all human goods depend on bees for pollination.

Butterflies in Peril

Increasing numbers of butterfly and moth species are becoming rare or even endangered. Their homes are lost when forests are cut down, hedgerows are pulled up, wetlands are drained and fields are sprayed with pesticides. All wild creatures have been endangered to some extent by human activity, but butterflies and moths have suffered more than most. The life of each species is dependent on a particular range of food plants. Any change in the habitat that damages food plants can threaten butterflies and moths. For example, the ploughing up of natural grassland has significantly reduced the numbers of Regal Fritillary in North America, while tourism in mountain areas may kill off the magnificent Apollo butterfly.

▲ **MORPHO PENDANT**
Millions of blue morpho butterflies are collected and made into jewellery. Only the brightly coloured males are collected, but this leaves the females without mates to fertilize their eggs.

▲ **WANTED DEAD OR ALIVE?**
In the 1800s, millions of butterflies were caught and killed by collectors. At the time, their activities had little effect on populations because so many butterflies remained in habitats that were undisturbed. The destruction of habitat since the 1800s has made some butterflies very rare. Collecting even a few specimens now could push some species towards extinction.

▼ **A RARE SIGHT**
The false ringlet is probably Europe's most endangered butterfly. The drainage of its damp grassland habitats has led to its disappearance from all but a few areas.

False Ringlet
(Coenonympha oedippus)

▲ **CLEARED AWAY**
Rainforests are cut down and burned by developers to create new farmland and towns. Many species of butterfly and moth are threatened by the destruction of rainforest habitat.

Did you know? The large blue butterfly became extinct in Britain in 1979, but has been reintroduced to certain areas.

▼ **TWO-PRONGED ATTACK**
The scarlet swallowtail butterfly is found only in the Philippines. It is now under threat because the rainforests it inhabits are being destroyed by urban development. Thoughtless collectors also trap this insect as a highly prized specimen.

Scarlet swallowtail butterfly
(Papilio rumanzovia)

▲ **NO HOME TO GO TO**
The Kentish glory moth became extinct in England in the 1960s. This happened because the birch woods in which it lived were destroyed.

WORTHY OF WORSHIP
The ancient civilizations of Mexico were fascinated by the many brilliant butterflies that inhabit that part of the world. The people of Teotihuacan (around 150BC – AD650) adorned some of their temples with butterfly carvings. The Aztecs (around AD1200 – 1525) also worshipped a butterfly god.

Saving Spiders

Most people are scared of spiders. With their long legs, hairy bodies and a habit of lurking in dark corners, these little creatures have not made themselves popular. Yet spiders are truly fascinating animals. Only a handful are dangerous to people, and medicines, called antivenins, can now help people recover quickly from a deadly spider's bite. Many spiders are useful in helping to control insect pests in our homes as well as on crops and in gardens. In most countries it is considered bad luck to kill a spider, but people are their greatest threat. We destroy their habitats and reduce their numbers in the wild by collecting some species to be sold as pets.

▲ NO FEAR
This man is obviously unafraid of spiders. He is quite happy to have a tarantula walk over his face. One of the greatest threats to spiders is our fear of them. People kill often harmless spiders just because they are scared. Some experts think we are born with a fear of spiders. This may be because a few were dangerous to our distant ancestors.

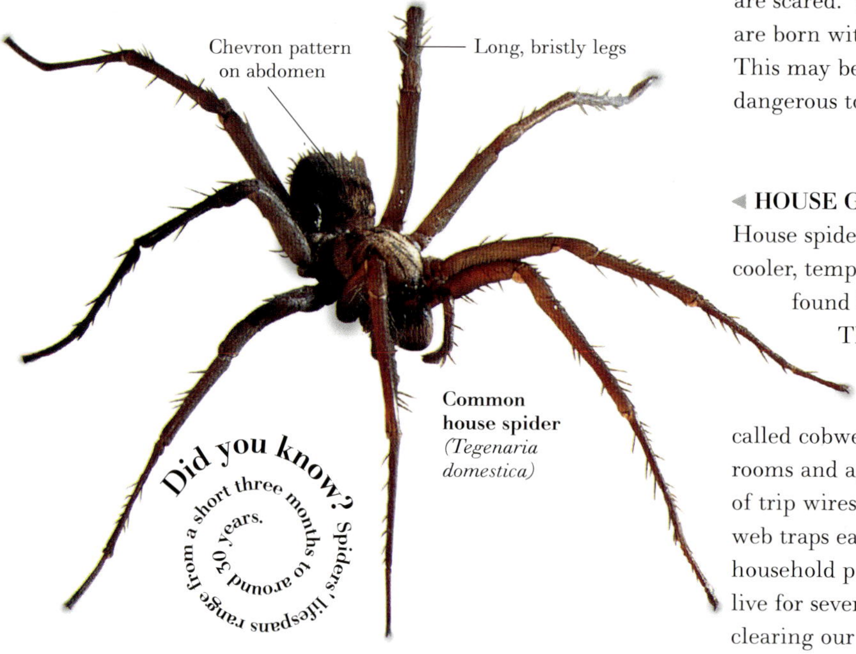

Common house spider *(Tegenaria domestica)*

Did you know? Spiders' lifespans range from a short three months to around 30 years.

◄ HOUSE GUEST
House spiders are far from rare. In cooler, temperate countries, they are found in most people's homes. The common house spider leaves unwelcome, dusty sheet webs, called cobwebs, in the corners of rooms and against windows. A maze of trip wires across the surface of the web traps earwigs, flies and other household pests. House spiders may live for several years, quietly clearing our homes of insects.

HABITATS IN DANGER

People destroy and pollute the places in which spiders and many other animals live. Clearing tropical rainforests, such as this one in Paraguay, South America, is particularly destructive. A huge variety of species of spiders live in the rainforest, many of them not yet known to scientists.

Little Miss Muffett

Miss Muffett was the daughter of the Reverend Thomas Muffett, a spider expert. When she was ill, her father made her eat crushed spiders as a cure. This made her terrified of spiders. A fear of spiders is called arachnophobia.

SPIDERS SAVING US

This Piaroa shaman (medicine man) from Venezuela, South America, uses a tarantula hunting mask as part of a ceremony. In Europe and America, spiders have been used in the past to treat malaria, the plague, toothaches and headaches. Sometimes the spiders were hung in a bag around the neck or eaten.

Ladybird spider
(Eresus niger)

REALLY RARE

Fewer than 20 species of spiders around the world are listed as threatened with extinction. They include the ladybird spider shown here. However, there must be hundreds or even thousands more spiders in danger that we do not know about yet. Spiders need our protection. For example, the Mexican red-knee tarantula is now rare in the wild because of over-collection by the pet trade. Mexican red-knee tarantulas that have been bred in captivity may help this species to survive.

Snakes Alive

Some snakes are killed because people are afraid of them. Farmers often kill snakes to protect their farm animals and workers, although many snakes actually help farmers by eating pests. In some countries snakes are killed for food or used to make medicines. To help snakes survive, people need to take action to preserve their habitats, so that snakes can live in safety.

▲ **FINDING OUT MORE**
Scientists use an antenna to pick up signals from a transmitter fitted to a rattlesnake. This allows them to track the snake. The more we can learn about snakes, the easier it is to protect them.

▲ **TROPHY**
There are still those who shoot snakes for recreation. The hunters put the snake's rattle or head on display as a trophy demonstrating their sporting achievements.

► **SNAKES IN DANGER**
Snakes, such as this Dumeril's boa, are in danger of dying out. Threats include people taking them from the wild and road building in places where they live.

▲ USING SNAKE SKINS
Snake skins have been used for many years to make jewellery. Some species have declined as a result of intensive killing for skins in some areas. Recently, countries such as Sri Lanka and India have banned the export of snake skins.

▼ ROUND-UP
This show in North America demonstrates the skill of capturing a rattlesnake. Today, rattlesnake hunts are not as common as they once were.

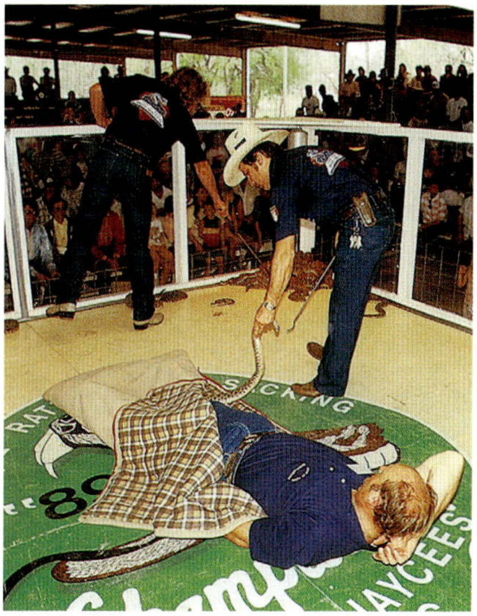

Did you know? Legend says St Patrick banished snakes from Ireland to rid the country of evil.

▼ PET SNAKES
Some people like to keep pet snakes. However, they can do very little and are not happy in captivity. Snakes can lose the ability to hunt and dislike being kept in a confined space.

Crocodile Conflict

Many people only ever see a crocodile or an alligator in a story book, on the television or at the cinema. These reptiles are often portrayed as huge, fierce monsters that attack and eat humans. Such images have given crocodiles and their relatives a bad name. A few large crocodiles, such as the Nile and saltwater crocodiles, can be very dangerous. But most are timid creatures that are no threat to humans. Humans are a much bigger threat to crocodiles than they are to us. People hunt them for their skins to make handbags, shoes and belts. Traditional Oriental medicines are made from many of their body parts and their bones are ground up to add to fertilizers and animal feed. Crocodile meat and eggs are cooked and eaten, while perfume is made from their sex organs, musk and urine.

▲ **LURKING DANGER**
The barely visible head of an American alligator proves why swimming is not allowed in this lake. Alligators do occasionally attack people but this usually happens only when humans have invaded their habitat or disturbed their nests or hatchlings.

► **CROCODILE DUNDEE**
One of the most dangerous and aggressive crocodiles is the saltwater crocodile, or 'saltie', which appeared in the film *Crocodile Dundee*. In the film, Mick 'Crocodile' Dundee, saves an American journalist from a surprise attack by a saltie. An adult saltie can grow up to 7m long and is likely to view a human entering its territory as a possible meal.

Krindlekrax

In Philip Ridley's 1991 story, Krindlekrax, *a baby crocodile from a zoo escapes into a sewer and grows enormous on a diet of discarded toast. It becomes the mysterious monster Krindlekrax, which lurks beneath the pavements of Lizard Street. Krindlekrax is eventually tamed by the weedy hero of the book, Ruskin Splinter, who wedges a medal down the crocodile's throat. He agrees to take the medal away if Krindlekrax will go back to the sewer and never come back to Lizard Street again.*

▲ **SKINS FOR SALE**
These saltwater crocodile skins are being processed for tanning. Tanning converts the hard, preserved skin into soft, flexible leather that can be made into bags, wallets, shoes and other goods. Some crocodile skin products are made from animals that were caught in the wild. But many skins come from crocodiles raised in specially created farms.

▲ **ALLIGATOR WALKABOUT**
An American alligator walks through a camp-site, giving the campers a close-up view. Attacks out of the water are rare – the element of surprise is lost and alligators cannot move as fast on land. Meetings like this are harmless.

A false, glass eye has been inserted into the head.

► **KILLED FOR A SOUVENIR**
A baby Siamese crocodile was killed so that its head could be made into this souvenir key-ring. Few tourists ever manage to see a wild crocodile, but if they buy souvenirs such as this, it means more animals will be killed for a cruel trade.

Croc Conservation

Although people are frightened of crocodiles and their relatives, they are a vital part of the web of life in many parts of the world. Crocodiles dig water holes that help other animals survive in dry seasons and they clean up the environment by eating dead animals. Scientists find crocodiles interesting because they are good at fighting disease and rarely develop cancers. They are also fascinating to everyone as survivors from a prehistoric lost world. We need to find out more about wild crocodiles so that we can help them survive in the future. Some species, such as the American alligator, the saltwater crocodile and the gharial have already been helped by conservation projects. But much more work needs to be done. If we are to save wild crocodiles, we must preserve their habitats, stop illegal poaching and smuggling, and breed rare species in captivity for release into the wild.

▲ **CROCODILE FARM**
Tourists watch a wrestler show off his skill at a crocodile farm. The farm breeds crocodiles for their skins, and attracts tourists for extra income. Farms help to stop crocodiles being taken from the wild. The Samutprakan Crocodile Farm in Thailand has helped to save the rare Siamese crocodile from dying out by breeding the species in captivity.

► **RESEARCH REFUGE**
Research at the Rockefeller Wildlife Refuge in Louisiana, USA, helped to work out the best way of rearing American alligators in captivity. They are brought up in hothouses where temperature, humidity, diet and disease can all be controlled. The alligators are played music so they will be less disturbed by outside noises. In these conditions, alligators grow more than 1m a year – much faster than in the wild.

▶ **IDENTITY TAG**
This tag on the foot of a black caiman helps identify it once it has been released into the wild. If the animal is caught again, it can be measured and weighed and the figures compared with previous records. This shows how well the animal is surviving in the wild.

▲ **INTO THE FUTURE**
This boy from Guyana is holding a baby dwarf caiman. Small numbers of caimans are sold as exotic pets. If people are paid more money for a living specimen than a dead one, they are less likely to kill crocodiles for skins. Educating people about why crocodiles are important is necessary to ensure their future.

▶ **FEEDING TIME**
A Nile crocodile is fed at a breeding station in South Africa. Crocodiles grow well on ranches or farms where they are fed properly. These places also provide information about the biology, health and feeding patterns of the reptiles.

◀ **OFF TO A NEW HOME**
A row of black caimans, reared on a ranch in Bolivia, wait to be flown to the Beni Biosphere Reserve, where they will be protected. The number of wild black caimans has dropped dramatically, and the animals they used to eat have increased as a result. This has caused problems for people, such as capybaras eating crops and piranhas attacking cattle.

Raptors at Risk

▲ **TRIGGER HAPPY**
A shooting enthusiast takes aim. A dog stands nearby, ready to retrieve the fallen bird. Raptors are shot by irresponsible hunters every year, especially as they flock together when migrating.

▲ **GRIM WARNING**
A dead hawk is left dangling on a piece of rope. This age-old practice is used by farmers and gamekeepers to warn other birds of prey to stay away from their livestock.

Birds of prey have few natural enemies. In many habitats they are the top predators. Wild birds of prey have only one thing to fear – humans. Over the centuries, people have hunted raptors as pests because they have occasionally killed livestock, such as game birds. Recently people have killed birds of prey indirectly by using pesticides on seeds and crops. When birds eat contaminated animals, pesticides build up in their own bodies and eventually poison them. Even when they do not kill, some pesticides weaken eggshells, which affects breeding success. Many birds of prey are now protected by law. This, and the use of safer farm chemicals, has led to a recovery in the numbers of several species. However, in some countries the indiscriminate shooting of migrating birds is still a threat, as is the destruction of habitats in which they live.

◀ **RARE GIANT**
The Philippine eagle is one of the largest birds of prey and also one of the rarest. This is because the tropical forest it inhabits is being destroyed to create farmland and places for people to live. The Philippine eagle gets its name from the Philippine Islands, where it lives. It eats large birds and sometimes even catches monkeys.

◄ **DEADLY BUILD-UP**
This sparrowhawk has been poisoned. It has preyed on smaller birds that have eaten seeds or insects sprayed with chemical pesticides. Gradually, the chemicals built up in the sparrowhawk's body until they made it ill, finally causing its death.

Did you know? Barn owls and kites are killed by eating poison-resistant rats.

Alice and the Griffin
A griffin sits next to Alice in a scene from Alice's Adventures in Wonderland. *The griffin is a mythical creature. According to legend, it had the head and wings of an eagle but the body of a lion.*

▲ **HIT AND RUN**
A barn owl lies dead at the roadside, battered by a passing vehicle the night before. Motor vehicles kill thousands of birds every day and every night. At night, owls often hunt for small prey, such as mice and voles, in roadside verges and hedges. Their habit of flying slowly, close to the ground puts them in danger from passing cars and trucks.

Falcons and Falconry

Hunting with birds of prey is called falconry or hawking. It has been a popular sport in the Middle East for thousands of years. Today falconry has many followers in other parts of the world. Falconers use a variety of birds of prey for hunting. In the past, many of these birds were taken from the wild, and some still are. This puts wild populations in danger. For example, the goshawk became extinct in Britain, partly because its eggs and chicks were taken by falconers. Today it is back in the wild and flourishing, after having been reintroduced. Falconers need skill and patience to train a bird. First they must gain the bird's trust so that it will sit and feed on the fist. Then the bird must be trained to get fit and to learn to chase prey. Falconers fly birds on long lines, called creances, before allowing them to fly free.

▲ **KEPT IN THE DARK**
This picture displays two essential features of falconry equipment, or furniture. The leather hood is used when the bird is on the perch and also when it is taken out hunting. Falcons such as the one above need a flat block perch to rest on.

▶ **ANCIENT PURSUIT**
An Arab falconer proudly displays a falcon as it perches on a strong leather glove on his fist. Falconry has been a popular sport in the Middle East ever since it began there more than 3,000 years ago. The favourite birds of Arab falconers are the saker and the peregrine falcon.

▶ **KITTED OUT**
This lanner falcon is about to fly back to its handler. A leash is threaded through a ring (swivel) on the jess, which is attached to the leg of the falcon. A bell helps the falconer to locate the bird if it flies off.

▲ **LURING AND STOOPING**
Moving at speed, a lanner falcon chases a lure being swung by a falconer. Falconers use lures to get falcons fit and agile and teach them to be persistent hunters. They swing the lure around their bodies or high in the air, tempting the bird to fly at it and stoop (dive swiftly).

Did you know? Many falconry centres breed birds to protect those in the wild.

▲ **A BIRD ON THE HAND**
The first stage in training a falcon is to get it to sit on the fist whilst tethered. When it first does this, the bird should be rewarded with a piece of meat. Soon, it should actively step up, then jump on the fist to feed.

▲ **A SPORT OF KINGS**
In one scene on the famous Bayeux tapestry, King Harold of England is seen riding with a hawk on his fist. The tapestry portrays events leading up to the Battle of Hastings and the conquest of England by the Normans in 1066. Hawking, or falconry, was a favourite sport of noblemen in the Middle Ages.

Wild Horses

While domestic breeds of horses and asses multiply, their wild cousins fight for survival. The only wild horse that is still plentiful in its natural range is Africa's plains zebra. All of the other species live in small, isolated groups, and many are in danger of extinction. Some horses are bred in zoos and then returned to the wild in protected reserves.

Feral horses and asses are also in danger. These domestic animals gone wild are often considered pests and are shot or poisoned. The feral burro (ass) in North America is blamed for the decline of native bighorn sheep. Burros damage the topsoil and compete with the sheep for food and water. Nevertheless, the burro is protected by law, and charities have been set up to help the free-ranging herds.

▲ **SAVED FOR THE FUTURE**
Przewalski's horse once lived in the Altai Mountains of Mongolia. It disappeared from its natural habitat in 1968. Before the species became extinct, 13 were taken into captivity and bred in zoos all over the world. Now their descendants are being returned to the wild. Sixty horses have been reintroduced in a specially created mountain steppe reserve in Mongolia.

◄ **UPSETTING THE BALANCE**
Like all feral herds living on islands off the east coast of North America, Cumberland Island horses may upset the delicate island ecology. Birdwatchers say the horses should be removed as they are not natural. But the National Parks Service protects the horses. There is a rich range of wildlife on these islands, including feral hogs.

◀ CONTROLLED POPULATION

Chincoteaguen feral horses are kept at the Virginia end of Assateague Island off the east coast of North America. They are kept separate from the Assateague ponies, another feral group. The Chincoteague Volunteer Fire Company keeps the herd to below 150 animals. By doing this, they hope to lessen damage to the island ecology. Each year, some Chincoteague ponies are sold to help pay for the upkeep of the feral herd.

▶ BACK FROM THE BRINK

The onager is one of the smallest, fastest and nimblest members of the horse family. It is a subspecies of the Asiatic wild ass and lives in northern Iran. Intense hunting caused a huge population decline, and many were pushed out by fighting in World War I. Recently, the onager's numbers have been increasing.

▲ PROTECTED MUSTANGS

Life is not always easy for feral mustangs. They must survive harsh winters in the mountains. In many states, people keep a watchful eye on them, and herds are protected by government organizations.

▲ BORN FREE

A feral foal has the chance of a more natural life than its domesticated cousins. But horses are one of the animals that have thrived because of humans. There are about 60 million domestic horses in the world, far more than could be supported naturally.

Brought Back to Life

▲ **HORSE OR ZEBRA?**
The quagga looked like a cross between a zebra and a horse. It had stripes on its forequarters, like a zebra, but its hindquarters were plain, like those of a horse.

In the past few centuries, numerous creatures have become extinct because of over-hunting, or the destruction of their habitat. But it is now possible to recreate extinct species for release back into the wild. Scientists in South Africa are breeding an extinct zebra subspecies called the quagga, which died out over 100 years ago. Analysis of DNA from the cells of a quagga skin in a museum showed that the animal was a subspecies of the plains zebra. Suitable plains zebras with paler stripes were selected to start a breeding programme to bring the quagga back to life.

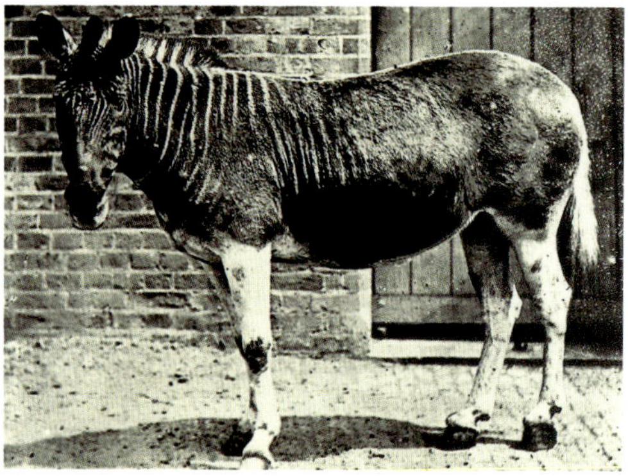

▲ **SWIFT DECLINE**
The quagga lived in a barren area of South Africa. Early settlers thought that it competed with their sheep and goats for the sparse grass. Millions of quaggas were slaughtered, many simply for sport. Some were transported to zoos. Breeding quaggas was not thought necessary because everyone believed there were plenty in the wild. The last quagga died in Amsterdam Zoo on 12 August 1883.

▲ **NEW BEGINNING**
Nine plains zebras like this one were chosen for the Quagga Project. In 1998, descendants of these nine were released in Karoo National Park. They are the only zebras there so will only breed among themselves. The offspring that are most quagga-like in each generation are selected for the next stage of breeding. It is a long process because it takes two to three years for a zebra to become sexually mature.

◀ **GETTING CLOSER**
One of the zebras from the Quagga Project shows that it is losing its zebra stripes. A descendant of the nine original plains zebras, it is browner and more quagga-like. It is hoped that eventually a foal will be born that matches the appearance of the extinct animal exactly.

▲ **SURVIVOR OF THE STEPPES**
The konik pony (above) comes from Poland. It is a descendant of the tarpan, a primitive pony that survived in the wild until the 1800s. The tarpan lived on the steppes of eastern Europe and western Asia. Its genetic make-up was identified by taking DNA from the konik and others of its descendants. Scientists selected the most tarpan-like animals and set up a breeding programme like the one for bringing back the quagga.

▲ **RETURNED TO THE WILD**
The Polish government are trying to recreate the tarpan. They released Przewalski's stallions (above) and tarpan-like mares, such as koniks and Icelandic horses, into two Polish nature reserves. Today, horses almost identical to the tarpan run wild there. Tarpans were victims of their own success. The stallions were fierce fighters and could take over harems of different breeds. This diluted the tarpan breed.

Elephants in Peril

Today wild elephants are in great danger. Experts warn that these animals must be protected if they are to survive in the future. Asian elephants are most at risk, with only between 36,000 and 44,000 individuals left in the wild. The main cause of their decline is humans taking their land. Activities such as building houses, mining, growing crops and constructing dams take up a lot of space. In Africa, the biggest threat to elephants is the ivory trade. African elephants have bigger tusks than Asian elephants and are therefore more valuable to hunters. Although the ivory trade was banned in 1989, it will take a long time for elephant numbers to recover.

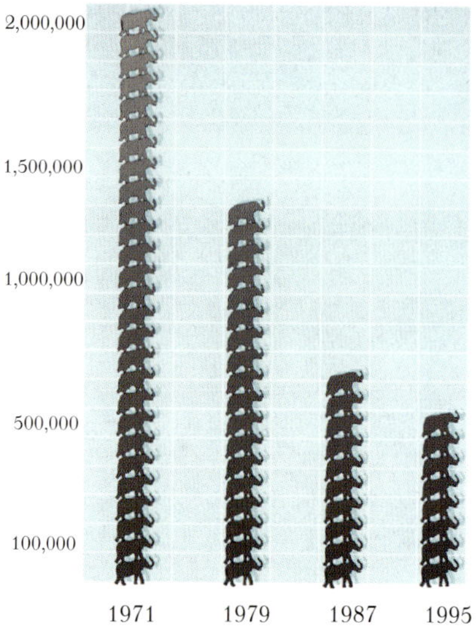

POPULATION CRASH ▲
Between 1971 and 1989, the number of elephants in Africa more than halved, from 2 million to 609,000. Up to 300 elephants were killed each day. More than 90% were killed illegally by poachers.

Did you know? Elephant meat is sold as food in some Asian countries.

◄ IVORY BONFIRE
In 1989, the Kenyan government burned US $3.6 million worth of ivory on this huge bonfire. They did this in order to support the worldwide ban on the trade in ivory. However, poachers will go on killing elephants illegally as long as people are prepared to pay huge sums of money for the tusks.

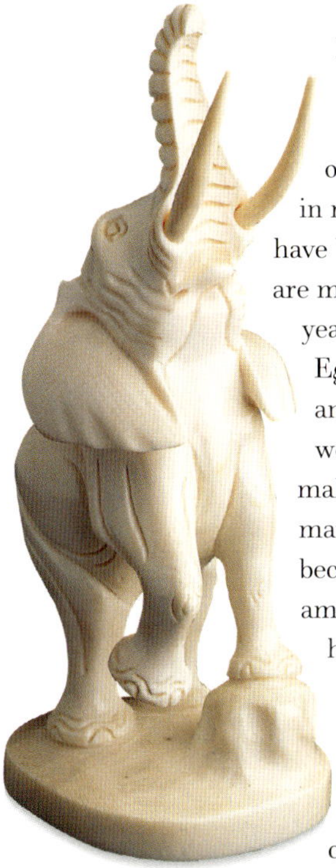

◄ **WHITE GOLD**
People have carved ivory for tens of thousands of years. Carvings in mammoth ivory have been found that are more than 27,000 years old. In ancient Egypt, both hippo and elephant ivory were carved. Ivory makes an ideal material for trade because even a small amount has a very high value. It is easy to carve but hard enough to last, and has a smooth, cool surface.

▲ **KILLED BY POACHERS**
When poachers kill elephants, they only want the tusks. They leave the rest of the elephant to rot. Before the ban on ivory trading was set up, an African poacher could earn hundreds of dollars for just one pair of tusks. It would take the poacher a year to earn this much money in an ordinary job.

▲ **TOO MANY ELEPHANTS**
African elephant feet are sometimes sold to raise money for conservation. These animals were killed legally in a National Park where elephant numbers had grown too high.

▼ **ELEPHANTS OR PEOPLE?**
These elephants are invading a farmer's home and fields in Kenya, east Africa. The human population of Kenya is expected to double by the year 2020, putting enormous pressure on the land. Finding enough land for both people and elephants will be a problem. Elephants will not be able to roam freely, as they have been able to do in the past. Instead, they will be confined to special areas.

▲ **WELL LOOKED AFTER**
A zoo elephant has its foot cleaned with a hoof knife. Zoos play a major role in conserving animals. But elephants are not often bred in zoos because bulls are difficult to handle and can be dangerous.

Protecting Elephants

Elephants need to be conserved if they are to survive. Many African and Asian countries have set aside areas of land called national parks or nature reserves. Here, elephants are protected from the threat of poachers. However, this is not a perfect solution. Elephants in reserves are so well protected that their numbers steadily rise. Confined to a protected area, they eventually eat everything within it. Rangers are then forced to kill some elephants to let others live. Other elephant conservation efforts include banning the trade in ivory. Several alternatives to ivory exist which are not a threat to wildlife, including plastics, resins and the nuts of a South American palm tree.

▲ **WALRUS WORRIES**
When the trade in elephant ivory was banned in 1989, poachers turned their attention to walrus ivory instead. During 1989, poachers in speedboats shot at least 12,000 Alaskan walruses, whose tusks can grow almost a metre long.

▲ **POACHING PATROLS**
Guards in a national park in southern Africa hold wire traps left by poachers. Protecting elephants from poachers is dangerous work. As well as removing traps left for elephants, guards may become involved in gun battles with poachers trying to kill elephants.

◄ **ELEPHANT TRAVELS**
Sometimes, elephants are moved to areas where they have better chances of survival. Moving elephants is not an easy thing to do. Getting these huge, heavy animals into a truck or an aeroplane can be a tricky business. Sometimes a whole elephant family is moved. This helps these sensitive animals get over the trauma of being captured and taken somewhere new. They then settle into their new home more easily.

BORN FREE FOUNDATION

ELEFRIENDS

◄ **SUPPORT GROUPS**
Conservation groups such as Elefriends in the UK raise money to help conservation work in the wild. They also persuade people not to buy and trade in ivory.

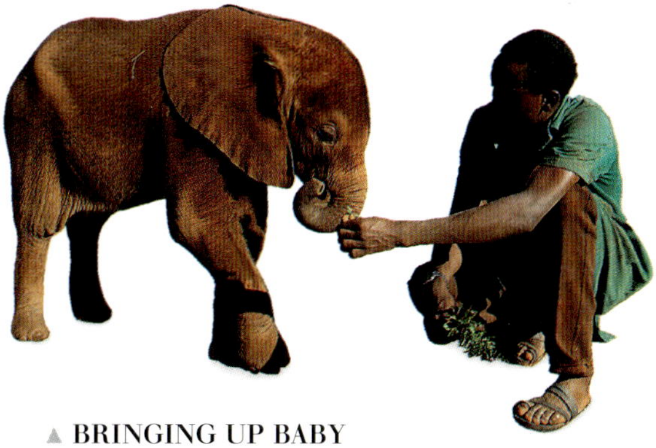

▲ **BRINGING UP BABY**
With a great deal of patience, care and understanding, orphaned baby elephants, such as this African elephant, can be raised in National Parks and returned to the wild. Raising a baby elephant is just as hard work as raising a baby human.

► **BIG ATTRACTION**
Tourists pay to watch elephants in national parks. This money is used to help run the parks and look after the elephants. It is also used to improve the lives of people living nearby. Many of these people have given up their land to save the elephants.

Bears in Danger

Of the eight species of bears living today, six are considered to be endangered. Only polar bears and American black bears are holding their own, and even they would not survive without considerable protection. Bears face many dangers. Their habitat is shrinking as natural areas are used to provide homes and farmland for people. Cubs are kept as pets but sold when they grow into troublesome adults. Many wild bears do not reach old age because they are shot by hunters. Hides and heads are used as wall hangings and trophies. In many parts of the world bear meat is eaten. Blood, bones and body parts are used in traditional Oriental medicines and as good luck charms. By far the biggest threat to bears is from poaching to supply the medicine trade.

▲ **DANCING BEAR**
A sloth bear is made to dance in India. Despite laws against it, bear cubs are taken from the wild. They are then taught to dance using cruel methods and kept in poor conditions.

◄ **CIRCUS ACT**
Bears have long been popular circus animals. Their ability to walk on their hind feet makes them appear almost human. These agile and clever animals are forced to perform tricks such as skipping, riding a bicycle and walking the tightrope. Performing bears are often badly cared for and may be made to work all year round.

▲ MAN VERSUS BEAST
Bears have been entertaining people for centuries. This carving from the AD300s depicts gladiators fighting bears in the arena. Both brown bears and polar bears were killed to entertain the audience.

◀ GOOD FOOD
We can learn a lot from bears. Native Americans discovered that many plants eaten by bears have medicinal properties. The Cheyenne treat diarrhoea with a plant called bear's foot and the Crow use bear root to cure sore throats.

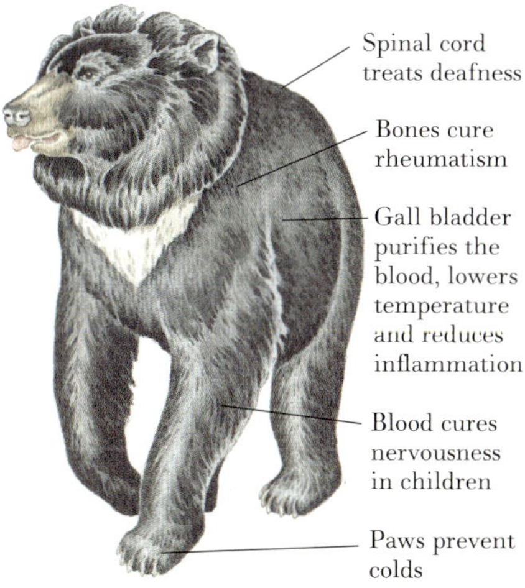

▲ MEDICINE CHEST
Bear organs are important in Oriental medicine. The most valuable part is the gall bladder, said to cure a whole host of ailments including fevers. Many bears are killed for their gall bladder alone.

▶ MEASURING UP
A scientist takes measurements from a tranquillized bear. A better understanding of the biology and behaviour of bears will hopefully secure them a safer future.

Churchill's

Each autumn, polar bears come into close contact with people at the isolated Canadian town of Churchill on the shores of Hudson Bay. The bears are on their way from the inland forests where they spend the summer, to the ice of the bay where they hunt. Often they arrive before the ice forms and cause a lot of trouble while they hang around with nothing to do. Some bears head for town and scare the local townsfolk. Others make for the town dump. The bears are chased away but some come back. Frequent offenders are tranquillized and taken somewhere safe. Despite the problems they cause, the bears have become a tourist attraction. People come from all over the world to see so many polar bears gathered together.

LOOKING FOR TROUBLE
This bear has picked up the tantalizing scent of tourists. Many visitors arrive to see the bears each year. They travel about in special buses called tundra buggies, where they are safe from the powerful and inquisitive bears.

READY FOR REMOVAL
A researcher cautiously tests a tranquillized polar bear to make sure it is fully sedated. He holds a gun in case the polar bear is not as sleepy as it seems to be and attacks. Polar bears at Churchill occasionally threaten people. They are tranquillized and moved a safe distance away or locked up in a trap until the ice refreezes.

Ice Bears

BEAR BACK
A polar bear keeps cool by rolling in a patch of snow while it waits for the ice to form on Hudson Bay. The days can be warm in the Arctic autumn. Polar bears have thick fur and may overheat if they are not able to cool down.

FAST FOOD
A bear scavenges through the town rubbish dump. This is a favourite rendezvous spot. Household rubbish provides easy food for hungry bears unable to hunt.

FREE FLIGHT
A sedated bear is carried away in a net strung under a helicopter. This is a quick way to move a large animal, but it is also very expensive.

THE SIN BIN
A rogue bear is released from a bear trap. Unfortunately, bears have a well-developed homing instinct and often appear in town again. Persistent offenders are kept in a polar bear jail until the ice refreezes.

Big Cat Casualties

▲ LION HUNT
Egyptian rulers hunted lions from horse-drawn chariots. Hieroglyphics (picture writing) tell us of Pharaoh Amenophis III (1405–1367BC) who killed over 100 lions in the ten years of his rule. Some experts now think that the Egyptians may have bred lions specially to hunt them.

The earliest record of people using big cat pelts (skins) dates from 6500BC. It comes from the archaeological site of Çatal Hüyük, in Turkey, where there is evidence that dancers wore leopard skins. Much more recently, in the 19th and 20th centuries, many wealthy people hunted big cats for the thrill of the chase. The skins of the animals killed were used to decorate the hunters' houses, and their heads were hung as trophies on the walls. Today, this kind of hunting is rare, and every effort is made to prevent it.

TIGER-HUNTING PRINCE ▶
This old painting on cotton shows an Indian prince hunting a tiger from the back of his elephant. Tiger hunting was a very popular pastime for many centuries in India. It was declared illegal in the 1970s.

▼ GREAT WHITE HUNTER

A hunting party proudly displays its tiger trophy. This photograph was taken in the 1860s. When India was under British rule, tiger hunting was considered to be a great sport by the British. Uncontrolled, ruthless hunting was a major cause of the tiger's dramatic fall in numbers.

▲ RITUAL ROBES

The Zulu chief Mangosothu Buthelezi wears wild cat skins on special occasions, like many African leaders and tribal healers. They are a sign of his rank and high status.

Did you know? The rarest of all the big cats is the snow leopard from the Himalayas.

◄ SLICED UP

A leopard is skinned, having been shot in the Okavango Delta in Botswana. Some game reserves raise money for conservation by charging huge sums to hunt. This only happens when numbers of a certain species are too large for the reserve.

SECOND SKIN ►

Some people continue to think it looks good to wear a coat made from the pelts of a wild cat. Many more, however, think that the fur looks much better on the cat. Designers now use fake fur and skins dyed to look like pelts, instead.

Conserving Cats

All big cats are in danger of extinction. They are hunted not only for their skins, but also for their teeth, bones and other body parts, which are used as traditional medicines in many countries. The Convention for International Trade in Endangered Species (CITES) lists all big cats under Appendix 1, which strictly controls their import and export. For cats particularly at risk, such as the tiger, all trade is banned. There are now many protected areas throughout the world where big cats can live without human interference. These areas are often not big enough, however, so the cats leave in search of food. They then attack livestock and sometimes local farmers.

▲ **IN ANCIENT TIMES**
This Roman mosaic shows a horseman hunting a leopard. Two thousand years ago, big cats were much more widespread. Until the 20th century, cheetahs lived throughout Africa, central India and the Middle East. Hunting big cats was not a problem when there were many of them but now the situation is desperate.

▲ **INDIAN PRIDE**
The last remaining Asian lions live in the Gir National Park in north-western India. There are fewer than 300 lions living in the forest park. The Asian lion is slightly different from the African lion. It has a smaller mane and a fold of skin running between its front and back legs.

▲ **SERENGETI LION PROJECT**
This lion has been drugged so that it can be fitted with a radio collar, before being checked and then released. In the Serengeti National Park in Tanzania, scientists use methods like this to study lion behaviour.

▲ **EYES ON THE BACKS OF THEIR HEADS**
Villagers in the Sundarbans mangrove forests in India wear masks on the backs of their heads. Tigers attack from behind, but will not usually strike if they see a face. The largest remaining tiger population in India is in the Sundarbans. Here 50 to 60 people die each year from tiger attacks. There is obviously not enough food for the tigers, so conservationists are trying to improve the situation. Another deterrent is to set up dummies that look and smell like humans, but give out an electric shock if attacked. There are also electrified fences in some areas, and pigs are bred and released as tiger food.

▼ **RADIO TRACKING**
Biologists attach a radio collar to a tigress in Nepal's Chitwan National Park. To save big cats we need to understand their habits and needs. For this reason, many scientists and conservationists are studying them. It is a very difficult task since cats are secretive and often nocturnal animals. One way of gathering information is to put a radio collar on a big cat and then follow its movements. By doing this, the animal can be tracked at long range.

The Biggest Big Cat of All
In Egypt, an enormous statue with a human head and the body of a lion guards the Great Pyramids at Giza. This statue is the Great Sphinx. A story written in 1419BC on the Sphinx tells of a prince called Thutmose IV who fell asleep between the paws of the statue. He dreamt that the Sun god told him to take away the sand covering part of the Sphinx and he would become a king. When he awoke, Thutmose did as he had been instructed, and the dream came true.

Wolves and People

Wherever wolves and wild dogs come into contact with people, the animals are regarded as dangerous pests that will kill livestock given the chance. They are poisoned, trapped and shot, not only for their skins, but for sport. Wolves were once the most widespread carnivores in the northern hemisphere. Now they have a much reduced range, often surviving only in small, scattered groups. Several wild dog species are endangered, including the Simien wolf, the red wolf and the African hunting dog. Much of the land where these animals once lived is now being farmed. Dholes have also become very rare as their forest habitat is destroyed. Some species, such as the Falkland Island wolf, a large fox, are already extinct.

▲ **WOLF HUNT**
In the Middle Ages domestic dogs were often used to kill wolves, as this Dutch engraving of 1880 shows. The last wolves were wiped out in England by 1500 and in Ireland by 1800.

Tame Wolf
This book is a first edition of the popular novel White Fang *by the American writer Jack London. Set in northern Canada, it describes how a wolf, named White Fang, is tamed and becomes a pet. In general it is not against the law to keep a wolf as a pet, but countries with restrictions require owners to have a special permit.* The Call of the Wild *by the same author describes how a pet dog joins a wolf pack and becomes wild.*

▲ **WOLF TERRITORY**
Grey wolves once had the greatest range of any wild land mammal. In the past, wolves were once common all across North America, throughout Europe, the Middle East and most of Asia. Their present range shows they have been exterminated in most of Mexico and the United States, in almost all of western Europe and over much of Asia.

◀ **NOWHERE TO RUN**
A hunter in Colorado, shoulders a coyote he has shot. In country areas, farmers shoot or poison coyotes because they kill sheep and other livestock, and spread disease. Elsewhere, when coyotes and other wild dogs enter towns to scrounge scraps, they risk being shot as pests.

▼ **A CRUEL LUXURY**
Fox fur was very fashionable in the early 20th century, mainly for coats.The fox fur stole (scarf) shown here uses the pelt (fur and skin) of an entire animal. In the past, furs were worn mainly to keep warm in winter. Today, however, man-made fabrics are as warm as fur, making it unnecessary and cruel to kill these animals for their pelts.

▲ **UNDER THREAT**
A Simien wolf howls high in the Ethiopian mountains. As the human population grows, more land is farmed and the animal's range is restricted. Simien wolves are shot for fur and killed by farmers as pests. There may be only 500 Simien wolves left in the wild.

Caring for Wolves

▲ **SUCCESS STORY**
Conservationists release a red wolf that was bred in captivity into a reserve in North Carolina, USA. Red wolves were once found throughout the southeastern United States. They nearly became extinct, but breeding programs have saved the species.

In many parts of the world, efforts are being made to save threatened wolves and wild dogs. Grey wolves have recently been reintroduced into areas where they had died out. Conservationists working to protect wolves face opposition from local farmers who fear that wolves will kill their livestock. In some reserves, wolves and wild dogs have begun to be promoted as tourist attractions. This helps people to learn about these animals and the entrance fees help to finance conservation work. Today, wolves and their relatives are gradually losing their bad image. More and more people are appreciating their admirable qualities – intelligence, loyalty and strong family ties. In the wild, these predators actually improve stocks of prey animals. By hunting mostly weak or sickly individuals, they help to ensure the survival of the fittest.

◀ **RADIO TRACKING**
This red wolf has been fitted with a radio collar. The collar allows scientists to track the animal as it roams the wilds. Radio tracking helps to provide scientists with valuable information about the red wolf's habits and range. Increasing such knowledge also helps conservationists with their work.

▲ STARS OF THE SHOW
Tourists on safari photograph African hunting dogs in a reserve. In recent years, such tourist attractions have earned much-needed cash for remote villages. The money helps to persuade local people not to hunt the dogs, but to see them as a valuable asset instead.

▲ KEEPING THE BALANCE
A pack of wolves feeds on a deer carcass. By targeting old and sick animals, the wolves actually help the rest of the herd to survive. They may be removing a deer whose sickness could infect others in the herd, or an old animal whose share of food could be better used to rear healthy young.

▼ SOUND OF THE WILD
For many people, the wolf is a symbol of the wilderness. In certain countries, wolves are now becoming a tourist attraction. At some centres, members of the public can even walk alongside tame wolves, petting them if they wish, accompanied, of course, by expert handlers.

▲ WOLF RESEARCH
Scientists check the teeth of a tranquillized Arctic wolf. Researchers sometimes capture the same wolves several times over the course of a number of years to study their life histories. This work helps to provide evidence of the strong family ties and keen intelligence of the wolf.

Monkeys and Us

Humans have often woven magical stories around monkey characters and some even worship monkey gods. However, people have also captured monkeys and used them cruelly.

By international law, it is illegal to buy and sell monkeys without a licence. This may be given, say, for the purposes of scientific experiments. Unfortunately, some monkeys are illegally exported, often travelling long distances in cramped and cruel conditions.

Many monkey and ape species are eaten in Africa and South-east Asia. Most are eaten by local people, for whom monkeys are a cheap source of 'bush meat'. However, more and more monkey meat is being smuggled around the world, especially into Europe and China, where it is sold illegally for very high prices. Conservationists believe that, if the bush meat trade is not stopped, many monkeys and apes could be wiped out within a few years.

▲ **AT YOUR SERVICE**
In Malaysia, macaques are trained to climb palm trees to pick coconuts. The agile monkeys easily scramble up to the tops of the trees, where the coconuts grow. The macaques have learned to throw the coconuts down to their human owner. Although the monkeys are captive, this task is similar to the behaviour of wild macaques.

◄ **UNNATURAL PERFORMANCE**
In parts of Asia, monkeys, such as this rhesus macaque, are trained to perform tricks to earn money for their human owners. Wild animals in captivity are often treated cruelly by being forced to perform in a way that is completely unnatural to them. Monkeys are not domesticated animals that have been bred to live with humans.

▲ **OBEYING ORDERS**
This monkey has been put in a cage to stop it escaping. The monkey will behave toward its human owner as a low-ranking male would do to a troop leader in the wild: it will cower to avoid confrontation and will try to do what the owner wants in return for access to food.

▲ **FOR THE SAKE OF HUMANKIND**
Live monkeys are sometimes used in scientific experiments. This is called vivisection. Some of these monkeys are injured or killed. Many scientists believe that vivisection provides important information that could reduce the suffering of human beings, but others disagree.

◀ **LIFT OFF!**
A space shuttle blasts off. In the early days of space travel, many monkeys were used in experiments to study weightlessness.

GUIDE MONKEYS ▶
Capuchins – the cleverest New World monkeys – have been taught to help disabled people. The monkeys can pick up objects such as telephones and take them to their owners, as well as perform tasks such as operating switches. Although their owners might benefit, not everyone thinks that it is right to use monkeys in this way.

▲ **LIFE IN A COLD CLIMATE**
Woolly monkeys come from the steamy jungles of Brazil. This one lives in English woodland. The monkeys' natural habitat in Brazil is being destroyed by humans and the species is disappearing fast. At its cliff-top home in the south-west of England, this monkey is given special foods to make sure that it gets the same minerals in its diet as it would in the wild.

Protecting Primates

When the last member of a species dies, that species is extinct. It is lost forever. In the last few decades, many people have worked to stop the rarest primate species becoming extinct. Some have started sanctuaries and zoos where animals are helped to breed away from predators. Nearly half of the world's total population of aye-ayes (one of the most threatened of Madagascar's lemurs) is in zoos because there is not enough of their natural habitat left to support them.

To save an endangered species, the cause of the threat must be addressed. This might be the destruction of the animal's habitat or the poverty of the people who hunt them. We can all affect the survival of species by making sure that we do not buy products that cause damage to their wild habitat.

Did you know? Thanks to conservationists, only one primate has become extinct in 100 years.

◄ **BACK TO THE WILD**
Gerald Durrell, a British conservationist, holds a red-ruffed lemur. Durrell set up a pioneering zoo on the island of Jersey. Many rare primates have been bred there, and the zoo has successfully reintroduced lemurs and tamarins to their natural habitats. The Jersey zoo teaches keepers from other zoos how to raise captive-born animals so they can be released back into the wild.

◄ **HOME FROM HOME**
This realistic rainforest has been created in New York's Bronx Zoo. The temperature, humidity and light are as close as possible to natural rainforest conditions. Captive primates raised in a habitat similar to their wild environment are less likely to become distressed. They will stand a better chance of survival if they are later released into the wild.

KEEPING TRACK ►
These two golden lion tamarins, born in a zoo, were released into a protected area of Brazilian forest. Scientists fitted them with radio transmitters to keep track of them. This species has been saved from extinction by being bred in zoos around the world.

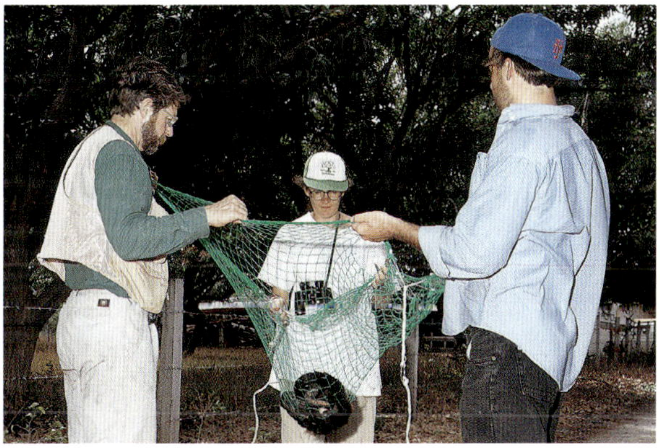

▲ **IN THE BAG**
Scientists have shot this howler monkey with a drugged dart. They will take some measurements, then give the monkey another drug to bring it back to consciousness. Their aim is to gain as much information as possible about the howler monkey's population structure, its diet and the diseases it suffers. This will help them to understand how to conserve the species better.

▲ **SAFE SANCTUARY**
This monkey, whose parents were killed by hunters, has been rescued and taken to an orphanage. Sometimes, young monkeys that were captured illegally are rescued and sent to zoos. They can't be set free, as they don't know how to survive in the wild.

Apes in Danger

Wild apes live in steadily shrinking habitats. Their woodland and forest homes have been gradually replaced by farms, grazing lands and villages. Vast areas of rainforest have been flooded by the water held back by dams, and other areas have been dug up by mining companies looking for precious metals and other minerals. Even in some protected areas, apes are still illegally hunted for their meat, or captured to be sold as pets or for medical research. In times of war, apes are further threatened by weapons such as land mines and the movement of large numbers of refugees into their habitat. People can also pass on diseases to apes, without even realizing that they have done so.

▲ **A POACHER'S TOOLS**
This is some of the equipment used by poachers to kill apes illegally in protected areas such as national parks. Wire snares concealed in the undergrowth can prove deadly to apes trapped in their tight grip. Traditional hunting weapons such as spears and arrows may also be used.

Did you know? There are just 630 mountain gorillas in the world.

GORILLA SKULLS ►
Ape body parts are sometimes sold as grisly souvenirs. These gorilla skulls are for sale on a traditional African medicine stall where they are used as fetishes (a type of good luck charm). There would be no reason for poachers to kill apes if people were not prepared to buy their body parts. Gorillas are also killed for meat. Some of it feeds workers cutting down the forests. The rest is sold in city markets.

▲ FOREST DESTRUCTION

The greatest danger to apes is the destruction of their habitat, especially the rainforests. An area of rainforest the size of over 100 football pitches disappears every minute. Rainforests are cut down for their valuable timber, or burned to make way for cattle ranches or plantations of cash crops.

▲ THREAT OF WAR

In the 1990s, war in Rwanda led people to raid the mountain gorillas' national park for food and firewood. Land mines were also left in the park.

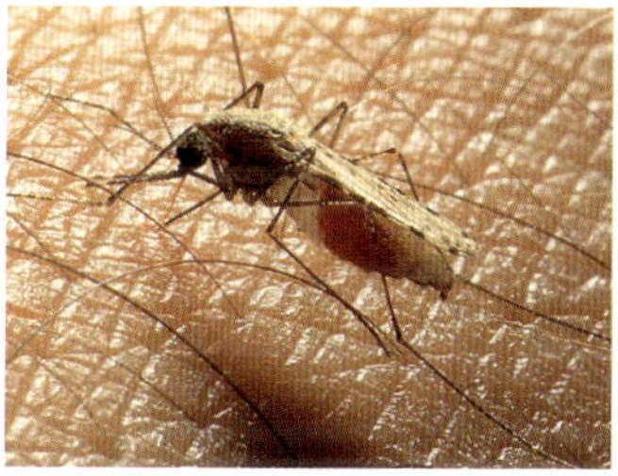

▲ DEADLY DISEASE

Apes are so similar to us that they suffer from many of the same diseases. For example, like us, apes can catch malaria, carried by mosquitoes.

FOREST FIRES ►

In the late 1990s, forest fires raged across Borneo and Sumatra, killing many orang-utans, destroying their habitat and causing breathing problems for the survivors.

▲ **GORILLAS IN THE MIST**
Dian Fossey wrote about her work with mountain gorillas in *Gorillas in the Mist*, later made into a film starring Sigourney Weaver (above). The film raised awareness of the gorilla's plight.

▼ **HABITAT ZOOS**
Some good zoos now keep apes in large, tree-filled enclosures, which are as much like their natural habitat as possible. Breeding apes in zoos helps to increase their numbers.

Ape Conservation

Gorillas, orang-utans, chimpanzees and bonobos are now officially recognized as endangered species. Laws have been passed to stop live apes and parts of their bodies from being bought or sold. However, laws can never give total protection to wild animals, especially when people can make large amounts of money by breaking the law. To help apes survive in the future, their habitat needs to be protected in national parks or reserves. Apes bred in captivity might one day be released into the wild, but only if suitable natural habitats can be found. Conserving apes takes much time and costs much money. Many of the countries where wild apes live have very little money and need help for conservation from richer nations. Apes are more like humans than any other animal. It will be tragic if we cannot find a way to share our future with them.

western lowland gorillas
(Gorilla gorilla gorilla)

▲ **TOURIST DOLLARS**

Many people pay a lot of money to get close to a wild great ape, but this is too close as the ape could catch human flu. If tourists are carefully controlled, they can help ape conservation.

▼ **POACHING PATROL**

These wardens are patrolling the national park where mountain gorillas live. They are keeping a sharp lookout for armed poachers and their snares. If there is a shoot-out, both the wardens and the poachers could be killed.

◄ **CHIMFUNSHI ORPHANAGE**

David and Sheila Siddle have converted their farm in Zambia into the Chimfunshi Wildlife Orphanage to look after rescued chimps from the Congo. The Siddles have walled and fenced off their land and allow the chimps to climb trees, build nests and live like wild chimpanzees.

► **LIVING ON THE EDGE**

In developing countries where most families grow their own food, there is an increasing need for more land. Forests are cleared right up to the park boundary, as can be seen in this photograph, which shows the edge of the Virunga National Park in the Congo. If gorillas and elephants wander out searching for food, they are labelled 'crop raiders' by local farmers, who are desperate to protect their only source of food or income.

Whale Slaughter

The baleen whales and sperm whale are so big that they have no natural predators. Until a few hundred years ago, the oceans teemed with them. In the 15th and 16th centuries, whaling grew into a huge industry. Whales were killed for blubber, which could be rendered down into oils for candles and lamps. The industry expanded following the invention of an explosive harpoon gun in the 1860s, and by the 1930s nearly 50,000 whales a year were caught in the Antarctic. In 1988, commercial whaling was banned.

▲ WHALE SOAP
The sperm whale was once a prime target for whalers. They were after the waxy spermaceti from the organ in the whale's forehead. This was used to make soap.

► DEADLY STRUGGLE
Whalers row out from a big ship to harpoon a whale in the early 1800s. It was a dangerous occupation in those days because the dying whales could easily smash the small boats to pieces.

Did you know? Whale blubber was made into lipstick and other sorts of make-up.

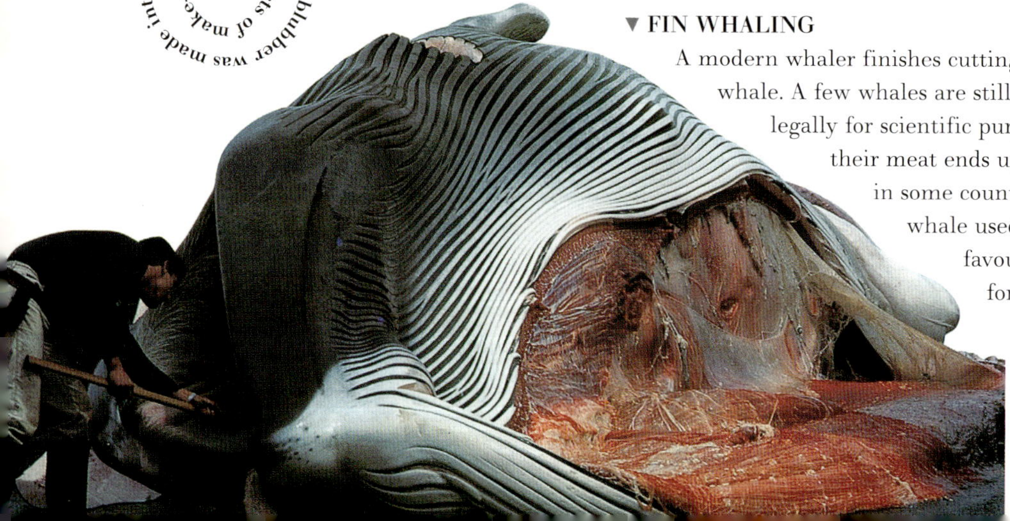

▼ FIN WHALING
A modern whaler finishes cutting up a fin whale. A few whales are still caught legally for scientific purposes, but their meat ends up on the table in some countries. The fin whale used to be a favourite target for whalers because of its huge size.

◄ PILOT MASSACRE
Every year in the Faroe Islands of the North Atlantic, pods of pilot whales are killed, a traditional practice that has not been stopped. The blood of the dying whales turns the sea red.

Did you know? Early whalers killed their prey by throwing harpoons from rowing boats.

► KILLER NET
This striped dolphin died when it was caught in a drift net. It became entangled and was unable to rise to the surface to breathe. Tens of thousands of dolphins drown each year because of nets cast into the oceans.

Did you know? In the 1800s baleen was used to make umbrellas.

Whale Tale

Moby Dick *was written by Herman Melville in 1851. The one-legged Captain Ahab searches for a great white whale (a sperm whale) called Moby Dick. Eventually he harpoons Moby Dick, but he and all but one of his crew die.*

Saving the Whales

If full-scale whaling had continued, many of the great whales would now be extinct. Even today, only a few thousand blue whales, right whales and bowhead whales remain. Because they are slow breeders, it will take a long time for numbers to recover. However the grey whale and the humpback whale appear to be recovering well. These two whales are favourites among whale-watchers because they are so approachable. Whale-watching has made people aware of how remarkable whales are and why they must be protected. Dolphins and killer whales are popular at aquariums, but it is not to their benefit to keep them in captivity.

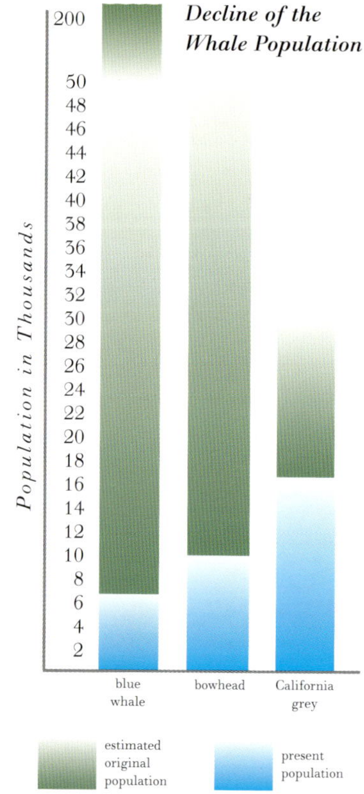

▲ **WHALE RECOVERY**

By the middle of the 20th century, the blue, bowhead and grey whales were close to extinction. Then whaling was banned. Now populations are recovering.

Did you know? The first whale sanctuary was set up in 1945.

▲ **GREY GREETING**

A grey whale rises to the surface near a tourist boat off the Pacific coast of Mexico. It is winter, and the grey whales have migrated to these breeding grounds from the far north. Because these animals stay close to the shore, they are easy to reach by boat.

▼ **HUMPBACK SPECTACULAR**

A humpback whale breaches. It hurls its 30-tonne bulk into the air, belly up, and will soon crash back to the surface. Out of all the behaviour whale-watchers come to see, this is by far the most spectacular.

▶ **FRIENDLY FLIPPER**

One bottlenose dolphin character, called Flipper (played by several dolphins) starred in a series of TV programmes and films. These focused attention on how intelligent dolphins are, yet how vulnerable they are, too.

Did you know? You can adopt your own whale by contacting your own local whale and dolphin society.

◀ **WHALE-WATCHING**

A boatload of whale-watchers sees the tail flukes of a humpback whale disappear as the animal starts to dive. The boat is cruising off the New England coast of the United States where some populations of humpbacks feed during the summer months.

▶ **PERFORMING KILLER**

A killer whale leaps high out of the water at an aquarium, drawing applause from the huge crowd watching. In the wild, the killer whale is a deadly predator, but in captivity – with all meals provided – it is docile and friendly. However, the benefits of keeping these creatures in captivity are not certain.

Did you know? Some countries continue to hunt whales.

Shark Encounters

Sharks are feared because they attack people. However, only a few such attacks take place each year. People are more likely to be killed on the way to the beach than be killed by a shark in the water. Fortunately, attitudes are changing. Today, people have a healthy respect for sharks, rather than a fear of them. As we come to understand sharks, instead of killing them, people want to learn more about them. Diving with sharks, even known man-eaters such as the great white shark or bull shark, is more accepted. People study sharks either from the safety of a cage or, increasingly, in the open sea without any protection. Such is our fascination with sharks that aquariums for sharks are being built all over the world. Here, more people will be able to learn about sharks at first hand, and not even get wet!

Jaws

The book and film Jaws *featured an enormous great white shark that terrorized a seaside town. The film drew great crowds and its story terrified people all over the world. It also harmed the reputation of sharks, encouraging people to see them as monsters, rather than the extraordinarily successful animals that they are.*

◂ **FREE LUNCH**
At tourist resorts in the tropics, divers can watch sharks being fed by hand. This activity is not always approved of. Sharks come to rely on this free handout, and may become aggressive if it stops. Inexperienced divers may also not know how to behave with sharks, resulting in accidents, although these are rare.

◄ **ANTI-SHARK MEASURES**
Anti-shark nets protect many popular South African and Australian beaches. Unfortunately, these nets not only catch sharks, like this tiger shark, but also other sea life, including dolphins and turtles. Less destructive ways of reducing people's fear of attack have yet to be invented.

► **SHARK POD**
Although a similar system is not yet available to bathers, one anti-shark invention seems to work for divers and, possibly, surfers, too. A shark pod can produce an electric field that interferes with the electrical sensors of a shark, encouraging the animal to keep its distance.

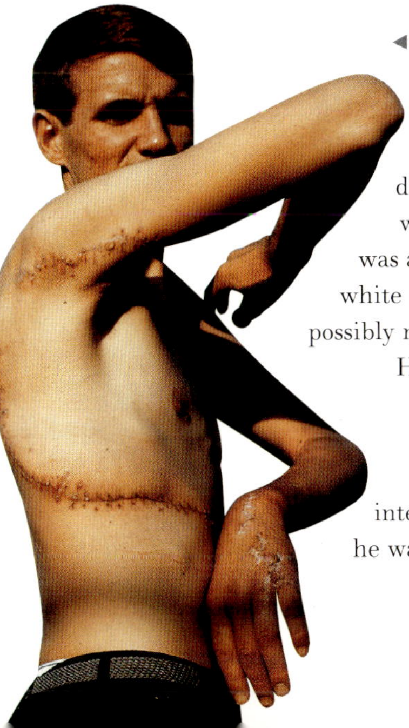

◄ **SHARK VICTIM**
Occasionally, sharks do attack people. While diving in Australian waters, Rodney Fox was attacked by a great white shark. Rodney was possibly mistaken for a seal. He is probably alive because he did not have enough blubber on him to interest the shark and he was able to get away.

▲ **SHARK WARNING**
On many beaches, shark warning signs are used to tell people that sharks might be present. During the day, danger of attack is low, but it increases at night, when the sharks move inshore to feed.

Sharks Attacked

Flying Tigers
The Japanese god of storms is known as the 'shark man'. In ancient Japanese legend, the shark man was terrifying. Encouraged by this fear of the shark, Allied airmen fighting the Japanese during World War II painted a tiger shark on their aircraft as a talisman. The pilots of these planes soon became known as the 'flying tigers.'

Sharks take a long time to grow to adulthood. They have very few offspring and may breed only every other year. Added to these factors, the hunting and killing of sharks can quickly reduce their numbers. This happened at Achill Island, on the Irish coast, where large numbers of basking sharks quickly disappeared, after they were killed for their oil. Off the coasts of South Australia and South Africa, the great white shark was hunted as a trophy for many years. Numbers of great whites were so reduced that the hunting of them has since been banned internationally. A few countries control the fishing of sharks, to try to conserve (protect) them. However, in other countries, sharks are still hunted for shark fin soup, unusual medicines and souvenirs. They are also sold to supermarkets as shark steak. Sharks, it seems, have more to fear from people than people have to fear from sharks.

◄ **WASTED SHARKS**
Each summer, many sharks are killed in fishing tournaments off the east coast of the USA. Sports fishermen are now learning to tag sharks, returning them to the sea alive instead of killing them. By tagging sharks, our understanding of shark biology is increased.

▶ CRUEL TRADE

Caught by fishermen, this whitetip reef shark has had its valuable fins removed. The shark was then thrown back into the sea, still alive. Without its fins, a shark is unable to move and, therefore, feed. It will quickly starve to death. This awful process, called finning, has been banned by some countries.

◀ TRAVELLING INTO TROUBLE

This tiger shark is being tagged to track its movements. Shark tagging programmes like this show that many sharks travelling great distances are being netted by several fisheries along their routes. Unless shark fishing is controlled internationally, sharks that travel long distances will probably disappear from the sea altogether.

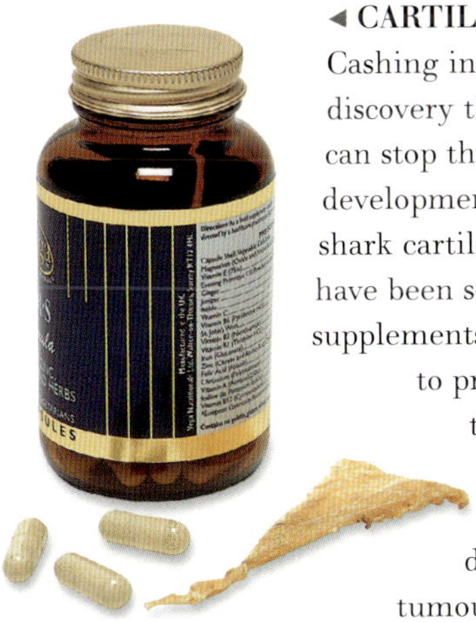

◀ CARTILAGE PILLS

Cashing in on the discovery that cartilage can stop the development of cancer, shark cartilage pills have been sold as dietary supplements. However, to prevent cancer, the cartilage has to be applied directly to tumours. Pills taken orally are unlikely to have any effect.

▲ EXPENSIVE SOUP

Shark fin soup is made from the dried fins of a shark. It has been prepared by chefs in oriental countries for over 2,000 years. The soup was once served to show favour to an honoured guest, and was also thought to be a health-giving food. Today, it is sold in cans and can be bought in supermarkets.

Glossary

abdomen
The rear section of an animal's body, which holds the reproductive organs and part of the digestive system.

adapt
To change in order to survive in altered conditions. It usually takes place over many generations in a process called evolution.

alarm
Sudden fear that is produced by an awareness of danger.

ambush
To hide and wait, and then make a surprise attack.

antennae (singular antenna)
The 'feelers' on top of an insect's head, which are used for smelling, touching and tasting.

artery
A blood vessel that carries blood away from the heart.

arthropod
An animal without a backbone that has many jointed legs and an exoskeleton on the outside of its body. Arthropods include spiders, insects, crabs and woodlice.

binocular vision
The ability to see things with both eyes at the same time. This enables animals such as cats and wolves to judge distances accurately.

bird of prey
A bird, such as an eagle, that catches and kills its prey with powerful hooked claws called talons.

bladder
Where waste urine is stored in the body before being expelled.

body language
The communication of information by means of conscious or sometimes unconscious bodily gestures and facial expressions.

bonding
To form strong emotional attachments, especially between a mother and her baby.

brackish
Water that is not fresh and is slightly salty.

bray
A loud cry that asses and zebras make, sounding like a loud laugh.

breaching
When whales and dolphins leap out of the water and fall back with a great splash.

breed
An animal that belongs to one species, but has definite characteristics, such as colouring, coat markings and body shape.

broad-leaved
Trees with broad, flat leaves. The term is often used to distinguish these trees from conifers.

brood
(1) The number of babies a mother has at one time.
(2) When a bird sits on its eggs to incubate them.

burrow
A hole in the ground, usually dug by a small animal for shelter or defence.

camouflage
The colours or patterns on an animal's body that allow it to blend in with its surroundings.

canid
A member of the dog family. The group includes wolves, foxes and African hunting dogs.

canine
A sharp, pointed tooth that grips and pierces the skin of prey.

captivity
When animals are captured and forced to live within certain areas that they are unable to leave.

carcass
The dead body of an animal.

carnivore
An animal that feeds on the flesh of other animals.

carrion
The remains of a dead animal.

caterpillar
The second, larval, stage in the life of a butterfly or moth, after it has hatched from the egg. A caterpillar has a long tube-like body with 13 segments and many legs.

chrysalis
The third, pupal, stage in the lives of butterflies and moths, during which the caterpillars are transformed into adults. Moth chrysalises are often enclosed in silken cocoons.

cloaca
A chamber at the very rear of the gut in fish, amphibians, reptiles, and birds. The reproductive and urinary systems open into it.

clutch
The number of eggs laid by a female at one time.

cocoon
(1) The shelter spun from silk thread by some insect larvae in which they turn into pupae. (2) A silky covering or egg case made to protect a spider's eggs.

cold-blooded
An animal whose temperature varies according to its surroundings.

colony
A group of the same species that live close together.

conflict
A disagreement or fight between two or more animals.

congregate
To gather in a crowd.

coniferous
Trees that bear their seeds in cones. They have needle-like leaves and usually grow in cool or cold areas. Most are evergreens.

conservation
Protecting living things and helping them to survive in the future.

constrictor
A snake that kills by coiling its body around its prey to suffocate it.

courtship
The process of attracting and establishing a bond with a mating partner.

crocodilian
A member of the group of animals that includes crocodiles, alligators, gharials and caimans.

cultivated
Land or soil that is especially prepared and used for growing crops.

deciduous
Trees that drop their leaves for part of the year. They grow in cool, temperate areas.

diaphragm
A sheet of muscle separating the chest cavity from the abdominal cavity of mammals. Its movement helps with breathing.

diet
The range of food an animal eats.

digestion
The process by which food is broken down so that it can be absorbed by the body.

domesticated
Animals that do not live in the wild but have been tamed by humans and are kept as pets, for example, cats and dogs, or farm animals, such as sheep.

dominance
A system between animals, such as lions, in which one or a few animals rule the group and have first choice over the other, more junior members.

down
Fine, hairy feathers for warmth not flight. Young chicks have only down and no flight feathers.

dragline
The line of silk on which a spider drops down, often to escape danger, and then climbs back up.

drought
A prolonged amount of time without any rainfall.

echo-location
The method used by toothed whales to find their prey. They send out pulses of high-pitched sounds and listen for the echoes produced when the pulses are reflected by objects in their path.

egg tooth
A small tooth that snakes and birds use to help them escape from the egg when they hatch.

endangered
Any plant or animal that is in danger of extinction in the near future.

environment
The surroundings or conditions within which an animal lives.

equids
Horses and horse-like animals, such as asses and zebras.

evolution
The natural change of living organisms over very long periods of time, so that they become better suited to the conditions they live in.

exoskeleton
The hard outer layer of an insect that protects the soft parts inside.

expression
A look on an animal's face that shows how it is feeling.

extinction
The total, worldwide dying out of any plant or animal species.

falconry
Flying falcons or hawks as a sport. Also called hawking.

feral
Domestic animals that have escaped or been abandoned and are now living freely in the wild.

fertilization
The joining together of a male sperm and a female egg to start a new life.

filter-feeder
An animal that sieves water through giant combs called gill rakers, for small particles of food.

fledging/fledgling
The time when a bird starts to fly is called fledging. A fledgling is a young bird that has just reached this stage.

flehmen
A behaviour shown by many male mammals, where they curl their lips back and smell the air, searching for important odours. Female equids and young also use the flehman response.

fossil
The remains of a once-living plant or animal that have turned to stone over thousands or millions of years.

fovea
The sensitive area at the back of the eye in birds and primates that enables them to see in sharp detail.

gait
The way an animal moves at certain speeds. It refers to the order in which an animal moves its legs.

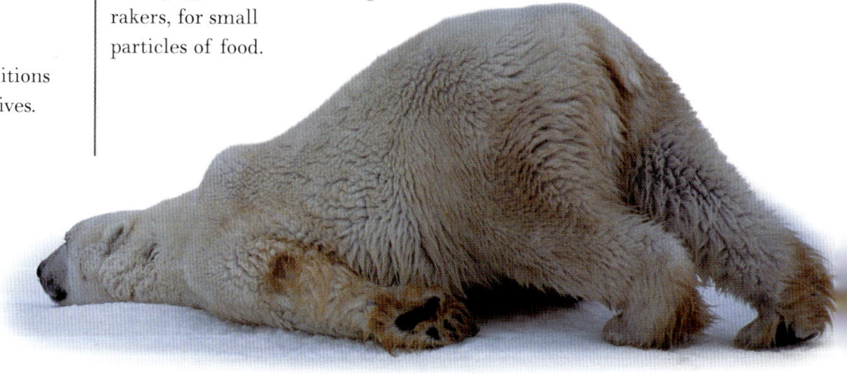

gene/genetics
The code for a physical trait and the way this is passed from one generation to another. Each gene contains a strand of DNA that is responsible for a feature, such as blue eyes.

gill
Part of an animal's body used for breathing underwater.

grassland
Open areas covered in grass.

grazer
An animal that feeds on grass, for example a horse or antelope.

groom
The way an animal cares for its coat and skin. It can be carried out by the animal itself or by one animal for another.

habitat
The particular place where a group of animals live, such as a rainforest or a desert.

harem
A collection of female animals overseen by a single male.

hemisphere
One half of the Earth, divided by the equator. The northern hemisphere lies above the equator, with the southern hemisphere below it.

herbicide
A substance used to kill weeds.

herbivore
An animal that eats only plant food.

herd
A group of particular animals that remain together, such as elephants or wildebeest. Elephant herds are made up of several family units, together with adult bulls. A large herd may have 1,000 individual elephants.

hibernation
A period of sleep during the winter when body processes slow down.

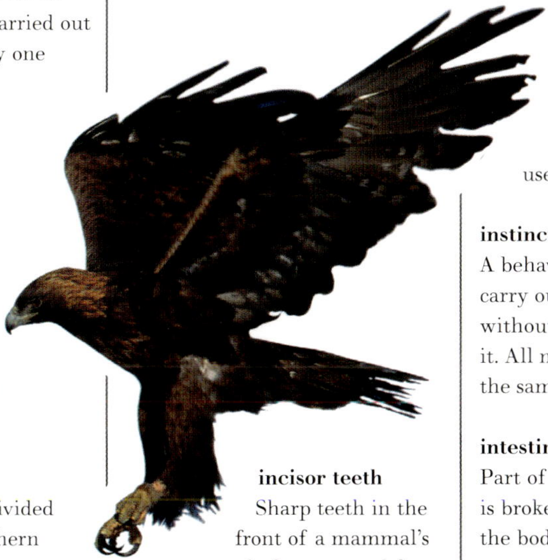

incisor teeth
Sharp teeth in the front of a mammal's mouth that are used for biting and nibbling food.

incubation
Keeping eggs warm so that development can take place.

infrasound
Sounds that have a frequency below the range of human hearing. They are made by crocodiles and other aquatic animals and can travel long distances through water.

insect
An invertebrate (no backbone) animal which has three body parts, six legs and usually two pairs of wings. Beetles, ants and butterflies are all insects.

insecticide
Any artificially manufactured substance used to kill insects.

instinct
A behaviour that an animal can carry out from a very early stage without having to learn how to do it. All members of a species have the same instincts.

intestine
Part of an animal's gut where food is broken down and absorbed into the body.

joint
The point of contact between two bones, this also includes the ligaments that join them.

juvenile
A young animal. In birds, juveniles have not grown their adult plumage.

keratin
A horny substance that makes up a snake's scales.

krill
Tiny crustaceans that are the main food for many of the baleen whales (toothless whales).

labour
The process of giving birth.

lagoon
A shallow, sheltered part of the sea, close to land.

larva (plural larvae)
The young of insects that undergo complete metamorphosis, such as beetles, butterflies and true flies. Larvae can be grubs, maggots or caterpillars.

Latin name
The scientific name for a species. An animal often has many different common names. For example, the bird called an osprey in Europe is often referred to as a fish hawk in North America. The Latin name is the same worldwide.

lens
The transparent part of an animal's eye that focuses the light on to the light-sensitive cells at the back of the eye.

life cycle
The series of stages in the life of an animal as it grows up and becomes an adult.

litter
The number of babies a mother gives birth to at one time.

liver
An organ that processes food from the digestive system (gut). One of the liver's main tasks is to remove any poisons from the blood.

livestock
Domesticated animals such as sheep, cattle, pigs and poultry that are kept for producing meat, milk and wool or for breeding purposes.

lung
An organ of the body that takes in oxygen from the air.

lyriform organ
A sensory organ, especially on the legs of spiders, that picks up vibrations.

malaria
An infectious disease that is passed to humans and some animals by the bite of a mosquito.

mammal
A warm-blooded animal with a backbone. Mammals breathe air and feed their offspring on milk from the mother's body. Most have hair or fur. Whales and dolphins are mammals, although they live in the sea.

mandibles
The jaw-like mouthparts that are present in some insects.

mantling
The behaviour of birds of prey where they spread their wings to conceal a catch. This is to prevent other hungry birds from stealing their kill.

mare
Adult female horse.

marsh
An area of land that is very wet for most of the year.

matriarch
The female head of a group.

mature
Developed enough to be capable of reproduction.

metamorphosis
The transformation of a young insect into an adult. Beetles and butterflies have four stages in their life cycle: egg, larva, pupa and adult. This is called complete metamorphosis.

migration
When animals, usually birds, travel (or migrate) regularly from one habitat to another because of changes in the weather or their food supply, or in order to breed.

milk teeth
The teeth of a young mammal that are replaced by adult teeth.

minibeasts
Small creatures such as insects, spiders and centipedes.

mobbing
When prey birds gang up against their predators and try to drive them away.

molar
A broad, ridged tooth in the back of a mammal's jaw, used for grinding up food.

moulting
(1) When a young, growing insect, spider or snake sheds its skin and grows a new, larger one.
(2) When a bird loses its feathers and grows new ones.

muscle
An animal tissue made up of bundles of cells that can contract (shorten) to produce movement.

native
An animal that originates in a particular place.

nectar
The sweet juice made by flowers that is the main food for adult butterflies and moths and many other insects.

nectary
A specialized gland in flowering plants that produces nectar.

nocturnal
Animals that are active at night.

nutrients
The goodness in foods that is essential for life.

oesophagus
Part of the gut of an animal, usually long and tube-shaped. It transports swallowed food from the mouth to the stomach.

organ
A part of the body or plant that has a special function, for example, a kidney in the body, or a leaf in a plant.

pack
A collection of animals that live and feed together in a group, e.g. wild dogs.

palps
Short stalks that project from the mouthparts of a butterfly, moth or spider and that act as sensors.

paralyse
To make an animal completely powerless and unable to move, even though it is still alive.

parasites
Animals that live on other animals and harm them by feeding on them, although they do not usually kill them. Fleas and ticks are parasites.

pecking order
A social hierarchy that exists among some animal groups.

pest
A living thing, such as an insect, that has a damaging effect on other animals or plants.

pesticides
Chemicals that are sprayed on to plants to kill pests.

pheromone
A chemical scent released by animals to attract members of the opposite sex and in some cases to attack prey.

photosynthesis
The process whereby green plants manufacture carbohydrates from carbon dioxide and water, using the light energy from the sun.

piracy
When a bird of prey makes a killing and is then intimidated by another bird into dropping its kill.

pits
Heat sensors located on either side of a snake's head.

placenta
The end of the umbilical cord, attached to the womb, through which an unborn mammal receives nutrients from its mother.

plains
An area of flat land without any hills.

plantation
An area of land that is planted with a certain crop which is sold to make money.

playfight
The games that young animals play to sharpen fighting skills that will be used in later life.

plumage
The covering of feathers on a bird's body.

poaching
Capturing and/or killing animals illegally and selling them for commercial gains.

pod
A group of animals. In crocodilians, this refers to newly hatched animals. In whales and dolphins, a pod is a group which hunt together.

polar region
The area around the North or South Pole, where it is very cold.

pollination
The transfer of pollen from the male part of a flower to the female part, so that the plant can be fertilized and produce seeds.

population
The number of people or animals or plants of the same species that live in a particular area.

posture
The way that an animal holds its body while standing, sitting or walking. Posture can show others that they are strong and dominant.

predator
An animal that hunts and kills other animals for food.

prehensile
A part of an animal that is adapted for grasping, e.g. a giraffe's lips. Monkeys have prehensile tails.

preserve
To keep safe from danger or death.

prey
An animal that is hunted by other animals for food.

pride
A number of lions that keep together as a group.

primates
A group of intelligent mammals that includes lemurs, bush-babies, monkeys, apes and humans. Primates mainly live in trees and have limbs adapted for climbing, swinging or leaping.

proboscis
The long, tongue-like mouthparts of certain insects, such as the butterfly, which act like drinking straws to suck up liquid.

prosimian
The group of primates that includes lemurs, lorises, pottos and tarsiers. Prosimians have smaller brains than other primates.

pupa (plural: pupae)
The third stage in the life of many insects, between the larval stage and the adult.

rainforest
A tropical forest where it is hot and wet all year round.

raptor
Any bird of prey. From the Latin *rapere* meaning to seize, grasp or take by force.

rare
Animals that only exist in small numbers and are not found often.

receptor
A cell or part of a cell that is designed to respond to a particular stimulus such as light, heat or smell.

regurgitate
To bring up food that has already been swallowed.

reproduction
When a male and female get together to produce offspring.

reptile
A scaly, cold-blooded animal with a backbone, including tortoises, turtles, snakes, lizards and crocodilians.

ritual
A procedure or actions that are repeated regularly.

ruminant
An even-toed, hoofed mammal, such as a cow, which eats and later regurgitates its food to eat again to extract as much nourishment as possible.

saliva
A colourless liquid that is produced by glands in the mouth.

salt gland
An organ on a crocodile's tongue that gets rid of excess salt.

savanna
A large area of grassland in a hot region, particularly found in Africa. Savannas may have scattered trees and bushes but there is not enough rain for forests to grow.

scavenger
An animal that feeds on the remains of dead animals.

scent
A smell. For instance, social insects give off scents to communicate a wide range of messages that influence the behaviour within the nest.

scrape
A patch of ground cleared by a bird to lay its eggs on.

scrub
A harsh, dry area of land dominated by low-growing bushes.

sedate
To calm or quieten an animal by giving it a drug known as a sedative.

semi-wild
Domestic animals that are left to run free over a large area of land for most of the year.

sense
Any of the five main faculties used by an animal to obtain information: sight, hearing, smell, taste and touch.

sensory system
The collection of organs and cells by which an animal is able to receive messages from its surroundings.

signal
A message in the form of sound or a gesture. A wolf's howl will gather a pack together for a hunt.

skeleton
The framework of bones that supports and often protects the body of an animal and to which the muscles are usually attached.

slaughter
The killing of animals, especially for food.

smuggling
Taking goods (or animals) into or out of a country illegally.

sociable animal
An animal that prefers to be in the company of other animals rather than being alone, e.g. lions.

social animal
An animal that lives in a group with other animals of its own kind. They co-operate with other group members e.g. horses and elephants.

solitary
Animals that prefer to live alone and without companions, e.g. snakes.

species
Animals and plants that belong to the same species are all so similar to each other that they can breed together successfully. All species have their own Latin name.

spinneret
An opening that is found at the end of a spider's abdomen. It is through this that silk is pulled out.

spiracles
The holes in the sides of an insect's body through which air passes into breathing tubes.

stimulus
Something such as heat or light that causes a specific physical response in the body.

streamlined
Shaped to slip through air or water easily without much resistance.

subspecies
A wide-ranging species may adapt to local conditions, and look different in some parts of the world. These different forms are called subspecies, but the animals are still able to breed together if they meet.

talon
A hooked claw, especially on a bird of prey.

tapetum
Reflective layer at the back of some animals' eyes that makes them glow when light shines into them.

temperate
Areas of the Earth that have a moderate climate. They are not as hot as the tropics nor as cold as the Arctic and the Antarctic.

termite
An ant-like insect that lives in highly organized colonies, in tropical areas.

territory
An area that an animal uses for feeding or breeding. Some animals defend their territories against others of the same species.

thorax
The middle section of an insect's body. The insect's wings and legs are attached to the thorax.

trachea
The windpipe running from the nose and mouth to transport air to the lungs.

tundra
The cold, treeless land in far northern regions of the world, which is covered with snow for much of the year.

umbilical cord
The cord running between an unborn baby mammal and its mother, through which it receives nutrients.

venom
Poisonous fluid produced in the glands of some snakes and by nearly all spiders that is used to kill their prey.

vertebrate
Any animal that has a backbone. For example birds, mammals and reptiles.

warm-blooded
An animal that maintains its body temperature at the same level all the time.

warning colours
Bright colours that show others that an animal is poisonous. Bright colours also warn predators to keep away.

whaling
The hunting of whales for their meat and blubber.

womb
An organ in the body of female mammals in which young grow and are nourished until birth.

yolk
Food material that is rich in protein and fats. It nourishes a developing embryo inside an egg.

Index

S

T

U

V

W

Y

Z

Picture Credits

ABPL: 104tl, 105bl, 105cl, 105br, 109br, 333t, 353tr, 353br, 407c /Daryl Balfour: 106b, 107t, 401bl /Nigel Dennis: 298t /Paul Funston: 289cl /Clem Haagner: 33c, 54–5c, 58b, 117cr, 296t, 367t, 403tl /Dave Hamman: 117t, 295tr /de la Harper: 334b, 335t /Martin Harvey: 33tl, 400b, 402tr, 402bl, 403bl, 424bl, 485tr /Gerald Hinde: 107bl, 409tl /C Hughes: 390b, 395t /Luke Hunter: 408–09c, 464br /Beverly Joubert: 294c, 367c /Philip Kahl: 400tr /Peter Lillie: 294b, 299t /Philip Richardson: 465tl /Anup Shah: 298c, 366b, 367b /Gavin Tomson: 107br. ABPL /Giselle Wurfsohn: 471tl. AKG London: 221br, 243r, 148bl. Brian & Cherry Alexander: 170br, 171bl, 181c, 239tr, 360tl, 405tr, 414br, 415tl, 469b, 477cr. Ancient Art and Architecture Collection: 162bl/ 94br /John R Bracegirdle: 393tl /Ken Lucas: 101tl. Heather Angel: 39bl, 35c, 28bl, 108tr, 113tl, 113tr, 115tl, 115tr, 185tl, , 281bl, 452b, 455tl. Animals Animals: 71tr, 130ct. Archaeological Museum, Sofia: 467tl. E.T Archive: 290tr, 388bl. Ardea London: 178b; 160bl, 351b, 444tr /Liz Bonford: 414bl /Stefan Meyers: 122b / Brian and Cherry Alexander: 120t /Francois Gohier: 124t /M Krishnan: 125tl. BBC Natural History Unit: 95t, 103br, 215c, 229tr, 158t, 412tr, 440bl, 441tr /Doug Allan: 468tl /Karl Amman: 165cl /Christopher Becker: 121tr /Erik Bjurstrom: 456bl /John Cancalosi: 348t /Bruce Davidson: 243tl, 307tl /G and H Denzou: 347br /Jeff Foott: 405br, 361tl /Gerry Ellis: 113bl /Jeff Foott: 293tl /Louis Gagnon: 61cr /Nick Garbutt: 216tr /Andrew Harrington: 121tl /Tony Heald: 279tr /Hamilton James: 369br /Peter A Hinchliffe: 39br /David Kjaar: 161bl /Hans Kristophe Kappel: 293br /Simon King: 124br /Leonard Lee Rue: 358tr /Lockwood and Dattari: 45br , 303br, 412tl /Alistair Macewen: 43cr /Thomas D Mangelson: 227tr, 358b /Klaus Nigge: 53bl, 392tr /P Oxford: 97br, 100bl, 125tr, 236bl, 466tr, 478bl /Chris Packham: 163c /T Pooley 395c, 333c /Colin Preston: 350tr /Ian Redmond: 483tr /Michael W Richards: 127tr /Rico and Ruiz: 328bl /J Rotman: 253tl, 253tr, 313tl, 491tl /Image Select: 289br /Keith Scholey: 399b /Anup Shah 69bl, 185bl, 242tr, 277t, 499cr, 423cl /Vadim Sidorovich: 300t /Lynn M Stone: 181b, 477tr /Roger Tidman: 361bl, 361c /Richard Du Toit: 179tr, 216br, 413b /Tom Walmsley: 393c, 359b /Tom Vezo: 231tl, 163tl, 179/Doug Wechsler: 65cl, 204bl.Biophotos: Adam Britton: 275cl. The Bodleain Library: 47al. Bridgeman Art Library: 27b, 125br, 177br, 213bl, 225cl, 294t, 302t, 342br, 411tr, 470b, 487b /M Chinery: 144tl /Bob Campbell: 184tr. Adam Britton: 35br, 96tr, 333br, 388tr, 389cl, 395br, 402cr. M. Chinery: 385cl, 444bl. Bruce Coleman: 30bl, 88bl, 88br, 91tr, 92cr, 92b, 98bl, 106r, 108cr, 122bl, 131t, 142br, 152br, 164tl, 183tl, 206tl, 207tl, 208t, 209b, 215b, 249tl, 270tl, 271cr, 286bl, 309tl, 310t, 311t, 321br, 322tl, 371b, 448tr, 449b, 459bl, 488t, 489c /Ingo Arndt: 82c, 84bl, 125tl, 306tl /Erwin and Peggy Bauer: 50bl, 118b, 235b, 290br, 296bl, 297b, 362c, 370t /J Brackenbury: 265bl /Jane Burton: 330tl /Thomas Buchholz: 466bl /Jane Burton: 149tr /RIM Campbell: 67tl, 129tl /Alain Compost: 106tr, 117tl & cl, 175t, 354bl /G Cozzi: 336b /Gerald Cubitt: 203b, 211t, 472bl, 483br Peter Davey: 165bl, 186tl /Bruce Davidson: 304t, 304b, 305cl /Adrian Davies: 326bl /Sophie and Michael Day: 359tr, 365tr /G Dore 82bl /Peter Evans: 83bl, 409b /Christer Fredriksson: 295b /CB & DW Frith: 451br /Jose Luis Gonzalez Grande: 100tl /Sir J Grayson: 263tl /D Green: 384bl /Janos Jurkai: 26br /M P Kahl: 169ac /Steven Kaufman: 459cr /Stephen Kraseman: 171br /F Labhardt: 145tc /Leonard Lee Rue: 233t, 297c /Robert Maier: 499t, 498br /Antonio Manzanares: 280tr, 295tl /L C Marigo: 97c, 337bl, 444cr /Antonio Manzanares: 329tr /Joe Mcdonald: 115b, 297t, 404tr, 411br /Rita Meyer: 233b /Dieter and Mary Plage: 87tr, 127b, 365br /Alan G Potts: 331tl Michael Price: 473c /Andrew Purcell: 86b /M. Read: 445tl /Hans Reinhard: 63br, 235c, 329c /John Shaw: 55b, 410b /Alan Stillwell: 148t, 205c, 326t /Jon Taylor: 145tl, 266t /Kim Taylor: 82tr, 263br, 268bl, 331c, 445bl /Norman Tomalin: 406t, 409tr /Paul Van Gaalen: 231tr /C. Wallace: 445cr /J and P Wegner: 182tr /Staffan Widstrand: 180b /Rod Williams: 117tr, 177c, 179, 243bl, 460t /Gunter Ziesler: 296br, 412b. Corbis Images: A Griffiths Belt: 479b /C & A Purcell: 481br. C M Dixon: 472t. Ecoscene: 207cr /Ian Beames: 455m /Robert Walker: 454m. ET Archive: 49cl. Mary Evans Picture Library: 25c, 32bl, 37b, 41bl, 52br, 91br, 114tr, 117cl, 210br, 217tl, 263cl, 281tr, 360bl, 371cr, 385tl, 455bl, 471tr, 474bl, 474br /Arthur Rackham: 447cr /Whittaker's Star Atlas, Plate 6: 170tr. FLPA: 70t, 70bl, 149br, 153tl, 153tr, 155tl, 155cl, 206c, 248t, 250c, 448br, 486b, 489t /Heather Angel: 159cr /Philip Berry; 232t /F Hartman: 49br /Mike Hill: 355br /E & D Hosking: 473b /L Lee Rue: 151br /Mark Newman: 52tr, 228bl, 229br /Philip Perry: 176t, 177bl /Fritz Polking: 234b /Sunset: 227tl /Kim Taylor: 57t /Terry Whittaker: 46ar, 55tl, 59t, 175b, 231b, /Terry Whittaker: 437t /W Wisniewski: 212b. FLPA: 84br, 85cr, 87c, 90b, 90r, 92–3, 93bl, 114b, 270bl, 309cl, 309cr, 341tr, 428b, 429t /M Harvey: 126tl /JJ Hinojosa: 98tr /Frank W Lane: 421cr /Mark Newman: 336t, 362tr, 362b /Philip Perry: 407tr /F Polking: 264tr, 298b, 299c /L S Sorisio: 433bl /Larry West: 267b /Terry Whitaker: 364t, 407b /DP Wilson: 343tr /Martin Withers: 288b. Michael and Patricia Fogden: 450bl, 211bl, 325b, 390t. Gallo Images: 38tr, 99tr, 175cbl & cbr, 215tl, 329bl /Daryl Balfour: 169bl /Peter Chadwick: 235t / Nigel Dennis: 99br, 177t, 234t /Thomas Dressler: 104tl, 105bl, 105cl, 105br, 218tl /Clem Haagner: 163bl, 176b, 281m /Roger de la Harpe: 175ctl /Martin Harvey: 158bl, 169cr, 186bl /Gerald Hinde: 230b /Peter Lillee: 331tl /Eric Reisinger: 281tl /Anup Shah: 244bl. Garden Wildlife Matters: M Collins: 265br /J Fowler: 320t. Gettyone Stone Images: Kathy Bushue: 180cr, 371tl. Gettyonestone /Art Wolf: 415tr. Ronald Grant Archive: 19tr. Grant Museum /A Lister: 57br. J M Gleeson in The Outing Magazine: 405tl. Griffith Institute, Ashmolean Museum: 470t. Heritage & Natural History Photography: 440tr, 443cl. Michael Holford: 44bl, 60t, 457br. Holt Studios International: 88tr. Kit Houghton: 40tr, 43br, 218br, 221tr, 396t, 398t, 349b. Images Colour Library: 282–3. Innerspace Visions: 342tl, 342bl, 345tl /M Conlin: 191cr, 343br /B Cranston: 253br, 432tl, 433br, 491bl /B Cropp: 313cl /S Drogin: 312tl /D Fleetham: 72tr /S Gonor: 191tl /SH Gruber: 492bl /H Hall: 72cr /P Humann: 432bl /R Kuiter: 190tl /J Morrissey: 190br /M S Nolan: 192tl, 313bl /D Perrine: 72bl, 73bl, 132br, 133bl, 252bl, 253cl, 253bl, 431c, 493c, 493bl, 493br /J Rotman: 191bl /F Schulke: 491br /M Strickland: 493tl /M Synderman: 312br /J D Watt: 133br, 430tr. Imagebank: 50tr /Paul McCormick: 467tr. The Kobal Collection: 244br /Ken Lucas: 48bl, 67cr. Microscopix Photo Library: 202b, 205b. Monkey Sanctuary: R Helvesi: 480tl. NASA: 189br. National Geographic: . National Geographic: 132tl, 492tl /N Calogianis: 133tl /Niall McInerney: 471br. NASA: 479bl /R Nannini: 479br /David Hiser: 468br. Natural History Museum: Carlo Dani and Ingrid Jeske: 365t /M Long: 351cl, 351tr. Natural Science Museum; 56b. Natural Science Photo Library: 364b /D Allen Photography: 166al, 406b /Carlo Dani & Ingrid Jeske: 473t /Lex Hes: 175b, 410–11t /Michael Kock: 471bl /David Lawson: 410c /Pete Oxford: 167al /S G Neginhal: 401c /M W Powles: 411bl /MS Price: 463tr. Natural Science Photos: 109tr, 308c /D Allen: 114t. Nature Photographers Ltd: 45ar, 71c, 204br, 388br, 325cr, 486t. NHPA: 30tl, 31tr, 31bl, 78t, 79br, 80t, 81b, 89tl, 89cl, 89bl, 91c, 92tl, 93tl, 98t, 102bl, 109bl, 111br, 130bl, 138b, 140c, 141b, 143tr, 152bl, 153bl, 153br, 155tl, 198c, 249b, 250tl, 250b, 255tl, 259tr, 259bl, 260t, 261tl, 261br, 267tr, 270br, 271tl, 317t, 346t, 346cl, 346b, 347t, 347cl, 399bl, 427t, 427b, 428t, 429b, 439br, 441tl, 446t, 486c, 489b /Daryl Balfour: 165br, 167ar & bl, 288cl /Anthony Bannister: 166br, 463bl /GI Bernard: 225tl, 483cl /Joe Blossom: 353bl /Mark Bowler: 356l /Steven Dalton: 217c /Manfred Danegger: 392b /Nigel Dennis: 104b, 243br, 337cl, 453c /K Ghani: 301t /Martin Harvey: 210bl, 161br, 185br, 481tl, 484b /D Heuchlin: 183br, 275t, 394t, 335c, 340cl, 453tl /V Hurst: 464bl /T Kitchin & V Hurst: 241br, 303br /Rich Kirchner: 413c /Stephen Krasemann: 469cl, 476t, 477bl /Gerard Lacz: 179c /Yves Lanceau: 220bl, 230t /Michael Leach: 67br /William Paton: 393b /Christopher Ratier: 126bl, 423br, 472br /Steve Robinson: 158br, 186br, 356r, 423bl, 425tr, 425bl /O Rogge: 212tl /Andy Rouse: 116t, 414t, 369tl /Jany Sauvanet: 123cl, 241c /Kevin Schaffer: 25tr, 192bl, 292bl, 389t /John Shaw: 405bl /E Soder: 451bl /Mirko Stelzner: 123t / Philip Ware: 106c. Only Horses: 287br, 348br, 348bl, 349cr, 349tl, 349tr //M Wendler: 33tr, 453tr, 453b /Alan Williams: 221cl /Norbert Wu: 164b, 193. OSF: 441cl, 443cr /D Cayless: 479 /R Davies: 478a, 478tr /B Kenney: 481cr /M Tandy: 481c, 481bl /C Tyler: 480br. Oxford Scientific Films: 19tl, 19br, 21c, 21br, 79t, 81t, 81c, 102br, 108bl, 110bl, 112tl, 112br, 115br, 115cl, 123cr, 130b, 130cr, 131b, 131t, 131bl, 138c, 139b, 141t, 141c, 188bl, 188br, 199, 221bl, 251b, 258r, 259br, 261tr, 261bl, 272–3, 308tl, 310b, 311b, 324b, 340t, 341b, 369bl, 426t, 426b, 427cl, 427cr, 429c, 438, 439bl, 447cl, 458cr, 461bl, 461t, 487t /Anthony Bannister: 301cr /A Bee: 451tr /Rafi Ben-Shahar: 477tl /Bob Bennett: 214bl /G I Bernard: 279br /Joe Blossom: 357tl /S Breeden 183cl /Matthias Breiter: 476b /Clive Bromhall: 187br, 187tl, 244tr, 357tr, 422br, 425tl, 425br /Alan and Sandy Carey: 220tl, 413tl /David Cayless: 305t, 305cr, 305b /Martyn Colbeck: 46bl, 106bl, 168bl, 225br, 289tr /Daniel J Cox: 51bl, 172tr, 226tr, 228tr, 229bl, 236tl, 239bl, 240tl, 240bl, 291bl, 359tl, 368t, 415b /D Curl: 182bl /R Davies: 95b /Richard Day: 300b /M Deeble and V Stone: 159cl, 213tl, 275tl, 391t, 391b, 337cr, 344, 345bl /Nigel J Dennis: 353tl /Carol Farneti-Foster: 217tr /David B Fleetham: 101br, 132cl, 491cr /M Fogden: 157 /David C Frith: 53br /David C Fritts: 292tr, 293bl /Carol Geake: 399bl /M Gibson: 490bl /Dennis Green: 329br /Dan Guravich: 170bl /Mark Hamblin: 99cr, 279tl /H Hall: 133cr /Dave Hamman: 285bl /David Haring: 65br /Mike Hill: 122t, 161tr, 311tr /Frank Huber: 110br, 173bl /Tim Jackson: 393tr /John R Jones: 47tr /R Kuiter: 190cl /Lon E Lauber: 238t, 239cr, 303bl /Martin Leach: 101cl, 301cl / S Leszczynski: 157cr /Ted Levin: 161tr /Alistair Macewan: 398bl /Victoria McCormick: 236br /Joe Mcdonald: 125bl, 424tl /Stephen Mills: 173tl /Owen Newman: 475cr /Rob Nunnington: 216bl /Ben Osborne: 219t /Stan Osolinski: 34tr, 63tr /Stan Osolinski: 95c, 278b, 288tr, 363tl, 422bl /Overseas: 123b /Nikita Ovsyanikov: 291tr /Richard Packwood: 370b /M Pitts: 96b / Andrew Plumptre: 67tr, 127cr, 128br, 129tr, 307br, 352t, 420tl /Ralph Reinhard: 245br / E Robinson: 32tr /J Robinson: 210tl /Norbert Rosing: 101tr, 173tr, 359cl, 467br /F Schneidermeyer: 157cl /Jonathan P Scott: 357bl /Krupaker Senani: 119c /Michael Sewell: 301b /David Shale: 360br /W Shattil: 211t /Nivek Sinha: 291br /G Soury: 313br, 430bl /Claude Steelman: 475t /Stouffer Productions: 172bl /David Thompson: 163tr /Gavin Thurston: 46al /M and C Tibbles: 368b /David Tipling: 287bl, 454tl /Philip Tull: 41cr /Steve Turner: 178t, 424tl, 462b /Tom Ulrich: 181tr, 397br, Tom Walker: 291tl, 292tr /Anna Walsh: 475bl /Peter Weiman: 119b /K Westerkov: 334t /Fred Whitehead: 41br, 460bl, 461br /Colin Willcock: 181tl /Konrad Wothe: 37tr, 185tr, 238br, 280bl, 355tl, 421c, 469cr //Belinda Wright: 225cr. Papilio Photographic: 27t, 54t, 80br, 87tl, 119bl, 143bl, 162c, 174t, 175ctr, 214tr, 233c, 242br, 252tl, 402tr, 407tl, 446b /Kim Taylor: 278tl, 282tl, 282tr, 283m, 283tl. Photo Researchers Incorporated: 187tr. Planet Earth: 99cl, 105tl, 109cl, 115tr, 119br, 122t, 129bl, 131c, 285tl, 308b, 309b, 397b, 321tr, 321cl, 321bc, 340br, 341c, 344br, 345br, 347bl, 355tr /K&K Ammann: 420b, 421br, 423tr /G Bell: 275c /Frank Blackburn: 328tr /G du Feu: 262br /N Greaves: 276tl/S Hopkin: 262bl /B Kenney: 263cr, 332b /D Kjaer: 337tl /K Lucas: 96t /D Maitland: 267tl, 320br /M Price: 94bl /J Scott: 276bl, 277b /J Seagrim: 343tl, 344br /A and M Shah: 277c /Anup Shah: 306br, 307cl, 354br /M Snyderman: 433tl. Planet Earth Pictures: 71bl, 188t, 208b, 219bl, 248b, 251t, 448cl, 449tl, 449tr, 487c, 488b /K & K Ammann: 463br, 482b /P Atkinson: 73tr /Andre Baertschi: 69br /M & C Denis-Huot: 156cl /Darrock Donald: 36bl /Georgette Douwma: 192br, 218bl /Geoff Johnson: 232b /Brian Kenny: 50br /K Lucas: 32–3, 63tl /D Mailland: 26t /Andrew Mounter: 456br /Nikita Ovsyanikov: 173br /D A Ponton: 159b /J A Provenza: 158tr /Roger Rogoff: 168al /J Scott: 213tr /Anup Shah: 66bl 165tr, 242bl, /P Stephenson: 452t /Tom Walker: 227br. Premaphotos Wildlife: 86t, 87b, 268t, 268br, 269b, 385tr, 385bl, 386bl, 386t, 386br, 324t, 325cl /K Preston-Mafham: 22tr, 203tl, 203tr, 265cr /Kim Taylor: 146tl, bl&r, 147tr, 262tl /Ian Redmond: 352b, 357br. Dr Rod Preston-Mafham/Premaphotos Wildlife: 149bl, 150t / Kim Taylor: 139t. Ian Redmond: 482t. Ann Ronan: 49ar. Science Photo Library /Tim Davis: 64tr. South American Pictures: 431tl. Spacecharts: 189b. SPL: 142tr, 441br, 442tr. Frank Spooner Pictures: Oliver Blaise: 168. Tony Stone: 54b, 396b, 397t /R Calvert: 237c /T Davis: 229tl /Momatiuk: 219br, 220br. Survival Anglia: 214c /M Linley: 450t /Nicholas Parfitt: 408b /Manoj Shah: 408t. Stouffer Productions: 112br, 363c. Kim Taylor: 18t, 19bl, 20, 22bl, 23ct, 37tl, 36–7m, 78b, 198t, 258l, 443tl. Roger Tidman: 404b. Twentieth Century Fox: 450b. Universal Pictures: 490tr. Visual Arts Library: 29br, 70cr, 249c /Artepot Roland: 83br. Volkswagen: 21bl. Warner Bros: 484tl. Warren Photographic: 18b, 21t, 79bl, 80bl, 139c, 140t, 140b, 143tl, 260b, 385cr, 321tl, 439t /Jane Burton: 26bl, 209c, 237tl, 330cl, 330c, 330cr, 387bl /Jan Taylor: 25tl, 205tl /Kim Taylor: 23cb, 25tr, 25b, 85tl, cl, & br, 144bl, 145br, 151tl & tr, 204t, 205tr, 217br, 264bl, 264cr, 269t, 279bl, 322bl, 322r, 323tl, 327c, 387tl, 387br, 457tl, 457tr. Bob Wilson: 364bl. Zefa Pictures: 93br. Zoological Society of London 458bl, 458tl.

This edition is published by Hermes House, an imprint of Anness Publishing Ltd, Hermes House, 88–89 Blackfriars Road, London SE1 8HA; tel. 020 7401 2077; fax 020 7633 9499

www.hermeshouse.com; www.annesspublishing.com

If you like the images in this book and would like to investigate using them for publishing, promotions or advertising, please visit our website www.practicalpictures.com for more information.

Publisher: Joanna Lorenz
Managing Editor: Judith Simons
Senior Editor: Sarah Uttridge
Editor: Elizabeth Woodland
Authors: Michael Bright, John Farndon, Tom Jackson, Robin Kerrod, Rhonda Klevansky, Dr Jen Green and Barbara Taylor
Illustrators: Julian Baker, Peter Bull, Vanessa Card, Stuart Carter, Linden Artists, Rob Sheffield, Sarah Smith and David Webb
Designers: Joyce Mason and Alix Wood
Production Controller: Mai-Ling Collyer

ETHICAL TRADING POLICY

Because of our ongoing ecological investment programme, you, as our customer, can have the pleasure and reassurance of knowing that a tree is being cultivated on your behalf to naturally replace the materials used to make the book you are holding. For further information about this scheme, go to www.annesspublishing.com/trees

A CIP catalogue record for this book is available from the British Library.

Previously published as *Life in the Wild: Animal Survival*

PUBLISHER'S NOTE

Although the information in this book is believed to be accurate and true at the time of going to press, neither the authors nor the publisher can accept any legal responsibility or liability for any errors or omissions that may be made.